THE CHARACTER OF THE POET

Wordsworth in *The Prelude*

THE CHARACTER OF THE POET

Wordsworth in *The Prelude*

BY RICHARD J. ONORATO

PRINCETON UNIVERSITY PRESS 1971

PRINCETON, NEW JERSEY

LCC 74-131126
ISBN 0-691-06049-5

This book has been composed in Linotype Baskerville
Printed in the United States of America
by Princeton University Press

For Jeanne Adrienne

PREFACE

To employ psychoanalytic concepts in discussing the "character" of a poet in an autobiographical poem invites criticism and requires explanation. It is my intention to consider the recollection and representation of character in two ways: character in the sense of *a* character, the character created by an imaginative construction based on memory, and character in the sense of the characteristics of oneself revealed through verbal behavior. Perhaps with the importance of neither would a reader disagree were it not the case that psychoanalytic considerations raise questions of unconscious intentions, repression and defenses, and elaborations of artifice that are said to conceal in one way and reveal in others. However discreetly managed the argument may be, it *is* being implied that a truth is latent in the text and that a reality, or a constellation of suggestions about realities, is to be recovered in the interpretation. Moreover, there is in all such interpretation that rests on theoretical assumptions generated from an attempt to be "scientific" an inherent reductiveness, which to some will always seem to be merely reductive and to others an appropriate way to question complexities freshly in the light of a few statable principles. I would go further and say outrightly that there is something inherently circular about interpretations that work back and forth between hypotheses about human experience and personal records of experience; but, while the circularity is a real limit on any claim of truth, the intention to make such a claim may be, and here is, the least important aspect of the undertaking.

My treatment of the Wordsworth revealed in his poetry begins in observations of unusual metaphors that recur and of recurrent experiences that are sometimes literal and sometimes figurative; it questions elusive and fugitive states of feeling and the peculiarities of image, diction, and tone of voice in which they are expressed. If I seem to discover obsessive concerns and suggest unconscious intentions, I would be obliged to call them thematic concerns and suggest ambiguities and obscurities of expression were it not the case that certain psychoanalytic assumptions seem appropriate and point to another way of ordering the observations. Here I should say, then, that my own predisposition to assume the importance of the traumatic loss of a mother at age eight (and father at thirteen) leads to close readings of many intricately related passages and, while seeking the significance of that trauma in and to the poet's characterization of himself and his growth, seeks to confirm the appropriateness of making that assumption. For some, perhaps Wordsworth's insistence on the rare "privilege" of his early freedom in nature—a freedom that dates from his mother's death—will be suggestion enough as to why one might question the attributes of nature and his pursuits of it in solitude; for others, I am sure, no amount of rendering plausible this line of interpretation will make much difference.

If I had approached Wordsworth through the kind of intuitive psychologizing that offers no account of itself but is implicit in many literary studies, this book would be heavy with arguments against others whose intuitions differed. My personal sense of obligation is strong to many fine scholars and critics for facts, insights, and general observations about the poet and the period; the Bibliography will suggest the range of such indebtedness. But in attempting an explicitly psychological interpretation of Wordsworth's long autobiographical poem, I have generally resisted the temptation to register specific disagreements with other interpretations of Wordsworth; the Appendix deals briefly with a few modern and cognate theories of Wordsworth's personality, from which I would distinguish my own. Of course, anyone who wishes will have his say about the appropriateness of applying psychoanalytic concepts to poets and poetry at all, but I have not sought to anticipate and contest that kind of criticism.

A word about the degree of explanation attempted here is also in order. I often found myself about to digress on some psychoanalytic point, but desisted rather than strain the patience of a reader willing to follow a basically psychoanalytic argument but more interested in Wordsworth than in the disputable speculations and formulations within psychoanalysis today. At other times I came near over-explaining some basic psychoanalytic point, and I hope desisted rather than patronize or bore the kind of informed reader I hope to have. I have also tried to avoid writing for the kind of reader more interested in psychoanalysis than in Wordsworth or poetry, and to resist explaining the basic relevance of the kind of psychology being applied merely for the sake of the kind of reader not likely to be interested in this book to begin with. In short, I have tried to keep in mind the kind of colleague and student with whom I have had some success while thinking out and writing the argument: those to whom psychological assumptions are not new or strange or unnerving, but who require the continuous and explicit attempt to render plausible the sense in which one uses them.

My indebtedness is of many kinds. For extended discussions of poetry or psychology or both, I am grateful to Drs. Stanley Walzer, Joan J. Zilbach, Stanley Cheren, and Stanley Palombo, and to Professors Allen Grossman and Aileen Ward. To David D. Perkins, in whose seminar at Harvard I sketched out the argument that was to be first a thesis and then a book, my gratitude is of long standing, as much for discussion and disagreement at the time as for advice and encouragement in the longer work. To Reuben A. Brower I am profoundly grateful for patience, frankness, and insight in reading a largely psychological analysis of a poet on whom he too has written and whom he understands in a different way. An enormous debt is mine to

Lionel Trilling in whose wise and friendly counsel I have continued to see what a teacher can be. With him, I first read Wordsworth and learned, perhaps more recklessly than he would wish, to value Freud.

I would like to acknowledge specially a few other debts: to the late Andrew Chiappe, who by precept and example fostered in all his students the fascination with things difficult, I owe the sense of wonder I associate with poetry; to John R. Northam, my tutor at Cambridge, I owe what command of prose I have to contain that sense of wonder; to Professor Stephen K. Orgel, with whom I first discussed the ideas in this book many years ago, I am indebted through the years for many friendly offices more memorable; and to Erik D. Wensberg, who cannot read a manuscript without a pencil in his hand, and yet can be persuaded to read a friend's manuscript, I have more debts than I could acknowledge adequately.

I would like to thank Brandeis University for funds to prepare this manuscript and Mrs. Richard P. Taub and my wife, Jeanne A. Onorato, for preparing, typing, correcting, and proofreading. Since they both knew that Wordsworth was notorious for spoiling with scribbled corrections all the fair copies of his manuscript prepared lovingly by his wife, relatives, and friends, they were indulgently forbearing in remaining good-humored at all hours, despite revisions.

It is a pleasure to acknowledge my oldest indebtedness in my first book to those from whom I had my first book.

R.J.O.

Eastham, Mass.
1970

CONTENTS

THE CHARACTER OF THE POET

Wordsworth in *The Prelude*

CHAPTER I

THE NATURE OF THE PROBLEM

1. "Wordsworth"

Anyone who has ever talked of Wordsworth's poetry has known the feeling that the subject of Wordsworth himself, his mind and character, would soon come to the fore. From his earliest ballads and lyrics to his most solemn odes and elegies, from his earliest meditative poems to the long autobiographical epic, one finds oneself commenting parenthetically on and attending with increasing care to the "Wordsworth" of Wordsworth's poetry. To proceed at all is first to yield to that necessity.

But any appraisal of Wordsworth's achievement in *The Prelude*, of his success at describing poetically the growth of his mind, must begin with a discussion of texts. Perhaps only scholars cherish alternative versions of a major work and a profusion of variant manuscripts, for collation is a labor of love. Yet "characters," too, at times thrive on discrepancies in texts: they live, or seem to have lived, other lives. *The Prelude* exists in eighteen partial or complete manuscripts and two distinct versions.[1] The 1850 version, a poem of 7,886 lines in fourteen books, was published posthumously and was for a long time "Wordsworth." In 1926, Ernest de Selincourt published the 1805-06 version of

[1] The various manuscripts of *The Prelude* are listed by Ernest de Selincourt and Helen Darbishire as: A, B, C, D, E, Alfoxden Notebook, JJ, Christabel Notebook, 18a, RV, U, V, J, W, M, X, Y, Z. They are described in the Introduction, under 1. Manuscripts, pp. xix-xxvii, in *The Prelude; or Growth of a Poet's Mind* by William Wordsworth, ed. E. de Selincourt, 2nd edn., rev. Helen Darbishire. [For full bibliographical data for works cited in the footnotes, see the Bibliography, pp. 421-427.]

The Prelude (8,479 lines), preserving its original thirteen-book form and adding in the *apparatus criticus* almost all of the MS variants. He gave to the scholarly world another "Wordsworth."[2] The critical reader, reading both versions, attending to poetic design and interpreting the poet's intentions, may find that differences of style, of sequence, nuance, and context lead to more basic questions about this autobiographical poem—about the poet creating and the character created.

I shall concern myself principally with the 1805-06 version, for reasons which I trust shall become obvious. But the problems in discussing a poetic autobiography—those we pose to ourselves from our own suppositions of what one might be—are immediately compounded by many insistent, less precise, and less manageable problems of context for this poetic autobiography. It would be difficult enough to hit upon a simple and consistent approach to the first version, which in its seven years of composition show signs of a mind changing *while* accounting for its first thirty-five years of life and growth; but it would prove impossible to discuss a single "Wordsworth," without inventing one, who will answer adequately to the eighteen manuscripts and the two versions. The second version is the result of revisions over a forty-five-year period by a man who remained attached to the earlier period of his life while changing radically from the person he had been.

This oft-mentioned "change" in Wordsworth often forces an overly simple and double sense of the poet—the "real Wordsworth" and the "later Wordsworth," the Wordsworth of the Great Decade and the Wordsworth of the years of decline—as if, against Wordsworth's insistence about human life, the child had not been father of the man. The older

[2] All references to *The Prelude* are made to the edition cited in n. 1 above. All extended quotations are followed by book and line reference (e.g. II, 592-600) to the 1805-06 version or have the 1850 version indicated (e.g. II, 592-600: 1850 version). Lines quoted within the body of the text, however often, are followed by a footnote reference.

Wordsworth is made to seem an unfortunate betrayal or reversal of the younger Wordsworth, rather than one quite possible development. Inevitably, the popular preference for the younger and greater Wordsworth makes for presuppositions in reading his poetry; and it is these presuppositions about what he was in his youth and what he "really" meant about himself in *The Prelude* that I wish to question.

We would all probably welcome some kind of simplification here, if only for the purposes of discussion and for the sake of having a whole and manageable poetic autobiography to study; but it is naive to suppose that we can have this by disregarding the many circumstantial peculiarities of the poem's composition and compilation. Since *The Prelude* is our only great example of poetic autobiography in English, it might be well to regard its many peculiarities, not as accidents which prevented a more ideal execution, but as significant to the very nature of the attempt. The generally sound scholarly practice of accepting as the definitive text the last corrected copy cannot be observed here if we are at all curious about the circumstantial nature of Wordsworth's attempt.

It seems strange that on the one hand there is the usual and often inordinate reaction to Wordsworth's preoccupation with himself, his self-elaborating egoism, and on the other hand a wish that he had been able to leave a more whole and poetically satisfying account of himself, implying the ability to have been even more perfectly preoccupied. If we are interested in poetic autobiography, the vicissitudes of such a preoccupation with the self, the poet's dissatisfactions with the project and with himself, his inability to finish with satisfaction, or even to finish, become of compelling rather than marginal interest. *The Prelude* is all we have as a record of a very complex intention, and we tend to ignore the nature of the complexity. When *The Prelude* has not simply been mined for its richest passages of Wordsworthian poetry, it has served mostly as a repository of quotations about Wordsworth himself for those who retell his story by alternately quoting and paraphrasing him. What I propose in a critical reading of the poem is to open another avenue of inquiry: there is the nature of the attempt to be considered.

In a poetic autobiographical account of the growth of a poet's mind, it would be useful to emphasize the inventive sense along with the recollective sense of the I-speaking character, and remember that the poet is creating a character, is "characterizing" himself, by using both Memory and Imagination. The selective recollection and the evaluation of facts are employed to exemplify what the poet "imagines" himself to have been and asserts that he is; for him, the remembered facts and their imagined and asserted significance are inseparable. He is accounting for the "Growth of a Poet's Mind." The selection, evaluation, and belief in exemplary experiences are simultaneous; they animate the poetry with metaphor, with a causal sense of what "growth" is and what becoming a poet is. Since the poet's skill at making poetry is being used to account for the making of himself in the character of poet, what we ordinarily associate with the imaginative invention of a character in literature is being used as the sustained activity of self-invention. By finding poetic connections between the facts of growth and the causation and development of imaginative powers, the poet invents himself as poet. Wordsworth's mind can account for becoming the poet only by accounting to itself for becoming Wordsworth. It follows, then, that the ability to write poetry is crucial to any sense that that mind has of being what it claims—to be not only a poet, but Wordsworth. When one compares the heightened self-consciousness of such a claim (and of such activity) with the random, mostly prosaic, and often inarticulate sense that people have of having become themselves, one should say at the outset that if Wordsworth is perhaps compelled to remember and imagine his growth, most people are, in some sense of the word, compelled not to. One should allow that it does not "just" happen that the poet does and most people do not.

First we should look at how *The Prelude* came to occupy so prominent a position in Wordsworth's life. The important poem was to have been *The Recluse*, a life work, "a philosophical poem, containing views of Man, Nature and Society, and to be entitled *The Recluse* as having for its principal subject the sensations and opinions of a poet living in retirement."[3] As preparation for this task and as a "prelude" to it, Wordsworth began a poem referred to always as "the poem on my/his life." It was entitled *The Prelude; or, Growth of a Poet's Mind* by his wife when it was published posthumously in 1850. The poem was to be a "review of his own mind to examine how far Nature and Education had qualified him" for the writing of a poem like *The Recluse*. The "poem on his life" was an unusual literary venture, and Wordsworth himself felt this. At no point in its composition did he consider publishing the poem in his lifetime; it was to be published only after the success of *The Recluse* had justified it. The Advertisement used for the first edition of *The Prelude* in 1850 was actually written in 1814, when *The Recluse* was still a cherished hope, though as early as 1814 *The Recluse* was no longer spoken of by Wordsworth with conviction. He refers to a long poem in three parts, of which only the second part, *The Excursion*, was executed. "The first book of the first part of *The Recluse* still remains in manuscript," the Advertisement tells us, "and the third part was only planned."

When *The Prelude* was published in 1850, Wordsworth was, in Keats's phrase, "among the English poets"; the body of his work and his considerable reputation were justification enough for its publication. Yet in all Wordsworthian criticism, the subject of his egoism is a considerable one. In allowing Wordsworth credit for the modesty of not plan-

3 *The Prelude*, Advertisement for edition of 1850, p. 509. The two quotations immediately following are from the same page.

ning to publish the long autobiographical poem until after the success of the really great poem had justified it, one is aware nevertheless of the vastness of the ambition: the review of the mind undertaken as a lengthy preparation for a subsequent great performance makes certain unmistakable assumptions about personal greatness, only partially dispelled by the diffidence of this poet about his pretensions to being that much idealized being, The Poet. We shall have occasions to examine carefully the relationship between the two roles—the poet writing about The Poet, the troubled and self-scrutinizing self accounting for the idealized self—but here I should like to observe another aspect of egoism prior to any attempt at evaluation.

The "long poem on his life" Wordsworth wrote to Coleridge, who believed him already qualified to write *The Recluse,* was originally to have been five books long and to culminate in the account of his dedication to poetry in a "memorable dawn" above Hawkeshead.[4] Despite Coleridge's encouraging insistence that the inventory of poetic capital should be brief and that the larger investment in the major work be made forthwith, *The Prelude* continued to grow. With an inner necessity that Wordsworth felt, a compelling urgency, it was gradually extended to include an account of the years after his Dawn Dedication to poetry in college. He wrote then of his residency in France, of the French Revolution and its disastrous effect on him, of his understanding of the impairment of his poetic spirit by circumstance and of its restoration by Nature and filial love. One can guess, if not readily understand, why there was to be a poem called *The Recluse*; by 1798, Wordsworth, then age twenty-eight, *was* a "poet living in retirement." There was the expectation that what he would write would proceed naturally through the years of his maturity from an acceptance of himself, self-evaluated and self-affirmed.

For the next eight years, evasively but compulsively, he

[4] See *The Prelude,* Introduction, p. 1.

dwelt upon the subject of how he came to be this "Recluse." As *The Prelude* delayed and then displaced the projected greater work by the difficult but steady fascination that it exerted over the mind of its creator, the permanent concern emerged—that of growth, as it has been called, or of identity, as it might be called. I shall argue, as modern psychologists do, that if growth through all the stages of one's life continues, necessarily the concern with growth changes, so that the word does not apply in the same sense to the early, middle, and late parts.[5] How exactly this statement applies to an interpretation of *The Prelude* I shall attempt to show, but "egoism" is what one must call the ego's lifetime concern with itself. It is crucial, however, that one put aside the fussy and embarrassed sense of the word if examples of explicit and detailed self-concern and self-observation are to be studied, since one hopes to learn from examples what one cannot learn from reticence.

In 1806, when Wordsworth finished the first draft of *The Prelude,* he was depressed. His peroration is an example of the rising tone of assertion of the last few books of the poem. Having assessed the tawdry facts of human life in the experience of history, Wordsworth sings out to Coleridge an ending that has assurances of poetic beginnings. He sounds like the Recluse promising in his retirement to turn his gaze outwards and to speak from visionary heights to the busy world of men. In posture, the statement is Miltonic.[6] He says:

[5] It will be plain to the reader who knows the work of Freud how generally my interpretations depend upon his theories. Footnotes throughout, kept to a minimum, suggest relevant passages and sometimes whole texts. Here I call attention to the work of Erik H. Erikson, who writes of growth in "The Problems of Ego Identity" and in *Childhood and Society.*

[6] The "visionary" view of history reminds the reader of Milton's influence on Wordsworth. Cf. *Paradise Lost,* XI and XII. Since I refer in Chap. III to both Milton and Lucretius, I should mention here the resemblance to Lucretius's view of man struggling, as observed by the Poet whose mind is well-fortified and elevated by Truth. Cf. *De Rerum Natura,* II, 1-28. With the epic form in mind, it is likely that Wordsworth was also mindful of Vergil; cf. *Aeneid,* VI.

Oh, yet a few short years of useful life,
And all will be complete, thy race be run,
Thy monument of glory will be raised.
Then, though, too weak to tread the ways of truth,
This Age fall back to old idolatry,
Though men return to servitude as fast
As the tide ebbs, to ignominy and shame
By Nations sink together, we shall still
Find solace in the knowledge which we have,
Bless'd with true happiness if we may be
United helpers forward of a day
Of firmer trust, joint-labourers in a work
(Should Providence such grace to us vouchsafe)
Of their redemption, surely yet to come.
Prophets of Nature, we to them will speak
A lasting inspiration, sanctified
By reason and by truth; what we have loved,
Others will love; and we may teach them how;
Instruct them how the mind of man becomes
A thousand times more beautiful than the earth
On which he dwells, above this Frame of things
(Which, 'mid all revolutions in the hopes
And fears of men, doth still remain unchanged)
In beauty exalted, as it is itself
Of substance and of fabric more divine.

(XIII, 428-452)

Poetry is to have a salutary effect on a few now, and perhaps on all later. One thinks inevitably of Milton's anticipated audience for *Paradise Lost* ("fit audience . . . though few")[7] when his hopes for man's spiritual estate in a Christian commonwealth that would transform history had failed, leaving in their stead hopes for the redemption of the virtuous minority. One finds Wordsworth here half expecting only "ignominy and shame" in history, but speaking nevertheless of "redemption, surely yet to come," a curiously

[7] *Paradise Lost*, VII, 31.

divided expectation. Despite, then, the personal confusion he felt whenever he tried to take people and their treacherous wills into account, Wordsworth *wanted* to speak of the redemptive work that could be done for them by poets who would speak to them of their spiritual lives.

The Recluse, as Coleridge conceived of it and discussed it with Wordsworth, was to be a philosophical poem about redemption for man in history.[8] But Wordsworth, I think, is only gesturing here toward the long poem already overdue. The philosophical poem about redemption is promised despite the conflict that has delayed it. If one were to suggest, even prematurely, that that conflict is greater and deeper than the tone of assertion in this passage, it would perhaps be clearer that Wordsworth was oppressed by the thought of attempting to extend the poet's role metaphorically to that of redeemer. His personal habit of observing himself and of accounting for himself to himself had other than ideal meanings; it served psychic needs that could not be put aside for a more difficult, even selfless, role. But it should not seem surprising that Wordsworth needed his pose of belief in this role for the poet, though he felt oppressed by the thought of it, in order to cover his abiding concern with a self animated by its unconscious doubts. It would be useful to observe right away, then, that there is a relationship between the tone of assertion and the animating doubts, because it suggests that the very strength of insistence is a denial of the exclusive self-consciousness that has preceded it. As for finishing *The Prelude*, merely *seeming* to have finished what compulsion could never allow to be finished while life lasted must necessarily depress him. To accept as finished the account of growth may confirm one's manhood, but it does so by exposing one to one's mortality. To make the claim that Wordsworth's true greatness resides elsewhere than in his own explicit expectations of himself, we must examine a variety of motives and executions, and

8 See Coleridge, *Table Talk*, July 21, 1832, quoted by de Selincourt, *The Prelude*, p. xxxviii.

convince ourselves, perhaps, of their real stature and worth. He expected ambitiously to turn a meditation on the present into great poetry; his great poetry, however, is predominantly retrospective.

In stating that *The Prelude* of 1805-06 was revised through the years and emerged as *The Prelude* in 1850, I am calling attention to a psychological fact of some importance: that the poem, after its first depressing completion, was never allowed to remain complete as an account of growth written at a certain time. It is less easy to evaluate that fact. In 1806, Wordsworth wrote De Quincey that the poem had a "dead weight about it" and that it came "so far below what I had seemed capable of executing."[9] As both Dorothy's and Wordsworth's letters testify, Wordsworth was always a fitful writer, one who composed in his head while walking outdoors or who scribbled in an almost illegible handwriting. He found the physical act of writing painful, enervating, depressing. In 1804, he apologized to De Quincey: "I have a strange kind of derangement . . . which makes writing painfull to me, and indeed almost prevents me from holding correspondence with anybody: and this (I mean to say the unpleasant feelings which I have connected with the act of holding a pen) has been the chief cause of my long silence."[10] More than the physical act of writing is involved, since it is inseparable from what one is writing; and it is a particularly unfortunate "derangement" for a writer.

If one observes Wordsworth's awareness of himself as a writer and as a poet—that he at times expressed dread of it, castigates himself as an idler, and laments his habits of evasion—one might suspect the derangement as symptomatic. Coleridge objected to Wordsworth's chronic hypochondria, which in the form of somatic ailments interrupted his work and made him at times too ill with pains

[9] *The Early Letters of William Wordsworth and Dorothy Wordsworth* (hereafter *Letters*), ed. E. de Selincourt, #497.

[10] *Letters*, #368.

in his side, headaches, eye and stomach trouble to compose at all. The explanations of himself Wordsworth offers seem too simple—that this, for instance, was why he could not become a lawyer like his older brother and their father before them; or that, in point of neglected correspondence, it was the physical act of writing that prevented him from writing, rather than the writing-of-what and the writing-to-whom. In addition to the letters that he would hesitate to write because they were simply tedious, there were the others—the kind, as to De Quincey, that had to be written to someone who regarded him as *the* Poet, who innocently expected something self-definitive from him, and who was therefore threatening. Wordsworth dreaded giving accounts of how his work was going, how the Poet was or what he thought of things, all subjects that tended to run too much together and to cause too much conflict. He was always struggling with the acceptance and the articulation of himself simultaneously, which is what *The Prelude* attempts in poetic form. *The Prelude* is also, unmistakably, a long *letter* to Coleridge, the friend (it is said often) who believed in him and who would never judge him harshly. It was, in the same sense, difficult to write.

One is always aware of a conscience supervising the task in *The Prelude,* if only that of an ideal of a Poet whose growth he hopes his autobiography exemplifies. Fairly ritualized and restrained self-criticism for not working at the poem was probably a welcome relief from, and a compromise with, greater fears of not doing it well enough, or unconscious fears of doing it too well. For if the desire to be a writer and the pain of writing are related in significant—that is, causal—ways, then doing it "well" would entail one kind of conflict about being the Poet, and not doing it "well enough" another. There is a psychic danger in excellence that we shall have occasion to observe; but the more obvious danger is in failure, in not being the Poet, and perhaps then of not being Wordsworth. Since being a poet was sufficiently different from being what most men become, the failure of Wordsworth's aspiration to superiority would surely result in the conviction of inferiority. It may seem strange, but the sense of powers withheld, used reluctantly, is an inner, if unprofitable, reassurance; whereas an achieved failure is unmistakably definitive. The aspiration to be a certain kind of poet (not a ballad writer but a major philosophical poet) was arrested by self-scrutiny: *The Prelude* came between the poet and his "great" work and extended itself until it became the expression of a dominant intention to get hold of oneself.

The psychological fact, however, can be put more precisely: the first version of the poem was subjected to revisions of various kinds. Awkward phrasing was often corrected and the sense made clearer. More appropriate images and metaphors were added; and often they were made to emerge from a specific passage as further developments or refinements, in the spirit of the original statement. Sometimes, stylistically, the opposite occurred, as when heavy latinisms replace the vital diction of the earlier version or when "poetical" metaphors decorate it.[11] Beyond this, we must wonder what Wordsworth may have intended by revision. Though dissatisfied by what he felt to be *The Prelude*'s "heavy weight," he did not recast the poem or try again. The modern editors of *The Prelude* describe the ideal text in this way:

"The ideal text of *The Prelude,* which the lover of Wordsworth may construct for himself from the material here presented to him, would follow no single manuscript. It would retain from the earliest version such familiar details as have any autobiographical significance. Of purely stylistic changes from that text, it would accept those only which Wordsworth might have made (and some he would certainly have made) had he prepared the poem for the press in his greatest period, changes designed to remove crudities

[11] For an interesting discussion of this point, see Donald Davie, *Articulate Energy,* pp. 106-116.

of expression, and to develop or clarify his original meaning: but it would reject those later excrescences of a manner less pure, at times even meretricious, which are out of key with the spirit in which the poem was first conceived and executed. Most firmly would it reject all modifications of his original thought and attitude towards his theme."[12]

With this wish for a variant text consistent with Wordsworth's original thought and attitude one can only concur and feel gratitude to the editors for presenting us with the material from which it may be imagined. But in the statement that follows there is a blandness of curiosity that I take to be a typically scholarly attitude; it makes of radical change nothing particularly interesting while finding it remarkable:

"To the student of the poet's mind the first version of *The Prelude* is chiefly valuable because it presents us with the history of his spiritual growth as he saw it when his powers were still at their height, and when he was writing those poems on which his greatness rests most securely. No man is the same at seventy years of age as he was at thirty-five, and Wordsworth, perhaps, changed more than most of us; for though, like others, he descended into the vale of years, he descended from more glorious heights."[13]

One becomes impatient with the limits so imposed on discussion and turns to literary criticism for enlightenment. But criticism, for the most part distrustful of any competence not strictly literary, has not ventured far to relate the problems of poetic autobiography psychologically to those of personality, though there has been no lack of explanations of Wordsworth's growth, change, and decline.

It is true that the attitudes of the man of seventy emerged so quickly after thirty-five that one hardly bothers to distinguish the man of forty, fifty, or sixty; and so it is that there are the two Wordsworths, young and old. It is both

[12] *The Prelude*, p. lxiii.

[13] *Ibid.*, pp. lxiii-lxiv.

true and meaningful that the older Wordsworth was in so many ways different from, and even antithetical to, the younger Wordsworth. Revising his story with politically conservative and Christian scruples, he sometimes seems to be his own earliest and dullest critic, unsure of the ardor, belief, and assertion of his younger self.[14] Yet in fact, the revisions of *The Prelude,* while indicative of profound basic change in the poet, are not extensive and are not all of them that severe. The differences between the younger and the older man are greater in letters and anecdotes, greater between early and late poems, than between the two versions of *The Prelude.* For a young radical grown conservative, for a pantheist and "semi-atheist"[15] grown pious and orthodox Anglican, Wordsworth allowed *The Prelude* to remain very suggestive and revealing of his younger self while taking on the supervisory and judgmental presence of his older self. If he was unable to leave the poem alone and go on to be the philosophical poet promised by it, he was also unable to recast what he had done and devote himself wholly to it as his "life work." But despite his unwillingness or his inability to persist with the work that had disappointed his expectations, *The Prelude* has become for us his principal work. It seems to contain a psychic truth by which he had been possessed and of which he was not quite in possession. The delays in composing and compiling the first version of *The Prelude,* the depression felt at its completion, the subsequent fussing with the poem, and the failure to write *The Recluse* all reveal the complexity of character that calls for a reconsideration of the younger Wordsworth rather than a dismissive caricature of the older Wordsworth. "The child is father of the man";[16]

[14] *Ibid.,* VII, 512-543. This apostrophe to Burke in the 1850 version should be read carefully as the clearest example of the intrusion of the older Wordsworth in the revision.

[15] ". . . at least a semi-atheist." Coleridge said this in 1796. It is quoted by David Perkins, *The Quest for Permanence,* p. 4.

[16] All references to Wordsworth's other poems will cite *The Poetical Works of William Wordsworth* (hereafter *Poetical Works),* ed. T. Hutchinson, rev. E. de Selincourt. "My heart leaps up . . . ," p. 62.

perhaps we should be reading *The Prelude* differently, allowing, as the inversion in the rubric suggests, more attention to the child.

2. Recurrent Metaphors and The Memory of Growth

Even the metaphor of growth is not itself clear and set for this poet who is remembering and imagining himself as a character exemplifying a kind of growth; generally a sense of significant change in time is rendered continuously, but variously. There is plainly the plant-likeness of growth, the feeling of rootedness in a natural place, for which "budding" and "blossoming" convey the metaphorical senses of growing, changing, maturing; and there is "transplanting," the metaphorical extension that means moving to live in another valley. That growth is also rendered as a journey in *The Prelude* is immediately recognizable to the reader who recalls that Wordsworth even uses the metaphor as a simple piece of structural artifice a few times, referring to himself as a traveller dallying along the road of the tale that he is telling of his growth. But the careful reader will have noticed that there are other and subtler uses of the journey-metaphor throughout.

Life is a journey; but in the sense that it is simply autobiographical time, it is a journey from childhood to manhood, implying the biological journey from birth to death. In the sense that a poet's growth is a growth to consciousness of himself and his function, it is a journey from the self-less and unself-conscious condition of birth to the special selfhood of a poet, from the thoughtless condition of general sensations to that of specific sensations and thoughts, and from irrecoverable states of feeling to those spiritual regions beyond thought of which poets sometimes write. In the sense that it is in some way a spiritual journey, it is a journey to an awareness of soul beyond self, of timelessness beyond time, of infinitude beyond the immediate footpath or highway of life. That most of Wordsworth's significant realizations about life and about yearnings that are great and insatiable take place while he is actually or figuratively a traveller must have struck the reader, as perhaps the simple literary metaphorical extensions of that sense of journey may have. Thus, life is a quest, an adventure, a pilgrimage, in which one is seeker, hero, or wayfarer.

The epic sense of journey, derived by Wordsworth from Milton, has its most precise analogue in *The Odyssey*: that a man realizes the complexity of his experience in art adequate to tell of it. In *The Odyssey*, the artist and the hero merge momentarily as Homer has Odysseus, that most fabulous of voyagers, tell his own tale at length. In *The Prelude*, experiences are not only reworked poetically in the exact sense in which Wordsworth meant "emotion recollected in tranquility,"[17] but they often serve as the basis for very complicated metaphorical representations of yearnings that are familiar and recurrent in the journey of life through its stages of growth and change. What is consciously selected as memorable experience is preconsciously selected to support what may be imagined on the basis of it. There is a metaphorical consistency which is structural in *The Prelude* and which provides the reader with significant connections between types of incident in their widest possible meanings, even when the meanings seem "mystical," as some say, or simply impenetrable, as others think. The critical attempt here to find those meanings is based on a belief encouraged by observation that Wordsworth was trying to characterize what he felt he could only in part explain. He did so with an imaginative fidelity of feeling which made for a coherency of representation, though the accompanying semblance of explanation certainly lacks that coherency.

When, for instance, Wordsworth speaks of the "visionary power" that he "drinks" while listening to "the ghostly language of the ancient earth," he has been describing his youthful predilection for walking at night in storm and

17 "Preface to *Lyrical Ballads*, second edition, 1800," *Poetical Works*, p. 734. (Quoted at length, below, p. 93.)

wind and pausing to stand in solitude. When he goes on to say that the soul,

> Remembering how she felt, but what she felt
> Remembering not, retains an obscure sense
> Of possible sublimity, to which
> With growing faculties she doth aspire,
> With faculties still growing, feeling still
> That whatsoever point they gain, they still
> Have something to pursue,
>
> (II, 335-341)

he is writing of a state of being, the sense of which fuses growth and pursuit. Faculties shared by self and soul seem to take over from each other: what he is accounts for his being here, having this experience; what more he will be will be revealed or imagined in a spiritual journey that can be characterized only by the use of intensely felt metaphor. New points will be gained; the pursuit will go on.

At another point (Book VI), while writing of the experience of being overwhelmed by his Imagination—his conscious self now figured as "the lonely Traveller" in the mountainous terrain of his own mind, and Imagination as an "awful power" that rises from "the mind's abyss"—he says that he becomes conscious of his soul's glory when he seeks "the invisible world." When, with a flash that reveals the invisible world, "the light of sense goes out," he realizes

> Our destiny, our being's heart and home,
> Is with infinitude, and only there;
> With hope it is, hope that can never die,
> Effort, and expectation, and desire,
> And something evermore about to be.
> Under such banners militant, the soul
> Seeks for no trophies, struggles for no spoils
> That may attest her prowess, blest in thoughts
> That are their own perfection and reward,

> Strong in herself and in beatitude
> That hides her, like the mighty flood of Nile
> Poured from his fount of Abyssinian clouds
> To fertilise the whole Egyptian plain.
> (VI, 604-616: 1850 version)

Here, one either attempts to analyze the complexity of metaphorical characterization or passes over it as an example of romantic afflatus, a kind of inspired but impenetrable rant. But it all could be made plainer by observing what is obvious in what is strange: the simple similarity between these two passages. The soul, which had been described as pursuing something in and through its growing faculties, here is undergoing a growth to consciousness of more of *itself*. In pursuing his being's destiny the poet is forced beyond ordinary self-consciousness towards something to be realized, "something evermore about to be." Our being, he says, sees into "the invisible world" when the ordinary consciousness is overwhelmed by Imagination, which comes from within and from an other-than-conscious source.

Too many related passages come to mind at once to be adduced here in an orderly way; but I should like to suggest how an associational method in criticism would be appropriate, since it resembles the associative mode of feeling and thought, of recollected experience and poetic construct, that Wordsworth himself held. To say, for instance, that these passages require a tracing out of such significantly recurring characterizations as those of wind, language, solitude, growth, power, journey, inside-and-outside, visible-and-invisible, etc., is to say that this autobiographical "character" is associated in the poet's memory with certain kinds of incidents that exemplify the emerging life-style of the Poet; and that the incidents, poetically rendered, have *become* psychologically associated in the poet's imagination with certain recurrent images and metaphors. Then we are saying that the fusion of the character created and the poet creating him is to be understood by understanding the significance of recurrent metaphors and the associational nature of metaphor itself. Metaphor always associates the present subject or incident figuratively with another one; and Wordsworth's recurrent metaphors add a further characterization of each memory by coming back to the reader's mind and bringing their associated contexts with them. The consistency of metaphor in *The Prelude*, which I find to be amazing, may be hidden in part by its density and complexity; but I think it is more significantly obscured by an obstructive emotional reaction we have to egoism. When someone else's "egoism" is too explicitly requiring of us the kind of attention we pay willingly in literature only to characters who have been projected from their creators rather than fused with them, we become inattentive to subtleties.

Without attempting now the reasoned critical construct I shall attempt presently, let me suggest by way of example how associated passages might be considered. For instance, when speaking of the "holy calm" that sometimes overspread his soul when he was alone in Nature, Wordsworth says, "I forgot/ That I had bodily eyes, and what I saw/ Appeared like something in myself, a dream,/ A prospect in my mind."[18] If one wonders why calm is "holy" and what "holy" means, one can trace through other contexts the recurrent religious metaphors applied to such states, and see what they have in common. Why something outside—a landscape, for instance—should appear as something inside may be traced too; and so may "dream" and "prospect in my mind" as recurrent characterizations of simple incidents. One of the Fenwick notes supplies this: "I was often unable to think of external things as having external existence, and I communed with all that I saw as something not apart from, but inherent in, my own immaterial nature. Many times while going to school I grasped at a wall or tree to recall myself from this abyss of idealism to the reality. At

[18] *The Prelude*, II, 368-371.

that time I was afraid of such processes."[19] Abysses, like the one of the mind, the deep, other-than-conscious source from which Imagination rises, have a suggestive meaning of realities inside one that are greater and more urgent than objects externally present to the senses. They are in some further suggestive way associated with the whole "invisible world" that Wordsworth seeks when "the light of sense goes out," or when with "growing faculties of sense," the soul aspires to attain the sublimity it has often felt as an "obscure sense."

The second passage quoted above, placed in its context in Book VI, shows that Wordsworth has been recollecting the profound feeling of disappointment in the past following upon his realization that he had "*crossed the alps*" without crossing a summit. There was no higher point to attain, though the aspiration to climb upwards was boundless. It is at *this* point that the recollection of himself as a traveller in the mountains becomes the figurative basis of a further metaphorical journey in the mountainous terrain of his own mind, in which the conscious self is the traveller going a further journey towards an "invisible world" within. A realization of the meaning of past experience, exacted by the writing of poetry, also comes at this point: that actual physical activity in this world as the poet has known it cannot satisfy the obscure aspiration towards something sublime that causes it; that such activity is a poor and disappointing approximation of ideal activity, which goes through but beyond the senses.

Strange, it may seem in its context, that eternity and infinitude ("our being's heart and home") are represented as both outside and distant, and inside and near, but consistent nevertheless. These lines in MS RV, written around 1800 but subsequently cancelled, perhaps convey more

19 Fenwick note on the "Immortality Ode." See *The Prose Works of William Wordsworth* (hereafter *Prose Works*), ed. A. Grosart, vol. III, p. 194.

vividly the sense of an infinitude at once within and beyond:

> By such communion I was early taught
> That what we see of forms and images
> Which float along our minds and what we feel
> Of active, or recognizable thought
> Prospectiveness, intelligence or will
> Not only is not worthy to be deemed
> Our being, to be prized as what we are
> But is the very littleness of life.
> Such consciousnesses seemed but accidents,
> Relapses from the one interior life
> Which is in all things, from that unity
> In which all beings live with God, are lost
> In God and nature, in one mighty whole
> As undistinguishable as the cloudless east
> At noon is from the cloudless west when all
> The hemisphere is one cerulean blue.
> (MS RV, 1-16)

And again:

> —In which all beings live with God, themselves
> Are God, existing in one mighty whole . . .
> (MS 2 of "Peter Bell")

But how we are to understand this, in what sense it was meant at the time and why Wordsworth may have felt this and then cancelled it, are questions that are worth pursuing to determine how Wordsworth stands revealed in such statements.

The observation that the younger Wordsworth had the feeling of great powers within him, fostered by Nature and creative like that of the God of creation's, would be best supplemented through other associations. How does Wordsworth say he felt godly, and when does he say he feels or felt that way?

So was it with me in my solitude;
So often among multitudes of men.
Unknown, unthought of, yet I was most rich,
I had a world about me; 'twas my own,
I made it.

(III, 139-143)

What the significant part of each of these experiences has in common with the others, we observe, is solitude; and solitude, at its simplest a physical circumstance, has an observable history of inner meanings for the poet. In solitude, the poet has acquired the habit of attempting to locate himself in his own special reality; his sense of self and his sense of reality undergo changes; and he is led on, imaginatively tempted and challenged in his ability to characterize and assess those changes poetically.

Of Genius, Power,
Creation and Divinity itself
I have been speaking, for my theme has been
What pass'd within me,

(III, 171-174)

he says, at one point, even more explicitly; and the account he attempts to give in poetry of what "pass'd within" him (though "in the main/ It lies far hidden from the reach of words") is to him "heroic argument."[20] "Points have we all of us within our souls/ Where all stand single," he says;[21] and the heroic task is to put in words the singleness of one's inner being. "There's not a man/ That lives who hath not had his godlike hours," he says; and "Each man is a memory to himself," to the extent that he is able to be.[22] This poet, in the solitude he seeks, is compelled to speak of what otherwise would be lost, unrealized, unremembered, unimaginable.

At another point early in the poem, he who had been

[20] *The Prelude*, III, 178-185.
[21] *Ibid.*, III, 186-187.
[22] *Ibid.*, III, 189f.

made to feel "perhaps too much/ The self-sufficing power of solitude,"[23] and who had felt too keenly the inward pull towards an "abyss of idealism," gives this key sense of having been left alone in the world, in briefest detail, as if mentioning it without intending to show feeling about it:

For now a trouble came into my mind
From unknown causes. I was left alone,
Seeking the visible world, nor knowing why.
The props of my affections were remov'd,
And yet the building stood, as if sustain'd
By its own spirit!

(II, 291-296)

Wordsworth refers to the death of his parents, incidents actually six years apart, here rendered as one memory. In its context in Book II the passage is suggested no doubt by his having been talking about the crucial relationship of Mother and Babe as the type of human relatedness to the actual world and of the origin of the first poetic spirit. Only with considerable difficulty can it be shown how much the poetic sense remains preoccupied with that original relationship and that lost object of love, wonder, and power. Here I shall only suggest this connection between the objects of the "visible world," in which one must continue to live, and the lost objects and relationships that constitute the awesome appeal of the "invisible world," which is revealed momentarily by Imagination when the light of sense goes out.

Wordsworth's recollection of the child being "left alone" —an aloneness that entailed "seeking the visible world" and resisting the frightening inward pull towards an "abyss of idealism"—must be related to his gradual realization of an even greater search beyond the ordinary consciousness of self. The man and poet emerge from the child, and upon them devolves this search or journey that makes of poetry an "heroic argument" about encounters with the "invisible

[23] *Ibid.*, II, 77-78.

world" and with inner reality. Elsewhere he describes this as "the Mind of Man—/ My haunt, and the main region of my song."[24] In pursuing these connections, I shall emphasize what seem to me to be their apparent causes—that is, the psychogenesis of this sense of significant experience that is rendered metaphorically as soul and search.

Here, for instance, is one such connection to be further elaborated later:

> whether we be young or old,
> Our destiny, our being's heart and home,
> Is with infinitude, and only there.
> (VI, 603-605: 1850 version)

This excerpt is from one of the two passages we began by reading for their similarity, in which we found the journey metaphor and the growth metaphor fused: the growing faculties of the soul sensing something more to pursue, the self sensing something glorious related to itself beyond its ordinary consciousness, when Imagination has overwhelmed it. Leaving aside being and becoming for the moment, let us observe the "heart and home" that are—different though they are as images—the object in infinitude of this metaphorical journey. The journey metaphor suggests, somewhat mechanically, that one goes towards the eternal and the infinite, as for instance in the Christian pilgrimage of life, through death to eternal life. But there is also very strongly the suggestion of "returning" in that journey "home" to the place one left, or of returning to the condition that obtained before the search or journey began, as indeed the Christian sense of the origin of the soul in Eternity has always had it. Yet that "home"—an image of a tangible object outside one—is curiously paired with a "heart" which one would suppose to be inside one, the way our undivided "being" must be contained if it is felt to be un-

[24] "On Man, on Nature, and on Human Life . . . ," "Preface to the Edition of 1814," *The Excursion, Poetical Works*, pp. 589-590.

divided. Children, some have suggested,[25] have a more easily divisible sense of being than we realize except under special circumstances of inquiry, as I think Wordsworth shows when recalling his mother for the second and last time in *The Prelude*:

> Early died
> My honour'd Mother; she who was the heart
> And hinge of all our learnings and our loves:
> She left us destitute, and as we might
> Trooping together.
>
> (v, 256-260)

Here Wordsworth represents his life as a journey undertaken in destitution, the children "trooping together" along the road of life with a crucial connection broken between the heart as the life-sustaining part within one's own being and the much-loved external object symbolized by it. Not only had someone disappeared from the visible world, but perhaps Wordsworth's sense of the wholeness of his being had disappeared as well.

Wordsworth's accounts of his seemingly "mystical" experiences, I shall maintain, contain within them indications of those psychic realities which are most often ignored in the criticism of his poetry.[26] His accounts contain, too, traces of unconsciously remembered past experiences metaphorically associated with remembered experiences. Such memory traces are ordinarily unavailable to the memory as clear memories, and perhaps are only sometimes so available to the imagination with any clarity or consistency as they were for Wordsworth. But I think it is plain that the semblance of explanation, corresponding as it does to the poet's immediate *feeling* of his grasp on the matter he is presenting, is what makes possible for him the imaginative inclusion

25 See *Love, Hate, and Reparation,* two lectures by Melanie Klein and Joan Riviere.

26 See F. R. Leavis, *Revaluation,* pp. 171-175. That I think Dr. Leavis seriously wrong will be apparent: see below, Chap. IV, pp. 151-152 and Chap. VIII, pp. 384-385; see also Appendix, p. 405.

of unconscious memories in his significant recollections. Wordsworth was aware of poetic statement as a kind of "modal proposition," a way of dealing declaratively, affirmatively, and generally with the possible, the necessary, the contingent, and the wishful in personal experience. He knew about "what we half-create and what perceive," but he seems to have trusted that the poetic representation of feeling would express the urgency of such activity in the self; and it is this activity—his attempt to take possession of his life by using the feeling of being possessed—that we value and study, if we respond to it. When Wordsworth speaks of fixing "the wavering balance of my mind," the reader is adverted to the perilous nature of such urgency: inactivity is not allowed to seem a simple alternative. The problem to be dealt with first is that of the relationship between expression and understanding as, on the one hand, it is managed by the poet within the poem, and, on the other, as it is interpreted by the reader.

CHAPTER II

FROM "TINTERN ABBEY" TO *THE PRELUDE*

1. The Speaker

"Tintern Abbey," written in the blank verse style to be adopted for *The Prelude,* and written a year earlier than the first longer passages of Books I and II, shares with *The Prelude* the common theme of growth. It also reveals in one poetic whole the characteristic problems of Wordsworth's habit of self-regard, and offers for critical inspection the problem of personality in Romantic art. The problems to be considered are: What is expressed and what is understood in the poem? What may be understood on the basis of the poem? Much of one's reading of Wordsworth is determined by presuppositions about what can be expressed and understood in poetry.

First one must say how one regards Wordsworth as the "character" of the poem, its speaker. There is not, as in a play, a relativity of viewpoint. The character is not making a statement in a context of previous and subsequent statements and actions; we cannot balance expression and understanding as in drama, which imitates life; nor is there any clear sense that Wordsworth is detaching himself as creator from himself as speaker. It is plain that, despite the seemingly dramatic utterance of the poem, the poet does not pretend to know more than his "character" says: he is expressing and understanding himself to the extent that he is able. One has no sense that the poet could consciously intend as an effect of the poem whatever in it may suggest an alternative understanding to the self-understanding of the expressive speaker. I do not mean merely that we know it was not Wordsworth's habit to regard anything that he said ironically or to allow the validity of alternative interpretation of himself generally; I mean something more critical. Wordsworth is representing himself, but is not, in the *usual* literary sense of the word, using himself *representatively*. This is, I realize, a commonplace distinction between Renaissance and Romantic poetry.

If we consider Shakespeare only in the sonnets, we can more easily imagine a "character" speaking each of the sonnets, distinct from Shakespeare himself and created for what the sonnet is to express, than we can imagine a "character" distinct from Wordsworth in "Tintern Abbey" and created for what the poem expresses. However complex the matter of a Shakespeare sonnet may be, it is representative; one can project oneself into the role of the speaker and have his experience in one's own person, whether it is a matter that is truly resolved or truly ambiguous. The relation of the poem to the facts of Shakespeare's life is irrelevant; perhaps one can imagine the man of the sonnets best by the nature of his interests and the nuances of representation, the tension of surface understandings and probable ironies, but the experience of reading the sonnets generally is that of "having" their experience, in the way that the mind synthesizes poetic experience by playing the role and regarding oneself in it at the same time. One's feelings, if they are alive and responsive to the play of mind in the poem, are being more finely organized than one's own lesser powers of articulation could manage. The poetry of the poet who uses himself representatively provides both the feeling of poetic expression and the feeling of comprehending oneself differently.

If, on the other hand, we consider the Wordsworth of "Tintern Abbey," we find a man in his own mood on his own occasion. One cannot project oneself into the role of the speaker simply by trying to, nor is one supposed to try in that sense. Rather, the speaker is offering himself for regard in one particular activity of the self, his own. We are tempted to say that by allowing the forces seeking expression in him to work through him, the speaker realizes what he feels and also understands the self that feels it; and so it seems to many that Wordsworth "realizes" himself in an experience of communing once again with Nature, which has a restorative effect on him, or of communing with himself in Nature. It may be, however, that certain disturbances which are insistent but obscure in the self at times reach a threshold at which they must be expressed in some form if the ego is to maintain its mastery over them by again demonstrating that mastery. The forces that seem to rise from within are of oneself; the ego, one's habitual way of being oneself, must restrain their insurgency even while allowing them occasionally greater expression. Often without realizing quite how, one earns one's composure. What Wordsworth actually realizes, then, is his need and his ability to reaffirm himself at times in this way, which is not quite the same thing as realizing truly the nature of the disturbance. This need is the cause of his seeking the occasion to commune with Nature, which has become implicated in his psychology, as a means of adjusting the one to the other, the disturbance to the affirmation.

The poem, in no simple or direct way, is "about" senses of things that are deeper than the sense of the present occasion; and the reader is being invited only to observe the process of response to the occasion. Wordsworth felt that the poet's function was to give "new compositions of feeling" to the reader;[1] and here we may say that the real success of the poem is in the appearance and feeling of "self-realization"—of expression, restraint, and affirmation—that the reader may take from it. One learns from the poem to appreciate the habit of response demonstrated in it. The occasional, consistent, and recurrent nature of such moods and the consequent sense of self achieved by a responsive relaxation in them are made to seem very attractive. From

[1] Wordsworth, *Letters*, #130.

this poetic account of the experience, one may learn to allow one's need to affirm oneself to engage one's own disturbances; or one may discover the pleasure of allowing sensation and thought to sustain a mood of attenuated trust, and learn from it, too, to make explicit the connections in one's personal history between the self and the places where it experiences renewal. To achieve any amount of trust and of connectedness in time is no easy accomplishment in life, and the Wordsworth who speaks of what we "half create and what perceive" was not naive about his own attempt to hold to his affirmative intention. It is a question whether or not the realization of self is true, but the process displayed by Wordsworth is an uncommon enough one—urgent, instructive, beautiful. To interpret the "character" of "Tintern Abbey" or of *The Prelude* is inevitably to interpret Wordsworth himself, to accept his self-understanding or oppose it with one's own understanding of him.

One gets the impression from the possessiveness Wordsworth showed towards his poetry that he felt that an understanding of it and of himself as the speaker in it could be conveyed only by the repetition of the poem, a recitation in his own voice with his personal tonal emphases. He was uncomfortable with any understanding of his poetry that merely described what it was about, necessarily in statements other than his own.[2] "But no one," he says, "has completely understood me—not even Coleridge. He is not happy enough. I am myself one of the happiest of men and no man who lives a life of constant bustle and whose happiness depends on the opinions of others can possibly comprehend the best of my poems."[3] This was said by the embarrassing "older" Wordsworth in 1812, but there is something about it generally suggestive of the man. The conditions

[2] The impression Wordsworth made on people was that of a man very much attached to his own utterances, in poetry or in conversation. See *Blake, Coleridge, Wordsworth, Lamb: Selections from the Literary Remains of H. C. Robinson*, ed. Edith J. Morley, passim.

[3] *Letters*, #49.

for such happiness, we who live in constant bustle might say, are elaborate in their seclusion; yet Wordsworth had attained them by 1795 at the age of twenty-five. With the aid of a small legacy, which had made him independent, he could disregard the opinions of others since he was willing to live frugally. "Tintern Abbey" was written in 1798.

Just as one might suspect that the insistent claim of happiness is somewhat forced, so too might one suspect that he set strange terms for understanding his poetry. But were one simply to describe the apparent affirmative intention of the poet, one would omit a crucial aspect or function of the poem to which Wordsworth's very possessiveness attests. For were Wordsworth to recite the poem he would again express more than the interpretation, if only because the syntax is so intricate and strains to accommodate varying impressions, with hesitations and assertions close together. Affirmations, like claims of such extreme happiness, are not generally made wholly for their own sake—without, that is, being animated by, and made against, some lingering and equally habitual doubt which dictates the tone and form of assertion to be made against it. So, when one critic says that the poem is "about the dissociation of sensibility from thought and their reintegration" and finds in Wordsworth's concluding vision "[William's and Dorothy's] love for each other and for Nature, *Nature's love for them* . . . ,"[4] he has taken his description of what has happened from the generally affirmative intention of the poet and has limited the poem's meaning to the apparent success of that intention. One would not guess, then, that there is much or serious doubt in the poem, even less that there is deeper doubt than that of which Wordsworth seems partly conscious. Of course it is Wordsworth's unequivocal statement that leads to this overacceptance of "Nature's love for them":

[4] Robert Langbaum, *The Poetry of Experience,* p. 43. Though I cite it for the purpose of taking issue with an interpretation, I recommend this excellent book to the reader.

this prayer I make
Knowing that Nature never did betray
The Heart that loved her . . .

Anyone who has not found something about the assertion in the poem troubled and troubling is unlikely to pause here to inquire.

What is troubling here? Is it just that "betray" sounds too heavily, resonates too inopportunely, having its own effect against the simple declarative sense of the sentence? One has difficulty imagining in what sense "betrayal" could be applied to Nature. Perhaps it is the oddness of the locution "never did betray" that calls too much attention to "betray," or perhaps it is the oddness of saying such a thing at such a moment at all. I mean only to suggest a way of questioning the as-yet unquestioned relationship with Nature. But except for death as Nature's possible "betrayal" of human life, one can think of no reason for distrusting her; and death as one of the many natural events of the future seems excluded from the future imagined in the poem.

In what way does Nature seem to love them? Nature, in that it is personified, has acquired the attributes of someone from someone; "she" can be seen more or less clearly as different from objective phenomena. Then, if we have raised a question about Wordsworth's Nature and possible reasons for distrusting "her," we have really raised the question about the relationship implied by those attributes and reasons for trusting or distrusting it. It is plain, I think, that this nurse, guide, guardian of the heart, soul of the moral being, is Nature as the *mother*, before whom brother and sister stand. Orphaned as children but grown up now, separated for years and only recently reunited, they stand here. The brother is exhorting the sister to allow her mind to become, like his, a metaphorical home, an imaginatively reconstituted dwelling place able to receive this Presence predisposed to feed their minds with lofty thoughts, receive their worship, and exchange love with them while continuing to supervise their growth. This is a very filial occasion. But if we pursue our original question, the distrust implied by the attributes that personify Nature, we must ask: why distrust mother? We must look at Nature since Wordsworth is talking about her.

In the context of the statement that Nature never did betray the heart that loved her, Wordsworth has been trying to value change by calling it growth; he has been trying to accept what has happened to him while observing wistfully his sister, to whom it has not yet happened:

> oh, yet a little while
> May I behold in thee what I was once.

Again, it is plain: it is this change that is the possible betrayal by Nature. Nature has led him to this—has he been betrayed? But what *has* Nature led him to? Most simply, to himself as he is through his experiences, for which Nature seems also responsible. Is it possible, then, that unconscious feelings about his mother are expressed in his present concern with trust and well-being?

It is worth pausing here to observe that Wordsworth, who seems so much older than Dorothy (the "dear, dear sister" he addresses), is in fact only two years older and that the difference between them is in Wordsworth's greater experience of the world. At the time of his first visit to the Wye Valley, alone, in 1793, he had already had a profound experience of the world, the consequence of which was a prolonged sense of impending crisis. This five-year interim between visits, we can show, was a time of the severest psychic crisis for him.[5] *The Prelude,* which he will start to write in this very year, 1798, will reveal how much he felt Nature had led him to all of his experiences; and in it, too, he will deal with that difficult retrospect of change

[5] For a brief but very judicious consideration of Wordsworth's crisis and of the scholarly interpretations of it, the reader should see the account given by de Selincourt in *The Prelude,* pp. 603-606.

under the heading of growth. At the time of his first visit to the Wye Valley, he had been already significantly different from what he feels he was in his youth, an innocent like Dorothy; and at that time he was unwilling or unable to let thoughts of his recent experience of the world and of his present self accompany him into the landscape in his attempt to regain a lost relationship: "more like a man/ Flying from something that he dreads, than one/ Who sought the thing he loved." I would suggest here the psychological term "regression" to describe the attempt to withdraw the self from a present reality into a previous one.[6]

In that regressive disengagement there figures a bodily metaphor that is of interest psychosexually: in 1793, Wordsworth fled to this landscape, as he tells us, feeling dread, and seeking to satisfy here "an appetite; a feeling and a love"—"drinking in" the landscape as he says of vision many times in *The Prelude*—with what was always for him an oral and incorporative eye. He left behind, symbolically, in France, the more phallic identification of himself as a man engaging in life—sexually with a woman, politically with people and historical issues. He had become a thinking man living in History, a man sympathetic with Republicanism and with the new revolutionary spirit of the people opposing oppressive authority. The man who was to "yield up moral questions in despair" at some point between 1793 and 1798 was first to flee thought and seek the simplest kind of delight in visual sensation. Shortly before his experience of despair he was to turn again and flee natural feeling, seeking in Godwinism pure abstract thought about man.[7] However one dates these shifts of activity, what one is observing is intolerable conflict within a young man and the wide swings of mood familiar in clinical observation.

[6] See Freud, "On Narcissism," Standard Edition of the Complete Psychological Works (hereafter CW, see Bibliography), vol. XIV, 67-102; also, briefly, "Psycho-Analysis," CW XVIII, 246-247 (the theory of repression). See, too, Anna Freud, *The Ego and the Mechanisms of Defense*.

[7] *The Prelude*, p. 604f.

The year 1793 had found him reacting with sustained perplexity to the September Massacres in France, about which he equivocated; to the imprisonment and subsequent execution of the French King, about which he felt dread; to the declaration of war between England and France, about which he felt an aggrieved dismay, since he had come to regard the principles of the revolution ideologically as "a higher creed" than nationalism;[8] and to the ascendancy of the opportunistic Robespierre as the champion of the revolution, about which he felt a fearful distrust. He had recently written the challenging and self-declaring "Letter to the Bishop of Llandaff," but he had withheld it from publication.[9] Most significantly, he had left behind, in France, Annette Vallon, his French mistress or then wife-to-be, who was pregnant and who was soon to bear him his illegitimate daughter Caroline. These are facts more significantly dealt with in relation to *The Prelude*, but they are relevant to "Tintern Abbey," at least in the sense that they suggest some of the circumstantial realities minimally indicated in the poem.

To return now to the context of the statement that "Nature never did betray the heart that loved her," notice that he is *not* saying that "Nature *never would* betray the heart that loved her"—a line that would fit well enough metrically and would be a more appropriate construction for a statement of probability expressing a feeling about Nature. If one thinks the statement inappropriate to begin with, the altered form of it would not make much difference to that effect; but actually he has hit upon, perhaps unconsciously, the oddest possible locution for it: "never did betray." Either we trust elementally by being unsuspicious or we overcome distrust, as all people capable of trust probably must. There is also such a phenomenon as denial when the normal degree of distrust is rigidly denied because its implications are unacceptable to consciousness.

[8] *Ibid.*, x, 285-286.

[9] "Letter to the Bishop of Llandaff, Apology for the French Revolution, 1793," *Prose Works*, vol. I, pp. 1-23.

"Never did betray" seems to be recalling a past betrayal, rigidly denied, that resembles the present sense of betrayal because of an unconsciously held resemblance between the mother and Nature. Why Nature should be implicated in so personal a relationship is a question we shall have occasion many times to raise; but here it is worth insisting on one of the usually ignored implications of the cliché "Mother Nature." It is indeed the case that mothers are the models upon which love is built and relatedness with the world is accepted (as Wordsworth knew well and himself elaborated); but they are also regarded ambivalently for a variety of formative reasons, irrationally blamed and raged against for betrayals of that too perishable security in which the infant thrives safe from reality, from the burdens of selfhood and the difficult possibilities and opportunities of life. If this is psychologically the case in normative growth, then surely there is no clearer model of betrayal than the mother who leaves her children orphaned early in life. It is this unconscious sense of grievance denied, I think, that is present in "She *left us destitute,* and as we might/ Trooping together," in that passage quoted earlier to show the journey metaphor in relation to the mother.[10]

It is no accident that "Tintern Abbey" expresses unmistakably and profoundly what can only be called aversion for those difficult possibilities and opportunities of worldly life. Dr. Johnson said: "When a man is tired of London, he is tired of Life!"[11] We may observe how little Wordsworth expects from the evil-tongued, rash, sneering, hypocritically-kind, dreary reality of daily life and other people. Wearied by the "burthen of the mystery" and the "unnatural self" that develops in relation to the "unintelligible world," he is relieved by the "joy" of a state of soul that is like self-loss. "Joy" becomes the key to the poem, since with his affirmative intention the poet will tell us that Nature leads us "from joy to joy."

10 *The Prelude*, v, 259-260.

11 James Boswell, *Life Of Johnson*, ed. G. B. Hill, rev. L. F. Powell, vol. III, p. 178.

Before analyzing the difficult logic by which Wordsworth arrives at his self-reassuring sense of growth and of Nature's benevolent intentions towards himself and Dorothy, we should observe something peculiar about poetic effects as distinguished from the apparent declarative sense of poetic statement: the effects may be inimical to the declarative sense of what is being said, and so subversively as to raise the question of intention. What does the poet "really" intend? and in which sense of "intend"? Let us observe here simply what follows "never did betray . . . ":

'tis her privilege,
Through all the years of this our life, to lead
From joy to joy: for she can so inform
The mind that is within us, so impress
With quietness and beauty, and so feed
With lofty thoughts, that neither evil tongues,
Rash judgements, nor the sneers of selfish men,
Nor greetings where no kindness is, nor all
The dreary intercourse of daily life
Shall e'er prevail against us, or disturb
Our Cheerful faith, that all which we behold
Is full of blessings.

Did Wordsworth not know, one wonders, that he was *not* presenting the sense of "from joy to joy," but rather the opposite? that he was not merely noticing the apparent signs of joylessness that threaten the cherished reality of joy, but rather expressing a profound sense of joylessness consistent with every other suggestion in the poem of the present reality he has left in revisiting the Wye Valley—the "lonely rooms," "the many shapes of joyless daylight?" The declarative sense simply does not survive the greater effect of a line like "The dreary intercourse of daily life," which gathers to itself the felt aversions of "evil," "rash," "sneers," "no kindness," and makes "dreary" the most expressive as well as the longest sounding word in the poem. (Notice, too, that one even tends to hold "daily" unusually long, as if repeating "dreary," intensifying in that way the effect of "dreary" against its context, as if the line had only two stresses: "The dréar-ry intercourse of daíl-ly life.")

It is very difficult to believe that Wordsworth "means" here what, unquestionably, he consciously wants to mean:

> that all which we behold
> Is full of blessings.

This affirmation makes clearer what is at stake: Nature has led him to this and it is a question of expressing one's sense of what one has been led to—a new joy in place of old ones, a reality full of blessings, or the opposite? The passage states one thing and expresses another. "Prevail against" makes us think of an assault made on one's "cheerful faith," and "cheerful faith," in its pathetic declarative flatness, seems less like an affirmation than a denial of an all but habitual cheerlessness. The assertion of Nature's benevolence is made simultaneously with the denial of possible doubt, though doubt is being raised by the effect of the passage. One might also say that Wordsworth asserts the conviction of joy along with and against the unavoidable expression of an intolerable sense of joylessness which is in part evoked by the Wye Valley and in part simply expressed there.

The passage seems to say that he has had a preferred relationship with benevolent Nature and that with his sense of a continuing and renewable relationship he can withstand the ways in which reality attempts to spoil the joy of that relationship. "Continuing" and "renewable" are the issues in the poem, for he has observed a change in his response to Nature; and in such matters there are no changes but "natural" ones. But does it not also seem that the preferences expressed in the poem (and their corresponding aversions) are extreme? Would it be unfair to consider for the moment that the need for this preferred relationship with Nature in fact precludes a more responsive engagement with other people and other places? and that that accounts for the sense of joylessness Wordsworth experienced in the city as a demanding reality? In offering its opportunities by making its own kinds of demands the city really was inimical to his predisposition to seek another kind of joy in Nature and solitude.

It would be best to approach this need for solitude through his representations of his sense of joy. His most recent sense of joy—"And I have felt/ A Presence that disturbs me with the joy/ Of elevated thoughts . . ."—must be considered last since it depends on what it is being distinguished from; it fits with the affirmative intention; it announces the willingness to trust that change is growth and that there are gains in loss. The evocation of the last visit—"And all its aching *joys* are now no more/ And all its dizzy raptures"—sets the quality of the past response against that of the present occasion. The representation of its particular joys, in other words, is presented in the poem only to convey his awareness of what he has been led away from by Nature. The significant difference between the response on the past occasion and the response now necessarily opposes the interim between the two visits to the immediate future. The most significant statement about joy is actually made about the interim between the two visits; and the apprehensions now felt about the immediate future of joy is the effective cause of the doubt of Nature in the poem. And yet it is most difficult to suggest what the apprehension is where profound doubt is to be seen as strongly denied doubt, as one might say "this would be very troubling were there cause to worry."

Consider that after presenting his immediate response to the landscape, he talks about what "these beauteous forms" have meant to him in the interim between visits, and then, for some reason, wonders whether what he has just said about the effect of those beauteous forms on the spirit is true or not: "If this be but a vain belief, yet oh! how oft . . ." It is one thing to assume that, having noticed that his present response is different from his past one, he wonders simply whether he can expect the same after-effects in the future;

but it is another thing altogether to interpret the degree of Wordsworth's awareness of his doubt. Have "these beauteous forms" as such ever had the complicated effect attributed to them? And what does it mean that he has wanted to believe that they do? Obviously, in wondering, Wordsworth knows that he is experiencing some doubt, and he knows it throughout the poem. I believe that he attempts to express, contain, and resolve a doubt in the poem in order to suppress a deeper experience of it. The depth of the doubt will be revealed only in the form of denial.

Let us observe here how these following lines are meant to shift our attention and fail to do so:

> And now, with gleams of half-extinguished thought,
> With many recognitions dim and faint,
> And somewhat of a sad perplexity,
> The picture of the mind revives again:
> While here I stand, not only with the sense
> Of present pleasure, but with pleasing thoughts
> That in this moment there is life and food
> For future years. And so I dare to hope,
> Though changed, no doubt, from what I was
>   when first
> I came among these hills . . .

The somewhat abrupt "And now . . ." at the beginning of this new passage (which follows the exclamation "How oft in spirit have I turned to thee!") is immediately qualified; and so much so that the simple effect of a statement like "And now . . . the picture of the mind revives again" is lost because of the qualifying "with" statements that intervene. Wordsworth could have left them out, but it would seem that acknowledging some kind of hesitation here was important to him. By observing the syntax, we can see that for him the hesitation is adequately "contained" in a larger syntactical statement meant to lead onwards. The reader's mind, of course, responds instead to the hesitation: which half-extinguished thoughts? thoughts of what? dim and faint recollections of what? and why a sad perplexity?

For Wordsworth, however, the colon after "again" emphatically shifts his attention to the present moment of his affirmative intention:

> The picture of the mind revives again:
> While here I stand, not only with the sense
> Of present pleasure, but with pleasing thoughts
> That in this moment there is life and food
> For future years. And so I dare to hope,
> Though changed, no doubt, from what I was
>   when first
> I came among these hills . . .

Not to say this would require of him the further elaboration of what precedes the colon. But here is an expression of that apprehensiveness I have related to doubt and denial: something saddening and perplexing follows from a momentary doubt of his "belief," and is relieved by a self-given assurance that literally does not follow anything except a colon. The "with" statements on this side of the colon—"with the sense of present pleasure . . . with pleasant thoughts . . ."—seem intended to balance, answer, or cancel the earlier ones in an almost rhetorically antithetical way. The last part of this reassurance—"And so I dare to hope/ Though changed, no doubt, from what I was when first/ I came among these hills . . ." has exactly that way of admitting off-handedly what would be very troubling were there much cause to worry.

I think this sequence must be interpreted in the following way: when he says "The picture of the mind revives again:/ While here I stand . . . ," he is taking a fresh look at the scenery in front of him; he is recovering himself from the sequence of associated thoughts and feelings that have preceded it. The sequence had begun with "these beauteous forms" and moved inwards, away from the present moment and place to other states of mind and other feelings suggested by the forms and associated with them; in mood, however, the sequence moves from assurance to uncertainty to doubt, and apparently even to the beginnings of a deeper recognition of doubt. But now he is returning to the habitual self-consciousness present at the beginning of the poem in "once again do I behold . . ." He is assigning to the present occasion a meaning that resembles the one he began by assigning to the last visit: "These beauteous forms . . . I have owed to them. . . ."

What actually has happened? Thinking about these beauteous forms upon seeing them again, he has had the momentary felt recollection of turning inwards, of having access to "that serene and blessed mood." The doubt he has just felt about the connection between these forms and that mood has something to do with his present response; it is thoughtful rather than sensuous. But by recalling the experience of turning inwards, by saying "turned to thee," and then repeating emphatically "turn'd to thee!" he again experiences momentarily what it has felt like to feel like that. The actual place, a close scrutiny of the poem will show, has less appeal to him than that feeling and mood. But *between* his saying emphatically "turn'd to thee!" at the end of one verse paragraph and his resuming speaking with the abrupt "And now . . . ," there has been some further mental activity, experienced and resisted, not articulated or set down here, and indicated minimally by the statement "with gleams of half-extinguished thought." It is "contained" by the construction that leads to the colon: "And now (. . .) the picture of the mind revives again."

But notice, too, that by saying Wordsworth is recovering himself from a sequence of thoughts that led both to doubts and the beginnings of a deeper recognition of doubt, I have been treating the poem as Wordsworth's behavior, the poet as character. It is true that Wordsworth often did what the title of the poem suggests ("*composed* a few miles above Tintern Abbey . . ."), that is, actually stood as the expressive speaker at the spot, composing lines in his head and carrying them in memory to be set down later exactly as he had felt them. But the question necessarily arises as to how he as artist, reading what he had set down, regarded as sufficient the clarity and meaning of these lines? If, as we must assume, Wordsworth felt satisfied that the statements expressed and related one kind of feeling to another, then he was consciously using a sense of doubt here, one that is contained and resolved *for him* by his strong intention to be affirmative. But I am arguing that in so fine an artist the art is truer and more revealing than the conscious intention as we infer it of the artist, and is accessible to criticism.

2. The Depths of Response

Having now raised the question of alternative meanings and other intentions, I would like to make a more basic observation about this tendency in Wordsworth as it may be seen first in the poetic effects of this poem. This tendency to move away from the present moment towards feelings and thoughts that are deeper and prior to it can also be seen as expressive of strong and unrealized preconscious wishes that bear upon the present occasion while remaining apart from and at variance with Wordsworth's apparent conscious intentions; the tendency qualifies psychically the generally self-affirmative statement of the poem. It is observable even in his present perception of the landscape, significantly revealing things that are not being said. The general motion of the poem from the beginning has been away from the actual scene, despite the marveling and specifying of "again I . . . once again I . . . again I," "these . . . this . . . these . . . these. . . ." Notice that the "wild secluded scene" is a kind of material notation of its elusive mental equivalent, "thoughts of more deep seclusion," or that the fixed details being specified are induced by the wishful metaphorical language to take on a motion that also proceeds from the mind, "clad in one green hue . . .

lose themselves . . . run wild . . . ," as he tells us *he* himself had done at his last visit.

Notice especially the motion towards the "Hermit" at the end of the first paragraph: from the actual through the imaginative to the "imaginary." Imaginatively, the woods take on human activity: dressed up in themselves and set free metaphorically, *they* seem to enjoy being there. Then the "vagrant dwellers" he mentions are simply inferred from the smoke "sent up, in silence, from among the trees!" The smoke is unsubstantial, but it is there. But the exclamation seems to be prompted by the wish: imagine! "*vagrant* dwellers!" "*houseless* woods!" These are people wishfully imagined by Wordsworth to be living in Nature, and living no doubt in the contentment that Wordsworth associated with Nature, rather than the actual destitution one associates with itinerant vagrancy. The Hermit, unlike the imaginary vagrant community that precedes him, is completely alone. He is the man who has renounced the world and the human community. The passage ends with the present indicative replacing the conditional: "The Hermit *sits* alone." It is hard not to believe that he is *there*, or there to Wordsworth. So, too, by wishful evocation, the Sylvan Wye seems to participate in a human way—"thou *wanderer* through the woods"—assimilated imaginatively to his mood; and from river through vagrant dwellers, through Hermit to Wordsworth, the representations of being here blend the natural and the human, expressing his volition, *wanting* to be here. The same longing that results in an actual revisiting of the Wye Valley on a tour affects talking about it when there, indicating on the part of Wordsworth a strongly wishful affinity with such natural or imaginary alternatives to his own lot.

With this in mind we should pursue the wishfulness underlying his further recollections of what these "beauteous forms" have been to him, since we have seen that even here in the Wye Valley his response to what is material and actual serves to evoke deeper wishes. The imaginary Hermit in his cave has been wishfully projected on this actual landscape in exactly the same way that this actual landscape has provided an occasion for Wordsworth's mind receiving, as from outside itself, "thoughts of more deep seclusion." Here, too, we should notice that Wordsworth has disregarded the ordinary way of saying things. He says:

> Once again
> Do I behold these steep and lofty cliffs
> That *on* a wild secluded scene impress
> Thoughts of more deep seclusion . . .

as if the cliffs were pressing thoughts of a deeper seclusion on the scene itself and he were perceiving the thoughts there, rather than simply that a secluded scene is making him think of even deeper seclusion.

Perhaps here too the wishful language is telling us a greater truth, that thoughts of a more deep seclusion are forcing themselves on the perceiver and that inner reality is affecting the perception of outer reality. The mind often seeks the external object on which it can best project what it unconsciously wishes most to perceive; and it is significant that, instead of expressing a wish directly, one should find it being expressed more or less impersonally, perhaps directed at one, because this attests to an important degree of unacceptability about the wish. The strange opposition of self-conscious marveling and specifying ("once again I . . . again I . . .") and the wishful blurring of the detail is in point here, because beneath the self-conscious activity of placing himself as the beholder of the landscape is clearly a wish to do what the wishful language makes the landscape do: run wild, lose oneself. The presentation of the landscape further suggests blurring and loss of self in the assimilation of the natural and the human to each other and, in the projection of the Hermit, of the real to the imaginary.

In a psychological way it is worth considering that an imaginary figure projected into a real external landscape corresponds to a real figure in an "imaginary" or internal landscape. What is internal or imaginary is nevertheless psychically real; and we shall have many occasions to observe how landscapes pass in and out of Wordsworth. To him, landscapes were imbued with perceptible powers of mind: the inner landscape of the poet's mind with Imagination, the outer mountainous landscape with God's Revelation. Wordsworth at times becomes a figure metaphorically wandering in the inner landscape of his own mind, but here, in "Tintern Abbey," the process begins, the poetic habit is revealed in its earliest form. Wordsworth has imagined a figure symbolic of a real but unacceptable psychic wish, the Hermit who would renounce the world and withdraw into the landscape and from it into a cave and "more deep seclusion." One might suppose rightly that Wordsworth is aware of his preference for where he is to where he has come from; but this is not all his preference means, nor does Wordsworth realize the implications of what he expresses. The Hermit and the "thoughts of more deep seclusion," taken together, suggest that Wordsworth's visiting this particular landscape cannot satisfy the inner needs that give rise to this visit.

The wishful quality of his recollections of "these beauteous forms" tells us what they have been to him in the interim since his last visit. How often, Wordsworth says, his spirit has turned to the Sylvan Wye and these beauteous forms when, "amid the many shapes of joyless daylight," his heart has been oppressed by "the fever of the world." That is, the beauteous forms are a landscape within Wordsworth's mind; and Wordsworth withdraws into his own mind and experiences there tranquil restoration. What Wordsworth withdraws from, as he characterizes it, is an impressively unpleasant reality. If by this he means the city, we can imagine that a place so intolerable to him, with its dreary style of life, should be rejected, especially with the rural alternative presented so attractively; but if he means, as he seems to, external reality too, the rejection of it in favor of something withdrawn and inner is a potential psychic disaster.

Is it fair to represent what the poem is expressing in this way? No, in the sense that his affirmative intention firmly governs what the poem states; but yes, in the sense that the feelings attached to the characterizing details and the details themselves express greater aversion than fits with the poem's apparent issues. Wordsworth is not simply expressing that there is something infinitely preferable about the country to the city, or even for him alone, but rather that there is something tedious about life and the world for him. Expressing his alienation from the life of society and of the city and his preference for the country as it exists in his mind helps him relieve that feeling of deeper aversion. Yet one need only notice that it is not the country itself—as for instance *here* and *now*, or even *then* in the past—but rather the state of soul induced in him by the after-contemplation of Nature that is so very preferable.[12] But the meaning of such contemplation, one suspects, is not in the actual recollection of a place that one has been or could go back to, but rather, in some way, in the psychic activity of withdrawal itself when a reality that is present and unpleasant recedes and one that is absent and pleasurable takes its place. As the representation of joy in the poem suggests, the beauteous forms seem to stand for a reality felt by Wordsworth to be both absent and within him. It is this feeling of a deep and absent reality that is so important to him that needs interpreting, and not simply the realistic differences between the country and the city and what the sense of the one and of the other allows to the spirit.

12 "After-contemplation" is more perfectly rendered by Wordsworth in "I wandered lonely as a cloud." Recalling the daffodils, he says:

> For oft, when on my couch I lie,
> In vacant or in pensive mood,
> They flash upon that inward eye
> Which is the bliss of solitude.
>
> (*Poetical Works*, p. 149)

The wishfulness that underlies this deepest sense of joy makes us think of his ways of pursuing joy, for if his expectation of joy in future life is being extended and affirmed at the present moment, it is being distinguished at the same time from other senses of active pursuit, physical and psychic. For instance, the present return to the Wye Valley is a physical activity; and I take the response on the present occasion to reveal the real but limited pleasure of the self at an actual, much loved, and very pleasant place. At the same time, it reveals the pressing wish for something more psychically real, something that this marveling and specifying self can neither name nor have, nor this landscape be nor continue to seem. But the reality of joy has at other times been pursued in a psychic way, as Wordsworth in part knows, a way curiously involving this very landscape as inner imagery and involving the extinction of the habitually conscious self.

The strenuous physical activity and the emotional intensity of his last visit as he represents it now are very revealing. Before this present visit, it must have seemed to him that there was some direct causal relationship between that intense response to the landscape and the after-effects of its "beauteous forms" in his mind. He says:

> when like a roe
> I bounded o'er the mountains, by the sides
> Of the deep rivers, and the lonely streams,
> Wherever Nature led: more like a man
> Flying from something that he dreads, than one
> Who sought the thing he loved. For Nature then
> (The coarser pleasures of my boyish days,
> And their glad animal movements all gone by)
> To me was all in all.—I cannot paint
> What then I was. The sounding cataract
> Haunted me like a passion: the tall rock,
> The mountain, and the deep and gloomy wood,
> Their colours and their forms, were then to me

An appetite; a feeling and a love,
That had no need of a remoter charm,
By thought supplied, nor any interest
Unborrowed from the eye.

At first the bounding roe conveys simply the sense of a physically vigorous response, as well as that of an instinctual and seemingly unself-conscious one. These qualities in the past are easily distinguished from that of the present in which a thoughtful and self-conscious person is saying: "the day is come when I again *repose* here . . . and *view* . . . while here I *stand* . . . ," though what I have called the wishful quality of the language actually preserves the frenetic past response in the present one. But then the mention of the "bounding roe" seems to have suggested a further recollection of himself—"more like a man/ Flying from something that he dreads"—because of the way in which bounding deer suggest startled deer fleeing into a protective landscape. The suggestion is of fleeing from man, as Wordsworth actually was at the time, but although he completes the sense of the startled deer with the figure of his own fleeing person, he leaves it in that peculiar form: the figure of a man suggests a deer who suggests a man. When he then says parenthetically that animal movements, "*glad* animal movements," characterize him truly only in the very distant past of his boyhood, one loses track of the metaphor; it has changed meaning to convey uncertain distinctions.

One suspects that Wordsworth was seeking in Nature an object for "an appetite, a feeling and a love" after having had a dreadful experience of the world of men; also, that what he sought was being projected into Nature and was associated unconsciously not simply with boyhood but with the truly unself-conscious and instinctual gratifications of infancy. For the infant, "an appetite, a feeling and a love" are barely distinguishable, nor is the self wholly distinguished from the primal external object in infantile narcissism.

Since Wordsworth in the present intends to affirm that change is growth, he must see primarily the continuity of past joy and present joy. Obviously, then, in avoiding any present sense of doubt, of dread, or of fleeing in spirit, he will pass over that past experience of dread from which apparently joy was achieved with some difficulty. When he goes on to affirm a connectedness in time that joins Nature and "the language of the sense" to his purest thoughts and his present "moral being," this large self-acceptance *is* his trust that continued change is continued growth. The losses, first of pure infantile gratification, then of the "glad animal movements" of boyhood, and then of the "aching joys" and "dizzy raptures" of a regressive response to Nature are all compensated for now, he hopes, with appropriate gains in this thoughtful and "joyful" enough present response. In this "trust" is also to be seen the strength of his denial of a profound doubt.

Nature, the landscape, has been both a protective place and the object of an "appetite, a feeling and a love." It is possible to say that here is an example of the way in which Nature "stands for" the protective and feeding mother unconsciously recollected and desiderated. The combination of this regressive search for pure pleasure with the attempt to extinguish self-consciousness suggests that the intense physical activity was an enactment of an unconscious wish. It is as if the projection of unacknowledged psychic needs into external reality momentarily makes possible the feeling that intense physical activity *could* satisfy those needs sensuously without their being named and known as such. That this is so is not surprising, for it is always so to some extent of the unconscious element in human behavior; but that it should be so apparent here is surprising. Wordsworth remembers himself as wholly given over to the experience, equally in flight from the world and from himself. The bounding *into* the landscape, the figurative feeding with the eyes, the exhilarated experiences of aching joys, dizzy raptures, and wild ecstasies suggest the same psychic wish for ecstatic loss of self and for satiation that the ancient cult-worship of Dionysus or Cybele provided in the sensational strenuousness of the orgy. In such worship the wish was not clarified; it remained the mystery of the worship.

If we are concerned with the relationship of affirmation and doubt, of denial and expression, we must observe that instinctual dread precedes the sense of joy expressed here. From it, it would seem, comes the compelling attractiveness of an earlier mode of gratification. Instinctual dread, however, reminds us of other joys renounced and present pursuits that are being determined by avoidances. Joy, rapture, ecstasy, and loss of self could, for instance, characterize the sexual union of lovers, as indeed they always have. The willing dependency on Nature ("wherever Nature led") limits the goals and the meanings of love to those felt within that dependency—"oh! with far deeper zeal/ Of holier love"—and the regressive pursuit has as its goal the ultimate state of satisfaction in that mode: contentment achieved in the continuous ingestion of love and power from Nature, the satisfaction of "an appetite, a feeling and a love."

Apparently, there is a deeper joy still; it is that "serene and blessed mood," the state of being "a living soul." It is connected with the beauteous forms; it has occurred in the interim between visits; and it is, unmistakably, Wordsworth's representation of the greatest joy as he speaks of joy in the poem. On the present occasion he subsumes the loss of past joy under the affirmation of present gains; but the immediate future of this greatest joy is left uncertain. Nevertheless, he says:

> While here I stand, not only with the sense
> Of present pleasure, but with pleasing thoughts
> That in this moment there is life and food
> For future years. And so I dare to hope,
> Though changed, no doubt, from what I was . . .

But the doubt is intercepted and set aside.

The passage in which he speaks of the "serene and

blessed mood" is of the kind in Wordsworth's poetry most likely to be regarded as impenetrable; it is a characteristic description of a recognizable state of revitalizing relaxation becoming at once more joyful and less recognizable as the state of soul becomes what is often called "mystical" in Wordsworthian criticism. No one cares to say what he supposes Wordsworth means that "we" see in

> that serene and blessed mood,
> In which the affections gently lead us on,
> Until, the breath of this corporeal frame
> And even the motion of our human blood
> Almost suspended, we are laid asleep
> In body, and become a living soul:
> While with an eye made quiet by the power
> Of Harmony, and the deep power of joy,
> We see into the life of things.

It is easier to see how the "beauteous forms" when called to mind during Wordsworth's long absence from the place may be said to cause "sensations sweet/ Felt in the blood and felt along the heart" than to see what follows or quite how it follows. That this mood is important to Wordsworth is more easily acknowledged than that an understanding of it is important to the poem.

The extension of this causal connection ("Not less, I trust,/ To them I may have owed another gift/ Of aspect more sublime . . .") is itself tentatively put. Wordsworth is not saying with certainty that the "serene and blessed mood" is a deepening or continuation of the tranquil restorative effect of calling the beauteous forms to mind, though perhaps before this present occasion he might have thought of one continuous mood as "that blessed mood," and then further as "that serene and blessed mood." What is presented here is a sense of spiritual relief, and it would simplify matters to say that the mood is continuous, that it goes from the initial sweet sensations to the blissful state of being laid asleep in body and becoming a living soul.

But Wordsworth says more tentatively "I may have owed. . . ." That these states may not be continuous seems to be what disturbs him momentarily when he says: "If this be but a vain belief, yet oh! . . . ," as if he were asking whether this ultimate state has some unknown cause instead of its apparent cause; or as if he were assuring us that he, too, knows that the cause of so wondrous a thing is strange and must seem discontinuous with what precedes it. But the tentativeness may also mean that he is not sure of what he now *wants* to believe about the cause of that mood, although he has had no reason to wonder until now. If the quality and intensity of his past response had been the cause of it, then very possibly his changed response now will be decisive to its future. It is only when he talks about the "Presence" shortly afterwards that he acquires the much desired feeling of control over moods that have seemed to depend on external objects or places. But the thought that the mood may have had no knowable cause is worse; for even the measure of control that his spirit has seemed to exercise would be lost, and such moods might simply cease to recur as he ages and changes. Having perceived significant change in himself, he will consider this doubt no further, although it may be what glimmers to him in the "gleams of half-extinguished thought."

If one assumes that these states of soul are continuous except for a momentary hesitation on Wordsworth's part to say so, then perhaps something even more "real" than the beauteous forms is seen by the soul when it sees "into the life of things." He may be seeing through the forms to what they stand for, or he may be describing the sensation of seeing in a different way from the figurative sense of "seeing" what things *mean.* Is it that the farthest reaches of such psychic withdrawal or inner contemplation occasion an ego state, a metaphysical sensation of seeing-in-depth, that the grosser physical activity of seeing does not occasion or now no longer seems to? His emphasis on being "laid asleep in body" and on an "eye made quiet" by the powers of harmony and joy suggests this is so. "Seeing"—by the cessation of all activity in this ego state—contrasts very strikingly with the vigorous activity of "seeing" Nature at the last visit, as does the quiet living soul with the active self. The wish we observed earlier (to lose oneself in the landscape as the wishful language of description makes the landscape lose itself in itself) comes to mind here; the bliss of "that serene and blessed mood" is that of loss of self when one has withdrawn into, and lost oneself in, the imagery within the mind. And that seemingly motionless activity results in the deepest feeling of completion that Wordsworth describes.

Seeing into the life of things seems to be a suspension of the breath and the blood because of the extinction of the usual bodily sense of the one-who-sees, of the ordinary conscious self that has seen all too clearly "this unintelligible world." In the past he had rediscovered the Nature from which the conscious self had been differentiated in growth, and in the interim he had discovered his desire to be assimilated as "soul" to that Nature, *or to what Nature stands for in his mind.* The "living soul," which is in some way within and beneath the ordinary self, and the permanent "life of things" seem to him to coalesce by the sensation of an inner seeing. In describing that state, the poet maintains only the minimal sense of subject and object that language forces upon any account of what has happened to one, even that of the coalescence of subject and object. There is consciousness without self-consciousness.

To Wordsworth, the soul is something deep within one; the self retains a recollection of pleasurable existence free from the experience of time as time relates to the self's cumulative awareness of itself.[13] The affections lead him

13 Wordsworth treats this phenomenon of the self in time and the recollection of "soul" as free from, or prior to, the life of the self in time in various places, to which I make several references in the text (e.g. the "Immortality Ode," MS RV, *The Prelude*, etc.). Cf. Freud, "On Narcissism" and "Instincts and Their Vicissitudes," CW XIV; also, "Civilization and Its Discontents," CW XXI, 64-73.

back to this sense of soul characterized by extreme physical passivity and associated further with sleep, harmony, joy, and vision. Wordsworth had described this elsewhere in a passage we have already observed:

> By such communion I was early taught
> That what we see of forms and images
> Which float along our minds and what we feel
> Of active, or recognizable thought,
> Prospectiveness, intelligence or will
> Not only is not worthy to be deemed
> Our being, to be prized as what we are
> But is the very littleness of life.
> Such consciousnesses seemed but accidents
> Relapses from the one interior life
> Which is in all things, from that unity
> In which all beings live with God, are lost
> In God and Nature, in one mighty whole
> As indistinguishable as the cloudless east
> At noon is from the cloudless west when all
> The hemisphere is one cerulean blue . . .
>
> (MS RV)

> —In which all beings live with God, themselves
> Are God, existing in one mighty whole.
>
> (MS A2 of "Peter Bell")

Here, too, growth and self-consciousness are an estrangement from the undifferentiated state of soul, and soul is an otherness at once within and without, greater and more real than the habitual sense of self. This passage on "the one interior life" which resembles the coalescence of "living soul" and "the life of things" was never used in the published version of *The Prelude*. Wordsworth would have transcribed it into the U and V MSS had he chosen to include it in Book II of the 1805 version, for which it was originally written, but instead he chose to find Divinity in himself in another way and celebrate growth and self-consciousness.

The part in Book II that the above passage from MS RV would follow speaks of Nature in this way:

> I was only then
> Contented when with bliss ineffable
> I felt the sentiment of Being spread
> O'er all that moves, and all that seemeth still,
> O'er all, that, lost beyond the reach of thought
> And human knowledge, to the human eye
> Invisible, yet liveth to the heart,
> O'er all that leaps, and runs, and shouts, and sings,
> Or beats the gladsome air, o'er all that glides
> Beneath the wave, yea, in the wave itself
> And mighty depth of waters. Wonder not
> If such my transports were; for in all things
> I saw one life, and felt that it was joy.
> One song they sang, and it was audible,
> Most audible then when the fleshly ear,
> O'ercome by grosser prelude of that strain,
> Forgot its functions, and slept undisturb'd.
>
> (II, 418-434)

It is particularly difficult for those who see Romantic "Nature poetry" as an intense response to the particularity of external objects in Nature to recognize here that all this particularity is used to render the sense of something underneath Nature which corresponds to the sense of something within oneself.[14] To Wordsworth, it is what is underneath Nature and what is deep within one that are real. To the realization of this, the responsive self occupied with particularity, its own or the details of the external world, is a hindrance. The paradox in this is that the responsive self and the actual place call so much attention to themselves, while the deepest bliss comes with the extinction of the marveling and specifying self in a psychic withdrawal from

[14] For a further consideration of what is perceived "underneath" Nature or projected from "within" oneself, see the discussion of "projected" and "real" by I. A. Richards in *Coleridge on Imagination*, pp. 145-146 and 152-163.

the actual place. Imagery is penetrated to a deeper sense of the "one interior life" and self yields to soul.

In this same book of *The Prelude* we find a precise characterization of this, recalling the "serene and blessed mood" of "Tintern Abbey" where the eye is "made quiet":

> among the hills I sate
> Alone, upon some jutting eminence
> At the first hour of morning, when the Vale
> Lay quiet in an utter solitude.
> How shall I trace the history, where seek
> The origin of what I then have felt?
> Oft in those moments such a holy calm
> Did overspread my soul, that I forgot
> That I had bodily eyes, and what I saw
> Appear'd like something in myself, a dream,
> A prospect in my mind.
>
> (II, 361-371)

It is in *solitude* as well as in Nature that this happens, which makes the preference for solitude as necessary for Wordsworth, who desires these recurrent experiences, as his better known preference for closeness to Nature. But what begins as an experience in Nature (seeming to be in some way "about" Nature) in fact becomes one of psychic withdrawal. He withdraws to the point where the soul beneath the self and the deep reality of Nature seem to fuse. This, for Wordsworth, is the joyful and holy "sentiment of Being." What is always felt as life within and beneath the self and what seems to be alive in and beneath the landscape coalesce when that landscape has been incorporated as imagery into the mind. How are we to regard this psychic and poetic phenomenon? The person is represented as sitting in the landscape, but the landscape then seems to be in his own mind; he is and is not himself, is and is not there. We may think of the withdrawn Hermit and the "thoughts of more deep seclusion."

When Wordsworth refers in this same book of *The Pre-*

lude to the death of his parents, but really to the death of his mother, he says:

> I was left alone,
> Seeking the visible world, . . .
> (II, 292-293)

This must mean that her death, her disappearance from the external world, profoundly affected his sense of reality. In the Fenwick Notes he speaks of the pull inwards away from the visible world towards an "abyss of idealism" within him.[15] In reaction to this recurrent experience which was frightening to him as a schoolboy, he protected his sanity by trying literally, physically, to grasp the reality of the visible world. But the experience that the child feared, the man as Poet gradually began to seek with an heroic sense of encountering the mysterious, invisible world in order "to fix the wavering balance of [his] mind."[16] The child could not approach, much less confront, his doubts and fears about inner and outer realities, and even the poet who writes in Book VI of *The Prelude* of wanting to approach the abyss to "look with bodily eyes and be consoled" does not actually do so.[17] In Book II, he recalls how his mind was then laid open to "Nature's finer influxes" and how he was able to live in the visible world, alone, with the props of his affection removed. But the way in which his sense of reality had been affected is, in one sense, obvious: the "invisible world," of which Wordsworth also speaks often, has a great reality and a powerful unconscious appeal to him. The power of Imagination, we learn, comes from the in-

15 *Prose Works*, vol. III, p. 194.

16 *The Prelude*, I, 650.

17 *The Prelude*, MS A2, VI, 70-75. See *The Prelude*, p. 198. Corrections in MS A could have been made at any time between the completion of Book VI in A and the copying of A, corrected as A2, in the new copy C; that is, between 1804 and approximately 1818. It is likely that these lines were added later rather than earlier and express sentiments that are Christian. For their other possible meaning (the confrontation of the "Abyss" in "the Mind of Man"), see below, pp. 116-118 and 141ff.

visible world and at peculiar moments usurps consciousness. The Poet becomes particularly concerned with that realm of the mind, desiring to penetrate the imagery of the material world to reach it; and we have now seen how external landscapes pass into him and become "something in myself," a world in the poet's mind into which he now withdraws serenely and through which later he will wander inquisitively.

There is, however, another connection between "Tintern Abbey" and *The Prelude* that is very important; the "Blest Babe" passage of Book II shows us how to understand the state of affection and the deepest joy spoken of in "Tintern Abbey" as "the serene and blessed mood." Wordsworth uses the Mother-Babe relationship in Book II to elaborate his sense of bliss and of first relatedness with the world, his sense of basic reality and of the first poetic impulse in life. We must not overlook the implications of the traumatic disruption of the relationship simply because the poet does not deal with them. He writes:

> Bless'd the infant Babe,
> (For with my best conjectures I would trace
> The progress of our being) blest the Babe,
> Nurs'd in his Mother's arms, the Babe who sleeps
> Upon his Mother's breast, who, when his soul
> Claims manifest kindred with an earthly soul,
> Doth gather passion from his Mother's eye!
> Such feelings pass into his torpid life
> Like an awakening breeze, and hence his mind
> Even [in the first trial of its powers]
> Is prompt and watchful, eager to combine
> In one appearance, all the elements
> And parts of the same object, else detach'd
> And loth to coalesce. Thus, day by day,
> Subjected to the discipline of love,
> His organs and recipient faculties
> Are quicken'd, are more vigorous, his mind spreads,

Tenacious of the forms which it receives.
In one beloved Presence, nay and more,
In that most apprehensive habitude
And those sensations which have been deriv'd
From this beloved Presence, there exists
A virtue which irradiates and exalts
All objects through all intercourse of sense.
No outcast he, bewilder'd and depress'd;
Along his infant veins are interfus'd
The gravitation and the filial bond
Of nature, that connect him with the world.
(II, 237-264)

The soul of the Babe is said to "gather passion from his mother's eye" (in the 1850 version the orality of vision is made even clearer: "who with his soul/ *Drinks in* the feelings of his mother's eye"). This feeding infant, "who sleeps upon his mother's breast," exists in serenity and blessedness, which recalls that "serene and blessed mood" recounted in "Tintern Abbey." And the affections that "gently lead us on" in "Tintern Abbey" lead back to this state of primal affection. But it will not do simply to observe the way in which this idealized condition underlies the description of deepest joy in the "Tintern Abbey" passage because in a crucial way the meaning of the activity described there is exactly the opposite. Here Wordsworth describes not only sleeping but awakening. The infant's *awakening* mind, under the influence of this "one beloved Presence," is also experiencing the coalescence of things, but of otherness *as* otherness. And self and soul are never represented by Wordsworth as closer together than here in his talking of the Blest Babe—"when his soul/ Claims manifest kindred with an earthly soul"—for "soul" here is closer in meaning to fullness of self than anywhere else in Wordsworth's poetry. Any awakening of self-consciousness must in one sense diminish the pure and timeless state of soul, but it is plain that Wordsworth idealized this approximate *wholeness* of being prior to the traumatic division of being into burdened self and deeply submerged soul. The "beloved Presence" makes the external world containing her real to the babe; she *is* its essential reality.

The relationships to be observed in Wordsworth's poetry between Imagination and Revelation, between powers that arise from within the mind and powers that seem to impinge from without, between the Poet's mind and God's mind as they express themselves creatively by imposing their wishful order on the matter of the world, are present in this difficult sense of the self's beginnings in relation to what is real:

> his mind,
> Even as an agent of the one great mind,
> Creates, creator and receiver both,
> Working but in alliance with the works
> Which it beholds. (II, 271-275)

This is a characterization of the earliest sense of the poet's mind, which "half-creates" what it perceives. The relationship of self and soul, then, is to be understood in the traumatic disruption of this ideal state of being. Imagination and Revelation, as Wordsworth characterizes them, are experienced as attempts of the pre-conscious mind to reunite the self and soul by giving to consciousness a knowledge of that traumatic disruption of one's being.

It is only one step further in psychological thinking to say that a severely traumatic disruption of this relationship may be only a special case of the general human case; for normative growth is in many ways a series of lesser traumas disruptive of that idealized relationship revealed briefly in infancy and supposed by the poet to be a human birthright that might remain "pre-eminent till death." When Wordsworth says

> Such verily, is the first
> Poetic spirit of our human life;
> By uniform controul of after years

In most abated or suppress'd, in some,
Through every change of growth or of decay,
Pre-eminent till death. (II, 275-280)

he has rightly observed that most people seem to lose, in the exigencies of growth, not only the powers initially fostered in that ideal relationship, but even the capacity to realize or be concerned about their loss. The Poet as a special case, in Wordworth's account of himself, acquires early in life an elaborately "privileged" relationship with fostering Nature and a permanent concern with the ideal of growth. In our account of Wordsworth he is seen as fixated to a trauma, obsessed by a vital relationship with Nature which has come to stand unconsciously for the lost mother.

We speak of symbolic losses in ordinary growth, and of the loss of the capacity to remember the experiences of loss, under the headings of repression and infantile amnesia.[18] The crises of normal growth are lesser traumas gradually transforming that private, unworldly, passive, and dependent relationship of infant to mother into an unconscious memory and erecting in place of it the ego "character" that deals with the external world; and the ego deals with the external world in ways determined by, and limited by, the success of its dealings with the unconscious.[19] Whereas we account for the acquisition of the characteristics shared by most people in terms of the normal resolution of infantile conflict through repression, we can observe in Wordsworth the insistent preoccupation with something unknown seeking expression, something which forced him to attend con-

18 See Freud, "The Dissolution of the Oedipus Complex," CW XIX, 171-179; "Repression," CW XIV, 141-158; and "Psycho-Analysis," CW XVIII, 244-247. See, too, Ernest Schactel, "On Memory and Childhood Amnesia."

19 See Freud, "A Note on the Unconscious in Psycho-Analysis," CW XII, 255-266, and "The Unconscious," CW XIV, 159-204. See, too, "New Introductory Lectures on Psycho-Analysis," Lectures XXXI and XXXII, CW XXII, 57-111; "The Ego and the Id," CW XIX, 1-66; and "Moses and Monotheism," CW XXIII, 72-80.

stantly to its prior and greater reality. He did not experience the normal resolutions of growth, but felt impelled instead to search for something unapparent to ordinary vision, to give himself up to a great unknown of experience, and in so doing to distinguish himself from other men.

Certainly, it is one of the abiding mysteries of the mind that natural endowments vary as widely and significantly from person to person as does the quality of their earliest fostering relationships in life. So it is believable that, in the conditions for neurosis and possible psychic debility, Wordsworth's creativity could fashion a neurotic but grand poetic obsession, whereas in so many cases of early and severe trauma and of fixation we see only the fantastic but uncreative clutter of neurosis itself. His creative sensibility, as a natural endowment, remains the mystery it was; but his use of his creativity in relation to his neurosis, so often remarked as the "egoism" of his art, should induce our belief in the relative happiness of the first eight years of his life and in the formation of an ego strong enough to seek to heal itself in this adventurous verbal way.[20] The "way" of Wordsworth's art is that of insistent utterance poured forth, however hesitantly at first and however intermittently during the years of composing *The Prelude*, with the *appearance* of "irresistible fervor" when one reads *The Prelude* as a compiled text. But the relationship, so difficult to assess, between creativity and neurosis, and even as the Romantics speculated about it, between genius and insanity, must first be seen as different from the more ordinary case of growth which adapts mental activity selectively and reductively to the habits of mind most necessary for ordinary life in society.

Language, as children begin to acquire it, is erotically based because it is learned in pleasurable association with the initial object of love and wonder in their lives; it has

20 For an interesting and often cited discussion of the use of creativity in relation to neurosis, see Lionel Trilling, "Art and Neurosis," in *The Liberal Imagination*. In the same volume, see, too, the essay "Freud and Literature."

the "birthright" potential of making lifelong connections between the "language of the sense" and the developing capacity to think—what Wordsworth so beautifully means by "A Babe, by intercourse of touch/ I held mute dialogues with my mother's heart." But education is plainly utilitarian, selective, and reductive; it anesthetizes language and makes the experience of learning the more developed modalities of language that of losing touch with the "unprofitable" richness of infantile experience. The very language being acquired lacks words and constructions to contain the intensely sensory but pre-rational experiences that will not serve the most immediate needs of growth in society, and the further development of the reasoning mind inhibits the "first poetic impulse."[21] Yet poetry, in its constant attempt to find new uses of language, new ways of accommodating the unknown to the known, may be attempting, as Norman O. Brown says, "to reopen the way to lost capacities for response and growth."[22] It is in this sense that Wordsworth, fixated to a trauma, is nevertheless representative of the plight of humanity. We may recall that Freud thought that repression is the cause of man's mysterious feelings of "soul"; and soul, which seem ineffable, is the unrenounced, and perhaps unknowable, deep and unconscious attachment to pleasure. "Ineffable"—inexpressible; against the mortal condition of repression, the powerful poetic self, as Wordsworth sought to attain it, is seeking to reveal "soul" in words, to express the joy of "being" in images and metaphors. That is, his poetic self sought to *imagine* what his unconscious mind sought at the same time to *reveal*. Imagination and Revelation needed a common word, he felt, and lacked it "through sad incompetence of human speech."

What Wordsworth does express freely is the truth of the

[21] Wordsworth deals with the phenomenon of loss in growth and the decline of the visionary faculty in the "Immortality Ode." For an interesting discussion of the poem, see Cleanth Brooks, "Wordsworth and the Paradox of the Imagination," *The Well-Wrought Urn.*

[22] Norman O. Brown, *Life Against Death,* pp. 55-67.

deep human longing for the pleasurable reality of "soul"; and it is this further revelation of human longing that makes the special case so significant. For most people, every figurative loss of the mother in the early stages of growth implies, metaphorically, a death; every increase of individuality adds to the sense of the perishable nature of human and individual things—one's earlier selves and those of other people in earlier relationships that change and pass away. But in the normative formation of the autonomous self, these obscure senses of lost objects and relationships are more lived with than understood; they are religiously and socially ritualized rather than individually recollected and meditated. For Wordsworth, an early, traumatic, and absolute loss made unacceptable the usual experiences that lead to normative autonomy, an autonomy formed by the gradual acceptance-in-living of separation from the mother. In place of those experiences was the recurrent search in solitude and Nature for "the life of things," an absent reality, the sense of which was retained deeply within as soul. The death-like sense of loss in the younger Wordsworth appears only in denied form, which is why, I think, the affirmative intention in "Tintern Abbey" is accompanied by language that suggests what that intention must continually master:

> And all its aching joys *are now no more.*
> And all its dizzy raptures. Not for this
> Faint I, *nor mourn nor murmur . . .*

By the time he wrote the end of the "Immortality Ode," his increasingly Christian sense of things had provided him with an acceptable form for expressing long-denied feelings of loss and death; and he was able to speak there of an "eye/ That hath kept watch o'er man's mortality."

The state of soul described in "Tintern Abbey" most closely approximates that of the feeding infant "Nursed in his Mother's arms, the Babe who sleeps/ Upon his mother's breast." But most significantly, in no way does it suggest what the analogy in Book II of *The Prelude* does, that this is the simple precondition of further involvement with the world as external and other. The similarity of the two passages makes clear what is desired regressively; the significant difference makes clear the futility of regressive goals. The mother, as an object that stands for the otherness of all objects, is also the person from whom the child acquires his sense of himself and of people as people. As this basic reality of the self is accepted, and its autonomy eventually desired, separation from her in living is accepted in greater measure, too. Wordsworth's preference for solitude suggests that the reality of other people is not deeply satisfying to him because they are less real than what he seeks in solitude. Regressive as it is, the predisposition leads to an impossible psychic attempt to regain absolutely a relationship which, by age eight, is normatively lost anyway. It can be shown, I think, that Wordsworth had already undergone that normative loss, a resolution of oedipal conflict which the trauma at age eight undid.[23]

It would be pointless, however, to contend that Wordsworth was indifferent to the external world and to other people. He sought them, too, just as he had sought the "visible world" as a child and had feared the pull inwards towards the "abyss of idealism." The resolution he reaches in "Tintern Abbey" is that of an adult man to resist the tendency towards passive psychic withdrawal expressed indirectly in the poem in several ways. The point of my closer scrutiny here is to establish something about the moments of deepest longing, when the most personal and seemingly insatiable longings are revealed, to the extent that they ever show clearly to anyone. When they are expressed, as in poetry, they can be seen as comments on habitual tendencies observable enough in living, implicit in attitudes towards life and the world.[24] Wordsworth's poetic thoughts, some-

[23] See below, pp. 205ff.

[24] See Wordsworth's poem "Personal Talk," a sonnet published in 1807. In preference to intimate conversation or social intercourse, he

what unacceptably as yet, tended towards "thoughts of more deep seclusion"—the Hermit and the Recluse as imaginative characterizations of himself as Poet, to which may be added the Lonely Traveller and the Wanderer.

The traumatically determined nature of this regressive longing shows, too, in the fact that even for an eight year old it would be regressive. Wordsworth as the happy child already had a developed sense of the reality of things and of people based on his experience of the mother and of the child's world. This normative sense of the world was something with which the later traumatic sense of himself regularly interfered; and it is the traumatic sense he is recalling when he speaks in the Fenwick notes of the opposition of the visible world and the frightening "abyss of idealism" in his school-boy years after his mother's death. Out of this traumatic sense of himself, however, comes the idealized sense of himself—the Poet as the "favour'd being," seeking, almost in spite of himself, a deeper reality in solitude and Nature. It is in *The Prelude* rather than in "Tintern Abbey" that the Poet enters "the Mind of man," which Wordsworth called "My haunt, and the main region of my song."

3. In the Presence of a Poetic Obsession

With an understanding of the opposed demands on child and man of the external world and its reality, on the one hand, and of a greater inner reality being sought regressively, on the other, we find that the peculiar expression "no outcast he, bewilder'd and depress'd" in the Blest Babe passage makes a kind of sense that it does not readily make in its context:

> From this beloved Presence, there exists
> A virtue which irradiates and exalts
> All objects through all intercourse of sense.

---

prefers, he says, "silence long,/ Long barren silence" and sitting, withdrawn and "without emotion, hope or aim . . . ," *Poetical Works*, p. 382.

> No outcast he, bewilder'd and depress'd;
> Along his infant veins are interfus'd
> The gravitation and the filial bond
> Of nature, that connect him with the world.
>
> (II, 258-264)

Why does it occur to Wordsworth to put that qualifying phrase in his characterization of perfect belongingness in the world and the universe? "Outcast" means cast out *from* this relationship into the world. If most people lose their recollection of this relationship *in* their growth, then the poet is in some way "remembering" the casting out, the disruption itself. The line, despite its impersonal quality, attests directly to an earlier sense of his own experience, characterizing it by associating it preconsciously with the ideal of which the analogy speaks: Wordsworth, at the death of his mother, felt outcast, bewildered and depressed. Although Wordsworth knew well enough how his adult self felt outcast, bewildered and at times depressed in the "unintelligible world," only in this preconscious way does he relate his present self to his younger self. He cannot say, however, how soon in life he felt this way, or why.

Nowhere does he tell us his feelings at his mother's death, but in "outcast" I find the implications of the journey-metaphor, as in "she left us destitute"—trooping and feeling destitute. The self feels alien in a world which, since childhood, has had only the illusion of reality for him. The "soul" entices the dissatified self with its unconscious recollections, projecting this beloved Presence into the appearance of the material world or adding it to the imagery of beauteous forms in the mind. How strangely this "luring" of the self is present in the language of "Tintern Abbey"; from the "beauteous forms" and the easing of burdens, the affections are said to "*lead us on* until. . . ." And it is a dissatisfied Wordsworth who has returned to the Wye Valley with thoughts of the strange power of its imagery on his mind and with an awareness, too, of the attractions of inwardness and of deeper states of soul. Yet the poet states, consciously intending to affirm the life of the self in the visible world, that a stronger sense of self may be taken away from this contemplation of the material world imbued with the Presence in Nature. It is a question of how much he believes this, and for how long.

Unlike the whole analogy of the infant's awakening to the otherness of the world in Book II, the passage recalling bliss in "Tintern Abbey" seems to suggest the cessation of activity or something all but indistinguishable from it. And yet, seeing into the life of things is itself an activity of the awakened "living soul." But the difficulty here is in the way we talk about such activity, since our language also derives from the external world and reflects the ordinary self. To experience that state of soul or to write poetry about it was a choice Wordsworth may not have known he was making; but in writing about it, he made the expression of the desire for self-loss an occasion for further self-consciousness. In this way, the "activity" of the soul becomes something to be observed, to be followed and described by the poetry-making self. Poetry would attempt to render such activity of soul metaphorically, as for instance in Wordsworth's characterization of that activity as a journey or a quest. "Discovering" the journey of the soul beneath ordinary life makes ordinary actions and the sense of place seem to be manifestations of latent spiritual or psychological intentions. One has climbed the Alps in the past, for instance, but one discovers in the later experiences of making poetry from the memory that the imagery acquires an efficacy of its own. Whatever the soul may have "led" one to do that the self at the time could not understand, the poetic self seeks in that imagery a revelation now. The account is of something in the mind, the poetry-making, I-speaking self having entered through the imagery into the region of soul. The poetic self will have returned, perhaps, to the source of intention, where the intention to *be* is primary. The successful joining of self and soul would repair a traumatically divided being and fulfill the feeling of "something ever more about to be."

The "Presence" spoken of in "Tintern Abbey" seems to account for the resolution of the poem, for Wordsworth's trust that a preferred relationship with Nature is renewable "through all the years of this our life." We are asking, then, why should the Wye Valley have been particularly evocative of the mother, whose attributes are found in the Presence? In *The Prelude* there are particular and recurrent recollections of the "vale" traceable to the original vale, the river valley associated with infancy, home and the mother. By referring to this poem as "Tintern Abbey," one tends to forget that the poem has nothing to do with Tintern Abbey itself and everything to do with a vale, as the title tells us: "Composed a Few Miles Above Tintern Abbey, on Revisiting the Banks of the Wye on a Tour. July 13, 1798." He came to this vale, which preconsciously recalls the original valley of the Derwent, and then he returned to it, both physically and psychically.

The journey-metaphor, which I shall trace further in *The Prelude,* begins with the death of the mother and her "disappearance" from the original vale. Immediately after her death, Wordsworth too left the original vale to attend school in the neighboring vale at Hawkeshead. It was there, in the solitude that he often sought, that he began gradually and preconsciously projecting into Nature his sense of the mother, finding again in that way aspects of the lost relationship with her. The road, he will tell us, fascinated him since childhood; it seemed "an invitation into space boundless,/ A guide into eternity," which is to say, beyond the vale, perhaps in the world and perhaps not. Journeys, too, as we shall see, are undertaken to find again a lost object and to recreate a lost relationship; and the several senses of landscape, road and journey, of burdened self, unburdened soul, and reality, are extended metaphorically to express a regressive need of the outcast, bewildered and depressed ego for something that could be described in terms of the world but not found in it. But how appropriately and how beautifully the enactment of this nostalgia shows in "Tintern Abbey": the imagery of the beautiful vale of the Wye is gradually related through the affections to the state of being a living soul, recalling to the reader of *The Prelude* his descriptions of the original valley of the Derwent, the relationship of mother and infant there, and the wholeness of being of soul and self.

The question of where people "go" when they "disappear" is not one that a child can really ask in the experience of severe traumatic loss. If the trauma is denied, the fact of the loss of the mother, for instance, may be accepted consciously, though the whole range of consequent feelings is lost or hidden by repression. The fantasies of *how* and *why* and *where* are repressed. In an observably affectless way, those subjects become somehow unreal. What is likely to result and to show especially in the concern for the nature and tenure of one's own being, is a permanent tension between the attempt of the mind to recreate and acknowledge the trauma and the simultaneous attempt of the mind to erect and maintain defenses against recognition. Freud, who observed this, observed also that in part we retain a separate sense of the lost object of love as "real" and refindable, and in part we identify with the objects we lose, passively remodelling the ego to resemble them.[25] One can project a sense of the mother into external reality in order to perceive, say, the maternal regard of Nature for oneself, and in that way recreate from within a lost affective relationship. So may the imagery of Nature recalled in the mind seem like the affections gently leading us on. But in a peculiar characterization of the Poet in Book XIII of *The Prelude*, we also find an example of identification with the lost object; the loss is denied by the poet's becoming like the mother:

[25] See Freud, "On Narcissism" and "Mourning and Melancholia," CW XIV; also, "New Introductory Lectures," Lecture XXXI, CW XXII, 57-80.

> and he whose soul hath risen
> Up to the height of feeling intellect
> Shall want no humbler tenderness, his heart
> Be tender as a nursing Mother's heart;
> Of female softness shall his life be full,
> Of little loves and delicate desires,
> Mild interests and gentlest sympathies.
> (XIII, 204-210)

The identification also makes the objects of the poet's regard (and his readers) like himself as he would be treated by the mother. Wordsworth knew how the human spirit wants to be treated, if not why, and the disclosure in this characterization is again simple and beautiful.

The Blest Babe passage from Book II (quoted above) provides us with another way of understanding what the Presence in "Tintern Abbey" means to Wordsworth. In "Tintern Abbey," he says:

> For I have learned
> To look on Nature, not as in the hour
> Of thoughtless youth; but hearing oftentimes
> The still sad music of humanity,
> Nor harsh nor grating, though of ample power
> To chasten and subdue. And I have felt
> A presence that disturbs me with the joy
> Of elevated thoughts; a sense sublime
> Of something far more deeply interfused,
> Whose dwelling is the light of setting suns,
> And the round ocean and the living air
> And the blue sky, and in the mind of man;
> A motion and a spirit, that impels
> All thinking things, all objects of all thought,
> And rolls though all things.

The "Tintern Abbey" passage was written first. Although Nature is a fostering Presence habitually alluded to by Wordsworth in his poetry, and especially during the period 1798-1805, it is in this passage that he first speaks of it.

There is the strong suggestion in the poem that he is first discovering here what he wants to say about Nature as well as first putting it in this way: "Well pleased to *recognize* in Nature. . . ." His affirmative intention leads him to this recognition of his trust in Nature, which seems then to result from the tensions in the present experience. The passage from Book II, written within about a year of this, elaborates one aspect of the ideal relationship of Mother and Babe, and seems to result from an even more consciously held affirmative intention. In writing *The Prelude* he hoped to determine "how far Nature and education had *qualified* him . . ." to be the Poet of *The Recluse*.[26] The assumption on which *The Prelude* was undertaken was that he would find a powerful confirmation of his trust in Nature and in himself, one that could be given a fully causal elaboration. Although that account of the growth of the Poet was to raise the problem of his desire for autonomy from Nature (and even for a God-like superiority to her), "Tintern Abbey" simply presents the discovery of a religious bond to Nature; and *The Prelude* begins in the mood of "Tintern Abbey."

In "Tintern Abbey" Nature is the divinity; Wordsworth speaks of holy love and worship. What he gains in the poem is this new personification of the Presence and, in his belief in it, a surprising degree of control over it. Most simply his present thoughtful response is being affirmed in place of past sensuous responses; and this greater ambience of Nature, which seems like an idea of Nature rather than a view of it, or like the immanence of the divinity "Nature" in the phenomena of Nature, seems to require the sense of a containing mind capable of that realization. Consequently, to the verbal characterization of the Presence that dwells "interfused" in everything has been added "and in the mind of man."[27]

[26] *The Prelude*, p. 509.

[27] Cf. William Empson, *Seven Types of Ambiguity*, pp. 151-154. On page 20 of the same volume may be found the following off-handed characterization of Wordsworth's inspiration: "Wordsworth frankly

One might borrow from the Blest Babe passage in Book II to say that the Presence described in this way seems to be the "gravitation and the filial bond of Nature" that connects this perceiver with the world, that connects "all thinking things" with "all objects of all thought/ And rolls through all things." The Presence, then, is doing here for a thoughtful Wordsworth what he says the "one beloved Presence," the mother, did for the awakening infant; "she" connects his feelings of belonging in the world with the activity of his mind and seems like a function of it. The sense of the Poet's containing mind ("and in the mind of man") recalls, too, "the one great mind." The poem seems now to be indicating a greater degree of acceptance of the reality of the external world; and it seems clearly to be moving away from what we have observed about the Hermit, the "thoughts of more deep seclusion," and the state of being "a living soul." In fact, "far *more deeply* interfused" seems significantly to echo "of *more deep* seclusion," relocating as everywhere in Nature outside him the meaningful "depth" of the landscape that the Poet as contented beholder seeks. The poem does not indicate, however, what will happen to the state of being a "living soul," which may or may not have been the effect of contemplating the "beauteous forms" in the mind; and this new sense of the Presence in a thoughtful response to the external world seems almost to will going against that tendency.

The Presence, a personification that has no one image, is Nature herself and has all of Nature's imagery. It is also the mother projected into Nature; she who was the "one beloved presence" that once made the imagery of Nature coalesce is now evoked as a Presence by the coalescence of the imagery of Nature. In *The Prelude,* Wordsworth will speak of "Ye Presences of Nature . . . and souls of lonely places" while speaking of his childhood, using the personi-

had no inspiration other than his use when a boy of the mountain as a totem or father-substitute. . . ."

fication of Nature "discovered" here to explain his past. But we should understand that just as the imagery (the mental equivalent of the landscape) is separable from the actual landscape, so is the Presence separable from the imagery which evokes it. It is plain that what has been sought all along, in vigorous physical activity and in psychic withdrawal, is the Presence itself—at first in his hunger for the landscape, then in his nostalgic returns to it through the beauteous forms in his mind and through this second visit.

It is with a sense of what is half-created in perception that he speaks of the Presence as *in* Nature "and *in* the mind of man." In "Tintern Abbey" Wordsworth has the affirmative intention of finding his future contentment *in* Nature and *in* the response to Nature of his thoughtful mind, a contentment of the sort that his poetry-making self can achieve by maintaining a very fine balance between projection and perception, by writing about himself in relation to a world that seems to have what he needs. But in intending to find his future contentment in this way, he believes confidently that he has the powers that he says he has and is free to employ them as he chooses.

In "Tintern Abbey," however, Wordsworth says simply, "and in the mind of man," unaware of how the appeal of his own inwardness will deepen for him in the next few years. The poetic self will pursue the elusive Presence, obsessively, through the imagery of the past stored in the mind; the spirit will not find its contentment in the present and in the external world. Hence, the tendency towards inwardness becomes dominant after all, but as a poetic awakening to the inner world rather than as the tendency, also observable, towards self-loss in "the one interior life." In 1798, however, at Alfoxden, Wordsworth wrote the lines that were to be the opening passage of *The Recluse*. In them, he speaks boldly of looking

> Into our Minds, into the Mind of Man—
> My haunt, and the main region of my song.

And he asserts:

Beauty—a living Presence of the earth,
Surpassing the most fair ideal Forms
Which craft of delicate spirits hath composed
From earth's materials—waits upon my steps.[28]

He speaks of Beauty, not fabled and illusory beauties, but of the simpler realities of present life from which man is separated by fond hopes and deep fears; and he speaks in a way that suggests he can confront and understand those hopes and fears, even his own about whether the "living Presence" and living in the present are the same thing. Unable, however, to continue in this vein and at this pitch of fervor and assurance, he is led in *The Prelude* into the mind of man almost in spite of himself, the Imagination questioning Memory about traces of a Presence in her store of images—"those phantoms of conceit," "the many feelings that oppressed my heart."[29]

To understand why the "Presence" spoken of confidently in the resolution of "Tintern Abbey" could not do for Wordsworth what he hoped it would do (and why many readers feel the poem ends with inauthentic resonance), one must ask finally what it would mean that Nature would, does, or did betray the heart that loved her? Is it that like the mother whose death did leave the child orphaned in the world, she too will leave him destitute? "Tintern Abbey" admits to no fears, but is it a young man's poem, in Hazlitt's sense, that no young man believes he will ever die?[30] The poem reveals how the present sense of things is dominated by the sense of the past and by past senses of things, but there is also a curiously forced anticipation, a reconcilement made in advance between the unknown of the future and this present mode of resolute understanding by which composure is attained. Would someone thinking about "all the years of this our life" expect from Nature

28 "The Excursion," *Poetical Works*, pp. 589-590.

29 *The Prelude*, I, 130-134.

30 William Hazlitt, "On the Feeling of Immortality in Youth," *Complete Works of William Hazlitt*, ed. P. P. Howe, vol. 17, p. 189.

simply a succession of joys, new ones in place of old ones, and continued growth? Autonomous being, for most people, tends to replace expectations with resignations, which implies for them the difference between a fostering and maternal providence early in life and, perhaps, a providential God who has made some provision for the amelioration of death. Death may be said to come from God who also makes this provision; otherwise it must be said to come from Nature, which makes none. Growth after some point in life is merely a figurative sense we have of character: one grows in character or individuality or wisdom, while one perceives the decline of physical vitality and considers the ultimate extinction of self that it implies.[31] But that is not what Wordsworth means here; the poem does not introduce the future in that way. Death may be a future event which, imagined, would greatly qualify some of his thoughts, but as an eventuality and as a subject it is not real to him. "Tintern Abbey" is a young man's poem in exactly the way that "The Immortality Ode," written only a few years later, but after a few significant events in his life, is not.

In the present of "Tintern Abbey" there is the disturbing perception of change and loss to be transformed by Wordsworth's insistence into growth and gain. I interpret that perception to be recalling the past in an unconscious way; and Death is its unconscious recollection. Death has always stood as the fearful ultimate of knowledge in individual experience and popularly as a caution against the individual pursuit of knowledge or the self-knowledge that is individuality. The ideal Poet, to Wordsworth, would have self-knowledge and would be "a soul of more than mortal privilege." We may think of the epic heroes (and some poets) who have descended to the underworld and returned to the world of the living as souls of more than mortal privilege, but only unconsciously does Wordsworth relate death and self-knowledge. Wordsworth's individuality—the Poet's awareness of his separateness from the ways of the commu-

31 Erik Erikson, *Childhood and Society*, part III, chap. 7.

nity—reveals itself primarily as an obsessive preoccupation with itself rather than as an independent style of action or of thought. It seems that his proper activity is his attempt to maintain that individuality by a self-conscious scrutiny of memory. In *The Prelude* he will reveal this activity even more clearly than in "Tintern Abbey"; he will attempt to infer the causes of his uniqueness and to characterize them imaginatively. The final cause is said to be Nature's *intention* to frame "a favor'd being." We have begun to observe the correspondence between "favor'd" and "traumatized," between Nature and the mother whose attributes she has acquired; but it is surprising nevertheless to substitute those terms and to see in that way the unconscious feeling that it was the mother's "intention" to "traumatize" the child and to force upon him this preoccupied individuality, this lonely separateness from the ways of the community.

The question of betrayal by Nature that "Tintern Abbey" raises has to do with her role in his life—what it has been, what it will be—and especially with her dependability as a source of providential and sustaining love. To discover now that Nature abandons one to changes and losses, or that Nature has "led" him to a sense of himself that might be called joyless, is to discover that Nature has never "intended" to give him a privileged sense of his existence since birth and that Nature has never "loved" him as he has felt it "natural" she should. Were he to question Nature in this way, he would be forced to wonder why he had ever thought of Nature in so personal a way at all. We think of the child. So very dependent on the mother as a figure of providential intention and of sustaining love, the child could not accept his feelings that she has betrayed him by leaving him in so incomprehensible a way, that his happy feelings of extreme privilege since birth have been made false by her death, and that, most unacceptable of all, she did not love him.

We do not know what kinds of things were said by consoling adults to Wordsworth as a child (the relatives into whose hands he eventually fell were Dickensianly bleak); but it is unlikely that the worst feelings that children feel in such circumstances could even have been imagined by the adults, much less understood by them were the child to express them. A child represses these feelings because he feels guilty for feeling angry and perplexed about what he cannot understand in a reality so radically altered. The late eighteenth century was not a time when the complexity of a child was much appreciated, a neglect of feeling about which Rousseau complained and with which Romanticism concerned itself. No doubt the child was consoled, but religious consolation often deepens the guilt feelings of unconscious grievance while teaching religious resignation. Wordsworth may have been told that his mother had gone away or that his mother had gone to heaven, that she was with God, that he should be happy for her there and that she would watch over him; but this suggests how Nature became psychically a personal watchful providence for Wordsworth, a disturbing Presence "far more deeply interfused" in everything, a Presence "haunting" him, as he says in *The Prelude,* in his lonely play.

Whereas many children who suffer from similar traumas are initiated early and deeply into the life of religious resignation, Wordsworth, with the idiosyncratic strength of personal insistence, seems to have found in the neighboring vale a viable form of solace in solitude and in Nature, with which he resisted traditional religious solace. In "Tintern Abbey" he first articulates what he had felt since then, revealing religious feelings for Nature rather than for a God irrelevant to his most pressing needs. His mother is *not* with God, the child had answered the adults, denying and excluding God in this unconscious adjustment that is fixation; she is within him and with him in Nature. When, after alluding to her dcath in Book II of *The Prelude,* he speaks of "the spirit of religious love/ With which I walked with Nature," it is as if a reaching out would find again a hand to be taken.[32] But the differences between the past needs of the child in solitude and the present needs of the poet in the late 1790's begin to show soon after the affirmation made in "Tintern Abbey." As Wordsworth attempts to find his self-sufficient present image as the Poet in *The Prelude,* he moves towards a Creator-God whose relevance to himself he was slow in admitting psychically.

Here, however, we should briefly observe the effects of denial in the conclusion of "Tintern Abbey." Wordsworth does not realize what most careful readers sense, that the effect of the end of the poem is actually quite uncertain while he attempts to seem assured and intends to be reassuring to Dorothy. From the moment that Wordsworth says "Nor perchance/ If I were not thus taught, should I the more/ Suffer my genial spirits to decay/ For thou art with me here . . . ," there is a subtle and persistent confusion of Dorothy with himself that impedes the intended simplicity of the conclusion. It is the involuted and essentially negative expression of "*nor* perchance, If I were *not* thus taught . . ." that introduces the denied doubt here, again; and what shows is Wordsworth's preference for what he was rather than for what he is persuading himself to accept at present:

> Oh! yet a little while
> May I behold in thee what I was once . . .

When he says this, it is difficult to see him looking at Dorothy ("my dear, dear Sister!") as herself, as someone particular and other; for in one aspect of her presence she simply embodies his sense of his own "former self" whom he must continually persuade to accept the change into himself as he is now, even while reluctantly imagining further change for himself.

This seemingly dramatic moment is simply Wordsworth talking to himself in someone else's presence; yet it is not just *any*one's presence, but Dorothy's. In these years since

32 *The Prelude,* II, 376-377.

his crisis in 1795, Dorothy herself has been the fostering maternal presence to him, soothing a distraught mind, encouraging and supporting his belief in his restoration to poetry by Nature.[33] In this other aspect of her presence, Dorothy is the cause of a momentary confusion in his mind as to who is to be a continued reassurance to whom. It is not Dorothy but Wordsworth himself who is to learn this lesson and accept its truth—that "nothing can disturb our cheerful faith" that change is growth. And growth, Wordsworth implies here, is the ability to stand on one's own and be a reassurance to others.

In the benediction that follows, the "therefore" of "therefore let the moon shine on thee . . ." sounds inauthentic; it sounds like: "If you believe what I'm saying, if I believe what I'm saying, then . . ." It is easy to see the role he assumes here; the worshipper of Nature points out Nature's way. He sounds priest-like, but there is also the suggestion of the Poet as Redeemer here that we shall find recurring significantly in *The Prelude.* As one might imagine Jesus speaking to the Apostles, Wordsworth offers the memory of himself as teacher and model:

oh! then,
If solitude, or fear, or pain, or grief,
Should be thy portion, with what healing thoughts
Of tender joy wilt thou remember me,
And these my exhortations!

[33] In "The Vale of Esthwaite," the following lines appear:

Sister, for whom I feel a love
Which warms a brother far above,
On you, as sad she marks the scene,
Why does my heart so fondly lean?

Why but because in you is given
All, all, my soul would wish from heaven?
Why but because I fondly view
All, all, that heaven has claimed in you?
(Quoted by Bateson, *Wordsworth*, p. 69.)

But he assumes a tone of voice for which the poem has not prepared us.

I shall argue presently that Wordsworth sought greater autonomy both in the French Revolution and in his introspective poetry by seeking unconsciously to repeat and to understand the traumatic ordeal of his childhood. The doubt or the denied doubt of Nature's dependability in "Tintern Abbey" should remind us that, psychologically, however painful "betrayal" is, it is in some sense necessary. Autonomy requires that the psychic dependency on the mother be broken. Here, at the very moment that his protestations become most ardent about a newly-discovered and annunciated bond between the Poet and Nature, what Nature has stood for may in fact be seen as a psychic burden to the grown man. The unconscious sense of the mother and the unconscious desire for the lost relationship with her so elaborately maintained in this way are actually encumbrances to the spirit, and weary it in life. The habitual preference for a withdrawn, passive, and beautiful solitude; the exclusion of people from the "all" that is said to be "full of blessings"; the lassitude and *tedium vitae* so plain in the sense of a mysteriously burdened, unintelligible, and "dreary" daily life suggest a sensitivity to life heightened morbidly. In the poem, Wordsworth indulges this tendency in himself, but he resists realizing it. He ends by asserting that the Presence in Nature connects him in widening response to the world in which he perceives his continued growth; the poem fails to convince us of that. In offering himself as the teacher and model to Dorothy, Wordsworth would like to confirm himself, even if only in this rhetorical way, as self-sufficient, as dependable instead of dependent. Still, he clings to Nature and to Dorothy.

The two uses of "sad" in the poem are indicative in the same way of his failure to realize the full force of his feelings. "With many recognitions dim and faint,/ And somewhat of a sad perplexity" comes at the first moment of doubt; and yet the significant recognition of personal sadness is averted. He does not mourn or murmur. Similarly, "the still sad music of humanity" as the other part of the "abundant recompense" of which he speaks is not further elaborated in the poem. Although the line is memorable, it is nevertheless difficult to say what it means. Why does this still sad music of suffering humanity come through to the poet *now*, when most senses of humanity in the poem are of a social reality for which he feels aversion? Abstracted from people and perceived as the human condition or as Man in History, humanity has a believable pathos comparable to his own unrealized pathos which oppresses him, which the poetry expresses, and which the poem denies. It will become a matter of deeper concern in *The Prelude* whether the *ethos* of the Poet denies or masters his *pathos* when he speaks of a poetic self-cure, of "fixing the wavering balance of my mind." *The Prelude* ends with his assertion that the Poet has redemptive work to do in History; and in a letter to John Wilson, Wordsworth says that the Poet must give to people "new feelings, new compositions of feeling and new thoughts."[34] That is, he must make their pathos meaningful to them in how they think of themselves. But here, in "Tintern Abbey," the sense of self-mastery is being offered only to Dorothy and himself, and confusedly.

It seems to me unmistakable that he gets reassurance from Dorothy and that he associates it with her being and remaining as she is, and her remaining in this relationship to him. Now, looking at her, he can catch in her voice

> The Language of my former heart, and read
> My former pleasures in the shooting lights
> Of thy wild eyes.

And this he hopes will not change too soon, though inevitably it will. Yet to reassure her further he projects his own present assurance into the future for her; she too then will make a connection with her former self when she too will

[34] Wordsworth, *Letters*, #130.

have changed, and, for the moment, he sounds like her older brother. But then, instead of saying:

> Nor perchance—
> If I should be where you no more can hear
> My voice . . . wilt thou then forget . . .

he says:

> Nor perchance—
> If I should be where I no more can hear
> Thy voice, nor catch from thy wild eyes these gleams
> Of past existence—wilt thou then forget . . .

I am surprised that no one has ever said clearly that he is saying the wrong thing!

The "Nor perchance" here echoes the earlier doubt of "Nor perchance/ If I were not thus taught . . ."; and the lines that follow merely repeat the description of her as she is now. But the point is that later she will *not* be as she is now, and she too (at best) will have been led to the realization of another kind of joy. If she is to be self-sufficient later, presumably she will have to be so as he is now. Even if he were here again with her then, hearing again her voice and seeing her eyes, he would not be seeing quite these gleams of his past existence that he sees now, for she will have changed just as he has from wild-eyed to reposed and thoughtful. This reminds us of how reluctant he is to see her change or undergo growth at all; and this slight confusion of his image of her comes from his own reluctance in the present to accept what he has said about the disturbing sense of change and loss. It is Wordsworth who values his former self over his present one, which is why he values the resemblance of Dorothy now to himself in the past and does not know how to imagine Dorothy later. And in the future, not Dorothy, but Wordsworth will have to be reassured, which is why he repeats the present description of her, unconsciously keeping her in that impossible role in the future.

In "Tintern Abbey" Wordsworth is adjusting his disturbed feelings about past and present to each other. The artist, composing the elements of his personal experience to present a continuous sense of himself in time, seems to achieve the feeling of composure. The complexity of the process is awesome; and one submits willingly to the control of the person attempting it. It is difficult even to master the several senses of self, time, and place as they are adjusted to each other; and this is not only the case by the time the poem ends, but after one has read it several times. When one begins to think about the argument, however, the spell of the poem is broken, and one begins to see the man who needs order beneath the artist who attempts to impose it.

What the poem means—what may be understood on the basis of it—seems to require a sustained attempt to understand the Wordsworth who means it. *The Prelude,* more than "Tintern Abbey," makes this problem of priority clear. Yet one may well ask why a particular poet should require so much of his reader, and why that reader should bother to comply. I believe that what Wordsworth demonstrates in *The Prelude* is the attempt of the mind to say things about itself worthy of the imaginative powers that inhabit it, as if an as-yet-unknown freedom from the mortal lot would come of its success. The self implied by such a mind is an ideal one ("of more than mortal privilege"), and perhaps of such interest as to sustain us through closer attention to personality.

CHAPTER III

BEGINNINGS THAT BECAME *THE PRELUDE*

1. The Scope of Unclear Plans

The Prelude, as it was to be called when published, was the final result of various poetic beginnings in the years between 1795 and 1799. Although preceded by brief passages written at Racedown and Alfoxden, a large number of crucial passages composed in blank verse and later compiled as Book I of *The Prelude* date from 1798-99, the winter that Wordsworth spent with Dorothy at Goslar in Germany.[1] These passages, reminiscing about boyhood, seem to have come in response to his own self-chiding for his inability to get on with *The Recluse,* which, by that winter of 1798-99, had already been projected as a major philosophical poem "by a poet living in retirement." "Was it for this," he asks himself despondently, that Nature had so favored him since birth? And one can see immediately the simple extension of Nature from the figurative nurse, guide, guardian, and Presence of "Tintern Abbey" to a providential power overseeing a personal destiny, nurturing a "favor'd being."

He was not learning the German he had come to learn, but in terms of his life's work, these passages were the most important things he did during that winter. The man who was to be the poet characterized by the sublimity of his egoism got to sketching out his meaningful memories nostalgically for himself and Dorothy, whereas Coleridge—who was

[1] Detailed descriptions of the Alfoxden Notebook, MS JJ, Christabel Notebook, and MS 18a are given in *The Prelude*, pp. xxv-xxvii.

not after all to become the poet of his own dearest hopes—learned German, read philosophy, and entered society. But Wordsworth's substitution of one activity for another, although seemingly forced on him at Goslar by the freezing weather, the scarcity of funds, and the peculiarity of his circumstances, is nevertheless characteristic of him: having gone to a new place that had its own attractions and afforded present opportunities, he used the occasion to rediscover something left behind in place and time. Whatever the preference means, it is certainly demonstrated by *The Prelude*. The symptomatic sense of not being "for that time or for that place" recurs significantly whenever a circumstance required of him its own kind of attention. Revolutionary France was the one exception for him, and his feeling that he *was* exactly for that time and place led him through excess of enthusiasm to the crisis we shall presently observe.

However attractive the idea of *The Recluse* may have been to him at first ("I know not anything which will not come within the scope of my plan"[2]), no sooner did he consider the execution of it seriously than he discovered compelling prior considerations. The excellence of the idea seemed to draw upon him an inordinate degree of self-regard. The poet who planned to deliver his considered observations about Man, Nature, and Society as they passed in meditation through his own person could not get his own person out of the foreground. It was not vanity that caused him to hesitate and observe himself instead, but profound self-doubt, which "Tintern Abbey" had denied, but which not even *The Prelude* was to allay. Whatever questions we may feel *The Prelude* answers, it did not answer satisfyingly the question that led him to write it in place of the projected *Recluse*: "to determine how far Nature and education had qualified him for such an employment." He was depressed by his answer.

As early as 1795 when Wordsworth and Dorothy set up

[2] Wordsworth, *Letters*, #74.

at Racedown on Raisley Calvert's legacy to Wordsworth, Wordsworth was "a poet living in retirement" and was already intent upon finding the subject of a great poem. This was before his intimacy with Coleridge, from whom he was to receive encouragement and advice. It is apparent, however, from Coleridge's description of *The Recluse* that the projected poem was one Coleridge would have liked to write or to see written[3]; and it is apparent, too, that in Coleridge's mind Wordsworth was to be the poet that he himself might have been. In 1797 Wordsworth was much concerned with *becoming* a poet; Coleridge, however, was encouraging him to think of himself as the heir of Milton, about to write this great philosophical poem. Something joined Wordsworth's thoughts about the subject matter of poetry to his private thoughts about himself, about his becoming and being the Poet—perhaps his intimate discussions with Coleridge whose curiosity about the phenomenon of Wordsworth may well have elicited *The Prelude*. The fact is that to the "poet living in retirement" the matter of *The Prelude* had greater psychic appeal than that of *The Recluse*. Our observations about "Tintern Abbey" suggest why.

"Tintern Abbey" ends with what I have called confusion about who is to be reassuring to whom and in what ways. *The Prelude*, as we shall see, reveals in its development Wordsworth's attempt to find his self-sufficiency as a poet, independent of reassurances given him by Dorothy or Coleridge; and he attempts to complete the poem with an image of the Poet as a figure reassuring to Mankind. One may wonder whether a person who finds it necessary to live in retirement could ever really speak reassuringly to Mankind or whether he would have to abandon the pose of "Recluse" in order to try, but between the "Hermit" of "Tintern Abbey" and the "Recluse" there is a suggestive similarity to be considered in light of our reading of "Tintern Abbey." The Hermit, the type of the man who has renounced the

[3] Coleridge, *Table Talk*, July 21, 1832.

world of men to live in solitude and concern himself with the state of his soul, is a Recluse with a difference; but in trying to follow Coleridge's interests Wordsworth was going against his own. Admittedly, Coleridge's encouragement fit well with Wordsworth's hopes at the end of "Tintern Abbey," but Coleridge's emphasis on "man as man" shows his thinking at that time to have been more of the eighteenth century than of the Romantic period: poetry, traditionally social in its orientation, was concerned with examples of General Nature; and so being a Recluse meant eschewing polite society in order to write, but writing meant concerning oneself with "Man, Nature and Society," much as Pope had.

If the Hermit actually symbolizes the psychic tendency towards withdrawal observable at the beginning of "Tintern Abbey," then Wordsworth was not preparing to concern himself with the world as it is or as it might be, but rather to contemplate his past life in the world and to examine the present state of his own soul as hermits do. I have already interpreted Wordsworth's sense of soul as a union with the real "life of things" being sought by a divided, dissatisfied self unconsciously recalling in that "serene and blessed mood" the contentment of the infant at the mother's breast. But the Hermit must now be further distinguished from the wishful tendency towards psychic withdrawal in which he was first observed in "Tintern Abbey," and seen more precisely; for to Wordsworth, he represents contemplative consciousness of a special sort. He represents, in fact, not the wish simply to withdraw into the passive state of soul that, in "Tintern Abbey," is beneath the apparent desire to revisit the much-loved Wye valley, but rather a preconscious, and of course unacknowledged, intention to contemplate that wish in relation to the whole of his past life in the world and to discover its meaning. In "Tintern Abbey," a limited expression of preconscious "intention" is made. The affirmative intention of the poem denies what the poem expresses of doubt, joylessness, betrayal, and apprehension, just as the ego regularly denies and keeps repressed what is painful and unacceptable to consciousness; but the adjustment made by the writing of the poem is in favor of more poetic activity, of further imaginative questioning.

"Tintern Abbey" not only goes against the desire for the deepest joy it speaks of (blissful self-loss), but the act of writing confirms the Poet in his acute self-consciousness more significantly—one might say obsessively—than Wordsworth knew. The Hermit stands for that positive aspect of the repetition-compulsion that Freud describes as the attempt to represent a repressed trauma to consciousness or to repeat it in some form so that it can be made real and be accepted as usable experience.[4] Wordsworth's failure to write *The Recluse* has to do first with its irrelevance to his unconscious need for expression; *The Prelude,* which "usurped" its place, better served Wordsworth's preconscious intentions. If in "Tintern Abbey" Wordsworth reveals that the present self is disturbed by its several senses of the past, it is in *The Prelude* that he attempts a fuller characterization of them. The affirmation made in "Tintern Abbey" that Nature herself has determined his growth providentially and will continue to do so accounts for his willingness to attempt this new and personal use of poetry. On the one hand, then, we can say that *The Prelude* is an attempt to extend that conviction into a theory about the identity of the Poet; and on the other hand, that it is the record of an unconsciously compelled fascination with the problem of identity. Consciously conceiving the image of oneself is one intention—among other and less controllable intentions to be revealed by Imagination. For Wordsworth, writing poetry was meant to maintain and extend the ego's

[4] See Freud, "Moses and Monotheism," CW XXIII, 72-80. Wordsworth's use of the word "usurpation" ("in such strength/ Of usurpation, when the light of sense/ Goes out, but with a flash that has revealed/ The invisible world . . . ," VI, 599-602: 1850 version) is part of a description of the Imagination as a power of Revelation in the writing of poetry. This is discussed at length in Chap. IV, below.

"composure," its feeling of control over the promptings of an inspired but still recognizable self; but writing poetry was also in the service of an unconscious and unacknowledged intention to reveal what the ego had disowned.

In *The Prelude* we observe how the poet who recollects the child in his experiences of solitude presents at the same time the artist's heroic determination to pursue his recollections and imaginings in solitude in order to find again the "special" sense of himself in his experience, and perhaps to determine its meaning. We would locate that special sense ultimately in traumatic moments; in another context, Wordsworth himself describes, with a dramatic sense of the moment, how contemplation works upon recollected experience. He says: "I have said that Poetry is the spontaneous overflow of powerful feelings: it takes its origin from emotion recollected in tranquillity: the emotion is contemplated till by a species of reaction the tranquillity gradually disappears, and an emotion, similar to that which was before the subject of contemplation, is gradually produced, and does itself actually exist in the mind. In this mood successful composition generally begins. . . ."[5] It is with the precariously maintained assurance of himself as the Poet that he will dare to contemplate even the faintest of past feelings in order to re-experience and express them. He will approach the other-than-conscious sources of Imagination and emotion, too; for Wordsworth, who was aware of the irresistible force of Imagination, was also aware of the shadowy nature of some of his inner imagery and of the distressful feelings attached to their elusive motion:

> I had hopes
> Still higher, that with a frame of outward life,
> I might endue, might fix *in a visible home*
> Some portion of those phantoms of conceit

5 "Preface to *Lyrical Ballads,* second edition, 1800," *Poetical Works,* p. 734.

> That had been floating loose about so long,
> And to such Beings temperately deal forth
> The many feelings that oppress'd my heart.
> (I, 127-133)

In the same opening passage of Book I, Wordsworth tells of his choosing "one sweet vale" in which to settle into the life of the poet. But the life of the Poet in his poetic activity is to be figuratively that of the contemplative Hermit. "I journey'd towards the vale that I had chosen," he continues; "a pleasant loitering journey . . . brought me to my *hermitage*."[6]

It is known, and it has been variously interpreted by scholars, that the opening lines of the poem (lines 1-55 and 56-270) stands apart from the more easily datable passages compiled as Book I. The problems attaching to the "beginnings of *The Prelude*"[7] however, are not all of equal interest. Rather than trace the apparent discrepancies of representation or argue about Wordsworth's lapses of memory in selecting sequence and detail, I shall begin by ascribing a good deal to conscious artifice, allowing that Wordsworth was most probably simplifying imaginatively several similar recollections in order to present one poetic account of a beginning, which the poem plainly required.[8] The poem also required a sustained and clear continuity as well as a beginning; and it is likely that Wordsworth knew that he could not begin *The Prelude* with a complicated account of its inception as *The Recluse* and of its gradual emergence as a separate poem, a preliminary "review of the mind" prior to *The Recluse*. He could not include the actual sequences of aspiration, doubt, despondency, renewed aspiration and renewed endeavor; nor could he include the changes of location, the settings off, the sense of new beginnings, and the passing of seasons and

[6] *The Prelude*, I, 100-115.

[7] For an account of this complex subject, see Mary Moorman, *William Wordsworth*, chap. XIII, "The Beginnings of *The Prelude*."

[8] See *The Prelude*, pp. xliii-xlv.

years through which the past intention to write a great philosophical poem became the apparent present intention to write this one.

The poem has simply what all narratives need, an implied present from which its temporal references may be fixed in his poetic representation of himself as a character, the Poet. And so, until the beginning of Book VII, there is no explicit mention of breaks in composition; there is no account at the beginning of Book III, for instance, of the several years between the composition of Books II and III. Rather, towards the end of Book II, Wordsworth is recollecting his feelings of around the age of seventeen, and Book III follows logically enough from it with the account of his arrival at Cambridge soon thereafter. The fact is that the conflict he again experienced about writing when he resumed writing with Book III in late 1803—the doubts felt about the identity of the Poet and the identity of *this* poet—are represented in the first 270 lines of Book I, which were first written down in some version at that time.[9] Here, too, conscious artifice is present: conflict is appropriate to the nature of the undertaking, and the representation of it is essential; but it is likely that a conscious choice to simplify the narrative is responsible for his putting the account of it appropriately at the beginning of the poem. Wordsworth was simply being true to a poetic necessity. One could easily see in this the Renaissance sense of imitation, the poetic imitation of the essential reality by an imaginative selection from natural and historical detail.

The opening lines of the poem (1-54) express in the present tense the dramatic and momentary sense of beginning, which is then set unspecifically in the recent past at line 55, and what follows gradually is the extension in

[9] Lines 1-54 may have been written down earlier, though no copy of them survives; they may have been carried loosely in memory, as was Wordsworth's wont, and recalled in some form to be set down as part of lines 1-270 in late 1803. The first surviving copy of lines 1-270 is in MS M, dating from March 1804 when the poem was once again underway.

time of the interim between the past moment and the implied present moment of composition. That the brief account of the interim runs together the events of several years is neither immediately apparent nor apparently significant until scholarly curiosity makes it seem so. The interim has been a difficult one, full of the apprehensiveness that the present act of writing has apparently resolved; but the artifice is uncommonly smooth. A reader could easily take the first Book as wholly what it seems, and what in large part it is, the Poet coming to power and imposing his order on a nervous state. For 270 lines the poet has wavered uncertainly, but a brief history of the aspiration to be a poet and of the search for the subject matter of poetry has been presented in such a way that what follows seems the natural discovery of Romanticism: the poet discovers himself to be the subject of his poetry. The nadir has been reached at line 269 when he declares himself "unprofitably *travelling* towards the grave"; and the self-affirming question that follows—"Was it for this/ That one, the fairest of all rivers, lov'd/ To blend his murmurs with my nurse's song?"—is the point from which the ensuing tale of growth proceeds almost as if the journey metaphor of "travelling" had suggested it accidentally. The inspired poet takes over. This, however, is the smooth surface of artifice. The first 270 lines date in fair copy from March 1804 and have been placed in front of an earlier passage which, when written in 1798, was a piece of rhetorical self-chiding about his inability to get on with *The Recluse.* Let us see if we can now make some further use of the facts as a way of looking at *The Prelude.*

Around October of 1803 when the first 270 lines of Book I were first set down in some form, *The Prelude* was to be a poem of five books including in Book V his vision on Mount Snowdon and culminating in an account of the Poet's dedication to poetry in a memorable dawn at Hawkeshead in about his eighteenth year. Coleridge, referring to Wordsworth's resumption of work on the poem, wrote to Thomas

Poole: "He has made a Beginning to his *Recluse*. . . ."[10] Like Dorothy, Coleridge refers to the unwritten work, *The Recluse,* as "a great work" or "his great work," confident of the excellence of something that did not as yet exist; Wordsworth himself was not at all confident that he was the person who could produce it. That implied wholeness-of-being of the Poet who could write a great philosophical poem of meditations in his own person was a possibility that Coleridge had despaired of in himself but attributed without hesitation to Wordsworth. And Wordsworth, pleased by Coleridge's confidence in him, though made nervous by it, continued to equivocate in his communications with Coleridge, allowing him to think that he was working on *The Recluse* in spirit. As yet, he could neither tell Coleridge nor himself about his change in plans.

A consideration of the projected five-book *Prelude* shows that Wordsworth was certainly attempting to create himself as the Poet by a use of artifice, by an imaginative selection from autobiographical facts. He planned to deal with formative experience in a highly positive way, showing how an imaginative predisposition in the experiences of early childhood matured into his habit of imaginative self-consciousness. This is the quality that enables the Poet to see the analogy between the "One Great Mind" and the infant's mind and between God's creative mind and the Poet's as revealed in his account of his own visionary experience on Mount Snowdon. The Poet realizes himself by his predisposition to see a providential design in personal experience, as when, for instance, he takes the "memorable pomp" of a common dawn as the moment of a personal consecration. The poem about becoming the Poet, however, implied the same wholeness of being necessary for the Poet's great philosophical poem; if it seemed to allow Wordsworth to postpone the anxiety of being greatly philosophical, it did so only by requiring him to explain how he became qualified to be so.

[10] Coleridge, *Letters,* #525.

With the extended thirteen-book *Prelude* in mind, one finds that the self-affirmative question—"Was it for this . . . ?"—sounds beautifully pathetic when it comes after the first 270 lines as we now have them. Their account of his baffled hopes of attaining his ideal and of his bleak fears of being nothing at all win our sympathy because the implied present moment of composition, as we learn in the poem, is that of the poet who is no longer a youth. He has survived an experience of despair, and, despite misgivings, is daring now to aspire again. But in the projected five-book *Prelude* Wordsworth would have had considerably more difficulty establishing sympathetically the relationship between the implied present moment of writing and the past, for he would seem only to be an older man recollecting what led up to his realization in his college years that Nature intended him to be a poet. The poem would present a few examples of his precocious habits of self-consciousness, his penchant for recollection, and his naive self-concern. It would be about a college boy who did not very much like college and who preferred the rural setting and boyish pursuits of the village school; it would be about an undergraduate poet who, in the years since college, has not been realizing his aspiration to become the heir of Milton. But, plainly, "Was it for this . . ." are the words of someone older, who had lived through the difficult years of 1791 to 1799, and not someone younger than the poet of "Tintern Abbey."

Wordsworth, making a "beginning" for this poem in October 1803 and again aspiring to get it and himself underway, must have sensed that in its projected form it was not only out of touch with his recent past but also with his present self. It was not serving his present psychic needs. While he composed Books III and IV, which he began in January or February of 1804, that sense of discrepancy must have grown stronger, for in writing of himself as an undergraduate he must have seen something of his own callowness. His realization of the personal necessity of extending the poem to its present form occurred between October 1803 and March 1804.[11]

The Prelude, whether or not Wordsworth or Coleridge would quite abandon the title of *The Recluse* for it, was what Wordsworth was trying to write. Yet the poem has, as a kind of modest covering device for its extremely personal nature, the form of a sustained verse-letter to Coleridge who believed in him. We know how much Wordsworth was dependent on Dorothy, and in much the same way he had become dependent on Coleridge in the late 1790's. The latter's exhortations ("I will hear of nothing but *The Recluse*!") must have been a constant provocation of anxiety to Wordsworth. To conclude the projected five-book *Prelude,* as Coleridge wished him to, Wordsworth could have offered himself as the Poet only within the limits we have just observed; but Wordsworth *had* to attempt instead to include his present self in his account of the Poet even at the risk of disappointing Coleridge and of further engaging what I have called his unconscious intentions. The repetition-compulsion, as we shall see, would use poetry to reveal repressed traumata as the poet attempts to deal with formative experiences and their consequences in later life, and especially since his recent experience had not been accidentally traumatic itself.

It is probable that between October 1803 and March 1804, Wordsworth resolved some important conflict in himself, of which the commitment to the extended form of *The Prelude* is the outward sign. He had known that he could depend on Coleridge as the intended sympathetic reader of the poem to supply in his own mind the necessary knowledge of how difficult the years between 1791 and 1799 had been, just as he could depend on Coleridge and Dorothy for a supportive belief in his excellence. But we may infer that just as the attempt at poetic autobiography was Wordsworth's independent determination to find that

[11] See *The Prelude,* pp. l-li. I deal with the significance of this decision to extend the poem below, pp. 235ff.

reassurance within himself, so too was the subsequent decision in the very nature of the attempt, to affirm himself as the Poet in the totality of his experience. We shall return to consider the period between October 1803 and March 1804 in Chapter VI.

2. Metaphors of Beginning and Where They Lead

It is to the metaphors at the beginning of *The Prelude* that we must attend. Through them Wordsworth expresses beginnings, conscious and unconscious aspirations, and memories of much greater consequence than those suggested by the scholarly concern for date, place, and factual representation. His conscious artifice, his desire to recall and imagine, to remember and invent, the principal character of the poem, reveals at the same time the kind of preconscious association that Imagination forces upon Memory; and the apparent inaccuracy of memory perhaps attests to deeper memories. The extended thirteen-book *Prelude* is attempting a greater self-acceptance and requires the introduction at the outset of a character seeking that.[12] To begin with, then, here are the first 54 lines of Book I.

> Oh there is blessing in this gentle breeze
> That blows from the green fields and the clouds
> And from the sky: it beats against my cheek,
> And seems half conscious of the joy it gives.
> Oh welcome Messenger! O welcome Friend!
> A captive greets thee, coming from a house
> Of bondage, from yon City's walls set free,
> A prison where he hath been long immured.

[12] I personally think it likely that the lost MS version of lines 1-270, which was probably written in October of 1803, was in some way different from the version we have in MS M. The original version of these lines was written with the five-book *Prelude* in mind, whereas MS M, dating from March of 1804 and containing Books IV and V substantially in their present form, probably had been adjusted to fit the poem as Wordsworth had reconceived it in the light of his decision. The "I" of line 56 is, in a sense, a different and older person.

Now I am free, enfranchis'd and at large,
May fix my habitation where I will.
What dwelling shall receive me? In what Vale
Shall be my harbour? Underneath what grove
Shall I take up my home, and what sweet stream
Shall with its murmur lull me to my rest?
The earth is all before me: with a heart
Joyous, nor scar'd at its own liberty,
I look about, and should the guide I chuse
Be nothing better than a wandering cloud,
I cannot miss my way. I breathe again;
Trances of thought and mountings of the mind
Come fast upon me: it is shaken off,
As by miraculous gift 'tis shaken off,
That burthen of my own unnatural self,
The heavy weight of many a weary day
Not mine, and such as were not made for me.
Long months of peace (if such bold word accord
With any promises of human life),
Long months of ease and undisturb'd delight
Are mine in prospect; whither shall I turn
By road or pathway or through open field,
Or shall a twig or any floating thing
Upon the river, point me out my course?
  Enough that I am free; for months to come
May dedicate myself to chosen tasks;
May quit the tiresome sea and dwell on shore,
If not a Settler on the soil, at least
To drink wild water, and to pluck green herbs,
And gather fruits fresh from their native bough.
Nay more, if I may trust myself, this hour
Hath brought a gift that consecrates my joy;
For I, methought, while the sweet breath of Heaven
Was blowing on my body, felt within
A corresponding mild creative breeze,
A vital breeze which travell'd gently on
O'er things which it had made, and is become

A tempest, a redundant energy
Vexing its own creation. 'Tis a power
That does not come unrecogniz'd, a storm,
Which, breaking up a long-continued frost
Brings with its vernal promises, the hope
Of active days, of dignity and thought,
Of prowess in an honorable field,
Pure passions, virtue, knowledge, and delight,
The holy life of music and of verse.

(I, 1-54)

Wordsworth speaks metaphorically of a condition of bondage being left behind, and while in fact he is setting off for the country and leaving behind the city, he is using the actual occasion to distinguish figuratively between senses of himself that come at such moments. As in the traditional Christian allegorical reading of the historical books of the Bible, "coming from a house of bondage" (the Exodus) is to be understood as a metaphor for the soul finding its freedom. (In *Purgatorio,* Dante has the souls crossing from mortal life to the Mountain of Purgatory singing "In exitu Israel de Egyptu."[13]) Wordsworth is being deliberately Biblical here, his spirit willing to follow "a wandering cloud," confident of its way. He is speaking of spiritual freedom, and he makes clear, in language suggestive of spiritual possession ("Trances of thought and mountings of the mind/ Come fast upon me") that he may become, momentarily, an oracle to himself in poetic utterance.

As we observed in our reading of "Tintern Abbey," what is being opposed here is not the relative merits of country life and city life, but rather the psychic possibilities for which the one and the other stand. City life stands for the "burthen of my own unnatural self/ The heavy weight of many a weary day/ Not mine, and such as were not made for me"; and the language unmistakably suggests "Tintern

[13] Dante, *Purgatorio,* II, 46.

Abbey," "the burthen of the mystery," the "heavy and the weary weight of all that unintelligible world," "the dreary intercourse of daily life." The country life, here as there, stands for what the Hermit stands for in "Tintern Abbey," which is why, I think, it occurs to Wordsworth to say "hermitage" soon afterwards. He distinguishes a real "me" which can withdraw from the life of the "unnatural self"—"unnatural" in so far as it has been "bound" to circumstance.

If we accept as fact that these lines were composed extemporaneously on the way to Racedown in 1795, why after all does he pretend in these lines not to know where he is going?

> Now I am free, enfranchis'd and at large,
> May fix my habitation where I will.
> What dwelling shall receive me? In what Vale
> Shall be my harbour? Underneath what grove
> Shall I take up my home, and what sweet stream
> Shall with its murmur lull me to my rest?
>
> (I, 9-14)

Why so elaborate a metaphorical characterization of following his newly-free spirit—"a wandering cloud," "a twig or any floating thing/ Upon the river shall point me out my course"—if he knows the actual direction well enough and even the roads he will take? Should we be concerned, as many scholars have been,[14] about the possible confusion in recollection between Racedown, which he knew something of but had never seen, and Grasmere which, in 1795, he did not know was his future home? Is it not, rather, that in his spontaneous attempt to imagine Racedown as the destined habitat for his free and contented spirit, he is anticipating it imaginatively in the imagery associated with spiritual contentment? Then perhaps he is doing so by preconsciously recalling the past—a grove, a home, a stream and a vale, something lost, now reconstituted as the spirit

[14] See *The Prelude*, pp. 510-511, footnote to I, 1-270.

wishes it were.[15] If Racedown is perfect, he was saying, it will look like that. The fact, of course, is that it didn't; neither did Alfoxden, where he next moved to be nearer Coleridge. Eventually, much to Coleridge's disappointment, he returned with Dorothy to the Lake Country. To settle permanently and write, he required again what his spirit desiderated, the mountain and valley scene which was for him the setting of the "first poetic impulse." Thus, while writing this passage down in 1803, he was sitting on a pleasant autumn day in Grasmere, which is not confused in his memory with Racedown, but is simply the fulfillment of a wish he had once expressed imaginatively and spontaneously about Racedown.

We have already begun to interpret the characteristics of that landscape and its appeal, its way of figuring in past states of relatedness with the mother; but even without a previously adverted eye no alert reader could miss the similarity between "and what stream/ Shall with its murmur lull me to my rest?" (I, 13-14) and the stream that stands for the infant condition:

> Was it for this
> That one, the fairest of all Rivers, lov'd
> *To blend his murmurs* with my Nurse's song,
> And from his alder shades and rocky falls,
> And from his fords and shallows, sent a voice
> That flow'd along my dreams? For this, didst Thou,
> O Derwent! travelling over the green Plains
> Near my 'sweet Birthplace,' didst thou, beauteous
>   Stream,
> Make ceaseless music through the night and day
> Which with its steady cadence, tempering
> Our human waywardness, compos'd my thoughts
> To more than infant softness, giving me,
> Among the fretful dwellings of mankind,

[15] The ways in which Wordsworth's imagination engages preconscious suggestions and unconscious wishes are treated here. The further significance of his doing so is treated in Chap. IV and V, below.

A knowledge, a dim earnest, of the calm
That Nature breathes among the hills and groves.
(I, 271-285; my italics)

As in "Tintern Abbey" where the beauteous forms of a river valley held within the mind stand for a state of soul modelled on the preconscious recollection of infancy and association with the mother, so here does the spiritual preference for a journey to a hermitage make clear what is anticipated by the inspired spirit becoming free of the "unnatural self" and imagining its goal at the moment of setting off. If these lines were composed on the way to Racedown in 1795, then we have as early as that an indication of the unconscious intention to return through imagination to the past, for the journey to contentment is a return.

This opening passage ends in as highly a metaphorical way as it begins:

if I may trust myself, this hour
Hath brought a gift that consecrates my joy;
For I, methought, while the sweet breath of Heaven
Was blowing on my body, felt within
A corresponding mild creative breeze,
A vital breeze which travell'd gently on
O'er things which it had made, and is become
A tempest, a redundant energy
Vexing its own creation. 'Tis a power
That does not come unrecogniz'd, a storm,
Which, breaking up a long-continued frost
Brings with it vernal promises, the hope
Of active days, of dignity and thought,
Of prowess in an honorable field,
Pure passions, virtue, knowledge, and delight,
The holy life of music and of verse.
(I, 39-54)

An actual breeze felt as sensation on the body seems to be

a heaven-sent sign for his poetry because of a more significant answering breeze felt within him—"A corresponding mild creative breeze." The potential of creativity, he finds, is no more easily controlled than it is easily realized, and hence it seems tempestuous; it either vexes what is being created (these spontaneous lines) or seems to have become vexed by them. Making poetry is self-conscious; in some way it vexes the contentment presumably sought. Wordsworth says at line 68 that he then gave "a respite to this passion" and settled into "a gentler happiness:"

> On the ground I lay
> Passing through many thoughts, yet mainly such
> As to myself pertain'd. I made a choice
> Of one sweet Vale whither my steps should turn
> And saw, methought, the very house and fields
> Present before my eyes . . .
>
> (I, 79-84)

He is going to Racedown; in contented musing, he anticipates the "sweet vale" that isn't there. But the contentment and passivity described here may remind us of the affections leading us on in "Tintern Abbey," away from consciousness of self:

> Thus long I lay
> Chear'd by the genial pillow of the earth
> Beneath my head, sooth'd by a sense of touch
> From the warm ground, that balanced me, else lost
> Entirely, seeing nought, nought hearing, save
> When here and there, about the grove of Oaks
> Where was my bed, an acorn from the trees
> Fell audibly, and with a startling sound.
>
> (I, 87-94)

Then, self-consciousness returns to startle his vacancy and remind him subsequently of poetry, the "work of glory" he had put from mind.

In any case, there is conflict in poetic utterance at present; the mild creative breeze has become a tempest. But in his own way, through the recurrence of poetic figures, Wordsworth makes perfectly clear to us, if we will only utilize his characterizations fully, that at one time these very sensations of an inner breeze were felt by the Babe without conflict. They came from Nature through the mother, the essential reality of the world. It was she who fostered "the first poetic spirit of our human life"; he says of the Blest Babe:

> Such feelings pass into his torpid life
> Like an awakening breeze, and hence his mind
> Even [in the first trial of its powers]
> Is prompt and watchful, eager to combine
> In one appearance, all the elements
> And parts of the same object, else detach'd
> And loth to coalesce.
>
> (II, 244-250)

And it is to her absent and traumatically introjected reality that both the present poetic urge, the "mild creative breeze," and its tempestuous force as a disturbance within him attest.[16]

He tells us early in his story of "that spirit of religious love in which/ I walked with Nature" when as a boy after his mother's death he was alone in life:

> But let this, at least
> Be not forgotten, that I still retain'd
> My first creative sensibility,
> That by the regular action of the world
> My soul was unsubdu'd . . .
>
> (II, 377-381)

The description that follows these lines is of a power held within, unmanageable but one's own; it seems to fit exactly the descriptions of the power associated with the mother

[16] See Freud, "On Narcissism," CW XIV.

that composes things beautifully and that power as it is subject to inner disturbance, "vexing its own creation":

> A plastic power
> Abode with me, a forming hand, at times
> Rebellious, acting in a devious mood,
> A local spirit of its own, at war
> With general tendency, but for the most
> Subservient strictly to the external things
> With which it commun'd. An auxiliar light
> Came from my mind which on the setting sun
> Bestow'd new splendor, the melodious birds,
> The gentle breezes, fountains that ran on,
> Murmuring so sweetly in themselves, obey'd
> A like dominion; and the midnight storm
> Grew darker in the presence of my eye.
> Hence my obeisance, my devotion hence,
> And hence my transport.
>
> (II, 381-395)

The "midnight storm," on which the poet remembers imposing his tempestuous imagination, was experienced in one of those many situations that the boy sought with fascination in solitude.

His fuller characterization of the necessary solitude supplies us with an amazing connection between the disturbances he experienced in it and the various imaginative senses of it he retained in memory:

> for I would walk alone,
> In storm and tempest, or in star-light nights
> Beneath the quiet Heavens; and, at that time,
> Have felt whate'er there is of power in sound
> To breathe an elevated mood, by form
> Or image unprofaned; and I would stand,
> Beneath some rock, listening to sounds that are
> The ghostly language of the ancient earth,
> Or make their dim abode in distant winds.

Thence did I drink the visionary power.
I deem not profitless those fleeting moods
Of shadowy exultation: not for this,
That they are kindred to our purer mind
And intellectual life; but that the soul,
Remembering how she felt, but what she felt
Remembering not, retains an obscure sense
Of possible sublimity, to which
With growing faculties she doth aspire,
The faculties still growing, feeling still
That whatsoever point they gain, they still
Have something to pursue.

(II, 321-341)

On the one hand, he is simply saying that he heard the stormy wind in the darkness and felt exhilarated by it; on the other hand, he says imaginatively that he was listening to Nature's disembodied voice, "the ghostly language of the ancient earth," and feeling the longing of the soul to pursue something sublime by the further growth of faculties capable of such pursuit. In a characteristic way, he "*drinks*" in this "visionary power" from the experience of "sounds that are/ The ghostly language of the ancient earth/ Or make their dim abode in the distant winds." It is the visionary faculty that must grow—the ability to "see" the presence in Nature, the ability to hear Nature's language more clearly, and, one supposes, the ability to speak that language expressively as poetry. The supposition is correct. Later, in Book v, he will echo these very words in talking about Poetry and the "great Nature that exists in works/ Of mighty poets. . . ."

he who, in his youth
A wanderer among the wood and fields,
With living Nature hath been intimate,
Not only in that raw unpractis'd time
Is stirr'd to ecstasy, as others are,
By glittering verse; but, he doth furthermore,

In measure only dealt out to himself,
Receive enduring touches of deep joy
From the great Nature that exists in works
Of mighty Poets. *Visionary Power*
Attends upon the motions of the winds
Embodied in the mystery of words.
There darkness makes abode, and all the host
Of shadowy things do work their changes there,[17]
As in a mansion like their proper home:
Even forms and substances are circumfus'd
By that transparent veil with light divine;
And through the turnings intricate of Verse,
Present themselves as objects recognis'd,
In flashes, and with a glory scarce their own.
(v, 610-629; my italics)

But there remains some uncertainty about poetic expression, about what exactly may be seen in moments of "vision," that has to do with Wordsworth's sense of human language itself.

What is the darkness that makes abode in the mystery of words, and what are the shadowy things that work their changes there, if poetry is a "light divine" by which objects are seen with a flash, recognized and glorified? How does one get from the mystery and the darkness of words to

[17] William Collins's "Ode on the Poetical Character" has the line "shad'wy tribes of mind," which seems to be in Wordsworth's mind here. Interestingly enough, Collins was celebrating the inimitability of Milton, whereas succeeding Milton was the subject often on Wordsworth's mind. Collins asks:

Where is the Bard, whose soul can now
Its high presuming Hopes avow?
Where he who thinks, with Rapture blind,
This hallow'd work for him design'd?

and he answers:

In vain—Such Bliss to One alone
Of all the Sons of Soul was known,
And Heav'n and fancy, kindred Pow'rs,
Have o'erturn'd th'inspiring Bow'rs
Or curtain'd close the Scene from ev'ry future view.

the spiritual illumination caused by their use in poetry? The "Great Nature that exists in works of mighty poets" is said to be accessible in a special way to one who has been intimate with Nature, who has heard the "ghostly language of the ancient earth." Here, too, Wordsworth is emphasizing hearing rather than speaking. He has heard something in Nature "speak" to him in the windy darkness, and he is using that experience to characterize what he has "heard" in the peculiar utterance of poetry. Why, though, has he relocated his visionary sense of something "in" Nature's darkness and mystery in language itself, in the "mystery of words?"

Fortunately, Wordsworth has already told us something else about the experience of poetry:

> Dumb yearnings, hidden appetites are ours,
> And they must have their food: our childhood sits,
> Our simple childhood sits upon a throne
> That hath more power than all the elements.
> I guess not what this tells of Being past,
> Nor what it augurs of the life to come;
> But so it is; and in that dubious hour,
> That twilight when we first begin to see
> This dawning earth, to recognise, expect;
> And in the long probation that ensues,
> The time of trial, ere we learn to live
> In reconcilement with our stinted powers,
> To endure this state of meagre vassalage;
> Unwilling to forego, confess, submit,
> Uneasy and unsettled; yoke-fellows
> To custom, mettlesome, and not yet tam'd
> And humbled down, oh! then we feel, we feel
> We know when we have Friends. Ye dreamers, then,
> Forgers of lawless tales! we bless you then,
> Impostors, drivellers, dotards, as the ape
> Philosophy will call you: then we feel
> With what, and how great might ye are in league,

> Who make our wish our power, our thought a deed,
> As empire, a possession; Ye whom Time
> And Seasons serve; all Faculties; to whom
> Earth crouches, th' elements are potter's clay,
> Space like a Heaven fill'd up with Northern lights;
> Here, nowhere, there, and everywhere at once.
>
> (V, 530-557)

It becomes quite plain: infantile appetite, the capacity for almost unlimited sensation and fantasy comes in a period that is rich and dumb. We have observed how language, which seems at first to enable the infant to express his wants and which is imbued with the pleasurable sense of association with the mother, is ultimately utilitarian and reductive. So language gradually limits the wonder of experience, darkens the vision and recollection of pleasure. Only the experiences offered by poetry, which is partially elusive of the limits of ordinary human speech, are capable of evoking the infantile and fantastic sense of alternatives to reality, of a prior and superior existence, perhaps as soul, from which the sense of self and time are a gradual estrangement.

Wordsworth also says here, as in "The Immortality Ode" that we come "from our native continent/ To earth and human life," which makes us imagine, whichever way we choose, a pre-existence to the "human life" of the self. The habituation to the world is through the mother: and, if we recall from Book II that Wordsworth uses language there too as a metaphor for the process, we must be struck by the consistency of his metaphorical sense of things:

> by intercourse of touch,
> I held mute dialogues with my Mother's heart.
>
> (II, 282-283)

But with this same metaphor of speech-without-words, representing the hearing or ingesting of primal lessons and earliest visions, he also describes the relationship between the mother-substitute, Nature, and the growing child:

A Child, I held unconscious intercourse
With the eternal Beauty, drinking in
A pure organic pleasure from the lines
Of curling mist, or from the level plain
Of waters colour'd by the steady clouds.
(I, 589-593)

the earth
And common face of Nature spake to me
Rememberable things.
(I, 614-616)

He remembers, too, that the pure pleasure of childish play seemed to absorb the beauty of the surroundings; and he says explicitly that in this way Nature "*Peopled* my mind with beauteous form or grand/ And made me love them . . . ,"[18] just as the ambience of the mother's love had once suffused the natural objects of the world for the infant with light, love, and wonder. (Notice, too, that "peopled" figuratively preserves in the beauteous forms of Nature a very human association.) And Wordsworth himself surmises that Nature's way of doing this for the child is a further development of the mother-infant relationship:

those first-born affinities that fit
Our new existence to existing things,
And, in our dawn of being, constitute
The bond of union betwixt life and joy.
(I, 582-585)

The "ghostly language of the ancient earth" heard in solitude in the windy darkness is a projection into Nature of a preconscious sense of a lost relationship, of the dialogue that the infant had with the mother's heart. Nature metaphorically "speaking" to him in solitude, wind, and darkness makes him want to speak that "visionary" language which he tells us later is poetry. To speak of visionary things is to use the imagination to evoke, and perhaps sub-

[18] *The Prelude*, I, 573-574.

sequently recognize, lost objects of love and wonder, to reveal in special utterance their ghostly or shadowy existence in the mind, called elsewhere "those phantoms of conceit," "the many feelings that oppressed my heart."

Here, too, we should notice how "heart" is associated with the mother and death. "Mute dialogues with my mother's *heart*" calls to mind: "the heart/ And hinge of all our learning and our loves . . ." and "our being's heart and home is with infinitude. . . ."[19] A revision made by Wordsworth in the Poetry passage from Book v suggests further that it is a knowledge of what has been lost in death that poetry might uncover and present ("as objects recognized in flashes") when the poet's ability to speak in a visionary way matches his sense of being spoken to. When he changes "the motions of the winds" to "the motions of the *viewless* winds," I think that he is also preconsciously recalling Claudio's speech from *Measure For Measure*, which supplies the context of the imagination attempting to deal with the fear of death as an incomprehensible journey:

> Ay, but to die, and go we know not where;
> To lie in cold obstruction and to rot;
> This sensible warm motion to become
> A kneaded clod, and the delighted spirit
> In thrilling region of thick-ribbed ice;
> To be imprison'd in the viewless winds,
> And blown with restless violence round about
> The pendent world . . .
>
> (III, i, 118-125)

Death and darkness are associated with the "*ghostly* language of the ancient earth" and with the "viewless winds" of poetry. But illuminating light and glory are also associated with poetry. We remember from Book II that the "one belov'd Presence," which so closely resembles the "Presence" in Nature of "Tintern Abbey," is one that "*ir-*

19 These lines, often cited in this work, are from *The Prelude*, I, 283; V, 257-258; VI, 604: 1850 version.

radiates and exalts . . . all objects through all intercourse of sense"; and this, I think, suggests why poetry is also said to have a "light divine" which suffuses objects and presents them "in flashes," whereas there is a darkness inherent in language.

3. The Hermetic Adventure

We have come by a train of associations a long way from the end of the opening passage of Book I, but curiously enough the Poetry passage in Book V which speaks of "objects recognized in flashes" leads directly back to it and to another train of associations about poetry. The breeze that has had an answering breeze within, reminiscent of the "awakening breeze" in the infant, has turned his thoughts from the imaginative anticipation of Racedown to an imaginative characterization of his activity there. The inner storm that symbolizes the conflict about creativity is recognized and accepted, which is its hopeful sign:

'Tis a power
That does not come unrecogniz'd, a storm,
Which, breaking up a long-continued frost
Brings with it vernal promises, the hope
Of active days, of dignity and thought,
Of prowess in an honorable field,
Pure passions, virtue, knowledge, and delight,
The holy life of music and of verse.

(I, 47-54)

The "long continued frost" has been his inability to create, and probably refers specifically to the period around 1795 when he had first begun to think of subjects for a great poem on a Miltonic scale. Wordsworth himself is metaphorically the land to be thawed and has received this "vernal promise" of spiritual rain—a plainly metaphorical and unseasonal spring storm on this autumn day. And the poet, who will work "active days" (by thinking) and show his "prowess in an honorable field" (by tilling the land of his spirit for the crop of poetry) is figured at the same time as a religious man engaged in an activity of soul, "the holy life of music and of verse." Racedown is to be a kind of hermitage where the lone and self-sufficient spirit works its fields and produces a metaphorical crop by its labors.

Surely, this is curious; unless it has some elusive but precisely poetic meaning, it must seem to be merely a loosely figurative way of speaking. But the figures reappear significantly, and it is their difficult precision, not their looseness, that is remarkable. For instance, in speaking of the Convent of Chartreuse ("an awful solitude") seen on the way to his memorable crossing of the Alps in 1791, he is moved to defend it in memory, for he remembers the "military glare of riotous men/ Commission'd to expel and overturn/ With senseless rapine." At this moment of writing, Wordsworth is no longer a republican himself, but is writing of a time when he was beginning to sympathize strongly with the French Revolution. He is recalling that even then he had felt reverence for the Convent of Chartreuse and what it stood for. He speaks of *feeding* the soul with darkness and wishing this convent to remain "one spot/ Of earth devoted to Eternity." He speaks, too, of the "sister streams of Life and Death" (the "Guiers vif" and the "Guiers mort") that join below the Convent to become the Guier, and hears them speaking to his "inward ear." They end by saying:

> These forests unapproachable by death,
> That shall endure, as long as man endures
> To think, to hope, to worship and to feel,
> To struggle, to be lost within himself
> In trepidation, from the blank abyss
> To look with bodily eyes and be consoled.
> (VI, 495; MS A2, 70-75)

This passage in Book VI anticipates another long passage

in Book VI, in which the recollection of crossing the Alps induces a profound experience of Imagination in him, which he attempts to characterize.[20] Of the experience of being overwhelmed by the Imagination (an "awful power" that arises "from the mind's abyss") Wordsworth writes:

> I was lost;
> Halted without an effort to break through;
> But to my conscious soul I now can say—
> 'I recognise thy glory': in such strength
> Of usurpation, when the light of sense
> Goes out, but with a flash that has revealed
> The invisible world, doth greatness make abode,
> There harbours; whether we be young or old,
> Our destiny, our being's heart and home,
> Is with infinitude, and only there;
> With hope it is, hope that can never die,
> Effort, and expectation, and desire,
> And something evermore about to be.
> (VI, 596-608; 1850 version)

We recall here one of the passages we have just been looking at (quoted above, pp. 108-109) in which the "ghostly language of the ancient earth" incites the soul to seek its proper activity in the further use of its visionary faculties. But the significant difference is that in the Imagination passage, he is *not* recalling actual stormy nights and their effect on his imagination, nor is he writing figuratively about poetry in terms of dark and viewless winds, but rather he is describing an experience he has just had in his own mind while *writing* poetry, while trying to use his "visionary power."

In Chapter IV we shall examine that remarkable passage in detail, but here we should observe that a sense of psychic

[20] More than likely it is the case that this passage in MS A2 was written years later than the passage VI, 520-590 in MS A. (See above, n. 17 to Chap. II.) The actual experience of seeing the Convent preceded that of crossing the Alps, and so Wordsworth may have inserted the passage into the revised text in that spirit.

possibilities is suggested by an extraordinary momentary event in the mind, though there is no accompanying realization of its meaning. The "flash that has revealed/ The invisible world" precisely resembles the potential of power discerned in poetry where objects are gloriously transformed and recognized in "flashes"; but Wordsworth does not know and cannot say what he saw or why his imagination discharged itself so peculiarly at that moment of imaginative recollection. He is in fact attempting to describe the desire to express unrealized visionary things in poetry, and he reveals in the process how close he is in imagination to saying that he would like to *reveal* something in his poetry about his invisible inner world. There is in "the mind's abyss" (where man "is lost within himself") something on which he could "look with bodily eyes, and be consoled."

"Consoled" might then call to mind the status of the repressed trauma, the inconsolable traumatic loss that had profoundly affected the reality of the external world for him. Landscapes—especially, as in all these passages, ones recalling river-valleys deeply associated with the original home, the vale, and the mother—strengthen the appeal of the inner world and its idealized reality. In the "holy calm" of the convent, however, the meditative man might approach the abyss "with bodily eyes," look into it and be consoled; whereas the boy, unlike the man, had sought blissful forgetfulness, a state ambiguously between the visible world relinquished and the invisible world realized:

> among the hills I sate
> Alone, upon some jutting eminence
> At the first hour of morning, when the Vale
> Lay quiet in an utter solitude.
> How shall I trace the history, where seek
> The origin of what I then have felt?
> Oft in those moments such a holy calm
> Did overspread my soul, that I forgot

That I had bodily eyes and what I saw
Appear'd like something in myself, a dream,
A prospect in my mind.

(II, 361-371)

The inner landscape makes psychic withdrawal and the loss of self an attractive state to him, but the "abyss," we have observed, seems to be another characterization of the tendency towards inwardness. The sense of the inner world he presents by mention of it seems recurrent and compelling, but resisted rather than sought. As he says in the Fenwick note: "I was often unable to think of external things as having external existence, and I communed with all that I saw as something not apart from, but inherent in, my own immaterial nature. Many times while going to school have I grasped at a wall or tree to recall myself from this abyss of idealism to the reality. At that time I was afraid of such processes."[21] His resistance suggests that he felt that to yield was not to yield momentarily, but wholly, permanently. Wordsworth has elsewhere characterized this as "the one interior life" in which, unself-consciously, "all beings live with God, are lost/ In God and Nature." ("Themselves are God.")[22] But as a description of a permanent state of mind it sounds like psychosis.

There are, then, let us distinguish, *two* approaches to inwardness, one active, one passive. One seeks the abyss in order to see into it and to realize what is there; the other might yield to it, as if to fall into oblivion. The Poet is active; he would descend, like Orpheus, with the intention of returning to the visible world, though we must say that repression hides from Wordsworth a knowledge of what he seeks in the underworld. If the Poet in his ideal self-consciousness is modelled on the infant awakening with his poetic powers to the visible world, the passive extreme is modelled on the infant who falls asleep upon the breast, relapsing into unself-conscious union with the universe

[21] Wordsworth, *Prose Works*, vol. III, p. 194.
[22] *The Prelude*, p. 525.

and with eternity from which its young life is barely divided as yet in time. Against this calm oblivious tendency, poetry is an heuristic assertion, a process by which the conscious self seeks the region of soul in order to assimilate its expression of need: "but to my conscious soul *I* now can say: '*I* recognize thy glory.'" One should preserve equally the weight of the I-speaking self and that of the soul to which it is being said. The Poet begins to describe an awakening to an inner and invisible world.

At the end of the Imagination passage in Book vi, there is another curious example of complex metaphor. Its picture of the soul made fertile by the mind further describes the poet's activity in an idealized condition for his spirit; the metaphor of fertility is exactly like that of the thawed earth at the end of the passage in Book i we began by examining. In the Imagination passage he says:

> the soul
> Seeks for no trophies, struggles for no spoils
> That may attest her prowess, blest in thoughts
> That are their own perfection and reward,
> Strong in herself and in beatitude
> That hides her, like the mighty flood of Nile
> Poured from his fount of Abyssinian clouds
> To fertilise the whole Egyptian plain.
> (vi, 609-616: 1850 version)

Unlike the worldly revolutionists who would take the Convent of Chartreuse as the prize of their militancy, the soul struggles for no such prizes; the poet will enter Racedown, his hermitage, in much the same way that the meditative man might retire to the Convent of Chartreuse. It will be the place of his spirit, his soul enclosed there and put out to the tillage of his art, as when he says that the thawed earth of his spirit gives him

> the hope
> Of active days, of dignity and thought,

Of prowess in an honorable field,
Pure passions, virtue, knowledge, and delight,
The holy life of music and of verse.
(I, 50-54)

For Wordsworth, as for Milton before him, fame may be the spur to prowess, but the holy life of cultivating the soul in poetry is the unworldly way he proposes to himself. In the Imagination passage, too, he anticipates the soul attesting "her prowess," blest with the activity of thought and enwrapt in Beatitude. What follows is a characterization of the soul fertilized by Imagination and stretched out like the Egyptian plain ready to yield to tillage in the fullness of time its crop of poetry. If one presses the analogy, as one ought to, it does not give way under the strain; the inner consistency of Wordsworth's metaphorical sense of things supplies us with other interesting connections.

For instance, the association of soul-and-tillage is everywhere apparent in *The Prelude* as part of the simple use of the metaphor of growth: "Fair seedtime had my soul . . . ," he says (I, 305). Recalling the sowing of dragon's teeth by Cadmus, he equates the account to be given of Imaginative Power with that of the race of heroes:

O Heavens! how awful is the might of Souls,
And what they do within themselves, while yet
The yoke of earth is new to them, the world
Nothing but a wild field where they were sown.
That is, in truth, heroic argument,
And genuine prowess; which I wish'd to touch
With hand however weak; but in the main
It lies far hidden from the reach of words.
Points have we all of us within our souls,
Where all stand single; this I feel, and make
Breathings for incommunicable powers.
Yet each man is a memory to himself . . .
(III, 178-189)

But notice here that two very different and somewhat ambiguous metaphors are forced on each other: one is that of the soul sown in the world, as if men, identified metonomously by their souls, were seeds that grow into plants; and the other is that of the soul as something in which or on which one might stand, as in an underground cavern or on a mountain. If one thinks of the natural growth of man, rooted in place from birth and fostered by Nature, as the growth of his spirit, then perhaps the metaphors of the fertilized mind and spirit and of the poet's labor, taken together, mean simply that his poetry is the bloom or crop of his spirit, specifically the harvested account of the "growth of a poet's mind." But Wordsworth has also talked of being "transplanted" to another vale; and I have suggested that the journey-metaphor begins with his sense of leaving the original vale. "Transplanted" cannot adequately convey the psychic complexity of that experience.

We have found instead unconscious distinctions between inner and outer realities, the visible and invisible worlds, and ordinary and "visionary" ways of seeing, hearing, and speaking. Soul, then, is also unconsciously associated with another kind of growth; it seems to reside in hidden or inaccessible places, and may be seen, as here, as the inner terrain itself. In this sense the poet self-consciously searches for what lies "far hidden from the reach of words" inside himself; and language—at once inherently dark, as we have seen, and capable of gloriously illuminating the soul in poetic utterance—is the means by which the search is conducted. Whereas the tillage metaphor implies that the growth of a poet's mind may be rendered by beautiful and rather simple metaphors, the journey metaphor, from which the topographical metaphors for the soul derive, suggests an obscurity and complexity of growth of which Wordsworth was also aware. It is the journey metaphor, of whose full significance Wordsworth remained unconscious, that leads us to deeper considerations of growth, in terms of repression, fixation, and obsession.

What the poetry-making self seeks is not simply a state of soul, but an increased awareness of longings unsatisfied in reality and a greater acceptance of what they mean. Such is the assertion that Wordsworth makes about poets ideally considered at the end of the poem; they are whole and in possession of themselves:

> in a world of life they live,
> By sensible impressions not enthrall'd,
> But quicken'd, rouz'd, and made thereby more fit
> To hold communion with the invisible world.
> Such minds are truly from the Deity,
> For they are Powers; and hence the highest bliss
> That can be known is theirs, the consciousness
> Of whom they are habitually infused
> Through every image, and through every thought,
> And all impressions; . . .
>
> (XIII, 102-111)

The "heroic argument" to be made by the Poet about himself is an hermetic adventure pursued in words: with words he will seek the points "within our souls/ Where all stand single," imagining and revealing to himself the truth of his unique individuality. The Poet, with powers similar to those of the One Great Mind, would have to achieve a wholeness of being, an individuality that is new. He could not simply have a sense of his personal difference from other men and a preference for solitude that unconsciously maintains a profound dependency on the mother. In speaking of "heroic argument," Wordsworth does seem to mean that the activity of being a poet is that of entering fearlessly into the caverns, as Keats said, "where airy voices lead."[23]

It would seem, however, that conscious artifice alone

[23] Keats wrote:

> He ne'er is crown'd
> With immortality, who fears to follow
> Where airy voices lead . . .
>
> (*Endymion,* II, 211-213)

could account for the other characterization of poetry as a crop. "Every man is a memory to himself"; poetry is the way in which the poet exacts something from his experience by remembering and reflecting upon it. Just as the sun brings out the crop of the fertilized Egyptian plain, so would the Memory, prompted by Imagination, bring out poetry. At the end of Book I, Wordsworth treats Memory as metaphorical sunlight. Speaking of his attempt in poetry "to understand myself" and "fix the wavering balance of my mind," he says:

> I am so loth to quit
> Those recollected hours that have the charm
> Of visionary things, and lovely forms
> And sweet sensations that throw back our life
> And almost make our Infancy itself
> A visible scene, on which the sun is shining.
> (I, 658-663)

But "the charm of visionary things" sounds momentarily flat here, coming from one who invests "visionary" with such dark portentousness. We have seen already some of the associations of poetry, visionary power, darkness, death, and the absent mother, so we may suspect that his description is too placid, that Wordsworth, momentarily, is hoping for an easier time of recollecting his growth than his own troubled sense of himself should lead him to suspect.

Perhaps psychology should account for conscious artifice and for why there should be this tendency towards simplification. If poetry may be seen as, at some moments, an heuristic assertion, a self-discovery, it may also be seen at other moments as a compulsive process of rationalization, a contrived way of rendering one's self and one's story. The Poet orders the facts and assigns them their meanings as he manipulates his narrative to imply them. Freud was the first to observe significantly the sense in which artifice, as in dreams, is employed with the intention to conceal rather than reveal the issues it elaborates in rich detail. What we have, then, though it may seem puzzling at first, are two opposed preconscious tendencies in the *activity* of making poetry, corresponding to the positive and negative aspects of the repetition-compulsion.[24] The one attempts compulsively to reproduce for consciousness the content of repressed traumata; the other, equally compulsively, attempts to deny, disguise, edit-out, the traces of repressed traumata that remain attached with peculiar insistence to other memories. Similarly, there are opposed tendencies in extreme passivity: one is that of yielding to the "calm, oblivious tendency" that eschews all self-consciousness, even that of active rationalization; the other is a predisposition to be overwhelmed, to submit to forces that intrude upon habitual consciousness and force upon it unsought disturbances, revelations.

When Wordsworth uses a metaphor like the "sunlight of the memory," he is consciously and beautifully simplifying what can be remembered and he is unconsciously denying what cannot be clearly recollected.[25] The "sunlight of the

[24] See Freud, "Moses and Monotheism," CW XXIII, 72-80.

[25] *The Prelude*, VI, 659f: 1850 version. Consider here how the metaphors seem to be about the mind unconsciously as well as consciously:

> Locarno! spreading out in width like Heaven,
> How dost thou cleave to the poetic heart,
> Bask in the sunshine of the memory;
> And Como! thou, a treasure whom the earth
> Keeps to herself, confin'd as in a depth
> Of Abyssinian privacy.

That is, the heart is the repository of poetic impressions, and Locarno, remembered as a lake in the sunshine, seems still to be lighted in the heart/mind by the metaphorical "sunshine of the memory." But Como, also a lake in Northern Italy, is kept metaphorically in a very ungeographical privacy ("Abyssinian"). In the earlier version, Como is "a darling bosom'd up," which makes it an infant held at the breast, certainly an attractive state of repose for Wordsworth's subconscious mind. But "Abyssinian" itself seems like an unconscious pun: Wordsworth had just been talking about Memory being overwhelmed by Imagination which rises in the mountainous terrain of the mind from "the mind's abyss." Hence, Abyss-inian. The various phenomena of the world given to the senses and of the processes of the mind become confused with each other when metaphors for the mind are

memory" in conjunction with the tillage metaphor cannot characterize those other senses of soul associated with the abyss. And yet on one occasion Wordsworth does use sunlight in conjunction with the topographical metaphor for the mind to say as much:

> Caverns there were within my mind, which sun
> Could never penetrate . . .
>
> (III, 246-247)

The caverns he imagines here are like the points in the soul "Where all stand single" and like the abyss of the unconscious where Imagination originates. I think it is no accident that the last great characterization of the Imagination (in Book XIII) takes place at night in the mountains lit by *moonlight* and is a negative image of the Imagination passage in Book VI, which was based on the daylight crossing of the Alps.

4. Milton and Beyond

To trace the journey metaphor as Wordsworth's unconscious metaphor for poetic growth to consciousness, we shall examine the Imagination passage in detail in Chapter IV. But the use to which that metaphor was put was so intimately associated with Milton in Wordsworth's mind that it was his Miltonic sense of himself that he sought to rouse in contemplating the poetic way before him, aspiring towards

---

turned back upon their icons in the world under the pressure of preconscious wishfulness.

This possible unconscious association of Ideas, I have since found, is also suggested by Geoffrey Hartman, who adds: "The earthly Paradise was sometimes placed in Abyssinia, near the hidden source of the Nile (see Dr. Johnson's *Rasselas*)"; Hartman, *Wordsworth's Poetry, 1787-1814*, p. 353. Since I find in Wordsworth's unconscious wishfulness the primary wish, according to the pleasure principle, for reunion with the mother, I believe the unconscious association of ideas leads back to what Wordsworth called "the Paradise/ Where I was reared," *The Prelude*, VIII, 144-145.

some philosophic Song
Of Truth that cherishes our daily life;
With meditations passionate from deep
Recesses in man's heart, immortal verse
Thoughtfully fitted to the Orphean lyre.
(I, 230-234)

A consideration of some examples of Wordsworth imitating and echoing Milton will shed light on what I have called Wordsworth's topographic representations of soul.

The "Orphean lyre," for instance, calls to mind the beginning of Book III of *Paradise Lost*—a context worth dwelling upon here. Milton's "Hail holy light . . ." invocation is addressed prayerfully to Light, the poet speaking in his own person about where his narrative—his own adventure of words—has taken him:

Thee I revisit now with bolder wing,
Escap't the Stygian Pool, though long detain'd
In that obscure sojourn, while in my flight
Through utter and through middle darkness borne
With other notes than to th' Orphean Lyre
I sung of Chaos and Eternal Night,
Taught by the heav'nly Muse to venture down
The dark descent, and up to reascend,
Though hard and rare: thee I revisit safe,
And feel thy sovran vital Lamp; but thou
Revisit'st not these eyes, that roll in vain
To find thy piercing ray, and find no dawn.
(*Paradise Lost*, III, 13-24)

For the moment Milton sees Satan's flight from Hell as his own, since within Imagination he has had "to venture down/ The dark descent, and up to reascend," which puts him in mind of Orpheus. Orpheus had sought his beloved Eurydice in the underworld and sung of the sorrow of his experience, which ended in loss. The further development, briefly, is of Milton's blindness and of his kinship through it with Homer, the model for epic descents to hell, and with Thamyris, who wrote of the wars of the Titans and the gods. When Wordsworth speaks of the "Orphean lyre," he speaks of meditations from the "Recesses in man's heart"; he does not say here that the poet would descend into the heart, as Milton has talked of adventurous descent into hell, but I think we can connect these "Recesses in man's heart," for instance, with the points within the soul "Where all stand single." We can also connect them with "the caverns within the mind which sun could never penetrate" and which memory finds inaccessible; also, with the abyss of the mind which Imagination inhabits or the abyss that the meditative man approaches at the Convent of Chartreuse, "lost within himself" and intent on looking with bodily eyes and being consoled.

The thought that to Wordsworth the recesses of the heart are like Hell in the epic sense, the abode of the shades of the dead, is a startling one to us, but one that the context of Milton adds to the echo of Milton heard in Wordsworth. It is further suggested by what Milton goes on to say about his blindness.

> So much the rather thou Celestial Light
> Shine inward, and the mind through all her powers
> Irradiate, there plant eyes, all mist from thence
> Purge and disperse, that I may see and tell
> Of things invisible to mortal sight.
>
> (*Paradise Lost,* III, 51-55)

The words "irradiate," "Celestial Light," and "things invisible" here remind us of what we have just been observing in Wordsworth, his recollections of visionary experiences in Nature, poetry, and his own mind, and their connections with the mother and the Blest Babe. The passage itself reminds one of the Homeric world, and especially of the favor occasionally shown heroes by gods who grant them *theoria,* purging their mortal vision so they can see gods and see as a god sees. In Milton, however, this passage reveals the occasional self-consciousness of the poet in *Paradise Lost*; whereas in Wordsworth self-consciousness distinguishes the Poet "of more than mortal privilege," self-conscious of his plight and of his powers. And "heart" with all its associations with the dead mother, could easily suggest the Eurydice that this Orpheus would seek in its recesses.

If we also consider here the lines Wordsworth wrote at Alfoxden as his prospectus for his "philosophic song," we can see the striking difference between Wordsworth's own thoughts at the time and the Miltonic sense of the Poet he was adapting to radically different intentions. The passage begins:

> "On Man, on Nature, and on Human Life,
> Musing in solitude, I oft perceive
> Fair trains of imagery before me rise,
> Accompanied by feelings of delight
> Pure, or with no unpleasing sadness mixed,
> And I am conscious of affecting thoughts
> And dear remembrances, whose presence soothes
> Or elevates the Mind, intent to weigh
> The good and evil of our mortal state.
> —To these emotions, whencesoe'er they come,
> Whether from breath of outward circumstance,
> Or from the Soul—an impulse to herself—
> I would give utterance in numerous verse.
> Of Truth, of Grandeur, Beauty, Love, and Hope,
> Of blessed consolations in distress;
> Of mortal strength, and intellectual Power;
> Of joy in widest commonality spread;
> Of the individual Mind that keeps her own
> Inviolate retirement, subject there
> To Conscience only, and the law supreme
> Of that Intelligence which governs all—
> I sing:—'fit audience let me find though few!' "
> (lines 1-23)

Book VII of Paradise Lost is alluded to; Wordsworth is idealizing himself as the Poet—not the imitator of Milton, but the heir, and perhaps ultimately, the rival in fame. In Book VII of *Paradise Lost,* Milton is about to have Raphael tell of the creation of the world, how God "after the expelling of Satan and his angels out of Heaven, declared his pleasure to create another world and other creatures to dwell therein;" how the Son was sent to accomplish this in six days; how the angels celebrated with Hymns his performance of the task; and how he reascends to heaven.[26] Milton prayerfully invokes Urania who has led him in flight higher than Olympus, "above the flight of Pegasean wing," for she was before Olympus and was with God before the Creation:

> Up led by thee
> Into the Heav'n of Heav'ns I have presum'd,
> An Earthly Guest, and drawn Empyreal Air,
> Thy temp'ring; with like safety guided down
> Return me to my Native Element:
> Lest from this flying Steed unrein'd, (as once
> Bellerophon, though from a lower Clime)
> Dismounted, on th' Aleian Field I fall
> Erroneous there to wander and forlorn.
> (*Paradise Lost,* VII, 12-20)

Merritt Hughes, an editor of *Paradise Lost,* explains this in a footnote: "In the myth of Bellerophon's attempt to storm Heaven on the wing'd horse, Pegasus, Milton saw an allegory of his own blindness in writing *Paradise Lost.* Zeus punished Bellerophon by throwing him down onto the Aleian marshes in remotest Lycia, where he wandered, crazed and . . . blind until he died."[27] Milton, who would "justify the ways of God to man," was fearlessly a Protestant individualist in matters of religion, though fearfully a mortal: he had followed where his Imagination led him.

[26] *Paradise Lost,* ed. Merritt Hughes, The Argument, Book VII.
[27] *Ibid.,* n. 18 to Book VIII, p. 217.

Here, it is as if, having dared to imagine "the ways of God" in this way, Milton feels he will be held accountable for his presumption.

But the Wordsworth with whom Coleridge became intimate in 1796, was, in Coleridge's words, "a semi-atheist." According to Hazlitt, Wordsworth said that he had read "the description of Satan till he felt a certain faintness come over his mind from a sense of beauty and grandeur."[28] With none of Milton's Christian scruples to temper his imagination, Wordsworth continues in this way:

> "So prayed, more gaining then he asked, the Bard—
> In holiest mood. Urania, I shall need
> Thy guidance, or a greater Muse, if such
> Descend to earth or dwell in highest heaven!
> For I must tread on shadowy ground, must sink
> Deep—and, aloft ascending, breathe in worlds
> To which the heaven of heavens is but a veil.
> All strength—all terror, single or in bands,
> That ever was put forth in personal form—
> Jehovah—with his thunder, and the choir—
> Of shouting Angels, and the empyreal thrones—
> I pass them unalarmed. Not Chaos, not
> The darkest pit of lowest Erebus,
> Nor aught of blinder vacancy, scooped out
> By help of dreams—can breed such fear and awe
> As fall upon us often when we look
> Into our Minds, into the Mind of Man—
> My haunt, and the main region of my song.
> (lines 24-41)

This passage too will go on to speak of the Creation, as does Book VII of *Paradise Lost,* but it is that of the Poet, that of the individual mind as it works in "blended might" with and on the external world. What Milton imagines The Redeemer doing, Wordsworth adapts to the Poet as Creator himself. But first we should attend to the assertion in this

[28] Hazlitt, *Works,* vol. 11, p. 457.

passage. Notice how the younger Wordsworth seems to patronize Urania here and facilely combines Milton's description of the awe-struck poet following the muse into heaven in Book VII with that of the poet's having followed Satan through darkness and hell in Book III. It is Wordsworth's way of grandly imagining his own activity as the Poet.

The statement that he makes is complex. It is now easy to pass over such utterance as wild, imaginative, inspired, or merely inflated; it is difficult, however, to sort out what is being said figuratively. Perhaps were we to introduce here the passage from Lucretius's *De Rerum Natura* that it recalls we would see at first glance the implications:

"Not fables of Gods, not thunderbolts, nor heaven with ominous menace, could intimidate him; they but roused the more his eager spiritual courage, stirring him with the want to be the first to shatter the fast bars of Nature's gates. Therefore the living strength of his soul conquered. On he passed, far beyond the flaming walls of this world, and pastured both mind and spirit upon the immeasurable void. Thence he returns, a conqueror, to tell us what can, what cannot, be created; briefly, on which principle each thing has its power defined, where its ultimate boundary lies. Therefore religion is thrown down at our feet, is trampled upon; his victory brings us level with heaven."[29]

Milton, the finer classical scholar, perhaps recalled the same passage and used it for suggestive descriptive detail; but Wordsworth has taken the implications of it as well, and has only slightly muted them. Though incongruously Wordsworth was to make use of this passage in 1814, when the "semi-atheist" had "submitted to a new control,"[30] no reader feels that these earlier lines fit with the pious spirit

29 Lucretius, *De Rerum Natura*, I, 57-73.

30 "Elegiac Stanzas. Suggested by a Picture of Peele Castle in a Storm, Painted by Sir George Beaumont," line 34. See also, "Ode to Duty," *Poetical Works*, p. 452 and p. 385.

of *The Excusion* to which they were then affixed. These lines say that neither our fearful imaginings of Heaven as they have been "put forth in personal form" as Jehovah, the unapproachable God who imposes banishment from Paradise, death, and judgment on mankind, nor our worst imaginings or dreams of chaos or hell, can exceed in fear and awe what happens in the descent into the self, into the mind, in which these figurative senses of reality originate and exist as a "veil" for the true reality. Does it follow, as it would for Epicurus as Lucretius recalls him, that with death the figurative senses of reality cease too? that when the mind gives up its life at its natural limit, so too do its imaginings die, though in fear of them the mind has lived impoverishing itself with the exotic clutter of its rituals? Milton's uneasy identification of Satan with himself and of himself with Bellerophon attests to his belief in the awesome greater reality of what seems to enter the inspired mind through the imagination; whereas Wordsworth seems fearless about the mind that invents its figures and can confront its inventions. But it is hard to imagine, taking all of one's sense of Wordsworth, that this "Epicurean" generative naturalism was ever more than a rather poetic and briefly-held view. It was expressed in a period of life when belief is as loosely held as is the sense of unlimited growth in youth, as Wordsworth tried to maintain in "Tintern Abbey."

One might say that these inspired lines have the ring of heroic rhetoric; they seem to assert more confidently than "Tintern Abbey" or the passages at the beginning of *The Prelude* what the poet will do and be. But they also sound merely rhetorical; they have the verbal assertiveness of one who refuses to be alarmed, as the Romantics so often merely refused to be alarmed, at what has alarmed most men and most great men in the past. Wordsworth's admission that the Poet is subject to an even more extreme "fear and awe" than other men (when looking "into the mind of man") passes almost unnoticed; "I pass them unalarmed" is the dominant tone of the passage. The evidence of his failure to sustain this level of assertion goes against Wordsworth here: he could not merely set aside the anxieties that most men feel in their communal acceptance of themselves and each other, nor could he make so little of the fears of his own hero Milton. But *The Prelude* should be seen in relation to this tendency; in *The Prelude,* he persisted in seeking a true individuality that he lacked by attempting to articulate a compelling sense of difference from other men. He had imagined a poet whose god-like powers would recreate the world by the life he imagined for man in it; and *The Recluse* was to show how. But with his attempt in *The Prelude* to determine whether he would be the poet to write such a poem as *The Recluse,* he brought himself closer to his fears than his hopes, and desisted.

One scholar has argued that these "dythyrambic" lines, rather than the lines he set down as the opening lines of Book I of *The Prelude,* are the ones that Wordsworth momentarily recalls when he pauses at the beginning of Book VII to say "I sang/ Aloud in dythyrambic fervour. . . ."[31] If it is so, as I tend to agree it is, it is because he had just been writing of the abyss of the mind in Book VI, which resembles the "mind of man" described here, and he had just had the shaking experience of Imagination of which he writes while trying to recall his feelings about a significant past experience in the Alps. It is, I think, the pressure of an unconscious intention that shows itself momentarily in that confused recollection of "beginning" a poem that was eventually to become this one. The Imagination passage in Book VI is an example of Wordsworth pursuing that desired sense of his own being into "the mind of man" and trying with the poetry-making self to assimilate distressing

[31] See again, *The Prelude,* pp. xliii-xlv. Notice, too, that Wordsworth later changes "in dythrambic fervor" to "in fervor irresistible" in MS A2, as if, upon re-reading the poem, he, too, found "dythrambic" inappropriate to the quiet opening passage of the poem, and was, in revising the poem, no longer subject to the pressure of preconscious suggestion from which the odd characterization came.

experiences. If the experience of Imagination described there is an example of how the force of unconscious intention may be released by the Poet's attempt to use the Imagination in conjunction with Memory, then Book VII is the real new beginning of the extended thirteen-book *Prelude*, for in it Wordsworth begins to deal imaginatively with his disturbing memories of the recent past, exposing himself again to his own uncertainties.

In writing of his experiences of London, France, and the French Revolution, he will have to deal boldly and imaginatively with his crisis and despair before celebrating his restoration. This is why the beginning of Book VII makes the first significant mention of breaks in composition of the narrative and, in doing so, perhaps accidentally recalls the earlier moment of greater daring when he wrote dithyrambically for what was then to be *The Recluse*. Whereas lines 1-54 of Book I emphasize the soul-and-tillage association of poetry, Book VI has touched again on "the mind of man," on the cavernous-mountainous topography of the mind and soul; and the "I" is figured there as divided from what it glimpses momentarily as its completion in consciousness. While we attempt to observe the important relationship between the extreme experience of disorder in his recent past and the repressed traumatic experience of his childhood, we shall see the peculiar coincidence of a climax in a personal history and in History itself.

CHAPTER IV

IMAGINATION AND REVELATION

The crossing of the Alps through the Simplon Pass was for Wordsworth the particularly memorable journey of a summer spent on the continent during a college vacation in 1791. In Book VI (lines 452ff.) his recollected journey is transformed by Imagination into another and more symbolic one, a figure for talking about the mind itself. Here, the journey-metaphor emerges as the principal metaphor in his attempt to extend the sense of growth and completion.

First, there is the recollection of his disappointment at seeing Mount Blanc, an odd but honest way of introducing the experience. He grieved that the "soulless image on the eye" had "usurp'd upon a living thought/ That never more could be."[1] He knew at the time that the actual experience would be less satisfying to him than his imaginative anticipation had been; so must Racedown, standing on a cliff by the sea, have been a disappointment to the imagination that had anticipated it. In light of our analysis of the same effect in "Tintern Abbey," we could say here that Mount Blanc in the imagination stands for something for which Mount Blanc itself will not suffice. The "*soulless* image" of the mountain as something tangible is momentarily threatening to the cherished reality of "the *living* thought." By the end of the poetic rendition of the experience, Wordsworth will have changed this fear to a hope of greater be-

[1] *The Prelude,* VI, 453-456.

ing. The otherness of the mountain and its "soulless image" will have been assimilated to the "living thought" in an experience of soul that maintains (and even extends) the necessary sense of a greater spiritual or psychic reality. He recalls, though, at first, his having been "reconciled to realities"—that is, again, to the visible world—by his immediate response to the beauty of "the wondrous vale of Chamauny."[2]

The immediate appeal of *vales* is constant in *The Prelude,* and it means, I have suggested, that sense of the otherness of Nature for which the mother had stood in his infancy and early childhood. Present to his eyes, the vale nevertheless evokes in him preconsciously the sense of the mother now. As we have already observed, his heightened response to the beauty of the natural world is usually attended by an increased and disturbing sense of an absent reality. This sense, which is constant and habitual, governs his restless need to seek satisfaction in certain kinds of activity, of which actual journeys are typical. The journey-metaphor is the most meaningful extension of the most intense moments of search.

Then comes his account of the realization that without having reached or crossed any summit, he had "*cross'd the Alps*"; dejection ensues—not "Dejection taken up for pleasure's sake," as was his youthful poetic bent, but dejection as a "deep and genuine sadness."[3] But let us observe what he was dejected about. The anticipated crossing of the Alps expressed his aspiration to find in physical activity a satisfaction for the feelings that prompt it, but the actual activity, it turned out, was only a disappointing approximation of the state in which such feelings would be satisfied. While recollecting and thinking about that, he is seized by his Imagination, and he interrupts the poetic account of the past to render poetically the state of feeling he has just experienced, his mind being overwhelmed by Imagination.

2 *Ibid.*, VI, 456-457.

3 *Ibid.*, VI, 492.

Imagination! lifting up itself
Before the eye and progress of my Song
Like an unfather'd vapour; here that Power,
In all the might of its endowments, came
Athwart me; I was lost as in a cloud,
Halted, without a struggle to break through.
And now recovering, to my Soul I say
I recognise thy glory; in such strength
Of usurpation, in such visitings
Of awful promise, when the light of sense
Goes out in flashes that have shewn to us
The invisible world, doth Greatness make abode.
There harbours whether we be young or old.
Our destiny, our nature, and our home
Is with infinitude, and only there;
With hope it is, hope that can never die,
Effort, and expectation, and desire,
And something evermore about to be.
The mind beneath such banners militant
Thinks not of spoils or trophies, nor of aught
That may attest its prowess, blest in thoughts
That are their own perfection and reward,
Strong in itself, and in the access of joy
Which hides it like the overflowing Nile.
(VI, 525-548)

The realization in a general way seems plain: it is of aspirations beyond the possibilities of human activity in this world. He experiences and accepts the glorious joy and fullness that come of knowing hope unlimited. He can hold within himself his excesses of desire about the world and relate them to "infinitude"; and in his "soul" he can feel satisfied by a kind of self-possession. One can see here how Wordsworth will become fully Christian, how the resolution to descend into "the Mind of Man" may result not in the psychological confrontation of his mortality and the understanding of it, but rather in the traditional Christian transmutation of it into continuing life. But here it is still a question whether the self will be assimilated to the soul or the soul to the self; we remember that when Wordsworth wrote in Book II of the idealized Mother-Babe relationship ("who, when his soul/ Claims manifest kindred with an earthly soul/ Doth gather passion from his mother's eye"[4]), soul seemed almost as earthly as self, expecting the satisfaction of its passions in the external world.

Past dejection here is being changed in poetry to present joy. The immense feeling of aspiration is being given Imaginative expression and relieved of the encumbering recollected experience that had stimulated and frustrated it. The experience of Imagination in the 1805 version is rendered "I was lost as in a cloud/ Halted . . ."; and perhaps the feeling of being lost itself comes directly from the preceding account of losing the path through the mountains, only to discover it again and to experience dejection. On the basis of the 1850 version it would seem so, for there Wordsworth further develops the similarity between the recollected journey through the mountains and the present experience of Imagination in his mind. This particular revision is peculiarly felicitous since it results in finer poetry without the older Wordsworth having changed the implications of the passage. It also shows Wordsworth at his best and most characteristic practice, that of using the details of an experience for a subsequent metaphorical elaboration of it. The substance of the two versions is the same; the second version invites the closer scrutiny because the added details relate it to the deep consistency of the entire poem.

The passage in the 1850 version comes out of several gradual revisions from which the image of a "lonely traveller" emerges:[5]

> Imagination—here the Power so called
> Through sad incompetence of human speech,

[4] *Ibid.*, II, 241-243.
[5] *Ibid.*, *apparatus criticus*, pp. 208-209.

That awful Power rose from the mind's abyss
Like an unfathered vapour that enwraps,
At once, some lonely traveller. I was lost;
Halted without an effort to break through;
But to my conscious soul I now can say—
'I recognise thy glory:' in such strength
Of usurpation, when the light of sense
Goes out, but with a flash that has revealed
The invisible world, doth greatness make abode,
There harbours; whether we be young or old,
Our destiny, our being's heart and home,
Is with infinitude, and only there;
With hope it is, hope that can never die,
Effort, and expectation, and desire,
And something evermore about to be.
Under such banners militant, the soul
Seeks for no trophies, struggles for no spoils
That may attest her prowess, blest in thoughts
That are their own perfection and reward,
Strong in herself and in beatitude
That hides her, like the mighty flood of Nile
Poured from his fount of Abyssinian clouds
To fertilise the whole Egyptian plain.
(VI, 592-616: 1850 version)

Here, again, we are dealing with conscious artifice which remains true to an unconscious intention as well. In this version of the Imagination passage, Wordsworth has taken the recollected experience in the Alps and used it figuratively. The baffled traveller and the mountain on which dejection is experienced are taken within the mind and *are* the mind in which Imagination liberates the sense of joy. The mountainous landscape is that of the mind itself, the "lonely traveller" the habitual consciousness of the mind. One then finds that in the following passage (VI, 549-572), he returns to his account of descending the mountain through the Simplon Pass ("Downwards we hurried fast . . ."), but describes the terrain with metaphors that imbue it with the workings of an Apocalyptic mind. For convenience, I shall distinguish the passage by calling it the Revelation passage. Although the Revelation passage seems to follow *from* the Imagination passage, like an extension and elaboration of the figurative sense of a mountainous-mind, the Revelation passage in the 1805 version was written, of course, long before this revised version of the Imagination passage.[6] As they appear in the 1850 version, Wordsworth has worked them to a consistency that relates Memory, Imagination, and Revelation. When he says in the later version of the Imagination passage that Imagination is "so call'd through sad incompetence of human speech,"[7] it is because he has worked out this consistency to his own satisfaction, having characterized Imagination and Revelation as analogous workings of the Poet's and God's minds through the common figurative basis of the mountainous mind. After examining the Imagination passage, we shall attempt to clarify this sequence.

Imagination, then, is an "awful power" that rises "from the mind's abyss" to enwrap the consciousness, the way an "unfathered vapor" might enwrap "a lonely traveller." Let us see the lonely traveller as consciousness, not to suggest unduly its possible meaning in a psychological vocabulary, but because in ordinary speech we would say as much: he is figured as part of the mind conscious of itself in an ordinary way encountering something extraordinary but also of the mind. "Unfathered"—that is, without a prior generative source—adds the weight of primal to the vapor that is

6 The sequence of the passages would be: Imagination passage, MS A; Revelation passage, MS A; revised Imagination passage, MS A2, C, D, E. Obviously, then, the Revelation passage in MS A influenced the rewriting of the Imagination passage, as Wordsworth gradually brought them into greater consistency with each other and with the preceding passages recollecting the experience of approaching the Simplon Pass and crossing through it. Here, see especially, Hartman, *Wordsworth's Poetry*, pp. 60-67, for an interesting discussion of the implications of the sequence of composition and revision.

7 *The Prelude*, VI, 592-593: 1850 version.

Imagination. Though the passage offers no reason for the word, "unfathered" perhaps suggests only the more forcibly that this is the landscape of the mind in which nothing is found that is not generated from itself. An earlier revision of the 1805 text (MS A3) has "that enwraps/ A way worn traveller on a lonely moor," but it would seem that Wordsworth saw the greater appropriateness of keeping to mountain landscape in presenting a realization about the mind based on the recollection of a mountain experience. It would seem, too, that he saw the greater appropriateness to the present experience of the image of a traveller in the mountain passes climbing through the low cloud levels that often creep up valleys. Billowing upwards in convections, clouds can seem to enwrap one from below. Here, consciousness is aware of being "halted," unable to make "an effort to break through." The figure of the traveller is stopped short because the account Wordsworth was giving of aspiration resulting in dejection was beyond his comprehension of it. Now Imagination has seized him. Cloud-enwrapped and presumably on uncertain footing near the abyss, cautious and "lost," he is perhaps particularly receptive to what is going to happen next because it will come from a source other than the faculty that watches things happen: it will happen to him, in the mind.

In retrospect—that is, moments later—Wordsworth recognizes the "glory" of his "conscious soul." The soul itself is figured here as capable of consciousness. It is not clearly said to have been made conscious of things or conscious of itself by the experience, but "to my soul" has been revised to "to my conscious soul." It is useful to read this passage preserving the distinction between the "I" of "I now can say" and the "conscious soul" to which it is being said; it presents clearly the recognition "within" of one part by another, or rather of the whole by the most habitually conscious part. It is meant to suggest a shift of metaphorical emphasis from a figurative and conscious self to a being conscious of itself as "soul." Wordsworth was always conscious of himself as the traveller in the mountains, the traveller was unconscious of himself as a soul, which is why, in the past, the traveller's disappointment at having crossed the Alps could obscure the issue of the soul's aspiration. In this way does the passage make sense (and belong where it is). At this distance in time, what Memory has held loosely and unrealized, Imagination has touched on, and now forces as an experience upon the consciousness, as one might say, in a new light.

It would be false, however, to say that self-expression results here in self-realization. What the poet presents as a result of a flash and not of a steady illumination is a sense of a realization, a greater awareness of something to be realized; he attempts to characterize that feeling, as he had earlier when he spoke of the soul:

> Remembering how she felt, but what she felt
> Remembering not . . .
>
> (II, 335-336)

But one must notice that "Imagination" is not exactly the word he wants and that he says that this "usurpation" of consciousness—"when the light of sense goes out" with a "flash"—is the cause of a revelation: the "invisible world" is "revealed." Revelation is probably always characterized as happening within one's soul. Though "caused" there by God, it is taken to be "sent" from God; yet here, in a sense we have already touched upon, it is in and of the mind. Imagination "so called," which imagines the truth, and Revelation, which presents it, are common attributes of some awful power for which there is no word that Wordsworth knows in human speech.

Before attempting to understand the feeling of realization in the Imagination passage, it would be useful to relate the Imagination passage to the Revelation passage which follows. Momentarily lost in his attempt to understand his experience, Wordsworth felt lost in the unfamiliar vastness of his own mind figured in terms of traveller, mountain, and natural forces. The characterization of Imagination is then completed by being made analogous to the characterization of Revelation which follows it. It is worth preserving this very slight distinction because it shows Wordsworth using the Poet's perception of Nature to characterize the power by which a Poet speaks. The Revelation passage returns to the actual past moment in the Alps:

> The melancholy slackening that ensued
> Upon those tidings by the peasant given
> Was soon dislodged. Downwards we hurried fast,
> And, with the half-shaped road which we had missed,
> Entered a narrow chasm. The brook and road
> Were fellow-travellers in this gloomy strait,
> And with them did we journey several hours
> At a slow pace. The immeasurable height
> Of woods decaying, never to be decayed,
> The stationary blasts of waterfalls,
> And in the narrow rent at every turn
> Winds thwarting winds, bewildered and forlorn,
> The torrents shooting from the clear blue sky,
> The rocks that muttered close upon our ears,
> Black drizzling crags that spake by the way-side
> As if a voice were in them, the sick sight
> And giddy prospect of the raving stream,
> The unfettered clouds and region of the Heavens,
> Tumult and peace, the darkness and the light—
> Were all like workings of one mind, the features
> Of the same face, blossoms upon one tree;
> Characters of the great Apocalypse,
> The types and symbols of Eternity,
> Of first, and last, and midst, and without end.
>
> (VI, 617-640: 1850 version)[8]

[8] Wordsworth is talking about Revelation, which he "sees" as analogous to Imagination and perhaps as identical to it; he says this immediately after having a profound imaginative experience while writing poetry. Compare this with his description of poetry in Book V, 551-557.

We have said already in speaking of the "thoughts of more deep seclusion" in "Tintern Abbey" that the poet unconsciously seeks a reality within, of which the ordinary self is only aware by its response to natural beauty and by its restless dissatisfaction with its ordinary circumstance. And we have said, too, that the inner reality is projected into the external world and perceived by consciousness as something external to the self, beneath or behind Nature.

It is also strangely appropriate here that the *whole* account of the actual experience in the Alps seems figurative because of Wordsworth's figurative use of it in the Imagination passage. The high point of the Alps (though no summit has been reached) resembles the figurative sense Wordsworth has already touched upon in talking about himself: "points have we all of us *within our souls*/ Where all stand single. . . ."[9] The poetic representation of the lonely traveller in the Imagination passage as Wordsworth in his own mind ("in the Mind of Man") makes the traveller Wordsworth, in the actual past in the Alps, seem to have been physically enacting this desired figurative sense of himself in his experience and his being. And then, when Wordsworth returns to the actual past, recollecting his descent from the high point in the Alps in the next passage, one tends to supply the figurative sense that it so plainly suggests of the "caverns . . . within my mind"[10] that the sun could never penetrate, and perhaps of the "Orphean dark descent" inwards. The abyss of the mind, where man may struggle "lost within himself," is mentioned in Book VI; and we may add to abyss, mind, and soul, "The recesses of the heart."[11] Wordsworth says:

Downwards we hurried fast,
And, with the half-shaped road which we had missed,
Entered a narrow chasm. The brook and road
Were fellow-travellers in this gloomy strait,

[9] *The Prelude,* III, 186-187.
[10] *Ibid.,* III, 245-246.
[11] *Ibid.,* I, 233.

And with them did we journey several hours
At a slow pace.

(VI, 619-624: 1850 version)[12]

This peculiar sense of Wordsworth as outside and inside at the same time, suggested by the powers of mind he perceives in the external landscape and by the features of topography he regularly uses for the mind, is most strikingly and beautifully presented, as we shall see, in the Mount Snowdon vision in Book XIII.

In the account that follows in Book VI, we have another sense of the "ghostly language of the ancient earth": in "the rocks that *muttered*"; the "black drizzling crags that *spake* by the wayside/ *As if a voice* were in them"; the "giddy prospect of the *raving* stream." The inspired earth is perceived as containing a sybilline, oracular power striving for utterance. The "*blasts* of waterfalls" are like the trumpets of the Apocalypse that is approaching and fit in with the general character of portentous sound in the passage. But the "winds thwarting winds, bewilder'd and forlorn" have a peculiar effect. Why, one wonders, "bewilder'd and forlorn?" Why should this phenomenon of Nature seem to be crying out, lost and alone? We are aware that the wind is associated with the "awakening breeze," the creative storm, poetry, and the mother. And Wordsworth says that the whole is "like the workings of one mind." What is being projected into Nature that makes the mountain seem a mind disturbed by its attempt to speak and the winds like an abandoned and frightened child? I attach particular importance to the poetic parallel here of the characterization of the idealized Mother-Babe relationship in Book II:

From this beloved Presence, there exists
A virtue which irradiates and exalts
All objects through all intercourse of sense.

12 Here, I continue to use the 1850 version. The difference between this passage and VI, 551-556 is negligible, but the 1850 version allows us to keep the consistency of the experience more simply.

No outcast he, *bewilder'd and depress'd;*
Along his infant veins are interfus'd
The gravitation and the filial bond
Of nature, that connect him with the world.
. . . .
Even as an agent of *the one great mind,*
Creates, creator and receiver both,
Working but in alliance with the works
Which it beholds.—Such, verily, is the first
Poetic spirit of our human life;
By uniform controul of after years
In most abated or suppress'd, in some,
Through every change of growth or of decay,
Pre-eminent till death.

(II, 258-264, 272-280)

The perception of Revelation in Nature by the poet requires of him the belief in a superior mind—God's, the "one great mind"—able to compose its apparent disturbance. Through the experience of Imagination working on Memory, the Poet struggles to realize something about himself, which requires of him the belief in a superior mind, too—the Poet's, analogous to the "one great Mind"—able to compose its apparent disturbance. And in fact this is the ideal of the Poet that Wordsworth presents in Book XIII, after a vision in the moonlight on top of Mount Snowdon:

in a world of life they live,
By sensible impressions not enthrall'd,
But quicken'd, rouz'd, and made thereby more fit
To hold communion with the invisible world.
Such minds are truly from the Deity,
For they are Powers; and hence the highest bliss
That can be known is theirs, the consciousness
Of whom they are habitually infused
Through every image, and through every thought,
And all impressions. . . .

(XIII, 102-111)

The ideal Poet would see clearly the relationships between

the objects of the invisible world and the suggestive traces of them in the visible world, between his dimmest memories and his most immediate personal experiences, and express these relationships clearly. Wordsworth, in this instance, is less than ideal, but it is his *imaginative* recollection of the descent through the Alps that makes these passages much more than a memory. In the Revelation passage, the Poet perceives the mountain as a mind like his own trying to utter something, a Revelation from its depths. Wordsworth knew that poetry had the power to present "objects recognized/ In flashes,"[13] even if, as I shall argue, we reconstruct what those objects may be, whereas Wordsworth presents only an urgent sense of something to be realized, which suggests them to us.

In the Imagination passage, the realization that "our being's heart and home/ Is with infinitude and only there" follows immediately, if not exactly clearly from the flash that reveals "the invisible world." I should mention here again the connections already made between the "abyss of idealism," recalled from childhood (here, the same as the "mind's abyss") and "the visible world." Opposed to the pull inwards to the abyss was the attempt to accept the visible world in place of what had been lost, even though such an acceptance is partial: "I was left alone,/ Seeking the visible world, nor knowing why . . ." (II, 291-293). It was not an acceptance of otherness for its own sake, but an acceptance of a substitute for the mother, upon which many of the dependent needs endangered by her loss could be projected. I have made, too, the connection between the journey-metaphor in "our being's heart and home/ Is with infinitude and only there" and the journey-metaphor in

> she who was the heart
> And hinge of all our learnings and our loves:
> She left us destitute, and as we might
> Trooping together . . .
>
> (V, 257-260)

What, however, is "infinitude"?

[13] *The Prelude*, V, 628-629.

The sense of eternity in Wordsworth resembles the narcissism of infancy before the differentiation of the "self" and "other" which is the beginning of a life in time. Yet despite the prolonged initial period of dependency in childhood, the gradual differentiation of the self begun in infancy implies an increasing necessity for autonomy, for a wholeness of being which, always completing itself, feels like "something evermore about to be." But when Wordsworth says

> Our destiny, our being's heart and home,
> Is with infinitude, and only there;
> With hope it is, hope that can never die,
> Effort, and expectation, and desire,
> And something evermore about to be,

we might mislead ourselves as to the goal of this journey by inferring only its latent Christian meaning. An actual journey expressive of human aspiration in the world had resulted in dejection, but a metaphorical journey modeled on it and interrupted by the flash of Imagination-Revelation has resulted in joy. It is easy to see how "hope that can never die" can sustain effort and expectation and desire; it is easy to imagine how the Christian sense of the continuous access to being—"something evermore about to be"—comes out of this sense that the soul never dies. In beatitude (at "mystical" moments in life and in salvation after death) the soul reaches its completion by coming to rest in God's order, which is infinitude and "our being's heart and home." By assuming Christian meanings for the soul here we will miss what else this meant to Wordsworth. One could say, for instance, that from such realizations Wordsworth strengthens his awareness of soul: life is the Christian wayfarer's transit to Eternity; and one would expect a consequent pious humility of the kind that the older Wordsworth struggled to attain. Wordsworth had expressed something like that desire for the extinction of self elsewhere:

By such communion I was early taught
That what we see of forms and images
Which float along our minds and what we feel
Of active, or recognizable thought
Prospectiveness, intelligence or will
Not only is not worthy to be deemed
Our being, to be prized as what we are
But is the very littleness of life.
Such consciousnesses seemed but accidents
Relapses from the one interior life
Which is in all things, from that unity
In which all beings live with God, are lost
In God and nature, in one mighty whole . . .
(MS RV 1-16)

—In which all beings live with God, themselves
Are God, existing in one mighty whole.
(MS 2 of "Peter Bell")

And yet, it is curious that *this* is the passage that Wordsworth never used in *The Prelude.* One might suspect instead, then, that in the Imagination passage the self is trying to master the longings of the soul as it discovers them, and to assimilate the soul to the self. Ultimately it was his failure in this attempt that resulted in the development of its latent Christian meaning by the older Wordsworth, but at this earlier time of life, the problem for Wordsworth was still to find in the troubled sense of himself the acceptable form of poetic self-consciousness with which to believe in his ideal self.

In the Imagination passage, what should be remarked, then, is not the intimations of a Christian soul, but the way the poet emphasizes the joy of increase in consciousness. "But to my conscious soul *I* now can say—'*I* recognize thy glory.'" And "greatness," a personal quality, is seen in the "*strength* of usurpation" of Imagination in one's own mind. Whatever "soul" is, its claims upon the attention of the self are increased by the self's feeling of dissatisfaction with its activities in the world. For Wordsworth, every response to the visible world and every journey somewhere is relieved of disappointment only by the journey-metaphor, which extends and completes the activity of the self by affording it a poetic access to the deeper feeling of soul. But one should say here, too, that the poetry-making self discovers that the powers released in the mind, if one could master them, are like God's. One can see in this experience of Imagination that the "awful power" of the mind might fuse in poetry facts and feelings that have persisted unrelated and unrealized in Memory. This power from an unconscious source, which can break through the repressions that ordinarily limit the self, can alter consciousness and the sense of personal worth. To understand the possible non-Christian meaning of "infinitude," one must question the moments of increased consciousness.

Speaking of exactly such moments as these, however, to be found everywhere in Wordsworth, F. R. Leavis once said, with characteristic conclusiveness:

"Perhaps it will be agreed that though Wordsworth no doubt was right in feeling that he had something to pursue, the critic here is in a different case. If these 'moments' have any significance for the critic (whose business it is to define the significance of Wordsworth's poetry), it will be established, not by dwelling upon or in them, in the hope of exploring something that lies hidden in or behind their vagueness, but by holding firmly on to that sober verse in which they are presented."

He then tells us how to hold on to that sober verse, from which Wordsworth's visionary moments may be dissociated: "The poetic process engaged an organization that had, by his own account, been determined by an upbringing in a congenial social environment, with its wholesome simple pieties and the traditional sanity of its moral culture, which to him were nature."[14] Of course I would say that "Nature" was quite definitely something else to Wordsworth, but what strikes one in reading Leavis's argument is that one would not gather from it that Wordsworth's childhood and youth were in any way out of the ordinary except in the extreme good fortune of so congenial a social environment, which takes Wordsworth at his word rather naively.

Leavis knew, and perhaps thought it not worth mention, that Wordsworth lost his mother when he was eight and his father when he was thirteen. There is no suggestion that such losses are important psychic factors in growth and as likely to affect the account Wordsworth gives of his growth as they did the child's experience at the time. To continue, then, as I have started, exploring what lies hidden in or behind such visionary moments, I would place the exemplary journey through the Alps and the subsequent "event" in the poetic mind in a larger context of Wordsworth's unconscious predispositions towards experience and his imaginative interest in the contents of memory. The unconscious predisposition towards certain recurrent types of experience governs an image of the self taken from them: the Poet—here, the lonely traveller—is compelled to experience his life in a set way and to seek in poetry its unrealized causes.

How much *The Prelude* is a matter of journeys, roadside encounters and realizations, has already been noted. And the psychic origin of the predisposition to make actual journeys shows partly in Wordsworth's ways of describing that urge. For instance, the "lonely traveller" in the mind as Wordsworth's figurative sense of the conscious self seems at other moments to be a simple sense of himself as Poet and observer of life. In Book XII, he says:

> Oh! next to one dear state of bliss, vouchsafed
> Alas! to few in this untoward world,

14 See Leavis, *Revaluation*, pp. 171-175. See, too, the Appendix to this book, below, p. 405.

The bliss of walking daily in Life's prime
Through field or forest with the Maid we love,
While yet our hearts are young, while yet we breathe
Nothing but happiness, living in some place,
Deep Vale, or anywhere, the home of both,
From which it would be misery to stir;
Oh! next to such enjoyment of our youth,
In my esteem, next to such dear delight
Was that of wandering on from day to day
Where I could meditate in peace, and find
The knowledge which I love, and teach the sound
Of Poet's music to strange fields and groves,
Converse with men, where if we meet a face
We almost meet a friend, on naked Moors
With long, long ways before, by Cottage Bench
Or Well-spring where the weary Traveller rests.
(XII, 127-144)

This is a very curious passage, at once general and particular, an observation about human life and a personal recollection, but one that suggests even more than it states. The representative "we" tells us of the bliss of youthful love in life's prime and of a contentedness so absolute and so firmly associated with a place—"some place,/ Deep Vale, or anywhere, the home of both"—that leaving it at all would be misery. He then says: "next to such dear delight/ *Was* that of wandering on from day to day/ Where *I* could meditate in peace . . ."; and the general becomes the particular, the "we" an "I," with "*was*," which places the kind of activity being described in the past. It is an activity which became habitual early in life.

One scholar, F. W. Bateson, attempts to discover which "maid" Wordsworth seems to be recalling as the one with whom he, like other youths, walked in Life's prime in the Deep Vale,[15] but I must say that the attempt seems idle

[15] See Bateson, *Wordsworth: A Reinterpretation.* Mr. Bateson infers —I think invents—an adolescent romance of Wordsworth's from a few

here; Wordsworth never wrote of one. With Annette, for instance, he could be said to have walked so in the Loire Valley; and with some unknown beloved of his adolescence, he could be imagined to have done this in his native hills and vales. But what I am struck by is the way in which his deepest sense of himself as poet, as wanderer in Nature, is here distinguished from this bliss of love and set in the past as something that, at some point, replaced it. There are no representations of youthful love in, say, Wordsworth's college years; there is in fact a disapproving retrospective regard for himself as occasionally distracted by some evenings of revelry from poetry, truth, and the "religious dignity of mind." As for the alternative delight of teaching "the sound/ Of Poet's music to strange fields, and groves," it fits with the Wordsworth we know from his own descriptions of his youthful self composing poetry while walking in Nature. We know, too, that his sense of poetry as visionary speech came early to him from his comparison of its "voice" with the disembodied voice of Nature, the "ghostly language of the ancient earth."

The passage just quoted follows one that recalls the unpleasant life of the city. Wordsworth exclaims:

> therefore did I turn
> To you, ye Pathways, and ye lonely Roads
> Sought you enrich'd with everything I prized,
> With human kindness and with Nature's joy.
> (xii, 123-126)

And this leads to his habitual image of himself—the seeker of solitude, the "lonely traveller" with "long, long ways before." What follows is a further associative recollection about roads:

suggestions. I must say that the picture of Wordsworth as the youthful lover seems even less plausible than the picture of the imaginary beloved; nothing in *The Prelude* prepares one to see the Wordsworth who sought solitude at that age in the way Mr. Bateson suggests.

I love a public road: few sights there are
That please me more; such object hath had power
O'er my imagination since the dawn
Of childhood, when its disappearing line,
Seen daily afar off, on one bare steep
Beyond the limits which my feet had trod
Was like a guide into eternity,
At least to things unknown and without bound.
Even something of the grandeur which invests
The Mariner who sails the roaring sea
Through storm and darkness early in my mind
Surrounded, too, the Wanderers of the Earth . . .
(XII, 145-156)

It occurs to him to relate this poetic longing to "the dawn of childhood," and we find that "eternity"—a rather adult and therefore late notion—has since then been associated with the road as "a disappearing line." For the "lonely traveller" of the Imagination passage who realizes the metaphorical extension of the journey-metaphor towards "infinitude," this early sense of the road as a line disappearing over the hill is a revealing one.

In the 1850 version, it is made even clearer:

when a disappearing line,
One daily present to my eyes, that crossed
The naked summit of a far-off hill
Beyond the limits that my feet had trod,
Was like an invitation into space
Boundless, or guide into eternity.
(XIII, 146-151: 1850 version)

Wordsworth in the Alps wanted to do what he had wanted to do since he was a child discovering the line that disappears on the horizon in the sky.

The editor's note to lines 149-150 is a simple biographical one: "*On one bare steep/ Beyond the limits* . . . : i.e., the road to the village of Isel, over the Hay or Watch Hill, which can be seen from the garden and the back of the house at Cockermouth where Wordsworth passed the first years of life."[16] The metaphorical journey in the Imagination passage, directed towards an "infinitude" that is "our being's heart and home" associated with the mother, is to be further explained by the passage about the public road and by the footnote. One can see the crossing of the Alps according to the child's imagination about the road across the "summit of a far off hill." Its meaning and the meaning of "infinitude" are made clearer by the more probable sense of "eternity" that the child had. In this simile "like a guide into eternity/ At least to things unknown and without bound," the road that Wordsworth now associates with "eternity" was really associated with *disappearance*, "a disappearing line"; and beyond that, with death-as-disappearance: the line that disappears over a summit from *here*—home, this vale, Cockermouth—towards "things unknown and without bound" is associated with not-here, away, gone, absent, distant. What has "disappeared" is missing from the known and the bounded. Death is as sophisticated a notion as eternity and as difficult for a child to comprehend in his feelings,[17] whereas this simpler childish sense of away and absent can deny the absoluteness of "lost." "Dead" would mean unfindable-in-place-or-time. Taking-the-road, with the repression of the traumatic reasons for doing so, is an unconscious attempt to go after and find again what has disappeared. It is an attempt which, on the literal level, becomes restless and dissatisfied searching for the unnameable lost object and a lost condition. There is present in this activity another unconscious attempt to repeat some-

16 *The Prelude*, p. 616; footnote to XII, 149-150.

17 See, for instance, Wordsworth's "We are seven" in *Lyrical Ballads*. In the Preface (*Poetical Works*, p. 737) he gives as one of the attributes of the Poet "a disposition to be affected more than other men by absent things as if they were present."

thing about the trauma in action: a lifetime of "wandering" and "setting-off" would repeat actively what, in the original disappearance, was experienced passively. But we shall observe presently how Wordsworth came to feel oppressed by his own ideal of the Wanderer and of the lonely traveller as the Poet fixed in his role.

In the passage "Oh! next to one dear state of bliss . . . ," I find this early and traumatic sense of disappearance. The passage seems not to be recalling an experience of adolescence or of early adulthood but rather a sense of road and traveller from deep in the poet's troubled identity—that is to say, from childhood. There was a beloved in earliest childhood, and a vale from which it would have been "misery to stir," especially to seek solitude. A traumatic disappearance was the cause of a subsequent melancholy preference for solitude and wandering; it came to seem to him the only alternative "delight." On the metaphorical level, journeying is more noticeably accompanied by the unconscious attempt of the repetition-compulsion to force upon the conscious mind the painful facts necessary to an understanding of the "journey." This is because on the metaphorical level, the conscious attempt to express in poetry the feeling of dissatisfaction with the activities of the self seems to provoke this preconscious phenomenon of "usurpation" in the mind.

We have already seen how early Wordsworth's predisposition towards solitude became associated with poetry, as if a visionary search through poetry could find what was first sought restlessly wandering in Nature. And here the density and inner consistency of his images and metaphors may be seen. In the same passage from Book XII in which he speaks of the public road having had power over his imagination since childhood and speaks of the disappearing line and of things unknown and without bound, he remembers associatively having seen the "Wanderers of the earth" with "something of the grandeur which invests/ The Mariner who sails the roaring sea/ Through storm and darkness. . . ."[18] This image of the lonely wanderer who also experiences things unknown and without bound in storm and darkness should recall here the passage from Book II in which he describes his youthful self and the predisposition that leads to poetry as a visionary quest:

> for I would walk alone,
> In storm and tempest, or in star-light nights
> Beneath the quiet Heavens; and, at that time,
> Have felt whate'er there is of power in sound
> To breathe an elevated mood, by form
> Or image unprofaned; and I would stand,
> Beneath some rock, listening to sounds that are
> The ghostly language of the ancient earth,
> Or make their dim abode in distant winds.
> Thence did I drink the visionary power.
> (II, 321-330)

There is, however, another interesting connection between this passage from Book II and the passages we have been considering from Book XII. In the passage that precedes the one just quoted above, he speaks of having held "by intercourse of touch . . . mute dialogues with my mother's heart" and then mentions her disappearance: "I was left alone/ Seeking the visible world, nor knowing why. . . ." In speaking of his lonely experience of Nature a few lines later in this passage, he says:

> Many are the joys
> Of youth; but oh! what happiness to live
> When every hour brings palpable access
> Of knowledge, when all knowledge is delight,
> And sorrow is not there. The seasons came,
> And every season to my notice brought
> A store of transitory qualities
> Which, but for this most watchful power of love
> Had been neglected, left a register

18 *The Prelude,* XII, 153-156.

Of permanent relations, else unknown,
Hence life, and change, and beauty, solitude
More active, even, than 'best society,'
Society made sweet as solitude
By silent inobtrusive sympathies . . .
(II, 303-316)

First, one must be struck by how the death of the mother is so lightly touched on and passed over, and then by Wordsworth's strange insistence on intense delight in the increase of knowledge that came with living in Nature. Again, it is as if the period being described were one of rare privilege, rather than one in which, because of his mother's death, he was thrown more upon himself, put out to school, and left to wander more in Nature. That it occurs to him to describe the time "when all knowledge is delight,/ And sorrow is not there," as if unconsciously *denying* sorrow may make us the more alert to what follows. He goes on to say simply that the watchful power of Nature's love impressed senses of Nature on his mind and made "solitude more active, even, than 'best society.'" This line, with its quotation from Milton, is puzzling and, I think, very revealing.

We have seen partly how Nature's love and the Presence in Nature result from Wordsworth's experiences of solitude—his projections of need into Nature and the perception there of maternal solicitude. But why does Wordsworth recall Milton here and recall a very peculiar context from *Paradise Lost*? The passage from Book IX of *Paradise Lost* is Adam's speech to Eve:

But if much converse perhaps
Thee satiate, to short absence I could yield
For solitude sometimes is best society,
And short retirement urges sweet return.
But other doubt possesses me, lest harm
Befall thee sever'd from me . . .
(*Paradise Lost*, IX, 248-252)

Solitude and "best society" do *not* come to mind here simply because Wordsworth found Miltonisms very moving and because he is attempting to give a touching characterization of a child's preference for solitude in Nature, a preference which will deepen in time into the predispositions and preoccupations of the Poet as lonely traveller. This, I think, is the recollection of a phrase because of the preconscious recollection of a context: Wordsworth speaks at one point of the "Paradise where I was reared"; and like Adam's Paradise, it had its Eve. But from Biblical and common speech and from Milton, Wordsworth could have had the figurative sense of Eve as "our first Mother." In Book IX of *Paradise Lost,* Adam is speaking of separation from Eve, allowing that, in some circumstances, solitude is agreeable; that is, when one has the expectation of a "sweet return." And Adam's fearful doubt is intuitively right: in Book IX of *Paradise Lost* something *is* about to "happen" to Eve, and, through her, to him. Betrayal, Knowledge, and Death are the subjects about to come up in the poem, the fall and the loss of Paradise—certainly subjects that have an unconscious appeal to Wordsworth, seeking the truth of his experience and a true knowledge of himself.

The real reference for the beloved and the deep vale in the passage from Book XII ("Oh! next to one dear state of bliss . . .") is the mother and the lost Paradise of his childhood; and the habitual preference for solitude in Nature is a way of denying death and loss by the unconsciously held expectation of her "sweet return." The wandering of the lonely traveller is Wordsworth's unconscious attempt to find again by search what has been lost, even though in his search he necessarily lacks a clear idea of the object sought because of the repression of the trauma of loss. The "sweet return," as we observed it in "Tintern Abbey," is a psychic phenomenon which completes the experience of solitude in Nature: the landscape evocative of the past, the Presence felt in its imagery, the withdrawal into the mind when the affections lead him on through "beauteous forms" to the serene and blessed mood, the visionary union of the living soul and the deep life of things.

But gradually the search in the world becomes the urgent poetic search—a search in and through poetry to find something that is elusive both in experience and in the recollection of experience. Poetry is itself an experience, which is what Wordsworth means when he says that it can "present" objects realized with a flash. The experience dealt with in the Imagination passage is a particularly important one because there, more clearly than anywhere else previously, an event takes place in the mind itself: what is ordinarily projected into external Nature and perceived as a reality underneath Nature is experienced entirely within the mind, an invisible world or an object momentarily glimpsed.

When Wordsworth says "our being's heart and home is with infinitude," he is unconsciously revealing division in the ego and describing feelings that have remained attached to the mother by unrenounced dependencies. This is the way "heart" symbolizes the mother—"heart" which should symbolize the centrality and wholeness of one's autonomous being, but which for him did not. The divided ego feels that one's self is not one's whole being and that the reality it inhabits is not its true one. As Freud observed in speaking of the Pleasure Principle, man's reluctance to relinquish the timeless sense of pleasure associated with his earliest sentient existence as undifferentiated ego, his unwillingness to achieve a truly self-sufficient individuality in time, accounts for his restless sense of lack in life and his constant search.[19] The "heart" can only be accepted as the center of one's whole being to the extent that a man accepts his own mortality. Wordsworth speaks of "heart" as a reality associated with a lost "home," both a specific and a symbolic home. "Home" is symbolic of a lost condition in which the child had felt included and in which, to a

[19] See Freud, "On Narcissism" and "Instincts and Their Vicissitudes," CW XIV.

degree, the surrounding otherness had been acceptable to him as real. The traumatic disruption of this condition forced upon him his unconscious feeling of being "outcast . . . bewilder'd and depress'd," of "trooping," "destitute," on the road of life. The life of the self is felt to be an estrangement from the true condition of being.

Wordsworth's circumstance—or the Poet's circumstance insofar as Wordsworth's account of his own development may be taken to exemplify it—differs from man's generally only by the way in which it makes clearer the human inability or unconscious refusal to relinquish the ideal of pleasure. The repressed trauma animates a stronger and more compelling process by which consciousness might be made to recognize what normative repression in man is sufficient to withstand. It is this sense of "Imagination-and-Revelation" as a compelling process that I find in Wordsworth's characterization of the power that rises from the mind's abyss and overwhelms the consciousness; for while regressively and unconsciously seeking a lost condition, the poet may experience instead a conscious realization of what he is seeking and why he is seeking it.

In *Totem and Taboo,* Freud describes the power of unconscious recollection in this way:

"When we, no less than primitive man, project something into external reality, what is happening must surely be this: we are recognizing the existence of two states—one in which something is directly given to the senses and to consciousness (that is, is *present* to them), and alongside it another, in which the same thing is *latent* but capable of re-appearing. In short, we are recognizing the co-existence of perception and memory, or, putting it more generally, the existence of *unconscious* mental processes alongside the *conscious* ones. It might be said that in the last analysis the 'spirit' of persons or things comes down to their capacity to be remembered and imagined after perception of them has ceased."[20]

[20] Freud, "Totem and Taboo," CW XIII, 93-94.

When Wordsworth speaks of the "presences of Nature" that "haunt" the child in his play and form by their influence the "favor'd being" who will be the Poet, he is demonstrating the capacity to remember and imagine as spirits in the world the formative beings whose reality he projects. The power of "Imagination" that comes in a flash within the mind comes when Nature, into which unconscious projections are ordinarily made, has been incorporated in the mind and is subjected to a more intense imaginative scrutiny. The glorious feeling of increasing consciousness and the equally strong feeling of something-to-be-realized in this kind of inner experience exceed the realization actually presented in the Imagination passage; but the sense of "something evermore about to be" suggests the desiderated wholeness of being sought in increased consciousness: the conscious acceptance of the fact of loss and the further acceptance of one's autonomy of being.

CHAPTER V

MEMORIES AND IMAGININGS

1. The Fiction of the Self

When Wordsworth recalls "one, the fairest of all rivers," he imagines the happiness of infancy and of childhood in one idealized picture of the river, the vale, and the first home. This is the river valley of the Derwent at Cockermouth from which all other vales gain their special affective power for him, even the "beloved vale" of his school years in nearby Hawkeshead, and Grasmere, which later became his "chosen vale." In the "beloved vale" of his school days he learned to live with the fact of his mother's loss and to compensate for his loneliness by finding *in* solitude his intimate and affectionate relationship with Nature. His unconscious feelings, projected into Nature and enacted, as we shall see, in his play, were given expression and found relief. To the extent that the child found contentment in his activities he could seem whole to himself and at home where he felt his heart was, in Nature. In this way, the trauma of separation and the loss of the true heart-and-home feeling of being were expressed in denied form, in activities fixated upon repressed experiences.

The first significant journey undertaken by the child was between these two vales, on the public road over the summit of the hill; and I have derived the emotional significance of the recurrent journey-metaphor from the death that led to the change of vales. Wordsworth simply omits to mention the cause of the change of vales:

> Fair seed-time had my soul, and I grew up
> Foster'd alike by beauty and by fear;

Much favor'd in my birthplace, and no less
In that beloved Vale to which, erelong,
I was transplanted. Well I call to mind
('Twas at an early age, ere I had seen
Nine summers) when upon the mountain slope
The frost and breath of frosty wind . . .
(I, 305-312)

In the seed-time of the soul, the soul seems like the self rooted in its natural life. As we shall see, the passage recollecting the first home is the most idealized, simplest, and happiest "recollection" in *The Prelude*; it is more a belief than a memory. But immediately afterwards, we begin to observe the remembered activities of the boy as they became habitual and, I think, indicative of the divided ego. The self is then not merely a transplanted thing, but one unconsciously aware of a lost home, strangely pleased in the activities by which it maintains itself, yet troubled in its pleasures. The metaphorical sense of natural growth as soul-and-tillage gradually changes; it ceases to express Wordsworth's growth and comes instead to characterize an ideal condition to be sought. The growth to poetic self-consciousness becomes a journey for Wordsworth—a journey in the world, through its imagery, and perhaps beneath or beyond it. Becoming the highly self-conscious Poet seems inseparable from attempting to be Wordsworth; and at the same time, having true being implies a return to a prior condition, now idealized as the natural habitat of the contented spirit and of the Poet's spirit.

It seems to me consistent with my interpretation of his unconscious search for the lost object and for the wholeness of being associated with it that Wordsworth imagines the completion of the "journey" as a place to live or as a state of being. Specifically, he imagines either an actual place, metaphorically idealized, like Racedown,[1] where there are the fields of the soul to be worked poetically; or he imagines

[1] *The Prelude*, I, 45-55.

a state of being which will result when a psychic experience of Imagination-Revelation increases consciousness and makes the soul fertile like the "fertiliz'd Egyptian plain."[2] Then his tillage can bring forth the crop of poetry. It is of great importance, too, that he feels he must achieve this condition, resisting the temptation to lapse into passive and unself-conscious states. As we have observed, the attractiveness of withdrawing into the "one interior life" or the possibility of falling into the "abyss of idealism" both express neurotic fears of being burdened by self-consciousness, and suggest psychosis and death.

When, in Book I, he imagines that "mellower years will bring a *riper* mind,"[3] as if time rather than some present activity will bring on the fertile condition for the "crop" of poetry, he feels himself to be weak, to be weakly himself, and to be untrue to himself:

> with no skill to part
> Vague longing that is bred by want of power
> From paramount impulse not to be withstood,[4]
> A timorous capacity from prudence;
> From circumspection, infinite delay.
> Humility and modest awe themselves
> Betray me, serving often for a cloak
> To a more subtle selfishness, that now
> Doth lock my functions up in blank reserve,
> Now dupes me by an over-anxious eye
> That with a false activity beats off
> Simplicity and self-presented truth.
>
> (I, 241-251)

The alternative, that of deliberately not trying, of taking refuge in renounced ambition and in the voluptuous condition of inactivity and vacant musing, *then* actually seems preferable to the self-told lies that counsel delay:[5]

[2] *Ibid.*, VI, 616: 1850 version. [3] *Ibid.*, I, 235-238.

[4] Wordsworth seems to be echoing *Paradise Lost*, the devils' synod in Book II. In spirit, the sentiment is closest to Moloch's speech, II, 51f.

[5] See *Paradise Lost*, II, 108-225. It is Belial who counsels delay and

—Ah! better far than this, to stray about
Voluptuously through fields and rural walks,
And ask no record of the hours, given up
To vacant musing, unreprov'd neglect
Of all things, and deliberate holiday;
Far better never to have heard the name
Of zeal and just ambition, than to live
Thus baffled by a mind that every hour
Turns recreant to her task, takes heart again,
Then feels immediately some hollow thought
Hang like an interdict upon her hopes.
This is my lot; for either still I find
Some imperfection in the chosen theme,
Or see of absolute accomplishment
Much wanting, so much wanting, in myself,
That I recoil and droop, and seek repose
In listlessness from vain perplexity,
Unprofitably travelling towards the grave,
Like a false Steward who hath much received
And renders nothing back.

(I, 252-271)

The questions of what sufficient power is, where it is located, where it comes from, and what inhibits its use are raised by Wordsworth's acute awareness that the pleasurable state of inactivity is a vacant one opposed to the poetic task of being Wordsworth. And it is immediately after his use of the journey-metaphor in conjunction with the prospect of death that the self, which has been set traumatically on its special journey by a death, is given the needed impetus to its task of being the *poetic* self. From the self-asked question: "Was it for this that one, the fairest of all rivers . . . ,"[6]

ease, II, 119-. The subject of the Poet's Godliness is to be raised in *The Prelude,* so the rhetoric of the fallen angels is not inappropriate to the conflict felt by Wordsworth about his own aspirations. Wordsworth greatly admired the "grandeur" of Milton's description of Satan; and here, I think, the grand Miltonic influence works with preconscious suggestion in Wordsworth's mind.

[6] *The Prelude,* I, 271f.

The Prelude, in all the peculiarities of its composition and compilation, may be said to follow.

The oblivion of the "one interior life" and the growth of poetic self-consciousness in the Imagination passage are so plainly opposed that the passage on the "one interior life" from MS RV finds no place in *The Prelude.* Both passages propose the union of the self with something greater ("infinitude" or "one mighty whole"), but antithetically in point of self-consciousness. The Imagination passage emphasizes the "I" and the potential of greatness in increased consciousness; the RV passage does the opposite, finding God wherever one cannot distinguish personal characteristics of oneself. Still, the striking inner consistency of Wordsworth's poetic sense of things may be seen by setting the characterizations of these opposite tendencies in him side by side. When he speaks of the "one interior life," he says:

> By such communion I was early taught
> *That what we see of forms and images*
> *Which float along our minds* and what we feel
> Of active, or of recognizable thought,
> Prospectiveness, intelligence or will
> Not only is not worthy to be deemed
> Our being, to be priz'd as what we are,
> But is the very littleness of life.
> Such consciousnesses seemed by accidents
> Relapses from the one interior life
> Which is in all things, from that unity
> In which all beings live with God, are lost
> In God and Nature, in one mighty whole . . .
> (MS RV)

> In which all beings live with God, themselves
> Are God, existing in one mighty whole . . .
> (MS 2 of "Peter Bell")

On the other hand, when he speaks so very beautifully of seeking himself in the uncertain imagery of Memory, he sees the same stream of the mind, its personal forms and images:

As one who hangs down-bending from the side
Of a slow-moving boat, upon the breast
Of a still water, solacing himself
With such discoveries as his eye can make
Beneath him in the bottom of the deep,
Sees many beauteous sights—woods, fishes, flowers,
Grots, pebbles, roots of trees, and fancies more,
Yet often is perplexed and cannot part
The shadow from the substance, rocks and sky,
Mountains and clouds, reflected in the depth
Of the clear flood, from things which there abide
In their true dwelling; now is crossed by gleam
Of his own image, by a sun-beam now,
And wavering motions sent he knows not whence,
Impediments that make his task more sweet;
Such pleasant office have we long pursued
Incumbent o'er the surface of past time
With like success . . .

(IV, 256-273: 1850 version)

This stream of the mind, the flow of the self in time since birth, is mentioned by Wordsworth several times and in different ways in *The Prelude*.[7] It is likely that the figure of speech is personal rather than conventional; it, too, is associated with the original vale, the home near the Derwent with the river outside the nursery window. This particular epic simile of self-regard reveals the characteristics and the degree of Wordsworth's self-consciousness perfectly: not only is there the usual difficulty of seeing clearly what is in the depths of the stream and of the self in time past, but as one both "solaces" oneself in looking there and "fancies" a certain amount of what one sees, one's own necessary presence adds one's own present motives to the

[7] *The Prelude*, IV, 39-55; also XIII, 166-184. See, too, the peculiar association of stream-road-dreams-soul in IV, 39-55.

task, distorting it. Having found intuitively a beautiful poetic analogy for his kind of poetic preoccupation, Wordsworth adds the detail that his own present image falls upon the surface of past time, so that he must look into the past by looking into and through himself—which is, in a visual sense, obvious. But at the same time the extended simile reminds us of how the image of his present self comes between him and his past, or rather, how his past tends to give back his own present image of himself while showing at the same time, and however imprecisely, a good deal more of himself beneath it. With a kind of optical inevitability, the simile adds the perceiver and his motives to his perceptions: unparted shadow and substance yield his image of himself as *he* tries to see it, not as someone might see him in his story.

Beyond solace and fancy is the synthesis of the self in time; poetry results from the peculiar tensions of self-consciousness, but as an activity, it moves beyond the acceptance of self-consciousness, hybristically seeking divinity in the consciousness of personal genius. Gradually, Wordsworth reveals the dimensions of the wish he cherishes, and unconsciously he reveals its origins. That Wordsworth joins the human desire to survive to the feeling of continuous and perhaps immortal life felt in poetry (and that he distinguishes both from the selfless "immortal being" of the Christian soul, which moves at death beyond these concerns), the following passage from Book v makes clear:

Thou also, Man, hast wrought,
For commerce of thy nature with itself,
Things worthy of unconquerable life;
And yet we feel, we cannot chuse but feel
That these must perish. Tremblings of the heart
It gives, to think that the immortal being
No more shall need such garments; and yet Man,
As long as he shall be the Child of Earth,
Might almost 'weep to have' what he may lose,

Nor be himself extinguish'd; but survive
Abject, depress'd, forlorn, disconsolate.
(v, 17-27)

Wordsworth implies that in creating or appreciating human things worthy of immortal life man expresses his own desire not to die. But there is also a poetic connection between what Wordsworth says here of man's desire to survive no matter what ("abject, depress'd, forlorn, disconsolate") and the early trauma in his own life that resulted for Wordsworth in such personal poetry. Poetry became the obsessive "commerce" of his nature with itself, revealing his desire to live and his way of being himself. But "depressed" calls to mind the line from the passage about the Blest Babe, which I have suggested characterizes his own unrealized feelings about himself at the time of his mother's death: "No outcast he, bewildered and depress'd."[8] Wordsworth the child had felt outcast, bewildered and depressed (one could add abject, forlorn, disconsolate), yet was "seeking the visible world" in order to survive in it. We have observed some of the ways in which becoming the Poet derives from that attempt to accept the visible world; but we have seen, too, how the mind further induces its psychic and spiritual experiences in a visionary relating of visible to invisible, of outside to inside, of present to absent, and of alive to dead. This is the commerce of Wordsworth's "nature with itself," the commerce of his habitual sense of himself with his spirit's original sense of its wholeness. What Wordsworth thinks poetry is to Man describes what it had gradually become to himself. The feeling of immortality with which poetry teases his mind is accompanied by a displaced acknowledgment of death: Poetry itself may perish. This opening passage of Book v leads to the remarkable Arab Dream (to which we shall return in Chapter VIII), which opposes the denial and the acceptance of death as they may be imagined or revealed in poetry.

[8] *Ibid.*, II, 261.

In its vigor, poetic self-consciousness opposes itself to the imagined union with God in the oblivion of the "one interior life," and seems instead to imagine no limit for itself. It is a temptation to the poetic spirit to find in itself and in its proper activity the very Godliness it seems to risk losing by the assertion of Self. God, Wordsworth says in the passage on the "one interior life," has centrality and wholeness of being within his nature. (One thinks here of Aristotle's self-contemplative God as engaged in the sole activity of the "commerce of his Nature with itself.") But Wordsworth seems consciously to seek his own centrality and Godliness in his poetic account of his growth. If he can fix "the wavering balance" of his mind and show himself how his own story leads to his ideal of himself as the Poet, he will have a Godly understanding of his own being. Poets, ideally described in Book XIII, have "the highest bliss that can be known. . . . The consciousness/ Of whom they are habitually infused/ Through every image, and through every thought."[9] But I have suggested, too, that in a more complex way, he seeks this knowledge unconsciously, unaware of what it entails.

If Wordsworth's sense of his "privileged" growth is to be understood as "traumatic," then the imaginable Godliness of the Poet depends in some way on the survival of the child who suffered in the artist who creates. Wordsworth would not accept the word "suffered," but the poet who said "The child is father of the man" would not have objected to our discerning the crucial presence of the child in the man. Wordsworth wished to make the case that the Poet of Nature, her special child, was comparable only to the God above Nature, as Imagination is to Revelation; and "God," who is not mentioned often, seems to be introduced only for the purpose of this high comparison. Let us first observe, then, that the Poet's autonomy as a creator is to be demonstrated by his powerful and personal use of Nature herself in his creations. Of course, this is not unusual, when

[9] *Ibid.*, XIII, 107-110.

one thinks about it; no poet could do less and be a poet. But the claim that Wordsworth makes for the Poet is so striking simply because it occurs to him to give the analogy that peculiar emphasis, exaggerating and insisting upon it. I think that it is to the relevant period of a child's psychology we must turn—the period of infantile omnipotence which culminates in the Oedipus complex.

The "Godliness" of the child is to be seen first according to the family triangle—in the child's desire to assert his autonomy from the mother by asserting his sexual powers in relation to her and his wish to deny the significance of the absent father. Rearranging the principal beings of his world in fantasy, and making the best of what he imagines, he uses his unchecked powers of wishing omnipotently. With them, he demotes the powerful and permissive mother to an object of desire, and at the same time excludes the father whose real power and significance he has begun to observe but has not yet significantly experienced and realized. It is this sense of the permissive mother who allows the self-exalting fantasy to develop that Wordsworth finds in Nature.

In observing what Freud called the fantasies and conflicts of the Oedipal period of growth, we should observe, too, that an eight-year-old child ordinarily has passed through and resolved these conflicts. In the figurative sense of the word, he has already "lost" the mother, and has instead an uncertain and distrustful recollection of her permissiveness which had "betrayed" him to his psychic conflict with the father. I shall attempt to show presently that Wordsworth had undergone that later experience of figuratively "losing" the mother, but that the literal event, the extreme trauma of loss in death, forced upon him the need to deny all loss. The subsequent expressions of regressive need may be understood in terms of this blocking of further normative growth, as may the subsequent unconscious poetic attempt at curing the self. It should hardly need saying that the apparent pathology of the poet affords us a closer look at something more interesting than normative growth and its many reductive adjustments. And that not pathology itself, but the use of the creative mind in a pathological circumstance is what is interesting here. There are many "cases" of unresolvable Oedipal fantasy and conflict, but one cannot even name another great poetic autobiography.

In normative growth, children repress the fantasies and the experiences in which their desire for the mother culminates, as well as repress their former awareness of such desires. Although wishes to possess her continue unconsciously, the figurative sense of the loss of the mother is felt; it is accepted-in-living, but it is not understood. On the one hand, she is still crucially the center of the life of the home, in which the son's growing identification with the father develops; on the other, she is ultimately the cause of his independent search for satisfaction in life. That "independence" is the real degree of autonomy he will achieve in his growth. His restlessness, his unconscious feelings of desire, of danger, of betrayal, and of loss, lead him specifically away from her as an object of desire after puberty, and yet towards something suggestive of her and of the original love relationship with her. Every finding in reality is a refinding, Freud observed.[10] What persisted for Wordsworth, however, because of the greater need to deny the experience of her absolute loss is the fantasy of unimpaired possession of the mother "within" him, and, in her projected form, around him as the Presence in Nature. His special sense of the power of a Poet derives from the enormous powers of fantasy originally associated with her permissiveness, now felt by projection as Nature's permissiveness.

Both the habit of action and the limits of imaginable action that sons acquire are normatively modeled on the father as they identify themselves with him after their initial conflict with him. But the need to deny the irrepara-

[10] See Freud, "On Narcissism," CW XIV.

ble loss of the mother, as Wordsworth experienced it, prevented further identification with the father and caused regression from it; so, too, did his actual separation from his father in the ensuing years in which the schoolboy saw his absent father only at holidays. Hence, both the habit of action and the limits of imaginable action reverted to those of an earlier period. This is to say that the fixated mind occupies itself with recreating the world it inhabits rather than with adjusting to the one that is there. Fixation is like an arrest of growth in the period in which play-fantasy dominates a child's being, limiting the extent and the kinds of action undertaken in reality. For the duration of childhood there is a latency period in which what is repressed may be comparatively quiescent, in so far as present reality does not make demands on the ego too great for it to answer while it attempts to maintain itself in this way. Many of the most ordinary habits of action, assertion, and competition are left undeveloped where fantasy predominates; for the ego can maintain itself even in solitude, and often more successfully so, without the impositions made on it by other people's needs and actions. But there is, too, the tendency in the self-aggrandizing and assertive fantasies of the pre-Oedipal and Oedipal periods to bring on the conflict with the father who seems to be sought out in order to be denied his significance. We shall see presently how this is applicable to Wordsworth's discovery of himself as "the favored being" of Nature. It is as if, beyond fantasy, his imagination were unconsciously seeking conflict.

Writing poetry, for instance, while not competitive and assertive in the usual sense of assertion among men, had for Wordsworth that same quality of fantastic and incestuous assertion present in the period of infantile fantasy I have been describing. The Poet's desire to name poetry as man's highest activity and to make the Poet's mind comparable to God's mind makes in fact the same connection between the Poet and God in point of Nature that the child once made between the child and the father in point of the mother. The Poet, Wordsworth says, fostered by Nature, can then use her as he wishes, creating out of her elements things of his own, as a God would. But when a child's fantasies initiate his Oedipal conflicts, it is because, among other things, he has already begun to perceive the finer autonomy of the absent father. The father is the man who comes and goes, who is and is not there, but whose power is believed by others. The child has begun to compare that autonomous power with his own powers as he has exercised them in his own willful pursuits. In wanting to render his father insignificant, he is only denying a model of power he has begun to admire and envy, and one that he has begun to perceive more or less accurately in relation to the mother and to himself. The ensuing experience of conflict with the father permanently fixes the normative sense of self and the subsequent degree of autonomy for a boy. One should observe that this, too, is a kind of fixation, a "normative" one.

When Wordsworth writes, in Book v, of growth as a diminution of powers, he gives a perfect characterization of poetry as the omnipotence of wishing opposed to the common acceptances of life. The Poet persists in using his powers of creation, imitating the God of creation:

> Dumb yearnings, hidden appetites are ours,
> And they must have their food: our childhood sits,
> Our simple childhood sits upon a throne
> That hath more power than all the elements.
> I guess not what this tells of Being past,
> Nor what it augurs of the life to come;
> But so it is; and in that dubious hour,
> That twilight when we first begin to see
> This dawning earth, to recognise, expect;
> And in the long probation that ensues,
> The time of trial, ere we learn to live
> In reconcilement with our stinted powers,
> To endure this state of meagre vassalage;
> Unwilling to forego, confess, submit,

Uneasy and unsettled; yoke-fellows
To custom, mettlesome, and not yet tam'd
And humbled down, oh! then we feel, we feel,
We know when we have Friends. Ye dreamers, then,
Forgers of lawless tales! we bless you then,
Imposters, drivellers, dotards, as the ape
Philosophy will call you: then we feel
With what, and how great might ye are in league,
Who make our wish our power, our thought a deed,
An empire, a possession; Ye whom Time
And Seasons serve; all Faculties; to whom
Earth crouches, th' elements are potter's clay,
Space like a Heaven fill'd up with Northern lights;
Here, nowhere, there, and everywhere at once.
(v, 530-557)

Invoking "the poets"—those of his and of everyone's impressionable years—Wordsworth simulates the wonder and implies the wisdom of the child. Philosophers and common men no longer know that once their wishes were powers, their thoughts deeds. Ultimately, poets gain only other poets as followers—seekers of truer homes, of deeper and prior realities, of invisible worlds, of fertile fields of the spirit, of lost empires and lost possessions. But in *The Prelude* Wordsworth is attempting to assure himself of his own possession of this very power; and, having considered the impoverishment of the human mind by man's loss of it, he intends in his future poetry to assault the dull minds of men, to remind them of their own lost feelings and powers. The Poet in his role is rather self-assertively some sort of God handling "the elements." Moralizing and beautifying the commonplace, like Jesus, he tells man to be instructed by regarding the lesser celandines and the daffodils of the field and by hearing the Apocalyptic blasts of the waterfall.

To many hungry in spirit, the Poet is Godly generous. But the Poet is also a spirit who tells man that there is no acceptable limit for knowledge, that he is to acquire again the Godly powers of mind that once were his and that should be his, as perhaps Satan would. If Jesus is the Divine Child of the Mother who must first free himself from her to go about his father's business, Satan, in Milton's version of him, would understand himself to be, like Imagination to Wordsworth, "unfathered."[11] But Wordsworth, of course, is not attending to these implications of the Poet's powers; he accepts only limited liability for his personal fiction. The Jesus who really "replaces" the father he perfectly serves and the Satan who cannot depose the father he will not serve are the two aspects of the ambivalent relationship of the Son with the Father as Western man has imagined the conflicts of his personal will to power. The Son is at one with the Father or at war with him. As Freud observed, Man seems unable to free himself of his unconscious ambivalence for the primary beings of his dependent childhood.[12]

But we should observe, too, that the feelings of dread felt at the beginning of *The Prelude* by the Poet—the "deadening admonitions," the hollow thoughts that "hang like an interdict" upon his hopes—must derive from this same circumstance of incipient conflict with the father. As Wordsworth intended to announce the Godly self-sufficiency of the Poet, he was unconsciously approaching the subject of freedom from the mother. He was also unconsciously approaching the repressed experience of Oedipal conflict with the father, an experience even more deeply "repressed" than the specific trauma and fixation from which he was seeking unconsciously to free himself. It is no accident, then, that in Book I, speaking of his inability to proceed with the poem, he speaks of

> Vague longing that is bred by want of power
> From paramount impulse not to be withstood,

[11] See *Paradise Lost*, V, 852-869.

[12] See Freud, "Totem and Taboo," CW XIII; "Moses and Monotheism," CW XXIII; and "The Future of an Illusion," CW XXI.

A timorous capacity from prudence;
From circumspection, infinite delay.
(I, 241-244)

He is echoing the devil's synod in Book II of *Paradise Lost*—the devils sullenly considering their own powers in rivalry with God's.

In his experience of fixated growth Wordsworth was not free to identify himself strongly with the father, whose own early death when Wordsworth was thirteen made the difficult psychic circumstance of the boy even more precarious. Circumstantially excluded from many of the normal experiences of identification from boyhood to manhood, Wordsworth discovered, adapted, and invented the role of Poet, his personal fiction. But one can see in his story his inability to learn simply the ways of men and to undergo their rituals of initiation. He could not imitate and accept. He habitually renounced action and competition, both at school and in the choice of career. His father had been a lawyer, but Wordsworth, in writing about his period of crisis (in Books X and XI) uses law, law-courts, and lawyers as a key metaphor for conveying his desperation: he felt unable to "defend" his own convictions, his feelings about the natural rightness of the Revolutionary cause. How, then, are we to see the psychological situation of the Poet in relation to what we might call the normative-historical experience of growth?

Freud derived the fear of death and the fear of individuality from the fear of separation from the mother and from castration anxiety. When the mother becomes an object of premature genital desire, the father is feared as a castrating figure; and the child's wish to do away with his father is perceived fearfully by the child, in its projected form, as the father's desire to kill the child. This psychic ordeal, which results in the fearful renunciation of the mother, the repression of unacceptable wishes, and the subsequent identification of the child with the father, is at the same time an historical ordeal, which fathers too have suffered in their growth. In this way, the structures and processes of historical societies come to reflect the personalities of men, since communities maintain institutionally the repressions by which men live. Repressed infantile wishes in men can neither gain the expression they continue to seek, nor be *seen* clearly so that possibly they could be relinquished when understood. Thus, repressed infantile conflicts permanently confuse man's feelings about desire, castration, and death, besetting him with unconscious fears that preclude true individuality. Between separation from the mother and ritual initiation into the community, there has always been the abnormality of neurotic self-consciousness, for which the human temperament has ever sought palliatives and employments; but when we discuss the abnormal "infantile" origins of the life-style of the Poet, we must bear in mind the implicit comparison with the normal "infantile" origins of the life-style of historical societies.

The Poet, to the extent that Wordsworth exemplifies him, is unconsciously compelled to return to infantile trauma. Unable to ignore the disturbance he continues to feel about loss and growth in his own past, he unconsciously expresses the doubts he feels compelled to deny; and still he achieves no lasting composure. Therefore, he undertakes to examine his growth more elaborately, with an imaginative theory about his growth that is a personal fiction. Consequently, he must express profound dissatisfaction with normative growth, and he indicts society and History. For if his growth is, as he believes, natural, then that of historical societies is unnatural. His sympathy with the French Revolution seems entirely natural to him; he was led to the Revolution by Nature.

In writing Books VIII-X of *The Prelude*, especially the parts dealing directly with France, the French Revolution and his crisis, Wordsworth was unsure of what to say his actions in that period meant. He could not say of himself what I think can be said about him in that period, that he was unconsciously seeking the ordeal that might free him from the fixated condition of his psyche, which had by then become such a burden to his young manhood. In idealizing the principles of the Revolution as they would be asserted against and tested by an historical reality and by men who were basically so different from the Poet, he was asserting himself as a "natural being in the strength of Nature." But unconsciously he knew about the undependability of the source of such strength. Were he to see that his natural sympathies with the Revolution were Nature's way of "betraying" him to the experience of what men in History are "really" like, he might bring upon himself the repressed traumatic feelings of the past. He would have to make himself understand why Nature had seemed to set him apart from men so early in life. And were he subsequently to see himself in this way in his poetry, he would see the young Poet standing alone in the middle of his ordeal, as in fact he did stand alone, though he did not see it clearly.

It is exactly his belief in his restoration to health and poetry *by* Nature that indicates how strongly he resisted realizing the meaning of that ordeal. Rather than continue to question Nature, as he was doing just before he "yielded up moral questions in despair,"[13] he ascribes to Nature the renewal of his ability to approach the story of himself for its meaning. As in "Tintern Abbey," the affirmative intention is maintained by denial. As he extends *The Prelude* from five to thirteen books, again assured of his belief in Nature and of his unshakeable bond with her, he again approaches that moment when the Poet figuratively stood alone. Reluctant as he had been to include the account of these distressing years, but feeling compelled to do so, he was not eager to explain the role of Nature in that recent experience. His experience had forced upon him some awareness that Nature had not prepared him to understand

[13] *The Prelude,* x, 901.

History, nor adequately protected him from his experience of it, even if he would still insist that she had rescued him from it finally. He knew, too, that in the experience of his despair he had forsaken Nature because of the intense pain of his disordered feelings. He was not eager to explain that period or to question his experience again for what exactly he had felt. To use Wordsworth's description of writing poetry, he was not eager to contemplate those emotions "till by a species of reaction, the tranquillity gradually disappears, and an emotion kindred to that which was before the subject of contemplation, is gradually produced, and does itself actually exist in the mind."[14] By using poetry to assert the Godliness of the Poet and by imaginatively questioning his feelings about significant experiences that persist in Memory, the Poet may provoke the unconscious force from the mind's abyss to reveal the invisible world. Having at times done just this, believing in it, and even finding his momentary experiences glorious and desirable, he was nevertheless afraid. How could he control revelations of what persisted unpleasantly in Memory? How could he imagine the deep truth that lies "far hidden from the reach of words" without excessive pain or terror? Understandably, then, denial and resistance increased to obscure the truth of his recent experience and of the repressed trauma in the distant past which he had sought unconsciously to repeat. And this unconscious resistance increased exactly because an opposed unconscious intention was compelling him to approach that moment of betrayal in his story.

2. Some Versions of Child and Mother

To return, however, to the seed-time of his soul in the Paradise where he was reared, we may begin by observing how beautiful is his recollection of being happily alive as a five year old in the original vale. The passage (I, 286-304)

[14] "Preface to *Lyrical Ballads*, Edition of 1800," *Poetical Works*, p. 734.

conveys the pleasure of life as thoughtless activity more perfectly than any of Wordsworth's later descriptions of his boyish activity, which often seems anxiously burdened with unconscious intentions. In the years between three and five, the developing feeling of mastery over the body makes motion more vigorous and sensuous, and the pounding heart gives pleasant sensations. The self encloses life, feeling at home in its being; and it is exactly the sense of assured possession of the parental home and of its principal figures to which this feeling of enclosure corresponds, and from which it derives. It is in misfortune that the child becomes confused about the whereaboutness of the "heart and home" of his being; and an impossible psychic task results when the child must try early in life to make himself metaphorically the building that stands when the props of affection have been removed. Here, instead, is a picture of the child in the world of the mother:

> When, having left his Mountains, to the Towers
> Of Cockermouth that beauteous River came,
> Behind my Father's House he pass'd, close by,
> Along the margin of our Terrace Walk.
> He was a Playmate whom we dearly lov'd.
> Oh! many a time have I, a five years' Child,
> A naked Boy, in one delightful Rill,
> A little Mill-race sever'd from his stream,
> Made one long bathing of a summer's day,
> Bask'd in the sun, and plunged, and bask'd again
> Alternate all a summer's day, or cours'd
> Over the sandy fields, leaping through groves
> Of yellow grunsel, or when crag and hill,
> The woods, and distant Skiddaw's lofty height,
> Were bronz'd with a deep radiance, stood alone
> Beneath the sky, as if I had been born
> On Indian Plains, and from my Mother's hut
> Had run abroad in wantonness, to sport,
> A naked Savage, in the thunder shower.
>
> (I, 286-304)

The "naked boy" who plays in the stream near his "father's house" distances simple reality, and makes himself a "naked savage" free and at large—absent from, and assured about, his "mother's hut." The father, as in the Oedipal fantasies of young children at this stage of growth, is acknowledged and is even being imitated, but held imaginatively at a convenient distance. He has not yet acquired his full psychic significance to the child's sense of reality, as he will when the further development of this infantile sensuousness forces the occasion.

The picture of the five-year-old boy is consistent with that of the "emphatically" alive Blest Babe; both have acquired from the mother's presence an impulse to vigorous response to their world. But the eight-year-old boy spoken of moments later as "transplanted" to his schoolboy existence (soon after his mother's death) has instead the disturbed feeling of "seeking" something nameless—a search that results finally in the journey-metaphor. This is Wordsworth's recollection of himself in the new vale:

> Well I call to mind
> ('Twas at an early age, ere I had seen
> Nine summers) when upon the mountain slope
> The frost and breath of frosty wind had snapp'd
> The last autumnal crocus, 'twas my joy
> To wander half the night among the Cliffs
> And the smooth Hollows, where the woodcocks ran
> Along the open turf. In thought and wish
> That time, my shoulder all with springes hung,
> I was a fell destroyer. On the heights
> Scudding away from snare to snare, I plied
> My anxious visitation, hurrying on,
> Still hurrying, hurrying onward; moon and stars
> Were shining o'er my head; I was alone,
> And seem'd to be a trouble to the peace
> That was among them. Sometimes it befel
> In these night-wanderings, that a strong desire

O'erpower'd my better reason, and the bird
Which was the captive of another's toils
Became my prey; and, when the deed was done
I heard among the solitary hills
Low breathings coming after me, and sounds
Of undistinguishable motion, steps
Almost as silent as the turf they trod.

(I, 309-332)

To Wordsworth, recollecting the excitement of his "privileged" boyhood in Nature, the event has the manifest appropriateness of boyish adventure. On the other hand, I think it has a latent associational appropriateness, too: it is unconsciously associated with the trauma omitted here from his account of traumatic times. He is not simply a "transplanted" child; he has acquired a strange new freedom, and experiences joy and anxiety in wandering alone "half the night," "hurrying, hurrying onward." The boyish adventure of catching birds in traps has the pleasurable acknowledgment of wishes that disturb the peace of Nature; and the act of stealing from the traps of others by yielding to a strong desire produces the unmistakable dread of being followed by something large and frightening from his own conscience. One of the things we ordinarily neglect commenting upon in reading such a vivid description of an adventure, perhaps because we reduce its significance by calling it a "boyish adventure," is the way in which it enacts a fantasy that most children have. Wordsworth is not giving an account simply of an adventure and of a child's "guilty conscience."

The "fell destroyer" who "in thought and wish" seems a "trouble to the peace" of Nature is enjoying the anxious feeling of asserting his will. Powerful in the capture and possession of birds, he is himself overpowered by impulses at times, and experiences dread. Here is a sexual fantasy of the child's separation from the mother, of the sort that children enact in their play, often making the weak object stand for the mother—the object stolen, used, mastered, *put in a new place* or *in a new relation to the child.*[15] Not the objects but the actions and the feelings about action are significant—his assertion of will, his capture and possession of weak objects, his taking what he wants from someone else and his being followed. He has experienced the pleasure of willfulness, anxious wishes, excess of pleasure, and dread. The Oedipal configuration is apparent in this: he asserts his sensual will, which then controls him; he provokes an awesome "being" whose steps pursue a now frightened child. This fantasy may be seen in simple play, sometimes in the home, often outside. Sometimes it occurs most vividly in dreams, but often, in permissive homes in rural circumstances, exactly as Wordsworth recalls it as part of his "privileged" childhood. But one should not miss the significant difference either: most eight-year-old children have the continued reassuring presence of the mother they have "lost" figuratively but continue to pursue in this unconscious fantastic way; and they have the real enough love of the father, with whom they frighten themselves and with whom they continue to identify themselves. But Wordsworth's "privileged" growth has the meaning of "traumatic" growth exactly because at this early age he *was* alone—orphaned from his mother and necessarily schooled-out by his father. The reality pursued through a succession of objects is a *totally* absent reality, and the pursuit acquires a correspondingly greater urgency in time until his preference for solitude and Nature becomes a profound one. Gradually emerging from Nature is the Presence in Nature, which we have observed has unmistakable attributes; and Wordsworth's preference for solitude and Nature shows the way in which other resolutions are not developing normatively.

Associated with this recollection is the next one of him-

[15] See Freud, "Infantile Sexuality," CW VII, 197-199; "The Infantile Genital Organization," CW XIX, 141-145; and "A Special Type of Choice of Object Made by Men," CW XI, 163-175.

self as a plunderer climbing the lonesome peaks in pursuit of birds' nests:

> Nor less in springtime when on southern banks
> The shining sun had from his knot of leaves
> Decoy'd the primrose flower, and when the Vales
> And woods were warm, was I a plunderer then
> In the high places, on the lonesome peaks
> Where'er, among the mountains and the winds,
> The Mother Bird had built her lodge. Though mean
> My object, and inglorious, yet the end
> Was not ignoble. Oh! when I have hung
> Above the raven's nest, by knots of grass
> And half-inch fissures in the slippery rock
> But ill sustain'd, and almost, as it seem'd,
> Suspended by the blast which blew amain,
> Shouldering the naked crag; Oh! at that time,
> While on the perilous ridge I hung alone,
> With what strange utterance did the loud dry wind
> Blow through my ears! the sky seem'd not a sky
> Of earth, and with what motion mov'd the clouds!
>
> (I, 333-350)

This recollection, too, has the appropriateness of the traditional "boyish adventure" of bird-nesting, but has a latent associational one as it is used here as well. While the mother bird is absent, the boy is stealing nests, himself dangerously loose in his adventure and "ill-sustain'd." He recalls that "on the perilous ridge I hung alone," that the loud wind "with strange utterance" blew around him and that the effect was one of reality seeming unreal. The feeling of significance accompanying the recollection exceeds its manifest significance; its latent significance is that he was unconsciously enacting his several unconscious senses of being utterly alone, of knowing the mother is gone from the home, of wanting to seek the lost home, and of wanting to make real the inner feeling of being in danger by doing dangerous things. Wordsworth recalls the strangeness of reality as the wind rather than the child cries out, and the sky looks unreal. Hanging alone on the perilous ridge is very similar psychically to grasping a tree or wall to resist the pull inwards towards the "abyss of idealism." We have seen already one revealing characterization of the wind that cries out, "bewilder'd and forlorn," in the Revelation passage as an analogy of his own mind.

How strangely, too, Wordsworth imagined support in the wind itself, dividing this ability of his to climb and explore, which he shares with other children his age, between his own inner powers and Nature's imaginary support of him. Here, too, the significant difference is that for him, all such "privileged" experiences seem meant to attach the boy as future poet to Nature. His recollections are of being supported, led, haunted, instructed, formed, by Nature, rather than of being freed by experience to discover and test "a boy's will." Of course there is will expressed in all his activities, but it is circumscribed and directed regressively at limited goals because the usual conditions of child's play had been traumatically altered for him. To maintain in fantasy a lost relationship was the object of his play, rather than to develop a greater degree of autonomous being and power. He was aware of how difficult it was to maintain the burden of his privileged lot:

> Ah me! that all
> The terrors, all the early miseries
> Regrets, vexations, lassitudes, that all
> The thoughts and feelings which have been infus'd
> Into my mind, should ever have made up
> The calm existence that is mine when I
> Am worthy of myself! Praise to the end!
> Thanks likewise for the means! But I believe
> That Nature, oftentimes, when she would frame
> A favor'd Being, from his earliest dawn
> Of infancy doth open out the clouds,
> As at the touch of lightning, seeking him

With gentlest visitation; not the less,
Though haply aiming at the self-same end,
Does it delight her sometimes to employ
Severer interventions, ministry
More palpable, and so she dealt with me.
(I, 355-371)

When he speaks of the "self-sufficing power of solitude,"[16] which he says he may have felt too deeply and too early, we know that solitude was his way of *not* being alone. It was only then that he felt strongly the necessary "sentiment of being" as the oneness and the joy of life because it was then that he could feel the proximity of the "visible" and the "invisible" worlds. When Wordsworth says:

I was only then
Contented when with bliss ineffable
I felt the sentiment of Being spread
O'er all that moves, and all that seemeth still,
O'er all, that, lost beyond the reach of thought
And human knowledge, to the human eye
Invisible, yet liveth to the heart,
O'er all that leaps, and runs, and shouts, and sings,
Or beats the gladsome air, o'er all that glides
Beneath the wave, yea, in the wave itself
And mighty depth of waters. Wonder not
If such my transports were; for in all things
I saw one life, and felt that it was joy.
One song they sang, and it was audible,
Most audible then when the fleshly ear,
O'ercome by grosser prelude of that strain,
Forgot its functions, and slept undisturb'd . . .
(II, 418-434)

he is not simply perceiving the quickness of life in Nature and feeling more alive for feeling himself to be part of it. He is asserting rather that the apparent life of Nature and

[16] *The Prelude*, II, 78.

the real life of invisible things that live "to the heart" (as he feels they *do* live) are what he feels as the joy of life's oneness. But one should note here that the picture of what lives in Nature, of what "leaps, and runs, and shouts, and sings/ Or beats the gladsome air, [or] . . . glides beneath the wave," corresponds so nearly to the one idealized picture of *himself* in Nature, bathing, plunging, leaping, running abroad from his Mother's hut in "wantonness." The significant difference between the two pictures is the present psychic needs expressed by them: whereas the one recalls life with the living mother—the child seeking excitement in external nature—the other is consistent with Wordsworth's present intention to assure himself of his hold on reality. For him that reality is deeper than the external life of Nature; and it necessarily includes "all that, lost beyond the reach of thought/ And human knowledge, to the human eye/ Invisible yet liveth to the heart." In the "recesses of the heart," in the "unlit caverns of the mind," something still lives, about which the mind cannot think, but to which the Poet passionately attests while remembering the history of such feelings in himself. When Wordsworth exclaims:

> Ye Presences of Nature, in the sky
> Or on the earth! Ye Visions of the hills!
> And Souls of lonely places! can I think
> A vulgar hope was yours when Ye employ'd
> Such ministry, when Ye through many a year
> Haunting me thus among my boyish sports,
> On caves and trees, upon the woods and hills,
> Impress'd upon all forms the characters
> Of danger or desire, and thus did make
> The surface of the universal earth
> With triumph, and delight, and hope, and fear,
> Work like a sea?
>
> (I, 490-501)

he is expressing a present sense of Nature that he urgently needed in the years between 1797 and 1800 in order to write. By writing, he resumes the kind of activity necessary to his attempt to be Wordsworth, and not accidentally reveals the continuity of need expressed in all his past activities, "haunted" as they were.

Before considering further the problem of the autonomy of the poet, I wish to examine the expression given to the unconscious desire for death by Wordsworth: occasionally, his images of child and boy strangely qualify the subject of growth. Death, the deepest passivity, has the same appeal of reunion with the mother we have observed in other passive states of soul, but reunion made perfect by its permanence.

In Book I, Wordsworth passes immediately from the idealized picture of the happiness of the five year old in the original vale to the experiences of the nine-year-old child immediately after the death of his mother. There is no further recollection of the earlier years; there is no transition to these crucial years immediately after that traumatic loss; and there is, as has been observed, a striking omission when he mentions the change to the new vale ("to which, *ere long,* I was transplanted"). In Book V, while talking about literature, Wordsworth recalls the same period, himself as a nine year old "transplanted"; and he makes another significant connection between search and poetry, poetry and death. He begins:

> Well do I call to mind the very week
> When I was first entrusted to the care
> Of that sweet Valley; when its paths, its shores,
> And brooks, were like a dream of novelty
> To my half-infant thoughts; that very week
> While I was roving up and down alone,
> Seeking I knew not what . . .
>
> (V, 450-456)

The brief account that follows is of a drowning discovered accidentally by the boy. It is used to make a point about art primarily, and about Wordsworth only secondarily:

> Twilight was coming on; yet through the gloom,
> I saw distinctly on the opposite Shore
> A heap of garments, left, as I suppos'd,
> By one who there was bathing; long I watch'd,
> But no one own'd them; meanwhile the calm Lake
> Grew dark, with all the shadows on its breast,
> And, now and then, a fish up-leaping, snapp'd
> The breathless stillness. The succeeding day,
> (Those unclaimed garments telling a plain Tale)
> Went there a Company, and, in their Boat
> Sounded with grappling irons, and long poles.
> At length, the dead Man, 'mid that beauteous scene
> Of trees, and hills and water, bolt upright
> Rose with his ghastly face; a spectre shape
> Of terror even! and yet no vulgar fear,
> Young as I was, a Child not nine years old,
> Possess'd me; for my inner eye had seen
> Such sights before, among the shining streams
> Of Fairy Land, the Forests of Romance:
> Thence came a spirit hallowing what I saw
> With decoration and ideal grace;
> A dignity, a smoothness, like the works
> Of Grecian Art, and purest Poesy.
>
> (v, 459-481)

Art can anticipate experience; it can prepare even a child's mind to accept the crude facts of reality by prior imaginative experiences. In art, reality can be sought and at the same time held safely at a distance. Why Wordsworth's mind should always use examples from his own experience and why they usually refer in some way to aspects of the trauma (death) or to the time of trauma ("the very week when I . . .") are questions that remind us both of extreme self-consciousness and of the nature of an obsession and a fixation. With this example of the efficacy of art, Wordsworth reveals that the nine-year-old child has been aimlessly "seeking" something while wandering in the new vale and that he discovered death there. One could not surmise from this recollection what the child was seeking aimlessly. The lost reality? Death itself? The acceptance of the fact of death? Wordsworth says simply that art had prepared the child's mind for the shock of the experience. Though Wordsworth does not say so, drowning was new to him, but death was not.

The details, however, suggest other contexts in *The Prelude*, and the associations, conscious and unconscious, are worth following. For instance, the calm lake at twilight with "shadows on its breast" appears in another association in Book v. After mentioning the early death of his mother in Book v (it is here that he recalls her as "the heart and hinge of all our learnings and our loves"), he reviles the kind of mother who, unlike his own, makes a monster of her child with her plans for him. In contrast, he then presents the effect of Nature on a sensitive child in "There was a boy":

> There was a Boy, ye knew him well, ye Cliffs
> And Islands of Winander! many a time
> At evening, when the stars had just begun
> To move along the edges of the hills,
> Rising or setting, would he stand alone
> Beneath the trees, or by the glimmering Lake,
> And there, with fingers interwoven, both hands
> Press'd closely, palm to palm, and to his mouth
> Uplifted, he, as through an instrument,
> Blew mimic hootings to the silent owls
> That they might answer him.—And they would shout
> Across the watry Vale, and shout again,
> Responsive to his call, with quivering peals,
> And long halloos, and screams, and echoes loud
> Redoubled and redoubled; concourse wild

Of mirth and jocund din! And when it chanced
That pauses of deep silence mock'd his skill,
Then sometimes, in that silence, while he hung
Listening, a gentle shock of mild surprize
Has carried far into his heart the voice
Of mountain torrents; or the visible scene
Would enter unawares into his mind
With all its solemn imagery, its rocks,
Its woods, and that uncertain Heaven, receiv'd
Into the bosom of the steady Lake.
(v, 389-413)

But this famous passage is made part of an argument about growth and seems peculiar in consequence. For instance, why should it seem a sufficient answer to those who educate children too solicitously that Nature does a better job of looking out for children and their natural growth, if the boy of Winander presented in "There was a boy" dies, as we learn next, before he is ten? (Or twelve, in the 1850 version.) The lover of Nature may not like to consider that death is natural, that it comes perplexingly from Nature, though it is hard to avoid that awareness once the subject comes up. And Wordsworth brings up the subject himself. It would seem an unrealistic explanation that the boy was happier for his brief nine years in Nature than are less favored children who continue to live.

This nine year old, standing by the glimmering lake at dusk and calling out to the owls in Nature, would sometimes be answered by all of Nature in a strange silence. Then the visible scene would seem to sink into the lake itself in the dimming of dusk. Is the "bosom" of the lake with the "uncertain heaven" received into it an image of death as an attractive state? What is he to feel about the "deep" calm suggested by Nature as she darkens the scene and silences the distracting owls whose clamorous cries echo his own spontaneous impulse to cry out for an answering voice in Nature? The image of the dead man rising "bolt upright . . . with ghastly face" is one powerful association that for Wordsworth as a nine-year-old boy death was beneath the "breast" of the lake described in the same way: the "beauteous scene of trees and hills and water," "the calm lake/ . . . with all the shadows on its breast." But what might make one think that the appeal of death is being expressed here is that Wordsworth does present elsewhere his imaginative recollection of something powerfully attractive and more conclusive than dusk on the lake, and again in very similar imagery. He recalls a boyhood outing in boats ending at dusk with:

> But ere the fall
> Of night, when in our pinnace we return'd
> Over the dusky lake, and to the beach
> Of some small Island steer'd our course with one,
> The Minstrel of our troop, and left him there,
> And row'd off gently, while he blew his flute
> Alone upon the rock; *Oh! then the calm*
> *And dead still water lay upon my mind*
> *Even with a weight of pleasure,* and the sky
> Never before so beautiful, sank down
> Into my heart, and held me like a dream.
> (II, 170-180; my italics)

Wordsworth imagines being held "under," as in a dream, with the weight of pleasure—"the calm and dead still water" on his mind; the boy of Winander, now dead, is described with the same scene in his mind.

The more developed sense of death presented in "There was a boy" reveals something about Wordsworth himself:

> This Boy was taken from his Mates, and died
> In childhood, ere he was full ten years old.
> —Fair are the woods, and beauteous is the spot,
> The Vale where he was born; the Churchyard hangs
> Upon a Slope above the Village School,
> And there, along that bank, when I have pass'd

At evening, I believe that oftentimes
A full half-hour together I have stood
Mute—looking at the Grave in which he lies.
(v, 414-422)

This nostalgia for "the Vale where he was born" suggests something very characteristically Wordsworthian apparently being felt by Wordsworth about the birthplace of a dead youthful comrade, one who died, we suppose, when Wordsworth was about his age and living in that same vale. MS JJ, however, makes clear that the boy of "There was a boy" was originally Wordsworth himself:

There was a boy . . .
. . . .
And they would shout
Across the watry vale and shout again
Responsive to *my* call with tremulous sobs
And long halloes & screams & echoes loud
Redoubled & redoubled a wild scene
Of mirth & jocund din. And when it chanced
That pauses of deep silence mocked *my* skill
Then often, in that sudden shock of mild surprize
Would carry far into *my* heart the voice
Of mountain torrents: or the visible scene
Would enter unawares into *my* mind
With all its solemn imagery its rocks
Its woods & that uncertain heaven received
Into the bosom of the steady lake
(S recto, v, 389 of MS JJ; my italics)

Of course the change to its final form does make "him" no longer *simply* Wordsworth; Wordsworth's conscious artifice directs our attention away from himself, though we may continue to wonder about both Wordsworth and the boy. For some reason, Wordsworth has invented the boy that the editors of *The Prelude* have been at pains to identify.[17]

[17] *Ibid.*, v, 397-98. See editor's footnote, p. 547.

In this way, however, Wordsworth may idealize a remarkable boy modestly: having made his own mother the type of the loving and permissive mother, distinguishing her from the too-solicitous kind of mother, he then presents his own mother's child after all as the ideal of boyhood, Nature's and the poet's favorite. But the mother who dies is, for the purposes of her child's growth, less than ideal; and the boy who dies at age nine can only exemplify an ideal of Nature's or the Poet's that is *not* one of growth and life.

In the Lucy lyric, "Three years she grew in sun and shower," Wordsworth writes in this same paradoxical vein. The poet imagines Nature saying of Lucy "This Child I to myself will take"; and Nature fashions her "darling" as a creature of pure response to Nature and to life, saying further:

> Such thought to Lucy will I give
> While she and I together live
> Here in this happy dell.

As described in the poem, she has become so like the landscape that her death seems appropriately to complete her translation to it. The poet then concludes the poem, himself left puzzling the paradox of death as perhaps ideal life *in* Nature:

> Thus Nature spake—The work was done—
> How soon my Lucy's race was run!
> She died, and left to me
> This heath, this calm, this quiet scene;
> The memory of what has been,
> And never more will be.

Again, the death is not his own, though the ideal of pure response to Nature exemplified by Lucy had been; and the emotion felt at being left behind *is* strangely like that felt by one who has in some way outlived himself or outlived a part of himself associated with the feeling expressed here "for what has been/ And never more will be." The poem "A slumber did *my* spirit seal," in which his spirit ("she") seems dead to him ("rolled round in earth's diurnal course/ With rocks, and stones, and trees.") carries this paradox to its extreme statement.[18] No one, or nothing, capable of *feeling* is left to mourn the passing or to celebrate the deathly union or fulfillment; for the poet is not half-mourning, half-envying someone who was very like himself and who may have Life-in-Death, but rather writing numbly about himself as one experiencing Death-in-Life. It is a small poem, but indicative.

In no direct way has Wordsworth "intended" these further thoughts about the "There was a boy" passage, and yet the richness and consistency of the text occasion them. Why does Wordsworth make himself into someone else in order to present imaginatively the sadness of his own premature death? In the sad and nostalgic regard for the boy of Winander we see Wordsworth imagining death and mourning a boy who "died" at age nine, about when Wordsworth's mother died.

There are other examples; I shall present two from Book VII because they reveal different aspects of the deep conflict about growth. While recalling London, Wordsworth recollects the theater and tells the story of the "Maid of Buttermere" because he had been deeply moved by it. It had been made into a bad play but was to him a story fit for

[18] "Three years she grew . . . ," *Poetical Works*, p. 148. And for convenience I quote the other poem:

A slumber did my spirit seal,
  I had no human fears;
She seemed a thing that could not feel
  The touch of earthly years.

No motion hath she now, no force;
  She neither hears nor sees;
Rolled round in earth's diurnal course,
  With rocks, and stones, and trees.

For an interesting discussion of this phenomenon in Wordsworth's poetry, see David Ferry, *The Limits of Mortality*, p. 81.

poetry, especially since the Maid was a native of his own hills. The Maid, the story goes, was joined in false wedlock to a man from the city who had courted her although he had a wife and children. She was then deserted by him when she was pregnant. Wordsworth associates his own childhood with the Maid's:

> For we were nursed, as almost might be said,
> On the same mountains; Children at one time
> Must haply often on the self-same day
> Have from our several dwellings gone abroad
> To gather daffodils on Coker's Stream.
>
> (VII, 341-345)

The passage could, I think, call to mind the picture in Book I of his own idealized innocence, himself as the child run abroad from his mother's hut "over the sandy fields, leaping through groves/ Of yellow grunsel. . . ."[19] The story of the disruption of the Maid's life reminds him of her prior innocence, and unconsciously of his own. The unconscious association proceeds, then; his childhood innocence has, in a sense, joined or replaced hers:

> These last words utter'd, to my argument
> I was returning, when, with sundry Forms
> Mingled, that in the way which I must tread
> Before me stand, thy image rose again,
> Mary of Buttermere!
>
> (VII, 346-350)

The whole story, which is simply an eighteenth-century sentimental piece, is obviously saved for Wordsworth by what, almost in spite of itself, it evokes.

The story, which seems so sentimental even to Wordsworth ("These feelings, in themselves/ Trite, do yet scarcely seem so . . ."), is not of his invention, but continues despite his willingness to let it go. As in the Imagination passage in Book VI, Wordsworth is describing a present

[19] *The Prelude*, I, 291-292.

event in the mind: the image of the Maid and Mother, like the power that rises from the mind's abyss, "rose again" to interrupt the on-going progress of the poem and to evoke further poetic associations:

> She lives in peace
> Upon the ground where she was born and rear'd;
> Without contamination does she live
> In quietness, without anxiety:
> Beside the mountain-Chapel sleeps in earth
> Her new-born Infant, fearless as a lamb
> That thither comes, from some unsheltered place,
> To rest beneath the little rock-like Pile
> When storms are blowing. Happy are they both,
> Mother and Child!
>
> (VII, 350-359)

Strangely, this husbandless mother is imagined by Wordsworth as a living being permanently watching over her dead-but-only-sleeping babe. The babe is "asleep" upon the breast of Nature but could "wake" and find the mother there, like the Blest Babe waking from sleep on its mother's breast. This may account for their strange happiness, if anything can be said to. The mother is a living Presence in Nature; and Wordsworth, who here regards in imagination the infant sleeping on the mountain slope in the graveyard near the mountain chapel, is exactly like the Wordsworth standing sadly over the grave of the boy of Winander, which is his own grave.

While Wordsworth develops the theme of "unnaturalness" in the life of London in Book VII, he is unconsciously developing the Mother-child-death association. For instance, he next recalls being struck by the appearance of a certain beautiful boy child in a theatre lobby in London, and again finds the memory peculiarly affecting:

> A rosy Babe, who, for a twelvemonth's space
> Perhaps, had been of age to deal about

Articulate prattle, Child as beautiful
As ever sate upon a Mother's knee;
The other was the Parent of that Babe;
But on the Mother's cheek the tints were false,
A painted bloom. 'Twas at a Theatre
That I beheld this Pair; the boy had been
The pride and pleasure of all lookers-on
In whatsoever place; but seem'd in this
A sort of Alien scatter'd from the clouds.
Of lusty vigour, more than infantine,
He was in limbs; in face a cottage rose
Just three parts blown; a Cottage Child, but ne'er
Saw I, by Cottage or elsewhere, a Babe
By Nature's gifts so honor'd. Upon a Board
Whence an attendant of the Theatre
Serv'd out refreshments, had this Child been plac'd,
And there he sate, environ'd with a Ring
Of chance Spectators, chiefly dissolute men
And shameless women; treated and caress'd,
Ate, drank, and with the fruit and glasses play'd,
While oaths, indecent speech, and ribaldry
Were rife about him as are songs of birds
In spring-time after showers. The Mother, too,
Was present! but of her I know no more
Than hath been said, and scarcely at this time
Do I remember her. But I behold
The lovely Boy as I beheld him then,
Among the wretched and the falsely gay,
Like one of those who walk'd with hair unsinged
Amid the fiery furnace.

(VII, 367-398)

Here, unfortunately, the poetry is more awful than the experience, which is melodramatically overblown and sentimentally gilded. But the point of the juxtaposition seems clear: at a London theatre one can see the sad story of a Good Rural Mother (and her Child) or witness the common reality of a Bad City Mother (and her Child). The crude vitality of dissolute city life draws from Wordsworth the somewhat puritanical tone with which he expresses aversion. The Beautiful Boy, seen as "a cottage rose," is made to seem a thing of Nature, as much out of the true place of life as a rose in the city or a cherub on earth, an "alien scattered from the clouds." As an infant "among the wretched and the falsely gay," the child is Innocence surrounded by Experience—Innocence not yet corrupted or destroyed by such life. But although Blake (who comes to mind) saw the city for what it was, he also made it the symbol of human imaginative adulthood. Unimaginativeness, which borders on depravity, makes London, but human poetic genius makes the New Jerusalem. The divine human does not dwell in mere Nature; his spirit makes its own habitat. In contrast, Wordsworth imagines his human cherub rather strangely in Nature:

He hath since
Appear'd to me oft-times as if embalm'd
By Nature; through some special privilege,
Stopp'd at the growth he had; destined to live,
To be, to have been, come and go, a Child
And nothing more, no partner in the years
That bear us forward to distress and guilt,
Pain and abasement, beauty in such excess
Adorn'd him in that miserable place.
So have I thought of him a thousand times,
And seldom otherwise. But he perhaps
Mary! may now have liv'd till he could look
With envy on thy nameless Babe that sleeps
Beside the mountain Chapel, undisturb'd!
(VII, 398-411)

As an afterthought, his own aversion to the "fallen" world makes Wordsworth imagine that the child grown to manhood in it might prefer the tranquillity of death, were he capable, paradoxically, of a moment of Wordsworthian detachment and vision. It is more likely that the cherub would simply become another Londoner, at home among the ribald, the wretched, and the falsely gay. But the kind of death implied here by Wordsworth, however, is different from the kind he has just been imagining in the story of the Maid of Buttermere, where death does not come of any bad experience of growth but blissfully precludes the necessity of it.

The real problem here is a familiar one: the subject of growth was not a clear one for Wordsworth; he could not easily imagine alternatives to his own problem-burdened sense of "ideal" growth, and really had very little interest in the subject beyond his preoccupation with himself as a changing being. Living in retirement in 1804, having cast off the "burthen of his own unnatural self" and its city life, Wordsworth can imagine death, too, as a suitable withdrawal from the life of the historical present, which often kills the spirit before the man. The poet survives the recent experience of "distress and guilt, pain and abasement" and believes himself restored by Nature; but looking back through the years in an effort to idealize his growth, he momentarily imagines and idealizes instead the arrest of growth in very early childhood: "through some special *privilege*/ Stopp'd at the growth he had, destined to live,/ To be, to have been, come and go, a child/ And nothing more. . . ." The "rosy babe" is about three at most; he is exactly at that ideal pre-Oedipal age at which "articulate prattle" and the recent mastery of bodily motion brings on the stage of freer and more exploratory play. With assured possession of mother and home, the child begins to play at being powerful and autonomous, and gradually replaces the Blest Babe. Unconsciously idealized, this was the ideal of "life" opposed to the ideal of sleeping death or the oblivion of "the one interior life . . ./ In which all beings live with God, are lost/ In God and Nature. . . ."

One must wonder, however, what the appeal of this particular idealization is to Wordsworth, strange as it is.

Wordsworth has imagined a kind of sentient exemption from life. It is as if, in "the years that bear us forward to distress and guilt, pain and abasement" the greatest "privilege" one can have is the conviction that Nature has intended something special, as when Wordsworth exclaims of himself:

> Ah me! that all
> The terrors, all the early miseries
> Regrets, vexations, lassitudes, that all
> The thoughts and feelings which have been infus'd
> Into my mind, should ever have made up
> The calm existence that is mine when I
> Am worthy of myself! Praise to the end!
> Thanks likewise for the means! But I believe
> That Nature, often times, when she would frame
> A favor'd Being . . .
>
> (I, 355-364)

And it is as if, at the same time, the Poet knew that an ideal of continued growth cannot even be adequately imagined. He gives perfect images of something young that could grow, and then reveals imaginatively that there is not so much difference after all between the ideal child in Nature and the ideal child prematurely trapped in the fallen world. How could one choose between country and city, Nature and History, on the basis of idealized images of the child dead or growing to wish himself dead? Perhaps the only difference is that Wordsworth can imagine the continuing presence of the good mother in Nature. Like the Maid of Buttermere, she watches over her child who "sleeps" in the earth, which is something Wordsworth imagines the city child envying. In imagination, Wordsworth takes the Beautiful Boy away from the Bad Mother, and gives him, too, ("embalm'd") to Nature and to Death.

Despite the bad poetry of both these examples,[20] it is

[20] It is only a speculation about passages of bad poetry in *The Prelude*, but I think it is curious that Wordsworth often expresses

significant that Wordsworth imagines a Good and Bad Mother so simplistically. The unconscious appeal of the Good Mother to him we have observed in many instances. But here he recollects a Bad Mother at the moment when she was *betraying* her child to the city world of dissolute men.[21] It is no longer an anticipation of my argument to say that this is placed in Book VII because Wordsworth is beginning to write about his own troubled experience of the City, of the world of men and of History. He is recalling reluctantly that his approach to adult life was made with the confidence that "comes from" Nature, but that he was repulsed in a way he could not understand at the time, nor show that he understood now. The sense of betrayal by both mother and Nature was strong in him after his crisis, though expressed only in its denied form.

3. The Truest Memory of Early Childhood

There is only one other passage in *The Prelude* that recalls vividly the period of the original home while both parents were still alive. Though it was composed as early as most of the passages now in Books I and II, it was not transcribed from MS U and V until Wordsworth placed it in Book XI. The passage is the first of two recollections used in an argument about significant particular moments in memory, "spots of time," to which his mind returns for strength. One is a recollection of himself as a five year old; the other, of himself as a thirteen year old just before the occasion of

strong feeling, himself affected, about certain incidents that most of his readers do not care for at all. The gross sentimentality, either implicit in them or superadded by Wordsworth, of "The Maid of Buttermere," the Beautiful Boy at the Theater, the "grave" of The Boy of Winander, the Shepherd and His Son, and Vaudracour and Julia, may have affected Wordsworth's ability to write well whenever he touched upon matters that unconsciously appealed to repressed infantile feelings in him.

21 In the 1850 version of the apostrophe to London (VII, 722f), Wordsworth makes London the Bad Mother who destroys her children ("what the mighty city is herself/ To thousands upon thousands of her sons . . .").

his father's death. The significance of the argument in which the two passages appear, the significance of the two passages taken together and of their position in the poem will be dealt with later. Here, I shall consider the indications in the first passage of the degree of normal Oedipal resolution the child had undergone by age eight, and the effect of the traumatic death of the mother on it.

At a time
When scarcely (I was then not six years old)
My hand could hold a bridle, with proud hopes
I mounted, and we rode towards the hills:
We were a pair of Horsemen; honest James
Was with me, my encourager and guide.
We had not travell'd long, ere some mischance
Disjoin'd me from my Comrade, and, through fear
Dismounting, down the rough and stony Moor
I led my Horse, and stumbling on, at length
Came to a bottom, where in former times
A Murderer had been hung in iron chains.
The Gibbet-mast was moulder'd down, the bones
And iron case were gone; but on the turf,
Hard by, soon after that well deed was wrought
Some unknown hand had carved the Murderer's name.
The monumental writing was engraven
In times long past, and still, from year to year,
By superstition of the neighborhood,
The grass is clear'd away; and to this hour
The letters are all fresh and visible.
Faltering, and ignorant where I was, at length
I chanced to espy those characters inscribed
On the green sod: forthwith I left the spot
And, reascending the bare Common, saw
A naked Pool that lay beneath the hills,
The Beacon on the summit, and more near,
A Girl who bore a Pitcher on her head
And seem'd with difficult steps to force her way

Against the blowing wind. It was, in truth,
An ordinary sight; but I should need
Colours and words that are unknown to man
To paint the visionary dreariness
Which, while I look'd all round for my lost Guide,
Did at that time invest the naked Pool,
The Beacon on the lonely Eminence,
The Woman, and her garments vex'd and toss'd
By the strong wind.

(XI, 279-316)

There is no suggestion of why the child is riding off, of whether he is being sent somewhere or being allowed to go along or simply being taken on an outing. In any event, the recollection of adventure begins with the feeling of inadequacy being overcome: a child whose hand "scarcely . . . could hold a bridle" is doing a man's things. Proudly mounted, the child masters a much larger and more powerful thing than his own body. Encouraged and guided by a grown man, he is one of "a pair of horse*men*." In comparison, playing with a hobby horse at home would be meaningfully but merely playing at something.

There is no suggestion of what caused his separation from his "Comrade," but then, an exact account of what happened is not what the recollection seems to intend or accomplish. For instance, there is no end to the story. The feelings presented are intensified; the poet associates "visionary dreariness" with describing what was seen in this condition of being frightened and lost; and the poet simply names a second time the things recollected as seen in this way. One may believe Wordsworth that this "spot of time" recollected has a "vivifying virtue" and invisibly repairs the mind, but Wordsworth does not say how it does. Instead, certain feelings are recalled, a situation, and some vivid images.

The fear felt at discovering the separation changed the entire experience, so that the vividness of what follows seems to make the recollection into an attempt to present the feeling of separation itself. The guide, who was probably found again, is not said to be found again, nor is the horse remounted. It would seem, too, that we have an account of how the sense of "visionary dreariness" was discovered: a child, feeling like a man, found himself fearfully alone and only a child. Wordsworth simply wants us to believe the example of his once having been strong, from which strength comes at other moments. Since, however, we can draw upon the other contextual meanings of "visionary" from our analysis, we should observe that "visionary" has been consistently associated with the sense of the mother and with the repressed trauma of separation from her by her death. Yet here is a vivid memory of a period earlier than the trauma being spoken of in the same way. Fixations to traumas color the account of all recollections and assimilate memories from the more distant past to their own enforced view of the life of the self.

We cannot say what fantasies the five-year-old boy had while feeling like a man, nor even what fantasies came to be unconsciously associated with this memory from the older Wordsworth who continued to feel its ineffable significance while writing about it. Some memories—those Freud deals with as "screen memories"[22]—have a specific relationship with repressed memories and fantasies, concealing them by taking their place in recollection, yet suggesting them by the significant configuration of elements present in the "screen." Earlier events can become screens for later traumatic events, as I think is the case here. Only speculatively does one attempt to say what an apparently symbolic picture means to someone else, but between Wordsworth's feeling for the significance of this "spot of time" and its otherwise apparent pointlessness, there is some encouragement to suggest another meaning.

The child, who dismounts in fear and stumbles along,

[22] See Freud, "Moses and Monotheism," CW XXIII, 72-80; also, "The Interpretation of Dreams," CW IV and V.

is for the time being on his own in reality; the difference between being like a man and being only a child is fearfully plain. What is reality to him? In earlier play fantasies most five year olds have already experienced their wishes to master things, and with continuing growth and increasing explicitness their wishes are to master the mother and exclude the father, thereby acknowledging first in the safe situation of play, their real separation from the mother and the real significance of the father they would exclude and replace. The period of initial conflict with the father would then be just beginning. The child emboldened by the success of his fantastic playing begins to behave in such a way as to bring on that conflict. But in this incident, we should observe that it was the delight of accepting men as men and himself as a man that the child was testing more in reality than in play. When in the incident he is lost, he cannot simply abandon a game that has started to go too far, as the child, exaggerating his mastery of things in play, has abandoned games in the past when his wishes have started to discomfort him with their too great explicitness. Here, instead, trust and emulation distinguish the sense of camaraderie. The recollection of his fearful separation from his guide throws him by mischance back upon childish inadequacy. (It is only later that the poet recalls this as a source of his strength.)

It is, then, exactly the vividly recollected pleasure of being-like-a-man that suggests that at age five-and-a-half the child had already achieved a quite liveable sense of separation from the mother, considerably greater than that presented in the idealized recollection of himself as "her" happy five-year-old naked savage. "Being-like-a-man"—the necessary willingness to identify oneself further with grown men—comes of Oedipal resolution and identification with the father. It would seem, then, that the child who is recollected at the beginning of the incident had already experienced relief from his futile and fantastic conflict with the father, and was living in the happier experience of the latency period of his growth. The eagerness to acquire manly and worldly skills which then manifests itself reveals the child's more realistic acceptance of the world.

In normative growth, we have said, the loss of the mother, in the figurative sense of loss, is repressed along with the kinds of unacceptable wishes directed at her and at the father; and from the inordinate nature of such wishes the child experiences relief. The too great dependence on the mother is relieved by this greater acceptance of the father; and through the father, primarily, the child can enter the less fostering world beyond the home. Of course the child has simply acquired a more realistic sense of the nature of his dependency on the real mother, who is still there; in "losing" her figuratively, he has lost only the overt infantile attachment to her, which persists dynamically, unconsciously. And in acquiring a more realistic sense of the father, he has also acquired a dynamic and unconscious fear of him. Freud also argued that the lasting consequences of repression were greater than their immediate usefulness to a child's growth. Repression determines, all but irreparably, the restless human sense of desire and of loss, as well as the fear of death and of individuality.

If Wordsworth's memory both conceals and reveals repressed traumatic matters, we must wonder how the repression of a later trauma affects the earlier and more normal repressions of growth, and we must wonder, too, whether or not Wordsworth's vivid feeling of recollection is accurately of a single incident, of an incident to which things have been added unconsciously, or of more than one incident run together. Most memories of the period covered by infantile amnesia and repression are screen memories—vivid but without apparent point, and something less than accurate. When one thinks about it, Wordsworth's only other "memory" of himself as a five-year-old "naked savage" is not a memory; it is a selective recollection of habitual activity, a collocation of images presenting an idealized picture of a five year old's life, from which all traces of psychic conflict are missing. There are no other memories of Wordsworth before age eight, except this one in Book XI, if it is a true memory. As a screen, however, it might be a compromise between things actually remembered and the very real things disowned by memory that cause the compelling and of course real feeling of significance for the person honestly recollecting. It is as this that I shall consider the incident Wordsworth presents, beginning by saying that Wordsworth most likely saw what he says he saw.

Let us return to Wordsworth's mention of "visionary dreariness" and our observation about his habitual use of "visionary." It is used in talking of the experiences of soul associated with the sense of the mother and of absent realities; it is the poetic self's way of seeing things in its poetic quest. When he says "visionary dreariness" he is characterizing what he saw "then" as he has since come to describe such experiences—that is, as he would describe it now. It is not what separation meant to the five-year-old boy that shows here, but rather what separation has come since then to mean to Wordsworth, a meaning that dates from the trauma. Unconscious matters that have the greatest urgency are, in this particular way, affecting the memory. For instance, a very young child, a three year old, would feel separation from the mother acutely, if he experienced that separation in any unfamiliar way. A three year old has barely begun to play at separation from the mother; he would not have, then, any of the sense of being-like-a-man that Wordsworth describes in remembering his setting off from home. On the other hand, Wordsworth's account of being lost, of his dismounting and stumbling on, of his looking round for his "lost guide," lacks exactly the appropriate resolution to the story that one would expect to be its point, from the point of view of the five-and-a-half year old. The story should go: lost, he was frightened, yet he continued on his own looking for his lost guide, and either did find him or found his way onwards or homewards again; or he was rescued by his guide or by someone. New reasons for trusting men and one's self identified with them are the exaggerated point of such memorable adventures,[23] all implying reasons learned in Oedipal conflict for separating oneself from women. Were a boy rescued by a woman, who would respond to his plight in that circumstance in a "motherly" way, he would not be so likely to remember that story as an adventure. But Wordsworth intensifies the feeling of separation from the man, of feeling lost, and of seeing with "visionary dreariness." It is to the Wordsworth writing in the present that these latter states have a compelling urgency, and this is what makes this memory different from whatever it was originally as an adventure to the child. Until age eight, he would have remembered it in terms of some simple "manly" resolution of the incident; afterwards, as here, it is recalled because it has acquired another meaning.

We may imagine what the five-and-a-half-year-old boy experienced. The fears felt at being separated in this way would have to do with the strangeness of the world beyond the home, which the child had entered feeling pleased with the exaggeration of his readiness to enter it and trusting the manly presence of his guide. All boys must learn to generalize that relationship of trust based on the recent resolution of conflict with the father. They have only recently experienced and renounced the violence of their wishes and achieved a measure of trust about themselves. So, too, the projected form of that violent wish, felt as the father's desire to kill the child, has only recently been resolved in such a way that there can develop a tentative further resolution in favor of trusting men. Here, he trusts "honest James, my father's servant." What else a child will undergo in his further experience of society as a structure reflecting the personalities of men awaits him at this point; he does not yet know by what political, economic, religious, and social rituals men maintain their trust and express their

23 See *The Prelude*, VII, 222-311 (the story of the Shepherd and His Son) and below, pp. 307ff.

distrust of each other with all the original ambivalence of the father-son relationship. Within the home the child continues to need the comfort of his mother, but in preparation for encounters with the world, it is not the mother that the man-child will seek, but his model. Beyond the home, there is still the danger of strangeness and strangers felt by the child because of the persistence in his unconscious of repressed violent wishes of "doing" and fears of "being-done-to." I should observe, then, that an encounter with a strange man in this circumstance, even one who is in fact "rescuing" the boy, would be likely to produce feelings of fear and distrust first, and then the reassuring feelings of trust-by-identification for men who behave in a "fatherly" way. Only the simple manly resolution of the incident would be memorable to the child afterwards.

The five-and-a-half year old came upon the spot where "in former times/ A murderer had been hung in iron chains." The mere strangeness of the mouldered apparatus itself might have frightened him away, but it is possible that so young a child already knew about murder and murderers, what a gibbet was, and even about the actual story attached to this spot. It seems more likely, it is true, that here after-knowledge of these local things has become attached imperceptibly to Wordsworth's recollection. It is possible that the murderer's name was something the child knew, in some way. Whether or not he could read, he could have been told that the characters spelled the murderer's name, though here too it seems likely that after-knowledge has filled out the story. In any event, he was frightened already, and this strangeness frightened him more. If unconscious fears of violence attach to strangeness, it is only an accidental appropriateness that makes the gibbet and the punished murderer seem appropriate here to the psychic reasons for such fears. A large piece of mouldering farm equipment that was strange to the child might have frightened him as much.

In this experience of separation, it is possible that the

child saw exactly what the poet says, the naked pool, the beacon on the summit, the girl who bore a pitcher on her head. They were not invested with "visionary dreariness" at the time, but the other relevant feelings actually felt by the child are lost, along with the simple ending of the story. The elements held in this "visionary" configuration are very interesting. Wordsworth names them twice; and the naming seems to convey to him again exactly the feeling he has in mind as a source of strength. Now whether or not these elements are actually being recalled from that particular incident or have become attached to it in other ways, the fact is that the feeling he has in mind has a history and these elements feel true to it, which suggests that they have symbolic meanings in relation to it. We should refer these "recollected" images to his habitual way of talking about himself to speculate about their meanings.

It is surprising, first of all, how very simply the images are very common dream symbols: the naked pool in a landscape enclosed by hills as woman or the mother; the mountain with the beacon on the top as phallic man or the father. The girl who bore a pitcher on her head is also woman or the mother; the pitcher, as something which holds and pours fluid to drink, is the symbol of the breast, here, as often in dreams, displaced but emphasized by that displacement.[24] But if one were simply to take poetic associations

[24] Displaced (on the woman's head) but emphasized by that very curious displacement, the object is a common enough symbol in dream and fantasy. Perhaps the displacement is crucial here instead of merely grotesque. The psychosexual stages of growth reveal a gradual evolutionary change in images of power—certainly from maternal to paternal, but actually, for boys, from breast to penis (see Edmund Bergler, *Counterfeit Sex*). The child contests the mother's powers over him by adducing his own. Wordsworth deals with power in *The Prelude* by speaking of powers originally "drunk" from the mother, later used freely and with superiority as one's own. Though the subject is one fraught with conflict for him, the picture is clear enough. It is also curious how sublimated his powers are; they are those finally of the mind. We have seen, too, how Wordsworth makes the Poet maternal (XIII, 204-210). It is perhaps less surprising, then, to find the pitcher on the head.

from Wordsworth, it becomes immediately obvious that the gentle aspects of the landscape form the earliest configuration of the "Presence" that is the mother in Nature. Associations of naked, pool, bathing, lake, vale are all vividly associated with the mother. So, too, in ways we have only touched on but shall treat later at greater length, does the mountain standing at a distance and dominating the landscape stand for the father.[25] Beacons, like all structures, are made by and associated with men ("the towers of Cockermouth . . . my father's House"). The child contemplating the summit of a far-off hill, in the passage on the public way,[26] unconsciously prepares the journey-metaphor of his growth; and the young man on his journey through the Alps, unable to cross the summit of the mountain, experiences dejection, which is a memory the Poet transforms to joy when he uses the mountain as the analogy of his own mind and of God's. We shall attempt presently to determine the significance of the mountain summit precisely by his use of it; first, in his moonlight experience of "boat-stealing" as a child, where the mountain strides after him; and then in the visionary experience on Mount Snowdon, in which the Poet stands emblematically on the mountain's summit between earth and heaven, like a lord and master.

If we see "the naked pool that lay beneath the hills" and "the beacon on the summit" as symbolic representations of the mother and the father in relation to the child beholding them, one simple sense of the basic family triangle is seen as it would be seen in its Oedipal phase. The mountain dominates the landscape, and the child is a very small figure in relation to the two. I have said that to the child the concentration of feeling about being separated from his guide would make the experience of being found in relation to the experience of being lost the memorable part of the incident. The reappearance of the "lost guide" would complete the symbolic picture by supplying again the already

[25] See below, pp. 270ff. and 286ff.

[26] *The Prelude,* XII, 145f.

acceptable image of the child's potential as a man as a way of resolving the relationships seen in the family triangle, where the child is too small and the parents too large. Here, the child is not calling out for his mother; *he* proceeds, though Wordsworth's recollection does not. Why, though, is "visionary dreariness" emphasized? and why is the last image "The woman, and her garments vex'd and toss'd/ By the strong wind"?

First, we should recall that we have already looked at connections between poetry and the mother, between poetry and the poet's desire to survive, and between the necessity of being the Poet and of being Wordsworth; then we should supply some of those connections here. If being the Poet is Wordsworth's strongest sense of his identity and if the "visionary" faculty is the "privilege" and power of the Poet, then his earliest sense of "visionary" experience while all alone will seem like the earliest memory of his strength. And that is exactly what Wordsworth is "recalling" here, though we shall say that the earlier incident is being recalled in an altered form adjusted to a traumatic need. It is only in retrospect that Wordsworth's mind is making this earlier memory into his *first* experience of what was to become the characteristic experience of the Poet, being alone in what could be a too fearful reality—the child at the death of his mother; the boy in his solitude; the lonely traveler "lost" in his own mind (in the Imagination passage) and on the verge of "visionary" experience. He has unconsciously changed a memory from an earlier experience based on Oedipal resolution to one that fits with his repressed trauma and with his powerfully fixated sense of his poetic identity since then. Because of the subsequent traumatic death of the mother, the child had to deny *all* earlier senses of loss and separation. The child did *not* cry out for the mother, but proceeded—to survive, to seek the visible world, to discover his "visionary" powers. The Poet, who grew out of that child, described as "visionary" the experiences by which that lost relationship was preserved;

and in consequence even such an earlier experience had to be unconsciously altered to fit the fiction in which the strengths of a Poet seem to be acquired and developed.

In several contexts I have treated the connections between the wind, the child, and the mother—such as the "awakening breeze," the "ghostly language of the ancient earth," the "midnight storm," the "mild creative breeze," the "tempest," the "viewless winds of poetry," the "strange utterance" of the loud wind, and the "winds thwarting winds, bewilder'd and forlorn."[27] With such contexts in mind, we should look again at the figure of

> A girl who bore a pitcher on her head
> And seem'd with difficult steps to force her way
> Against the blowing wind . . . . .
> . . . .
> The Woman, and her garments vex'd and toss'd
> By the strong wind . . .

What is expressed here in a limited way, in a way that disguises it by attaching it to an earlier and simpler incident, is some of the fearful and dreary sense of the "privileged" prospect for life of the child whose adventure was interrupted. His normal motion forward in growth was blocked, and his vision was fixated on this one disturbed and disturbing image that would take many "visionary" forms, but remain, as a psychic necessity, the same: the mother in the vexing wind. The emphasis on separation and "'visionary dreariness" in this "spot of time" fits with the time of the trauma when the child, in the period after Oedipal resolution, was feeling like a man and found himself fearfully and unaccountably alone and only a child. It is from this later circumstance that the imperatives we have observed as those directing Wordsworth to survival and "visionary" search derive.

It may be said that the desire for autonomy persists un-

[27] *The Prelude,* II, 245; II, 328-329; II, 392; I, 43; I, 46; V, 619-621 and V, 595-597: 1850 version; I, 348; VI, 560.

consciously associated with the desire for possession of the mother. If we have observed in Wordsworth an unconscious tendency to repeat the trauma in action or in imagination (so that it can be consciously realized), then here we may say that the poet is unconsciously seeking a way out of his own unduly constricted psychic landscape, in which the child is too small, the parents too large, the guide lost, and the "visionary" faculty fixated on this last significant symbolic image of the mother. To Wordsworth, for whom the vale and its imagery retained such significance and appeal, the vale is the limiting vale of childhood, to which he returns from his experience of the world beyond it, trying to imagine the genesis of his unique sense of himself in it. The journey "over the naked summit of a far-off hill" is a psychic quest, for which the public road early in his life symbolically became "an invitation into space boundless, a guide into eternity." One should notice that not the world as it is, but eternity is imagined beyond the vale, which indicates again how the disappearance of the mother from the actual vale implied the disappearance of the visible world's reality. The boy who grew and sought the visible world experienced life as a journey beyond the vale, and gradually realized along the way his dissatisfaction with the life of the self in the visible world. The poet who emerged from that frustrated search in the visible world became poetically obsessed with the experience of Mind—his own, the Poet's, Man's, and God's. Through memories and imaginings, he consciously sought the visionary truth and unconsciously sought the truth about the "visionary" obsession.

In this unconsciously altered memory of early separation, the poet presents his discovery in retrospect of the "visionary" obsession and of the deep feeling acquired early in life of having no model and no guide. What he seeks, when he is true to this sense of himself as the Poet, is not in the visible world; and therefore he communicates that he could not have been guided by men in his search nor profit from what they could tell of him of what may be found in life or the world. It was when he discovered the resemblance between the winds as the "ghostly language of the ancient earth" and the voices heard in poetry that he found models and guides. The Poet would seek through the imagery of the "visible world" for the visionary truth of the "invisible world" that "liveth to the heart" replete with its lost objects and lost relationships. It was in this way that Wordsworth unconsciously sought both the mother through Nature *and* true autonomy from her; for once to have found her shade in the unlit caverns of the mind or in the recesses of the heart, illuminated finally and clearly by his own imaginative descent or by an awful revelation, would have been to experience what Orpheus did: reunion, recognition and loss. There was a tradition, of which Milton knew, that Orpheus was "the first interpreter of the physical and spiritual secrets of heaven and hell."[28] Wordsworth's "Orphean dark descent," we have said, would lead him to confront the projections of mortal hopes and fears with the realities of their psychic origins in "the mind of man," in his own mind. Wordsworth had an uncommonly strong sense of himself as "a mind beset/ With images, and haunted by itself."[29]

[28] See Merritt Hughes, ed., *Paradise Lost,* p. 79, footnote to III, 17.
[29] *The Prelude,* VI, 179-180.

CHAPTER VI

THE WORLD BEYOND THE VALE

1. Cambridge

Early in *The Prelude,* Wordsworth gives a description of himself as Nature's chosen youth, the young Poet at the moment of his Dedication to poetry about to enter upon his ministry. It was obviously very important to him, both as an experience and as a passage of poetry, for he had intended to use it as the symbolic conclusion of the projected five-book *Prelude.*[1] As the passage appears in Book IV of *The Prelude,* it has perhaps been simplified to fit his revised intention to seek his present image in his whole story, but it nevertheless stands very fittingly as a picture of the young poet, as Wordsworth remembers and imagines himself then. We find in it the particular image of the young poet on the road that we are most likely to bear in mind while Wordsworth continues his account of journeys and realizations in the intervening years, and its exalted and strongly self-affirming tone makes clear how Wordsworth carried a mantle of aspirations with him into his further experience of life beyond the vale.

It is very striking that in his account of his dedication to poetry in his young manhood his attachment to Nature shows more noticeably as a habitual reserve which has behind it a whole history of psychic predisposition; but the formal "dedication" spoken of here is a religious dedication, solemnly opposed to other tendencies he had recognized in himself at that time. Lifted out of its context in the argument, his Dawn Dedication appears in Book IV in

[1] *The Prelude,* p. xxxvii.

this way: he is walking home at dawn from a party during his summer vacation from Cambridge:

Ere we retired,
The cock had crow'd, the sky was bright with day.
Two miles I had to walk along the fields
Before I reached my home. Magnificent
The morning was, a memorable pomp,
More glorious than I ever had beheld.
The Sea was laughing at a distance; all
The solid Mountains were as bright as clouds,
Grain-tinctured, drench'd in empyrean light;
And, in the meadows and the lower grounds,
Was all the sweetness of a common dawn,
Dews, vapours, and the melody of birds,
And Labourers going forth into the fields.
—Ah! need I say, dear Friend, that to the brim
My heart was full; I made no vows, but vows
Were then made for me; bond unknown to me
Was given, that I should be, else sinning greatly,
A dedicated Spirit. On I walk'd
In blessedness, which even yet remains.
(IV, 327-345)

His description of the beauty of the sunrise landscape is intensely animated. The sea that was "laughing" at a distance, the brightness of the mountains, the sweetness of the dawn, the melody of birds, all become associated with the party described at length in the preceding passage. The world is alight, gay and pleasant, spirited and musical. This evocation of the dawn, then, like that of the fullness of his heart, seems to follow simply from the experience of the party:

In a throng,
A festal company of Maids and Youths,
Old Men, and Matrons staid, promiscuous rout,
A medley of all tempers, I had pass'd

The night in dancing, gaiety and mirth;
With din of instruments, and shuffling feet,
And glancing forms, and tapers glittering,
And unaim'd prattle flying up and down,
Spirits upon the stretch, and here and there
Slight shocks of young love-liking interspers'd,
That mounted up like joy into the head,
And tingled through the veins. Ere we retired . . .
(IV, 316-327)

There are other connections between the party and the realization that takes place in the dawn. The "slight shocks of young love-liking" that mounted "like joy into the head/ And tingl'd in the veins," were like intoxication; and the heart, which is said moments later to be full of joy, is full "to the brim" and is the cup of life with its heady drink. He has come away from the party flushed with the joyful sense of life. How much does he realize the connection between the night and the dawn?

It would seem that the Poet who finds a dedication of spirit in the dawn should mean that festive spiritedness has been fully awakened in him; he is a dedicated spirit, a celebrant of Life. The context makes plain, however, that Wordsworth means something more restrained. The "blessedness" he speaks of has not that sexually-suffused and fully spiritual meaning to be found in Blake's "For everything that lives is holy."[2] And the religious metaphors that follow in Wordsworth's dedication—"vows . . . bond . . . sinning . . . blessed"—make the heart, as the cup of life, into a chalice at an altar. The spiritual distance from the earlier sense of "festal" as gay and mirthful is great. The labourers observed in this dawn "going forth into the fields" may then remind us instead of the very opening of *The Prelude* when Wordsworth proposes to seek a "hermitage"

2 William Blake, *The Marriage of Heaven and Hell*, in *The Poetry and Prose of William Blake*, ed. G. Keynes, p. 193.

and labor at tilling the fertile fields of the spirit: "the holy life of music and of verse."[3]

In the immediate context of the dawn experience Wordsworth has been talking about an "inner falling off" in his imaginative life:

> I loved,
> Loved deeply, all that I had loved before,
> More deeply even than ever; but a swarm
> Of heady thoughts jostling each other, gawds,
> And feast, and dance, and public revelry,
> And sports and games (less pleasing in themselves,
> Than as they were a badge glossy and fresh
> Of manliness and freedom) these did now
> Seduce me from the firm habitual quest
> Of feeding pleasures, from that eager zeal,
> Those yearnings which had every day been mine,
> A wild unworldly-minded Youth, given up
> To Nature and to Books . . .
>
> (IV, 270-282)

"Heady thoughts," "gawds/ And feast, and dance, and public revelry," are seen as seductive. The "trivial pleasures of youth" are a distraction from a deeper and prior seriousness, his love of Nature and of books. What he seems to be describing here is the way that young manhood has brought a more insistent sexuality with it, from which he has seemed free in early adolescence. His youth has seemed like an extended childhood or latency and, at the same time, like a precocious adulthood. Of course, his youthful predisposition to solitude and his early moral seriousness are being reported here in retrospect by the older man, so it is impossible to tell from his account what else the boy and young man may have felt about people, from whom he seems to have been temperamentally quite distant—among them but not of them.

[3] *The Prelude,* I, 54.

But the older man—of course, not much older, at this point the thirty-four-year-old poet living in retirement—remembers himself in his Cambridge years very much as he imagines the young Milton in *his* Cambridge years, walking "with conscious step of purity and pride."[4] Recalling his own occasional indulgence in revelry, in "these vanities," Wordsworth describes certain "observable" changes in contemporary life in this ambiguous way:

> But, sure it is that now
> Contagious air did oft environ me
> Unknown among these haunts in former days.
> The very garments that I wore appear'd
> To prey upon my strength . . .
>
> (IV, 289-293)

Either the older man writing this has observed that manners have become looser, even in the lake country, and is recollecting that at about the time that he was coming of age such looseness was becoming more common, or he is simply saying unthinkingly that what was "unknown among these haunts" in the former days of his boyhood was only unknown then to him. He adds to this:

> Something there was about me that perplex'd
> Th' authentic sight of reason, press'd too closely
> On that religious dignity of mind,
> That is the very faculty of truth;
> Which wanting, either, from the very first,
> A function never lighted up, or else
> Extinguish'd, Man, a creature great and good,
> Seems but a pageant plaything with vile claws
> And this great frame of breathing elements
> A senseless Idol.
>
> (IV, 295-304)

"About," in "something there was about me," seems to mean "about myself"; but Wordsworth's way of dissociating him-

[4] *Ibid.*, III, 293.

self from what "press'd too closely" makes "about" seem more like "round about me." The resulting feeling of aversion seems peculiarly strong; and the very excess in the characterization, which makes "contagious air" and "press'd too closely" seem like great external pressures on him, makes one wonder, too, whether Wordsworth is not describing unacknowledged pressures from within, to which, for a while, he gave way because he wanted to. The grotesque image of "Man"—"a pageant plaything with vile claws"—may fit that depraved creature who has no "religious dignity of mind," but in this context, used to describe the vanities or even the sexuality of young manhood, it seems excessive.

How firmly he has Milton in mind here may be seen in how puritanically he recollects his own experience, retrospectively admonishing himself "to scorn delights and live laborious days." One suspects that what shows here nevertheless is the basic attachment of poetry to pleasure, a prior and unconscious attachment, which even his attempt to impose an intellectualized spiritual rigor upon cannot wholly subdue. Having spoken harshly of "the vague heartless chace/ Of trivial pleasures," he introduces the Dawn Dedication with a hesitation:

> And yet, in chastisement of these regrets,
> The memory of one particular hour
> Doth here rise up against me . . .
>
> (IV, 314-316)

True that actually nothing in the ensuing account quite redeems the party itself for Wordsworth, but the recollection of it persists, qualifying for the reader Wordsworth's understanding of his own character. The regret expressed about time wasted stands, despite the fact that on this one occasion a night of festivity had set him on the road home in what proved to be a memorable dawn. What he will call his "thankful blessedness" seems to triumph over such folly, and he observes of his mind:

> Strange rendezvous my mind was at that time,
> A party-coulour'd show of grave and gay,
> Solid and light, short-sighted and profound,
> Of inconsiderate habits and sedate,
> Consorting in one mansion unreprov'd.
> I knew the worth of that which I possess'd,
> Though slighted and misus'd. Besides, in truth,
> That Summer, swarming as it did with thoughts
> Transient and loose, yet wanted not a store
> Of primitive hours, when, by these hindrances
> Unthwarted, I experienc'd in myself
> Conformity as just as that of old
> To the end and written spirit of God's works,
> Whether held forth in Nature or in Man.
>
> (IV, 346-359)

The line "consorting in one mansion unreprov'd," with its suggestion of above-stairs sobriety and below-stairs mirth, makes of Wordsworth's mind, which is often figuratively spoken of as a house maintained by his spiritual efforts, the very world of *Twelfth Night,* with the present Wordsworth as Malvolio commenting on it humorlessly. One retains from this the impression of division and conflict insufficiently realized or appreciated, of youthfulness put down and the poetic impulse diverted from its source.

Recollecting that at moments he had neglected his true calling and had acted indecorously, Wordsworth makes it seem he had acted "out-of-character." He would like it to appear that most of the time, like the young Milton, he had walked "with conscious step of purity and pride." And he probably did.

Recollected impressions of himself at Cambridge show how much he stood apart from life, despite his occasional other recollections of himself as sociable:

> And, as for what pertains to human life,
> The deeper passions working round me here,
> Whether of envy, jealousy, pride, shame,

Ambition, emulation, fear, or hope,
Or those of dissolute pleasure, were by me
Unshar'd; and only now and then observ'd,
So little was their hold upon my being,
As outward things that might administer
To knowledge or instruction.

(III, 531-539)

His habitual reserve extended from social to academic life. He felt free from the aggressiveness and competitiveness of normal adolescence; he gave himself up to Nature and the uses of Imagination instead. He says:

—of important Days,
Examinations, when the Man was weigh'd
As in the balance! —of excessive hopes,
Tremblings withal, and commendable fears,
Small jealousies, and triumphs good or bad
I made short mention; things they were which then
I did not love, nor do I love them now.
Such glory was but little sought by me,
And little won.

(III, 64-72)

or again:

I griev'd to see among the Band
Of those who in the field of contest stood
As combatants, passions that did to me
Seem low and mean; from ignorance of mine,
In part, and want of just forbearance, yet
My wiser mind grieves now for what I saw.
Willingly did I part from these, and turn
Out of their track . . .

(III, 511-518)

That lowness and meanness are inevitable traits of combatants may be doubted, though to the youth who eschews competitiveness they may seem so. As gentle a being as

Christopher Wordsworth, one of the poet's younger brothers, did well at the same university and remained a lifetime there—a fact which reminds us that traumatic events within a family affect the children in different ways and according to their ages and temperaments.

Although Wordsworth was aware that his unwillingness or his inability to resemble others was baffling his guardians and making his future prospects even more distressingly uncertain, he knew also that what he felt was profoundly in his character, and not casually or even alterably so:

> But it is right to say
> That even so early, from the first crude days
> Of settling-time in this my new abode,
> Not seldom I had melancholy thoughts,
> From personal and family regards,
> Wishing to hope without a hope; some fears
> About my future worldly maintenance,
> And, more than all, a strangeness in my mind,
> A feeling that I was not for that hour,
> Nor for that place.
>
> (III, 72-81)

The feeling of discomfort in the new situation and the "strangeness" *in* his mind may suggest the distress felt by the ego whose limited habits of action are proving inadequate to the new demands made by present realities. By turning away to private pursuits, he resisted demands he could not have met. However we may attempt to account for Wordsworth's dedication to poetry, its apparent and real imperatives, it is important to observe first the conflict he experienced.

Wordsworth in his early thirties, writing with renewed hope about the aspiration to be a poet, is very solemn about the dedicated life. He remembers the ordinary vanities and the exuberance of young manhood as life in a "promiscuous rout"—life, as it were, with Comus. But even in 1803 this avowed seriousness of his was questionable from the point of view of the adult and conventional world which regarded a poet as an idler; and Wordsworth, whose grander claims are unmistakable, had difficulty at first opposing the conventional expectations of his guardians with the personal ones he was discovering in his own identity. Whereas the young men who behaved frivolously, as they were "expected" to behave at Cambridge, had the kind of sanction given from generation to generation that the future poet has always lacked, Wordsworth at the time had felt guilty for his lack of gratitude and obedience, blocked in his aspirations, and incapable of personal discipline. And the poet now recalls his hesitancy disapprovingly:

> some personal concerns
> . . . hung about me in my own despite
> Perpetually, no heavy weight, but still
> A baffling and a hindrance, a controul
> Which made the thought of planning for myself
> A course of independent study seem
> An act of disobedience towards them
> Who lov'd me, proud rebellion and unkind.
> This bastard virtue, rather let it have
> A name it more deserves, this cowardice,
> Gave treacherous sanction to that overlove
> Of freedom planted in me from the very first
> And indolence, by force of which I turn'd
> From regulations even of my own,
> As from restraints and bonds.
>
> (VI, 34-48)

The "proud rebellion and unkind" has a Miltonic-Satanic sound. Satan had found sufficient cause for rebellion in "the debt immense of endless gratitude/ So burthensome, still paying, still to owe."[5] But for the while that Wordsworth felt guiltily that he should reconcile his own will with the sober expectations of family and society, he was driven to resist the expectations of others passively by refusing to

[5] *Paradise Lost*, IV, 52-53.

acknowledge any demands, even his own on himself. His older brother Richard had become a lawyer, like their father before them, and had set up in London. The family disapproval of Wordsworth as an idler was strong, of his willfullness constant, and of his discovery of the Poet in himself total. Only Dorothy, his younger sister, but comparable to mother and Nature in her favoring regard for him, was delighted.

By giving priority to his own needs, gradually he opposed both Cambridge and family with his belief in a prior vocation and duty, as may be seen in his recurrent use of religious metaphor for characterizing his activities in solitude:

> I was a chosen Son.
> For hither I had come with holy powers
> And faculties, whether to work or feel:
> To apprehend all passions and all moods
> Which time, and place, and season do impress
> Upon the visible universe, and work
> Like changes there by force of my own mind.
> I was a Freeman; in the purest sense
> Was free, and to majestic ends was strong.
> I do not speak of learning, moral truth,
> Or understanding; 'twas enough for me
> To know that I was otherwise endow'd.
>
> (III, 82-93)

He was less assured of his freedom than he claimed, but he became, in his incipient rebelliousness and in his claim of being "a chosen son," the Poet chosen by Nature. Incited by her maternal permissiveness, he elevates the maker of fantasies:

> I had a world about me; 'twas my own;
> I made it; for it only liv'd to me,
> And to the God who look'd into my mind.
>
> (III, 142-144)

The future Poet, who creates private worlds in his mind, feels observed by the God above Nature; but this God, so slightly acknowledged in these early books of *The Prelude,* has none of "His" usual characteristics, which inspire a dread humility. Wordsworth felt as yet none of "His" admonishments and has felt no need to deal with Him.

What is most significant, though, is that in his "first absence" from his native hills, Wordsworth's search for solitude became a more self-conscious pursuit than it had been in his boyhood, in which it had been merely one aspect of his continuous life in Nature. He speaks now of "turning the mind in upon itself" and finding

> What independent solaces were mine,
> To mitigate the injurious sway of place
> Or circumstance; . . .
>
> (III, 101-103: 1850 version)

and he says that the earth is "nowhere unembellish'd by some trace/ Of that first Paradise whence Man was driven." The process we began by observing in "Tintern Abbey" is being described here at its inception: in absence from the beloved vale, the mind seeks traces of its own early Paradise in Nature and then turns inwards to regard the "beauteous forms" within itself. In that way it sheds the "burthen of the mystery" of the "unintelligible world" and resists the "injurious sway of place/ Or circumstance."

To the objects of external Nature he "gave a moral life" and found correspondences between all passions and all moods "in" Nature and those in his own psyche, between the appearances of Nature and his own imaginings:

> all
> That I beheld respired with inward meaning.
> Thus much for the one Presence, and the Life
> Of the great whole; suffice it here to add
> That whatsoe'er of Terror or of Love,

Or Beauty, Nature's daily face put on
From transitory passion, unto this
I was as wakeful, even, as waters are
To the sky's motion; in a kindred sense
Of passion was obedient as a lute
That waits upon the touches of the wind.
(III, 128-138)

In the "Preface to The Lyrical Ballads" he was to state confidently that such habits of thought and feeling become in the Poet the talent by which he relates the feeling to the object for the reader, the feeling giving importance to the object and not the object to the feeling. The Poet, who has "learned" to perceive feelings in Nature can, by arranging images of Nature, transmit feelings "from" Nature and make his reader experience *those* feelings. What we are observing, however, is the source of those "natural" feelings in the poet's mind. His feelings about the "one Presence and the Life/ Of the Great Whole," we have seen in other contexts; and when he speaks of "*inward* meaning" here, we recall how in his projections he "saw one life, and felt that it was joy."[6] Nature gives him greater access to his own deeper feelings.

Wordsworth believed that the Poet acquired this talent of relating the feeling to the object from Nature; it is also exactly what he says of the Mother in relation to the Babe in the 1850 version of the Blest Babe passage:

Is there a flower, to which he points with hand
Too weak to gather it, already love
Drawn from love's purest earthly fount for him
Hath beautified that flower . . .
(II, 245-248: 1850 version)

That is, the feeling and the manner of presentation makes the object beautiful and to-be-loved by the time it is known. The Poet, then, makes the reader re-experience lost feelings

[6] *The Prelude*, II, 430.

from infancy and childhood by being "natural" or "maternal" to him. The Poet, as he says later, "Shall want no humbler tenderness, his heart/ Be tender as a nursing mother's heart,"[7] which is how Matthew Arnold remembered and praised Wordsworth in "Memorial Verses."[8] But Wordsworth, in his Cambridge years, lived emotionally withdrawn from others, feeling only the personal satisfaction that he knew the "natural" connections between feelings and objects, as he was learning to perceive or to imagine them.

In the spirit of self-justification, he says:

> So was it with me in my solitude;
> So often among multitudes of men.
> Unknown, unthought of, yet I was most rich,
> I had a world about me; 'twas my own,
> I made it.
>
> (III, 139-143)

He imagines, too, that his eccentric habits of preoccupied observation outdoors, his gestures and expressions, made him appear mad or ridiculous to others; and he resorts to lofty irony:

> Some call'd it madness: such, indeed, it was,
> If child-like fruitfulness in passing joy,
> If steady moods of thoughtfulness, matur'd
> To inspiration, sort with such a name;
> If prophesy be madness; if things view'd
> By Poets of old time, and higher up
> By the first men, earth's first inhabitants
> May in these tutor'd days no more be seen
> With undisorder'd sight: but leaving this
> It was no madness . . .
>
> (III, 147-156)

The elevated tone in which he announces possession of the Higher Truth of Nature reveals the degree of assurance

[7] *Ibid.*, XIII, 206-207.

[8] Matthew Arnold, "Memorial Verses."

Wordsworth was to feel in dealing with the lesser realities and the unnatural and mistaken aspirations of other people:

> But peace! it is enough
> To notice that I was ascending now
> To such community with highest truth.
> (III, 118-120)

Like Moses, he ascends this mountain, the receiver and giver of the immutable laws of Nature to Man. His desire for more than mortal privilege is also present a few lines later when, from an "eminence" that is metaphorically a mountain, he says:

> And here, O Friend! have I retrac'd my life
> Up to an eminence, and told a tale
> Of matters which, not falsely, I may call
> The glory of my youth. Of Genius, Power,
> Creation and Divinity itself
> I have been speaking, for my theme has been
> What pass'd within me . . .
> (III, 168-174)

And it will be with the ascent of Mount Snowdon, and with the visionary experience at its summit, that Wordsworth will conclude the poem making his fullest idealization of the Poet. And yet, in the account of his Cambridge years, there is a curiously unconscious kind of self-characterization, too. Recalling the life from which he lived apart, he presents a moral allegory of the Cambridge pageant with perhaps an unconscious pun placing him at the end of it:

> For all Degrees
> And Shapes of spurious fame and short-liv'd praise
> Here sate in state, and fed with daily alms
> Retainers won away from solid good;
> And here was Labour, his own Bond-slave, Hope
> That never set the pains against the prize,

Idleness, halting with his weary clog,
And poor misguided Shame, and witless Fear,
And simple Pleasure, foraging for Death,
Honour misplaced, and Dignity astray;
Feuds, Factions, Flatteries, Enmity, and Guile;
Murmuring Submission, and bald Government;
The Idol weak as the Idolater;
And Decency and Custom starving Truth;
And blind Authority, beating with his Staff
The Child that might have led him; Emptiness
Followed, as of good omen; and meek Worth
Left to itself unheard of, and unknown.

(III, 626-643)

"Meek Worth" left no mark on the place, like Wordsworth who has just said of himself "So was it with me in my solitude;/ So often amongst multitudes of men;/ *Unknown, unthought of,* yet. . . ."[9] Wordsworth's aspiration to change the human condition by confronting historical reality with the natural wisdom of the youth who has been intimate with Nature is apparent in Book III, but here "Blind Authority" still had the unconscious obedience of "the child that might have led him."

2. Three Figures of the World

Earlier we noted that in October of 1803 Wordsworth resumed work on *The Prelude,* probably by writing some draft form of the first 270 lines of Book I, before continuing with Book III. By March of 1804, he had decided to extend *The Prelude* beyond five books; and by March 17 he had written through Book V (as we know it in the 1805 thirteen-book version).[10] As I have interpreted that decision, it grew out of a need to find the image of himself as the Poet in all of his experience, not simply in the youthful period prior to his crisis. His beginning *The Prelude* was a hopeful sign of his recovery, but he realized in writing what he

[9] *The Prelude,* III, 139-140.

[10] See *The Prelude,* pp. l-li.

must do to reassure himself in the present. Wordsworth had decided to let go of Dorothy and Coleridge and attempt to prove in poetry his mastery of experiences that had overwhelmed him in reality. His decision must reflect the partial resolution of conflict about being the Poet.

One cannot say with certainty that the resumption of the poem on his life, which soon resulted in a significant alteration of its scope and intent, was the result of thoughts occasioned by his first wedding anniversary, but the fact that he resumed work within days of his anniversary does, I think, call attention to itself. The resolution of conflict at this time in favor of a more difficult but greater independence may also be observed in an important poem written a year before in the months just prior to his marriage: "Resolution and Independence." This poem was written in May of 1802 after a visit by Dorothy and Wordsworth to Coleridge at Keswick, a visit which found Coleridge's spirits at a very low point. As Lionel Trilling points out about the relations of the two poets at that time, the first part of the "Immortality Ode" had been composed and was probably read at that time to Coleridge, who, in answer, began to compose "Dejection: An Ode."[11] The "Immortality Ode," concerned as it is with a poet's resources, was written at intervals between 1802 and 1806, and expresses Wordsworth's feelings about the role of the poet and about his access to those resources. But Wordsworth's marriage was a significant modification of a role he had seemed to choose for life, and one might suspect that the thoughts before marriage and the thoughts one year later are about what one gives for what one gets.

In any event, the depression felt and spoken of in "Resolution and Independence" is, as Professor Trilling observes, about Wordsworth's "past indifference to the means of getting a living":

[11] Lionel Trilling, "The Immortality Ode," in *The Liberal Imagination*, pp. 139-140.

"He thinks of what may follow from his carefree life: 'solitude, pain of heart, distress, and poverty.' His black thoughts are led to the fate of poets 'in their misery dead,' among them Chatterton and Burns. The second specific fear is of mental distress: 'We poets in our youth begin in gladness;/ But thereof comes in the end despondency and madness.' Coleridge, we must suppose, was in his thoughts after the depressing Keswick meeting, but he is of course thinking chiefly of himself. It will be remembered how the poem ends, how with some difficulty of utterance the poet brings himself to speak with an incredibly old leech-gatherer, and, taking heart from the man's resolution and independence, becomes again 'strong.' "[12]

Professor Trilling thinks that "this great poem is not to be given a crucial meaning in Wordsworth's life. It makes use of a mood to which everyone, certainly every creative person, is now and again a victim"; but with this I do not agree. It was written at a time when Wordsworth was about to act in a way that nothing in his poetic account of himself has prepared us to understand. True, *The Prelude* attempts to present his growth to poethood rather than more generally to manhood, but we have so far observed how being the Poet and being Wordsworth seemed indistinguishable to him; how the spirituality of poetry and the sexuality of manhood seemed to preclude each other; and how the continuing attachment to the mother is dynamically present in the Poet's "bond" with Nature. Marriage is so significant an act that the particular poem associated with it must have considerable significance if it deals with feelings about changing attitudes and roles. And it is on the anniversary of that decisive action that Wordsworth resumed *The Prelude,* which he was soon to alter in scope and intent.

[12] *Ibid.*, pp. 139-140. Professor Trilling mentions Coleridge's very unhappy marriage, but does not attach the same importance to the fact that I do in the interpretation that follows.

In "Resolution and Independence," Wordsworth is a young man discovering the extent of his uncertainty. He is unsure of how men endure the world and is himself on the verge of making a significant attachment to it. He thinks that possibly "by peculiar grace,/ A leading from above" he has been providentially guided to his encounter with the old man on the lonely moor. His feeling that heavenly providence may be leading him to experience the wisdom of men, or of certain kinds of men, is consistent with a theme that emerges after Book VI in *The Prelude*, that of the father and of the Christian God. But as we shall see, he had been in the habit of opposing the wisdom of worldly experience with the unworldly wisdom of the youth who has had a prolonged intimacy with Nature.[13]

In "Resolution and Independence," he feels doubt as well as fear. He says:

> My whole life I have lived in pleasant thought,
> As if life's business were a summer mood;
> As if all needful things would come unsought
> To genial faith, still rich in genial good.
> But how can he expect that others should
> Build for him, sow for him, and at his call
> Love him, who for himself will take no heed at all?

One may be struck, first, by the description seeming to be that of a child, and then of someone realizing he is no longer a boy. The poet has had no settled life and none of the worldly responsibilities that force men to deal with the world in the world's ways. He has traveled, and he has been living frugally but pleasantly on a small bequest with his sister. Even in remembering himself in Book VII as a

[13] Wordsworth's epic simile in stanza IX describing the Old Leech-Gatherer includes "Like a sea-beast crawled forth . . . to sun itself" and seems to recall the scene in *The Odyssey* in which Menelaus recounts to Telemachus how he trapped Proteus sunning himself in the shape of a sea-beast. From Proteus, he learned what he would have to endure; he tells young Telemachus of his absent father Odysseus and of heroic endurance and survival.

young man in London, Wordsworth communicates a detachment greater than that of, say, tourism; and he was outside the events of the French Revolution, which he describes in Books IX and X, though emotionally and imaginatively involved. His love affair in France with Annette Vallon, of which he omits mention, could not—or in any event did not—become the beginning of his responsibilities.

At the time of "Resolution and Independence," Wordsworth was feeling all too keenly the anxiety and depression that may alternate with feelings of anticipation and delight when one has resolved to change familiar ways for unfamiliar ones, as he had resolved to change his temperamental preference for solitude in Nature for an even greater intimacy in life than he had with Dorothy. But Wordsworth was not finally to give up his dependency on Nature, which had taken precedence over, and often precluded, other relationships in the past, until he had found in Christian worship a form of dependency he could share with other men as a man. Whereas the poet in the "bond" of Nature seems to be withheld by maternal Nature from the likeness to other men that is psychically necessary to a man, part of the very likeness of men to each other in Christian and especially Protestant worship is that of each man's normative autonomy as a soul.

"I was a Traveller then upon the moor," says Wordsworth, introducing his characteristic presence into the golden look of the world in springtime; and I think it is not fanciful to say that ordinarily we might supply here Wordsworth's characteristic mood when wandering contentedly in solitude in Nature on a sunny morning. In *The Prelude,* examples abound. But in his elation, inexplicably, he experiences sudden dejection—"fears and fancies," "dim sadness and blind thoughts, I knew not, nor could name." It is possible that with marriage on his mind subtly qualifying even the elation felt in the familiar birth and beauty of the morning, he is unaware of the connection between new expectations of joy and new causes for dejection. He has been feeling "happy as a boy"; and he thinks of himself still as a "happy child" in Nature. The future may prove different, hold some unknown danger. While it is reasonable to suppose that thoughts about his impending marriage may bring fears about its obligations—the young man who walks "far from the world, and from all care" becoming the man who must be personally more dependable —it is likely that something other than uncertainties about worldly maintenance brings thoughts of despondency and madness to mind. If Coleridge is on his mind, as is likely, we should observe that Coleridge's low spirits were not caused by money worries, as Wordsworth well knew, but rather by his own sensibility (which Wordsworth then considers as "poetic" sensibility) *and by his very unhappy marriage.* Reasons for mad poets but not for bad marriages are being considered in the poem.

In Wordsworth's dependency on Nature, we have said, he denied his feelings about his mother's undependability. If we wonder, then, in what way his being on the verge of marriage may occasion fears and fancies, dim sadness and blind thoughts, we shall have to consider what it might mean to him that he intends to take a woman as his own, one that will change his relationship with Nature by more than merely increasing his worldly responsibilities. It is likely that his personally exaggerated spiritual kinship with Coleridge, to whom he is writing *The Prelude* as if he were talking to himself, made Coleridge's depression fearfully personal to him. He had himself already known the despair to which the poet's sensibility is prey; and whether or not he was ever to interpret his prolonged dependency on maternal Nature, or to realize his unconscious distrust of woman's love as undependable, he seems to have been unconsciously responsive to the bleak picture of Coleridge as both poet *and* husband. Still, he was resolving on his own to do what for him was a profoundly difficult thing, to risk the danger of loving and of seeking happiness in the external world. The desired wholeness and completion of love means to man risking the danger to his own well-being in a woman's separateness, as symbolically and woefully that of Eve's from Adam, or as once the mother's from the child.

One may imagine that the intensity of Wordsworth's latently incestuous intimacy with Dorothy had stirred in him both desires and fears, while strengthening the will to trust in intimacy with a woman.[14] Dorothy, who thought of her brother as strong and manly and who referred to Coleridge always as "poor Coleridge,"[15] may have been a good deal responsible for the strength of his resolve. Having presided over their friendship, she also provided Wordsworth with a crucial feeling of difference from Coleridge. But resolution is greatly facilitated in a young man by his identifications with men rather than simply by the good opinions of himself he gets from maternal women. This basic identification, of course, refers psychically to the father, a matter with which Wordsworth must also have been preconsciously preparing to deal.

In examining the beginning of *The Prelude,* for instance, we spoke of castration anxieties in relation to his reluctance about writing a great work "as becomes a man"; and we found there something very like this "dim sadness and blind thoughts, I knew not, nor could name" spoken of here in "Resolution and Independence." He had spoken of his mind being baffled by "some hollow thought" that "hung like an interdict upon his hopes"; he had spoken of irresolution and want of power. The figure of the Old Leech-Gatherer who appears in a suggestively providential way seems to evoke from Wordsworth the resolution to ap-

[14] See Bateson, *Wordsworth: A Reinterpretation,* p. 151ff. Professor Bateson directs attention to the latent incestuousness of the relationship of William and Dorothy and makes quite a plausible argument about the "Lucy" poems.

[15] *Ibid.* "Poor" is an often-used adjective for Coleridge in Dorothy's letters and journals. Professor Bateson finds Dorothy's frustrated love for Coleridge expressed in her concern for his sickness and unhappiness; he believes she saw the cause of Coleridge's unhappiness primarily as marital.

proach his fears and to be independent. Wordsworth married soon afterwards; but it was in the portion of the autobiography that he had not as yet resolved to write that his fears persisted. I think I can say that the extension of *The Prelude* does derive from the same resolution as that of his marriage, and merely suggest the likelihood that the first anniversary of his marriage was an occasion that reminded him of his need to locate his powers and his present self in his whole story.

Before proceeding with Wordsworth's approach to the subject of his recent past, we should examine briefly the contradictory needs and intentions that begin to show here. Certainly throughout *The Prelude* Wordsworth intended to affirm himself as a poet, though his confidence in idealizing himself as *the* Poet waned as he completed the first version of the poem. But the confidence in himself he showed in his decision to marry, and subsequently in his decision to extend *The Prelude,* reveals at the same time a significant change in attitude towards poetry. The way of "visionary" poetry, the poetic obsession with a lost object and a deep, absent reality, had seemed to preclude satisfaction with the visible world and attachments to objects in it. His marriage must be taken to mean that Wordsworth unconsciously *wanted* to stop being the poet poetically obsessed, as much because the psychic burden of the visionary search was too great as because the possibility of "godly" consciousness was too small.

If, however, Wordsworth had unconsciously intended in *The Prelude* to remember, imagine, and reveal the truth of his unique sense of himself, it remains likely that the tendency shows despite the increasingly strong unconscious tendency to conceal and deny the truth; we shall continue to observe these discrepancies of intention. For one thing, we can observe that Wordsworth recorded feelings about a change in himself at this time by which he was disturbed; his concern about the visionary *resources* of the poet begins to show, both in *The Prelude,* which he resumed in 1803, and in the "Immortality Ode," which he began in 1802 and worked on intermittently until 1806. It is likely that he felt his "resources" diminishing even while he continued to deal with the origin and nature of a poet's powers, because he was now living a life significantly different from the lonely one he had unconsciously associated with those visionary powers.

It is very significant that the first "spot of time," his memory of visionary strength, is immediately followed by another kind of memory, himself on the same lonely moor with his wife and sister. He now associates with that place his present contentment with a life very different from the "visionary" way of the poet. The image of "the woman, and her garments vex'd and toss'd/ By the strong wind . . ." is followed immediately by:

> When, in a blessed season
> With those two dear Ones, to my heart so dear,
> When in the blessed time of early love,
> Long afterwards, I roam'd about
> In daily presence of this very scene,
> Upon the naked pool and dreary crags,
> And on the melancholy Beacon, fell
> The spirit of pleasure and youth's golden gleam;
> And think ye not with radiance more divine
> From these remembrances, and from the power
> They left behind?
>
> (XI, 316-326)

He does not explain himself further, but the allusion to Mary and Dorothy here seems symbolic because Wordsworth then speaks of his diminishing visionary resources; and he speaks of them without distress:

> Oh! mystery of Man, from what a depth
> Proceed thy honours! I am lost, but see
> In simple childhood something of the base
> On which thy greatness stands, but this I feel,

That from thyself it is that thou must give,
Else never canst receive. The days gone by
Come back upon me from the dawn almost
Of life: the hiding-places of my power
Seem open; I approach, and then they close;
I see by glimpses now; when age comes on,
May scarcely see at all, and I would give,
While yet we may, as far as words can give,
A substance and a life to what I feel;
I would enshrine the spirit of the past
For future restoration.

(XI, 329-343)

Something is being spoken of elegiacally here. It is not the power by which poetry is made that has passed, but there has been a significant lessening of the compelling need by which this poet has sought the invisible world in visionary experiences. One suspects that the contentment of domestic life has eased a compulsion and dissipated the force of an obsession.

When Wordsworth says, "I see by glimpses now; when age comes on/ May scarcely see at all . . ." we may imagine him looking dimly about him, like an aging man unable to see clearly. What he means, paradoxically, here as in the "Immortality Ode," is that this will be the case when he can see the visible world only as itself. The lines leading up to the statement—

The days gone by
Come back upon me from the dawn almost
Of life: the hiding-places of my power
Seem open; I approach, and then they close;

—give again the sense that the "I" in them was once the poetically obsessed self that followed his visions in order to realize and assimilate those experiences. But the poetic self seems calmer now, if still curious, about the realm of the soul, the lost rest-of-the-self. The hiding place of power, which could be approached only partially by memory and by the imagination pursuing a disturbing Presence in Nature through the imagery of Nature, seems less accessible now—sadly, but somehow appropriately so. When the poet can "no longer see," when he squints at the visible world that has been darkened to "vision" by the simple "light of common day,"[16] it is because the poet no longer feels compelled as a man to keep something long since lost alive to the heart by projecting it into Nature.

What may seem perplexing to the reader of *The Prelude* is that it is *this* person who is telling the most exciting part of the story, of the poet's young manhood in the world beyond the vale and on the scene of a crisis in contemporary History itself. Unconsciously drawn to the subject of crisis in his poetry, unconsciously resisting its meaning, Wordsworth is at the same time seeking a revised and acceptable image of himself, and the composure in telling his story that he has begun to feel in living his life.

THERE ARE two significant and similar incidents in *The Prelude* to which the encounter with the Old Leech-Gatherer may be effectively compared: one is the roadside encounter with the Old Soldier near home (in Book IV), the other the encounter with the Blind Beggar on a London street (in Book VII). The account of the Old Soldier is found first in the Alfoxden MS (1798) and The Christabel NB and MS 18a (1798-99), and therefore was one of the earliest passages of *The Prelude* Wordsworth set down in some form; it is earlier, that is, than the actual inception of *The Prelude* in either its projected five-book or actual thirteen-book form. "Resolution and Independence" dates from 1802, the time of Wordsworth's marriage; and the Blind Beggar passage dates from 1804, the period after his decision to extend *The Prelude*. All three accounts are of

16 The "Immortality Ode," *Poetical Works*, p. 460.

encounters with older men while the young man is "travelling," and each account reveals significantly the present attitude towards the incident of the person writing.

His encounter with the Old Soldier is significantly placed; it follows the Dawn Dedication to poetry immediately, at once resembling it and contrasting with it. If the image of the young poet at his dedication came to seem an insufficient conclusion for the poem, perhaps the incident placed immediately after it, but actually composed before it, suggests why. In the "bond" given to him and the "vows" made for him in the Dawn Dedication, we see Wordsworth's belief in Nature; it is consistent with statements like:

> That spirit of religious love in which
> I walked with Nature.
>
> (II, 376-377)

and:

> and that I, so long
> A worshipper of Nature, hither came
> Unwearied in that service . . .
>
> ("Tintern Abbey")

and:

> But I believe
> That Nature, oftentimes, when she would frame
> A favor'd Being, from his earliest dawn
> Of infancy doth open out the clouds,
> As at the touch of lightning, seeking him
> With gentlest visitation;
>
> (I, 362-367)

In the Dawn Dedication, Nature seems to be choosing him again, reserving him for some special purpose; his dedication seems like an acceptance of a role and a renunciation of alternative ways of life: what was "intended" for him in the metaphorical dawn of infancy is realized by him in a memorable dawn of young manhood. Here, the metaphorical consistency of Nature's poet comes naturally, but too patly.

Wordsworth's encounter with the Old Soldier is more mysterious; an unexpected confrontation is strange to one who experiences Nature in solitude. Showing some interest in the stories of men who have experienced the world, Wordsworth, very insistently, wants to hear the soldier's story—a story which, in its barest outline, contrasts strikingly with the poet's preoccupation with his own "privileged" history of growth. As in the Dawn Dedication, Wordsworth is walking home along the road, this time late on a summer night, alone. The public way, fascinating to him since early childhood, is deserted for the night and has assumed "a character of deeper quietness/ Than pathless solitudes." We might observe the characteristic representation of a physical circumstance as a psychic condition: the deserted road *is* a solitude, suggestive of one's way into a state of mind, which is then seen peculiarly as "pathless." We need only call to mind Wordsworth's other description of the road to see the consistency: "an invitation into space boundless/ A guide into eternity" or to "things unknown and without bound."[17] He mentions "an exhausted mind worn out by toil," struck pleasurably by near objects that intrude upon its own listless motion:

> Thus did I steal along that silent road,
> My body from the stillness drinking in
> A restoration like the calm of sleep
> But sweeter far. Above, before, behind,
> Around me, all was peace and solitude,
> I look'd not round, nor did the solitude
> Speak to my eye; but it was heard and felt.
> O happy state! what beauteous pictures now
> Rose in harmonious imagery—they rose
> As from some distant region of my soul
> And came along like dreams; yet such as left
> Obscurely mingled with their passing forms
> A consciousness of animal delight,

[17] *The Prelude*, XII, 151-152 and XIII, 151-152: 1850 version.

A self-possession felt in every pause
And every gentle movement of my frame.
(IV, 385-399)

The stillness, peace, and solitude make him feel something like the restfulness of sleep, so that the activity of mind in the passing notice of objects outside him just described, gives way to the inner noticing of imagery that rose

As from some distant region of my soul
And came along like dreams;
(IV, 394-395)

And it is in this state of pleasurable "self-possession" that he notices the Old Soldier.

In his account of the Old Soldier, Wordsworth does not further develop the suggestion that the actual external figure also seemed like one that had risen from within him. This is because Wordsworth intends to make a different point, that at such moments one's greatest sensitivity shows and pleasurable self-possession yields to natural concern with the real needs of others. Book IV is "about" the deeper discovery of his love for his rural home and its people, after an experience of the meaner and more aggressive life of Cambridge which prefigured the city world of London. With the confidence that the people of his rural home can be counted upon in a "natural" way to lend "timely furtherance and help" if asked to, Wordsworth can admonish the Old Soldier for not having simply requested help, and can accept the rejoinder—"my trust is in the God of Heaven/ And in the eye of him that passes me" with no disquieting thoughts about what people or the world are like. He seems to prove himself right in easily securing the Old Soldier a willing host, but he does not learn what else the Soldier knows about the likelihood of charity in the world.

There is, however, more to the experience. Wordsworth's account of this incident follows manifestly from the preceding one of the Dawn Dedication to poetry: the spiritual bonding of the poet has just been recalled, and it is followed immediately and appropriately by an account of the young poet walking the same road soon afterwards and pausing to minister spiritually to the needs of wayfarers.[18] So, too, in a preconsciously associational way, the account of this follows from the preceding one; a startling figure from the world of men seems to rise in Wordsworth's imaginative recollection now just as he had seemed to appear at the time from within Wordsworth. He is an almost hallucinatory challenge to what the poet has just been saying about the exaltation he had experienced in the Dawn Dedication. But to the poet writing about his religious bond, the Poet *is* exalted above the profane world with its historical and masculine character, and so Wordsworth deals with his recollection of the Old Soldier in a manner consistent with his beliefs in himself. To us, the incident with the Old Soldier seems incongruous when we consider the assured tone of the youth admonishing the older man who has suffered and endured; but to Wordsworth, the youth did not lack experience. Rather, he possessed a more important kind of it to a greater degree from his prolonged intimacy with Nature. At first the recollection seems unsettling to Wordsworth who remembers his "specious cowardise"; but Wordsworth also remembers that he overcame his diffidence. The youth's assurance of his powers—

18 In the 1805-06 version, the Good Samaritan has an objectionable tone, the "I" sounding imperious:

At the door I knock'd
Calling aloud 'my friend,' here is a man
By sickness overcome; beneath your roof
This night let him find rest, and give him food,
If food he need, for he is faint and tired.
(IV, 483-487)

The passage is sensibly altered later to read:

At the door I knock'd
And earnestly to a charitable care
Commended him as a poor friendless man,
Belated and by sickness overcome.
(IV, 449-452: 1850 version)

and Wordsworth's memory and present acceptance of them—again affirm the providence of Nature here.

At the same time, although his "specious cowardise" seems merely to add a dramatic heightening to the incident and no more, it is as if Wordsworth had to remember to behave "naturally" to unfamiliar people seen startlingly in the moonlight landscape:

> slipping back in the shade
> Of a thick hawthorne, I could mark him well,
> Myself unseen.

In the 1805 version, Wordsworth says:

> He was of stature tall,
> A foot above man's common measure tall,
> Stiff in his form, and upright, lank and lean,
> A man more meagre, as it seem'd to me,
> Was never seen abroad by night or day.
> His arms were long, and bare his hands; his mouth
> Shew'd ghastly in the moonlight; from behind
> A milestone propp'd him, and his figure seem'd
> Half-sitting, and half-standing. I could mark
> That he was clad in military garb,
> Though faded, yet entire. He was alone,
> Had no attendant, neither Dog, nor Staff,
> Nor knapsack; in his very dress appear'd
> A desolation, a simplicity
> That seem'd akin to solitude. Long time
> Did I peruse him with a mingled sense
> Of fear and sorrow. From his lips, meanwhile,
> There issued murmuring sounds, as if of pain
> Or of uneasy thought; yet still his form
> Kept the same steadiness; and at his feet
> His shadow lay, and mov'd not. In a Glen
> Hard by, a Village stood, whose roof and doors
> Were visible among the scatter'd trees,
> Scarce distant from the spot an arrow's flight;

I wish'd to see him move; but he remain'd
Fix'd to his place, and still from time to time
Sent forth a murmuring voice of dead complaint,
Groans scarcely audible. Without self-blame
I had not thus prolong'd my watch; and now,
Subduing my heart's specious cowardise
I left the shady nook where I had stood,
And hail'd him.

(IV, 405-436)

His hesitation is real, and of course it is caused by his not knowing what to make of the figure—how to "take" him. What we observed earlier about fear and distrust, strangeness and strangers, is in point here,[19] but here let us recall that it is from repressed feelings about the father that such reactions principally derive, from wishes repressed in the Oedipal period, which persist, generating unconscious fears. At night anyone would be startled by such an ominous figure, but the fact that this figure may be seen as the last one to appear "as from some distant region" of Wordsworth's own soul reminds us that all was not really harmonious in that inner landscape.

Whatever other significance the Old Soldier has, the fact that Wordsworth reacts to him as the figure of Solitude and as a possible figure of Death is revealing. Solitude derives its pleasurable meanings from Nature, from unconscious contact with the mother and from the harmonious sense of life associated with her; and the pleasurable quality of self-possession Wordsworth has been describing has that same quality of psychic lulling, of self-cradling with "beauteous forms." But solitude for him ultimately derives its significance from the repressed traumatic experience of the mother's death and the child's fear of being left alone. The unconscious process of the mind is quick to seize upon suggestive detail and threatens to intrude upon consciousness. Here, in a startling way, in the strange figure of the

[19] See above, pp. 212-213.

Old Soldier, these opposed meanings of solitude are momentarily concentrated.

The mouth of the Old Soldier "Shew'd ghastly in the moonlight"; his figure was "stiff," "upright," "propp'd." "I wish'd to see him *move,*" Wordsworth says, recalling his own hesitation, himself unseen. "But he remain'd/ Fix'd to his place, and still from time to time/ Sent forth a murmuring voice of *dead* complaint. . . ." The description vividly recalls the drowned man who rose from beneath the calm bosom of the lake:

> the dead Man . . . bolt upright
> Rose with his ghastly face; a spectre shape
> Of terror even!
>
> (v, 470-473)

As a nine-year-old boy, Wordsworth had seen death in Hawkeshead vale, an experience he remembers from soon after his mother's death. The drowned man, encountered abruptly when the boy in the new vale was "seeking I knew not what," is presented in Book v after Wordsworth significantly omits mention of the fact of the death of his mother. In Book v, the accidental discovery of death in the new vale is a "screen memory" for the more significant death in the original vale; and it is with comparable significance that in the encounter with the Old Soldier the fear of solitude and death suddenly intrudes upon the poet's pleasantly vacant state of mind, affecting his perception of an unexpected figure standing nearby. Perhaps, then, the encounter with the Old Soldier is recollected in this association exactly because the "bond" Wordsworth is claiming for life in the Dawn Dedication of the poet is a version of the complex bond of child and mother in reality long since broken, psychically felt to be indestructible.

The public road here has the character of "pathless solitudes." The road and solitude both derive their mysterious appeal from the strangeness of death as disappearance and from the "unknown" world beyond the vale. For the young poet pictured in the Dawn Dedication, the actual journeys from the vale had not been many, nor had the sense of the unknown been much explored yet in words by the poet writing about it. For instance, even his realization that "our being's heart and home is with infinitude," which comes to the poet living in retirement and writing the Imagination passage for Book VI of *The Prelude,* has not happened yet to the poet writing this particular account for Book IV about the young poet of the Dawn Dedication who was first to seek in the world for what he wanted. In part I am suggesting that in writing of this particular incident Wordsworth felt preconsciously the association of solitude and death, and of the road, disappearance, journey, and death, at a time when journey still meant unconsciously to him finding or refinding in the world and in life what had disappeared from the vale. But at the same time, I am suggesting another and inevitable emphasis: the figure is a man coming into the vale from "beyond." We have observed already that the psychic significance of the father to the child as "guide" into the world of men was a normative resolution achieved by Wordsworth and then blocked by a subsequent trauma and his fixation to it. We shall examine presently the significance of the death of Wordsworth's father when Wordsworth was thirteen; but here let us wonder whether the Old Soldier, who was real and who also seemed to arise "as from some distant region of my soul" evokes an unconscious sense of the father in Wordsworth. "Beyond" may seem a spatial representation of time—from "beyond" or from back further in time than the fixation governing the mind. The sense of the father is one deeply repressed and in an equivocal relation to the mother who is still primary in Wordsworth's mind.

The second "spot of time" in Book XI is Wordsworth's recollection of himself as a thirteen-year-old schoolboy sitting on a small mountain crag above the meeting place of two highways, down either of which his father's horses might come to bear him home for the Christmas holidays.

Feeling such "anxiety of hope," "restless" and "impatient," he looked down those roads expectantly. Ten days later he "followed his father's body to the grave." The account reveals, I think, that he had begun again to discover power in his father who, as a lawyer in the world beyond the vale, was becoming again a model for him or a guide at an appropriate time in the boy's life. But with the loss of his father, Wordsworth was left during puberty with exactly those modifications of the ego we have observed in his adolescence at Cambridge. There was to be no saving contact with his living father; and Wordsworth, unlike his older brother Richard, felt that he could not become, like their father before them, a lawyer. Although Wordsworth felt that Nature had reserved him for her own service in poetry, his "dedication" did not preclude the possibility that unconsciously his own imagination might conjure his father's shade from the "invisible world" to disrupt that bond. For that bond, however beautifully described, was a burdensome fixation Wordsworth unconsciously wished to break.

The lesson Wordsworth learned from the Old Leech-Gatherer is very different from the admonishment he himself gave to the Old Soldier, though the meetings are in obvious ways similar. The Old Leech-Gatherer's ability to endure confirms Wordsworth in his resolution for independence, an independence that is not that of habitual solitude in Nature but the opposite; and to Wordsworth he seems

> Like one whom I had met within a dream;
> Or like a man from some far region sent,
> To give me human strength, by apt admonishment.

"Region" and "dream" in "Resolution and Independence" call to mind the setting we have just looked at, the "harmonious imagery" into which intrudes the figure of the Old Soldier as the figure of solitude suggestive of death. In "Resolution and Independence," however, the real external incident seems providential to Wordsworth while it also suggests to him this other kind of inner experience associated with dream and soul. We should observe, then, that characteristically Wordsworth was experiencing external events as symbolic representations of inner needs, but events that now seem to him susceptible of a newer kind of "providential" interpretation. We should simply observe the changing characteristics of Providence in his feelings; it is not maternal, solicitous, and natural, but uncanny, austere, more difficult to comprehend, and supernatural: "Now whether it be by some peculiar grace/ A leading from above, a something given. . . ."

In the encounter with the Old Soldier, Wordsworth had heard: "a quiet uncomplaining voice/ A stately air of mild indifference," but to the young poet in the encounter and to the poet writing down his recollection of it very early in his career, the solemnity and sublimity of the Old Soldier's speech are qualified by his "strange half-absence," his "weakness and indifference." That is, both the young poet spoken of and the poet speaking of that encounter felt no limit to the potential of the Poet; the one was close to his "god-like hours," living with "majestic sway" as a "natural being in the strength of Nature,"[20] and the other was attempting to reconfirm himself in that assurance by talking about it. In the encounter with the Old Leech-Gatherer, written several years later, the poet hears something very similar, but is aware of a difference in himself hearing it; this old man seems providential in so far as Wordsworth is prepared to hear the wisdom of endurance in the world and of trust in God. If this contrast indicates a significant difference in Wordsworth, it suggests at the same time that the resolution and independence sought by the poet at the time of his marriage implied a significant change in his feelings about poetry and manhood.

In 1804, in Book VII, Wordsworth begins to deal directly with the years after Cambridge, at once maintaining his conscious intention to reaffirm the bond between providen-

[20] *The Prelude*, III, 191-194.

tial Nature and the Poet with which he began the poem and revealing his present tendency to resolve the stresses of poet and man in another way. The general observation of London in the book prepares the reader for its climax, the grotesque vision of Bartholomew Fair, which we shall consider presently. Book VII sustains the image we have observed of the austere young poet taking the high and "natural" view of Cambridge life, of its passions that to him seemed "mean and low," but strangely enough, the encounter with the Blind Beggar, which comes immediately before the climax of the book, is suggestive of the later tendency we have just observed in "Resolution and Independence." Wordsworth hesitates momentarily, and recollects himself caught up in the dense flow of London; here, the force of Imagination threatens him with another kind of revelation:

> O Friend! one feeling was there which belong'd
> To this great City, by exclusive right;
> How often in the overflowing Streets,
> Have I gone forward with the Crowd, and said
> Unto myself, the face of every one
> That passes by me is a mystery.
> Thus have I look'd, nor ceas'd to look, oppress'd
> By thoughts of what, and wither, when and how,
> Until the shapes before my eyes became
> A second-sight procession, such as glides
> Over still mountains, or appears in dreams;
> And all the ballast of familiar life,
> The present, and the past; hope, fear; all stays,
> All laws of acting, thinking, speaking man
> Went from me, neither knowing me, nor known.
> And once, far-travell'd in such mood, beyond
> The reach of common indications, lost
> Amid the moving pageant, 'twas my chance
> Abruptly to be smitten with the view
> Of a blind Beggar, who, with upright face,

Stood propp'd against a Wall, upon his Chest
Wearing a written paper, to explain
The story of the Man, and who he was.
My mind did at this spectacle turn round
As with the might of waters, and it seem'd
To me that in this Label was a type,
Or emblem, of the utmost that we know,
Both of ourselves and of the universe;
And, on the shape of the unmoving man,
His fixed face and sightless eyes, I look'd
As if admonish'd from another world.

(VII, 592-622)

The Blind Beggar is the starkest figure that the young Wordsworth encounters, a puzzling image of human identity. The man who cannot see and the poet who has been observing everything; the man whose lot can be reduced no further and the poet who has been recounting his privileged sense of unlimited growth; the man whose story in a few words seems as complete as at death, though he has still a spectral life, and the poet whose story has so far taken six books and will take seven more—are plainly juxtaposed in the reader's mind. And the poet writing about the confrontation momentarily sees his opposite as a limit, and again senses Providence in the encounter.

The feeling of "admonishment" from another world here reminds us of the same feeling in the encounter with the Old Leech-Gatherer; both check the tendency of the poet to continue his elaboration of the analogy between the clarity and self-knowledge of the poet's mind and God's. The Beggar is observed here as a very different kind of "emblem" of man's story: "the utmost that we know/ Both of ourselves and of the universe." The observation made by Wordsworth has mortal humility—a humility that will deepen in Wordsworth into Christian humility as the attributes of Providence for him become clearer; and the contrast with the analogy of the Poet's mind and the apocalyptic "one great mind" is striking. The clearest statement of the analogy of the Poet and God, so important to the younger Wordsworth, will be presented nevertheless in the Snowdon vision in Book XIII when he speaks of "an emblem of a mind that feeds upon infinity . . . ," but when he does present it, he does not apply the analogy confidently to himself.

In speaking of the Old Leech-Gatherer, Wordsworth associates "dream" and the unspecified "far region" as alternative similitudes of the source from which this Providential figure has been "sent" to give him human strength by "apt admonishment." Here, in the encounter with the Blind Beggar, the reality of London itself seems to be the analogue of both "dream" and "far region." "Oppressed/ By thoughts of what and whither, when and how," he seems to be carried along in both a crowd *and* a mood; he seems to be remembering both being in the crowd and the dream-like experience he seemed to be entering: "A second-sight procession, such as glides/ Over still mountains, or appears in dreams." Again we observe how an external situation and a psychic condition seem interchangeable, so that when he says "And once, far-travelled in such a mood, beyond/ The reach of common indications, lost/ Amid the moving pageant . . . ," he seems to be saying, "And once in a crowd, carried far into such a mood and lost in the moving dream-pageant . . . ," and simply saying, "once in such a mood, carried far beyond what of the city was familiar to me, lost. . . ." The abrupt confrontation with the Blind Beggar intensifies the feeling of ambiguity preceding it, so that we feel that we have been looking at external reality with the sense of dream.

Wordsworth has come from the thought that "the face of everyone/ That passes by me is a mystery," to the realization, in looking on this "fixed face and sightless eyes," that he is himself a mystery. It is not, then, simply that the masses of city people in crowds seem mysterious to poets who themselves have the "natural" vision of life and the assurance that in rural life people know them and know each other; it is, rather, that one presumes to self-knowledge in setting aside the human mystery and talking of a limited experience of life in so knowing a way. While the implication of the passage is plainly that God is admonishing the poet for exalting himself, Wordsworth does not develop that implication further. An extended consideration of the inimitability of God at this point would unsettle Wordsworth's interest in his own "godly" powers, originally had from Nature and then restored providentially by her. But coming just before the climax of Book VII, the incident qualifies that climax when one thinks about it.

Earlier in *The Prelude* Wordsworth had acknowledged a God who is in some way "above" Nature, though Wordsworth continued to feel that it was maternal Nature who was providential. For instance, he says in Book III:

> I had a world about me; 'twas my own,
> I made it; for it only liv'd to me,
> And to the God who look'd into my mind.
> (III, 142-144)

But this God is not a demanding one; he is, we have observed, something like the father of the pre-Oedipal or early Oedipal period: a somewhat absent model of truly autonomous power—such a God as one might be oneself in relation to the permissive mother; such a God above Nature as the Poet is tempted to proclaim himself in relation to permissive Nature. But in Book VII, the feeling of "admonishment" from God is remembered when the poet is approaching the matters of the recent, distressing period of his life. And it comes at a time in the present when his ability or willingness to maintain his exclusive attachment to Nature has been changing. The connections between the Old Soldier, the Old Leech-Gatherer and the Blind Beggar are plain; they serve to elucidate each other. We should add here, then, that where it is least appropriate to the general thesis of *The Prelude,* the appearance of the Blind Beggar is like a psychic intrusion into the narrative. Wordsworth may persist in maintaining that Nature restored in the poet what Nature had originally formed in him, but it will be impossible for him to communicate a consistent interpretation of self for the period about which he feels unconsciously that Nature betrayed him to an ordeal, as once his mother had. So it is that here an old event has insisted upon its relevance, and a newer way of feeling has prevented the poet from doing with his account of his confrontation with the Blind Beggar what he had done earlier with his encounter with the Old Soldier.

3. Bad Dreams and London

It was in response to London that Wordsworth began to articulate a deeper perplexity of his own. To him, its low and misguided life was an extension and intensification of the worldly meanness he had already observed at Cambridge. As the youth without employment and without a plan that would draw him into its life, he was still the detached observer; but London, unlike Cambridge, was too formidable a reality for him to dismiss with a few fond recollections of his native vale.

Notice how in associating "dream" with "some far region" of the world and of the soul, Wordsworth refers different kinds of experiences to each other to characterize the feeling of significance. Perspectives of inner and outer distance are figuratively interchangeable. And Wordsworth, who says that the road beyond the vale led mysteriously to "things unknown and without bound," as if they were moods as well as places, also represents London in Book VII as "a far region." "London," the name of an unknown and distant place, stands for the mystery of the world itself as the child had imagined it, something magically different from the vale.[21] But the London the young man actually sees plainly becomes the analogue of a bad dream and be-

[21] *Ibid.*, VII, 81-120.

comes associated in this way with older and more perplexing matters.

Of Cambridge, the half-way station between the vale and the world beyond, Wordsworth wrote in Book III:

> I was the Dreamer, they the Dream; I roam'd
> Delighted, through the motley spectacle;
> Gowns grave or gaudy, Doctors, Students, Streets,
> Lamps, Gateways, Flocks of Churches, Courts and
> Towers . . .
>
> (III, 28-31)

Although he begins by simply recording the excitement and the first impressions of a "mountain youth," he then recalls Cambridge too as a spectacle of "passions that did to me/ Seem mean and low" as it turns at times into a bad dream prefiguring London. In Book VIII, recapitulating the themes of the first seven books, he again describes the transition from the vale to Cambridge, and to London beyond it, in the same way:

> Erelong transported hence as in a dream
> I found myself begirt with temporal shapes
> Of vice and folly thrust upon my view,
> Objects of sport, and ridicule, and scorn,
> Manners and characters discriminate,
> And little busy passions that eclips'd,
> As well they might, the impersonated thought,
> The idea or abstraction of the Kind.
>
> (VIII, 641-648)

But in alluding to what the dream "thrust upon" his view, he also reveals feelings that are less moralized:

> being brought more near
> As I was now, to guilt and wretchedness,
> I trembled, thought of human life at times
> With an indefinite terror and dismay
> Such as the storms and angry elements

> Had bred in me, but gloomier far, a dim
> Analogy to uproar and misrule,
> Disquiet, danger, and obscurity.
>
> (VIII, 657-664)

His argument in Book VIII is "Love of Nature Leading to Love of Mankind," but to him the great crisis in his life was between the ideal of mankind and the reality of people. Nature, as the poet understands her intentions, has led the poet to idealize himself and to love mankind; but "human life" (or human nature) is unaccountably vaster than the poet's understanding of Nature, Mankind or himself. The poet finds that he cannot love what he cannot account for in the city and in History; and what he cannot account for in those far regions of humanity reminds him of dreams.

Since we have asked in other contexts what states of pleasurable feeling are being unconsciously projected into Nature and perceived there, affecting his relationship with Nature, we shall have to ask presently whether states of "terror and dismay" are being unconsciously projected into the city and perceived there, affecting his relationship with people. What is the connection between the "indefinite terror and dismay" accompanying his thoughts of human life and the "Storms and angry elements" in Nature with which he associates them as a "dim/ Analogy to uproar and misrule/ Disquiet, danger and obscurity"? The analogy suggests too that there is more to Nature than is suggested by his most characteristic use of the word.

Certainly he felt a difference between the nature in which things happen and the "Presence" in Nature whose providence he inferred from his experience. Repression prevented him from fully considering Nature's "intentions" in everything that had happened to him. For the ego to deny its doubts and allay its anxieties about Nature's "intentions," he attempted to believe instead that it was Nature who, in her love for him, had exposed him to terror and dismay, early in his life and for his own good. Nevertheless, his belief in what was for his own good led inevitably to something he could not account for wholly in terms of Nature—his need to be independent of her and even superior to her. His inspired belief in the powers of the poet necessitated beliefs that went beyond Nature and which came unaccountably from his own imagination—from unconscious sources of feeling.

The suggestion, then, is that Wordsworth characteristically used "Nature" to exclude other feelings about causation he had experienced, though unconsciously they persisted, increasing in intensity and giving rise to grand and fearful imaginings. These other feelings came from the repressed earlier trauma of Oedipal conflict with the father, in which the power of the father had revealed itself and had impressed the imagination of the child, who felt *admonished.* But to the poet, any suggestion of these earlier matters, at odds with the fixed form taken by his obsession with the mother and Nature, seemed troubling, unnatural, or supernatural, as did dreams, the City and God. Wordsworth's feelings about powers outside and inside himself change in the course of *The Prelude* as his self-assurance rises and falls. The relationships of Nature to himself, of Nature to God, and of God to himself seem generally ambiguous; and these ambiguities, which we must now consider, are like those of mother, child, and father to someone uncertain of how he identifies himself with, and distinguishes himself from, each parent.

When in Book I Wordsworth says:

> Wisdom and Spirit of the universe!
> Thou Soul that art the Eternity of Thought!
> That giv'st to forms and images a breath
> And everlasting motion!
>
> (I, 428-431)

he is characterizing a kind of Godhead above Nature, but one with even less discernible attributes than the "God" in Book III—"the God that look'd into my mind." If the

"Soul" that is the "eternity of thought" is above Nature, it seems merely to reflect Nature's intentions; and Nature seems to "intend" whatever the poet imagines. For Wordsworth, here, God has not the personal attributes of God the Father, who inspires awe "in the Mind of Man." In fact, in the earlier version of these lines in MS V, the manifestations of powers in Nature are more crudely or primitively imagined:

> Ah! not in vain, ye Beings of the hills
> And ye that walk the woods and open heaths
> By moon or starlight . . .

The lines are echoed slightly later in Book I:

> Ye Presences of Nature, in the sky
> Or on the earth! Ye Visions of the hills!
> And Souls of lonely places! can I think
> A vulgar hope was yours when Ye employ'd
> Such ministry, when Ye through many a year
> Haunting me thus among my boyish sports,
> On caves and trees, upon the woods and hills,
> Impress'd upon all forms the characters
> Of danger or desire, and thus did make
> The surface of the universal earth
> With triumph, and delight, and hope, and fear,
> Work like a sea?
>
> (I, 490-501)

And the earlier version of these lines in MS V read:

> Ye Powers of earth, ye genii of the Springs
> And ye that have your voices in the clouds
> And ye that are familiars of the Lakes
> And standing pools, Ah, not for trivial ends
> Through snow and sunshine, through the sparkling plains
> Of moonlight frost and in the stormy day
> Did ye with such assiduous love pursue
> Your favorite and your joy. I may not think . . .

In talking about himself in relation to Nature, Wordsworth begins by expressing his earliest sense of powers around him. "Presences" in Nature were not at first the one maternal Presence, nor were "Powers" the power of the "one great mind."

What is called pantheism in the younger Wordsworth's style may be seen to derive from the experiences recollected here. As he characterizes the feelings and mysterious perceptions of the lonely child in Nature "haunted" in his play, he preconsciously attests to the strangeness of that circumstance by preserving the recollection of variety—the "beings, powers, presences"—all momentary projections, startlingly perceived. Furthermore, Wordsworth's projections and perceptions reveal a vestigial infantile sense of powerful and sexually undifferentiated beings around him—very appropriately, I think—for although the child had already lost his mother, he did not know whose attributes he was "finding again" in Nature; and since he was experiencing a discovery of "intentions" in Nature, it is psychologically appropriate that the poet remembers and imagines, and so recapitulates, the earliest infantile and mysterious perceptions of powers outside one from which one's powers will derive. Gradually, between 1798 and 1804, as Wordsworth wrote about his powers, he further characterized these "powers" and "beings," and he grandly imagined their "intentions." There was *then* a maternal Presence in Nature and a God that looked uncritically into his mind. Only as Wordsworth was compelled to imagine further the extent of his own powers did he begin to concern himself with Godliness; Godliness then became greatness of mind. The Wisdom and the spirit of the universe gives "to forms and images a breath/ And everlasting motion"; and Wordsworth, in saying this in Book I in 1799, is preparing himself to announce the analogy between the "first poetic impulse" of the Blest Babe and the "one great mind" in Book II in 1800. Later, he would elaborate the analogy between the Poet and God in Book VI in 1804. The Babe without realizing it and the

Poet consciously realizing it are Godly, giving "to forms and images a breath/ And everlasting motion." So conceived, God gradually becomes like the Blest Babe and like the Poet so that the Poet may be like God. It would be "Romantic" to go on in that vein about the Poet, but when *this* poet begins to reconsider his recent despair, he imagines himself "admonished" in Book VII for his presumption, and talks differently of God and himself in the later books of the poem in 1805.

These passages (quoted above), especially the earlier versions from MS V, echo Prospero's speech in Act V of *The Tempest* unmistakably.[22] Why should Wordsworth have Prospero in mind here, consciously or preconsciously? Prospero, a God-like figure in the world of his island—himself the product of the "God-like" mind of the poet, Shakespeare, who is himself more present in this figure and in this dramatic world of his own creation than in any of his other plays—is a brainteasing figure to contemplate at any time, and especially in this association. I think that the likelihood of preconscious association of language with figure with *context* by Wordsworth is strong here, just as earlier in the echo of the "viewless winds" from Claudio's speech in *Measure for Measure* where the imagination attempts to deal with the fact of death and the fear of it as an incomprehensible journey.[23] Wordsworth is unconsciously alluding to a context that expresses his own doubts and fears about himself in Nature. The echo of Prospero-Poet calls to our minds the figure of the powerful father—Prospero *is* a father and to childlike Miranda is a "God of Power"[24]—and makes clearer at the same time the paternal character of the Godhead which Wordsworth has been characterizing by a single poetic attribute, the power of Imagination in the "eternity of thought." The echo also calls to mind Death—"graves at my command/ Have wak'd

22 William Shakespeare, *The Tempest*, V, i, 33ff.

23 See above, p. 114.

24 Shakespeare, *The Tempest*, I, ii, 10.

their sleepers, op'd and let 'em forth/ By my so potent art"[25]—in one of the unconscious associations we have observed of death and poetry in Wordsworth's mind. And death in another sense, too: Prospero abjures his poetic magic finally to return to life with common humanity and to contemplate death. Death is to him the real mortal limit at which analogies between the man of poetic genius and his God cease. Although in youth's season of disbelief, Wordsworth would beguile himself with analogies and deny specific traumatic fears, unconsciously he wishes to contemplate death—death and *past* sufferings associated with it.

Prospero's control of the appearances of Nature is significantly different from Wordsworth's, though Wordsworth, I think, was preconsciously struck by the similarity. Prospero's knowledge of human nature and of *himself* gives him his power over the appearances of Nature; and although Wordsworth speaks of studying the appearances of Nature, of turning his mind "in upon itself," and of acquiring the power to transform familiar objects in ways that excite wonder, he believes this process to be the simple privilege of his growth in Nature. "Privilege" here separates Wordsworth's description from Shakespeare's. Prospero has "prospered" in suffering; through introspection, he has seen the weakness of his own youthful character and he has transmuted painful losses into imaginative and spiritual gains. When Wordsworth says "privilege," then, we think of trauma, of losses, and of suffering dynamically present but repressed and denied in him. The young Wordsworth, unlike Prospero, mistakes the efficacy of his art, forgets the tenure of his own being, and imagines himself a "God of power."

Long before conceiving of a maternal and providential Nature, Wordsworth had experienced Nature without thinking about it, as he makes clear enough in "Tintern

[25] *Ibid.*, v, i, 48-50.

Abbey" and *The Prelude*. In Nature he experienced passively the beauty, stasis, enclosure, and peace associated unconsciously with love and the mother; at times, more aggressively, he enacted his more disturbing unconscious fantasies in his play. If at times in these experiences the child dimly perceived "powers" and "beings" in Nature "haunting him"—the psychic monitions of an increasingly disturbed self-consciousness—it was the highly self-conscious poet who subsequently imagined that he had mysteriously perceived Nature's "intentions." To the reader, it is always plain that Nature's choice of Wordsworth is Wordsworth's imaginative choice of Nature; but Wordsworth's suggestive formulation of Nature's intentions is inadequate to explain his early experiences of the uncanny in Nature, and it is in the unexplored subject of "terror and dismay," "dreams," "storms and angry elements," "disquiet, danger and obscurity" that we seek an alternative understanding of the poet whose reliance on Nature gradually changed to submission to the traditional God above Nature. For instance, the Boat-Stealing episode.

In MS JJ, which contains the earliest surviving drafts of a large part of Book I, there are two of Wordsworth's attempts at the Boat-Stealing episode, from as early as 1798. That is, Wordsworth wished to write of it before there was a *Prelude* and a theory of growth to "explain" it. Like the other adventures of the school boy "transplanted" from the original vale, this one has the mark of unconscious intentions burdening the activity described. In a manifestly associational way, the account is used by Wordsworth as another example of "privilege"; we may find in it the corresponding sense of trauma. Speaking of how Nature, "when she would frame a favor'd Being," also uses "severer interventions, ministry more palpable" than the "gentlest visitation" of Love, Wordsworth cites this experience to exemplify Nature's use of "pain and fear." He believes that in this way, early in his life, Nature had harmonized in him "the passions that build up our human soul" and that the mind of the child had acquired "mighty forms" associated with "high objects, with enduring things." In comparison, he disdains "the mean and vulgar works of Man."

In so contriving to explain his growth, Wordsworth implicitly denies the significance to growth of the masculine and paternal, separating them from the "natural" and relegating them to the city and History as respectively the place and chronicle of man's meanness and vulgarity. His encounter with History, then, with historical societies as they reflect the personalities of men, had the psychic inevitability of conflict between modes of identity maintained in opposed ways. In his "journey" from the vale to the world beyond—Cambridge, London, France—he exposed himself to the nominal "reality" of the world as it obtains for most people. And we can see, for example, as early as the encounter with the Old Soldier who enters the vale from the world beyond, how Wordsworth confronts men with an opposed "natural" wisdom. We shall see how the French Revolution provided him with an occasion for confronting all of human History with the same inspired audacity. But if the Old Soldier, the Leech-Gatherer and the Blind Beggar seem, to the slightly older Wordsworth writing about them, to have come from within, from the "far region" of the soul, from dreams, and from a Providence above, as well as from the nominal reality of the world far beyond the vale, then the suggestion is that as Wordsworth approached the subject of the recent crisis in his life, he unconsciously felt that his dream-like conflict with the world and his gradual rediscovery of the father in his psyche had been providential. Through conflict and crisis, despair and recovery, he achieved, as we shall see, a normality he had always lacked, but achieved it in place of the greatness of mind he had sought and the true consciousness he was seeking in poetry. That achievement must seem ironic to the reader who has found Wordsworth's poetic obsession a great one, his audacity the earnest of a psychic truth by which he was possessed, of which he was not quite in possession. First, however, we should observe the Boat-Stealing episode and his attempt to explain the recollection by his belief in Nature as a loving and disciplining mother.

The "schoolboy traveller at the holidays," alone in a strange vale, finds a shepherd's boat by the shore and takes it out on the lake at night:

> The moon was up, the Lake was shining clear
> Among the hoary mountains; from the Shore
> I push'd, and struck the oars and struck again
> In cadence, and my little Boat mov'd on
> Even like a Man who walks with stately step
> Though bent on speed. It was an act of stealth
> And troubled pleasure; not without the voice
> Of mountain-echoes did my Boat move on,
> Leaving behind her still on either side
> Small circles glittering idly in the moon,
> Until they melted all into one track
> Of sparkling light. A rocky Steep uprose
> Above the Cavern of the Willow tree
> And now, as suited one who proudly row'd
> With his best skill, I fix'd a steady view
> Upon the top of that same craggy ridge,
> The bound of the horizon, for behind
> Was nothing but the stars and the grey sky.
> She was an elfin Pinnace; lustily
> I dipp'd my oars into the silent Lake,
> And, as I rose upon the stroke, my Boat
> Went heaving through the water, like a Swan;
> When from behind that craggy Steep, till then
> The bound of the horizon, a huge Cliff,
> As if with voluntary power instinct,
> Uprear'd its head. I struck, and struck again,
> And, growing still in stature, the huge Cliff
> Rose up between me and the stars, and still,
> With measur'd motion, like a living thing,

Strode after me. With trembling hands I turn'd,
And through the silent water stole my way
Back to the Cavern of the Willow tree.
There, in her mooring-place, I left my Bark,
And, through the meadows homeward went,
  with grave
And serious thoughts; and after I had seen
That spectacle, for many days, my brain
Work'd with a dim and undetermin'd sense
Of unknown modes of being; in my thoughts
There was a darkness, call it solitude,
Or blank desertion, no familiar shapes
Of hourly objects, images of trees,
Of sea or sky, no colours of green fields;
But huge and mighty Forms that do not live
Like living men mov'd slowly through my mind
By day and were the trouble of my dreams.
(I, 383-427)

It is often felt that in the Boat-Stealing episode the boy feels a guilty conscience because he has the moral knowledge that when one steals one knows one is stealing. Conscience rises up against him. But when Wordsworth talks about "stealth and troubled pleasure," he is not really talking about stealing, which does not even describe accurately what the boy is doing. Surely, the boy intended to return the boat, even if he was not innocent in taking it in the first place. It is rather the desire to possess momentarily, and to use to one's own passionate satisfaction, what belongs to another man that is the "guilty" wish here. Psychologically, the appearance of the feeling of guilt should remind us of the formative causes of conscience rather than the interpretations made in juvenile court.

"Even like a man," he says, making implicitly a comparison of boy with absent man: with the oars he "struck . . . and struck again," making the boat, propelled by him, move "even like a Man." Proud of his skill, sensually enjoying the rhythm of rising upon the stroke, the boy masters the boat: "she" moves to his "lust." It is *then* that a coincidence of unconscious fear and optical illusion takes place, which makes his experience of a guilty conscience so memorable. As the boy rows away from the shore (facing, of course, the receding shore line as he rows), the huge cliff seems to lift itself suddenly above the horizon, above the "craggy steep" of the mountain which had been the horizon for the boy's eye until then. The towering cliff seems "like a living thing" "striding" after him; and as fear increases the rhythm of his strokes, the very attempt to get away seems to increase the speed of pursuit, the striding and towering effects of the cliff. In panic the boy persists, but then fearfully submits; he must row to the shore, offering his back meekly to his pursuer, able to escape the cliff in his field of vision only by surrendering to it.

Despite his explanation of Nature's intentions, Wordsworth has unconsciously recollected and characterized a strikingly Oedipal experience, reminding us that guilt in this kind of symbolically enacted sexual fantasy derives from an earlier climax of fantasies, a psychic confrontation with the paternal Presence. Here, the reader—Wordsworth's or mine—must decide for himself whether the "huge cliff" that stands towering over the boy is or is not an unconscious projection of the paternal presence. The boy, his pride in manliness cast down, is a guilty child; he meekly renounces his wish and his pleasure. Wordsworth, of course, cannot say that this is the case, but he does more than simply not say so. The point is that to most of us it would be simply more "natural" to "imagine" the frightening father than the disciplining mother in this massive representation of conscience. But describing the "huge and mighty forms" in his mind that trouble his dreams, Wordsworth says that they "do not live/ Like living men," which reminds us that live men are the logical comparison in point of fear for the child and unconsciously for Wordsworth, even though Wordsworth says "men" only to distinguish between what is human and alive and what is inhumanly and uncannily life-like. If he did not need to believe that Nature loved the boy and intended merely to instruct him with fear, he could easily believe she had "led" him through desire to terror and had abandoned him there; but despite his inability to say what these "unknown modes of being" are like, one continues to think that they look like the "huge cliff" and are like the paternal presence. Perhaps, as in the Oedipus complex, Nature, like the permissive mother who has "led" him, has also seemed to summon the absent father; and this, the poet has unconsciously remembered. It is curious that Wordsworth believes that in this way Nature purified his passions, settling the matter of low passions early in his life.

The experience took place at night in the moonlight, and if it supplies the trouble of dreams, we can see why: the experience had become so like a nightmare that it seemed in consequence less like an actual experience in Nature. The darkened landscape is a "faceless" one—without its familiar daylight features; and the stark imagery of the setting is like the imagery of Nature usurped unnaturally by the tyranny of dream. His afterthoughts, then, are darkened—Nature, who led him to the experience, absent from them:

> in my thoughts
> There was a darkness, call it solitude,
> Or blank desertion, no familiar shapes
> Of hourly objects, images of trees,
> Of sea or sky, no colours of green fields;
> But huge and mighty Forms that do not live
> Like living men mov'd slowly through my mind
> By day and were the trouble of my dreams.
> (I, 420-427)

There is, then, a feeling of desertion associated fearfully with solitude and there is a Presence in Nature, or a Presence in some strange relation to Nature, that is terrifying, although in being at the same time dissociated from "Nature" as he generally uses the word, it is more like *an Absence.* He has "a dim and undetermin'd sense" of something that can manifest itself in Nature. It attaches itself to other things that seem unnatural; it appears suddenly and fearfully like the "huge cliff"; and it is associated with dreams.[26]

I think that the Old Soldier, in Book IV, appearing suddenly as from within, associated with dreams, attended by fear, perceived at night in the moonlight, is momentarily suggestive of the same immanence of the paternal presence in Wordsworth's psyche. Like the Boat-Stealing episode, the poetic account of the Old Soldier recalls earlier betrayals to terror—"blank desertions" associated with the mother. Before the traumatic loss of the mother, there had been the Oedipus complex and its resolution for Wordsworth. If the frightening confrontation in the climax of the Oedipus complex is a psychic ritual of growth necessary to manhood and to man's likeness to other men, then in his poetic intention to seek the latent meaning of his life, Wordsworth was unconsciously seeking to free himself from his obsession with the mother and from the very bondage to Nature he

[26] See Reuben A. Brower, *The Poetry of Robert Frost.* Professor Brower writes: "In passages like this Wordsworth did succeed in writing *philosophical* poetry, poetry in which he moves from one level of consciousness (outward seeing and primitive terror) to another (inward reflection and metaphysical interpretation) in a single unbroken act of expression." Professor Brower's reading of the boat episode is a fine one, but my objection is to the word "philosophical" here; for what is philosophical about the implied inward reflection of "my brain/ Work'd with a dim and undetermin'd sense/ Of unknown modes of being?" I think that Wordsworth often intimates metaphysical concerns by the substitution of abstract words for vivid images and metaphors, but what Brower is describing is how Wordsworth's diction changes when he is feeling "philosophical." Whereas the implied philosophy cannot be inferred, except in the most general ways (and hence, the loosely descriptive adjectives regularly employed to describe Wordsworth's thoughts and metaphysical states), the metaphors he often associated with strong and recurrent feelings can be traced to other contexts, providing some connections between the kinds of experiences from which they derive.

was celebrating; he was seeking to experience again, in imaginative form, the providential conflict with the father he had once experienced and resolved. In young manhood, tempted to test the natural strength of the Poet, he had sought in the French Revolution conflict with men; later, inspired to give a poetic account of himself, he sought to imagine the child-like divinity of the Poet and discovered instead, in talking of crisis, despair and recovery, his common humanity and a saving father-God above Nature.

In looking from the Boat-Stealing episode to the far region of London in Book VII, we should remember the contrast of the "peace of Nature"[27] and the trouble of dreams in the Boat-Stealing episode and the connection between them: Wordsworth's wishes trouble the peace of Nature, his dreams are troubled in consequence. In troubled dreams, it is what is excluded from Wordsworth's very "partial" sense of Nature that becomes the trouble; and the city, oppressively lacking in natural imagery, becomes to Wordsworth a disturbing analogue of a troubled dream. We may infer, then, that what Wordsworth unconsciously excludes from Nature he unconsciously projects into the city and experiences there. Thus, in remembering the aggressiveness and the implicit sexuality of the Boat-Stealing episode and the evocation of conscience that troubles dreams, we may see how human passion and sexuality, observed by Wordsworth in city life, are significant in his feeling of aversion for the city. His belief in the purity of his passions, effected by Nature in the poet, is affronted by the city. Human nature, closed in upon itself, seems unnatural and questionably like his own.

Book VII is about London. It concludes with Wordsworth's vision of Bartholomew Fair, in which he brings the book's poetic effects and implications to a sharp focus. The fair provides Wordsworth with an occasion for a profound

[27] Saying "peace of Nature" is a convenience to the author; the phrase reads: "a trouble to the peace/ That was among them." *The Prelude*, I, 323-324. For my analysis of the bird-stealing episode, see above, pp. 184-186.

self-justification, an exaltation of the Poet who cherishes his detachment from the city. He introduces the spectacle of the fair by asking ominously

> What say you then,
> To times, when half the City shall break out
> Full of one passion, vengeance, rage, or fear,
> To executions, to a Street on fire,
> Mobs, riots, or rejoicings?
> (VII, 644-648)

We should keep in mind this characterization of passion as lacking all control for his account of the French Revolution, to be dealt with presently, and notice that he introduces the description he is to give with a strong dissociation of it from himself:

> there see
> A work that's finish'd to our hands, that lays,
> If any spectacle on earth can do,
> The whole creative powers of man asleep!
> (VII, 651-654)

Perhaps the spectacle keeps the "creative powers" of its city participants *asleep,* but he actually means that his own mind received this spectacle already formed, which seems to put "the creative powers of man asleep." Wordsworth, however, invokes the muse's help to present it, and in doing so, regains poetic control; but he calls the spectacle a bad dream and expresses his revulsion. The people of the city, lacking the Poet's detachment and imagination, live this dream. One can read his description of it many times without realizing that in fact ordinary people are having a very good time:

> what a hell
> For eyes and ears! what anarchy and din
> Barbarian and infernal! 'tis a dream,
> Monstrous in colour, motion, shape, sight, sound.

Below, the open space, through every nook
Of the wide area, twinkles, is alive
With heads; the midway region and above
Is throng'd with staring pictures, and huge scrolls,
Dumb proclamations of the prodigies;
And chattering monkeys dangling from their poles,
And children whirling in their roundabouts;
With those that stretch the neck, and strain the eyes,
And crack the voice in rivalship, the crowd
Inviting; with buffoons against buffoons
Grimacing, writhing, screaming; him who grinds
The hurdy-gurdy, at the fiddle weaves;
Rattles the salt-box, thumps the kettle-drum,
And him who at the trumpet puffs his cheeks,
The silver-collar'd Negro with his timbrel,
Equestrians, Tumblers, Women, Girls, and Boys,
Blue-breech'd, pink vested, and with towering plumes.
—All moveables of wonder from all parts,
Are here, Albinos, painted Indians, Dwarfs,
The Horse of Knowledge, and the learned Pig,
The Stone-eater, the Man that swallows fire,
Giants, Ventriloquists, the Invisible Girl,
The Bust that speaks, and moves its goggling eyes,
The Wax-work, Clock-work, all the marvellous craft
Of modern Merlins, wild Beasts, Puppet-shows,
All out-o'-th'-way, far-fetch'd, perverted things,
All freaks of Nature, all Promethean thoughts
Of Man; his dulness, madness, and their feats,
All jumbled up together to make up
This Parliament of Monsters. Tents and Booths
Meanwhile, as if the whole were one vast Mill,
Are vomiting, receiving, on all sides,
Men, Women, three-years' Children, Babes in arms.
(VII, 658-694)

We have already seen most of the images of this passage in his poetic "tour" of London, which precedes it: the "hubbub," the exotic foreigners and "all specimens of man," the screaming venders, the ballad singers, the jostling crowd, the performing people and animals. What he says of their grotesque reality—"those mimic sights that ape/ The absolute presence of reality"—attaches to all the spectacles of the city and to the city itself as a vast spectacle, a "blank confusion." And with this suggestion of unreality, he enhances the alternative of the detached and natural view; the Poet prepares his reader for his final vision, and then presents Bartholomew Fair as at once the freak show and the emblem of the city.

The suggestion is that belief in the reality of these illusions is "delusion bold." The poet presents at the same time his view of simple people beholding these various spectacles, and in such a way that they are really being contrasted with the poet as viewers of London. Seated amongst the "rabblement" at a show, he observes them:

> Nor was it mean delight
> To watch crude nature work in untaught minds,
> To note the laws and progress of belief;
> (VII, 296-298)

City people are a permanent uncomprehending audience of spectacles and of the spectacle in which they live. The audience at the theatre is Hydra-humanity, "the many-headed mass of the spectators"[28]; the fair, the emblem of the city, is "alive with heads," its monstrous life that of an unnatural beast.

His apostrophe affirms his privilege as one who can see with vision and detachment:

> Oh, blank confusion! and a type not false
> Of what the mighty City is itself
> To all except a Straggler here and there,
> To the whole Swarm of its inhabitants;

[28] *Ibid.*, VII, 466-467.

An undistinguishable world to men,
The slaves unrespited of low pursuits,
Living amid the same perpetual flow
Of trivial objects, melted and reduced
To one identity, by differences
That have no law, no meaning, and no end;
Oppression under which even highest minds
Must labour, whence the strongest are not free;
But though the picture weary out the eye,
By nature of an unmanageable sight,
It is not wholly so to him who looks
In steadiness, who hath among least things
An under-sense of greatest; sees the parts
As parts, but with a feeling of the whole.

(VII, 695-712)

His belief in his own passions purified and disciplined by Nature is being contrasted with his observation of passions seen in men who cannot see themselves with detachment:

The slaves unrespited of low pursuits,
Living amid the same perpetual flow
Of trivial objects.

(VII, 700-702)

In speaking of Nature's purifying discipline in the Boat-Stealing episode, let us recall, he had used almost the same words about man, disdaining him:

Not with the mean and vulgar works of Man,
But with high objects, with enduring things,
With life and nature, purifying thus
The elements of feeling and of thought,
And sanctifying, by such discipline,
Both pain and fear, until we recognize
A grandeur in the beatings of the heart.

(I, 435-441)

Although he says of himself in London,

> This did I feel in that vast receptacle.
> The Spirit of Nature was upon me here;
> The Soul of Beauty and enduring life
> Was present as a habit, and diffused,
> Through meagre lines and colours, and the press
> Of self-destroying, transitory things
> Composure and ennobling Harmony,
>
> (VII, 734-740)

the reader must wonder what is the possible connection in human nature between the poet who feels "a grandeur in the beating of the heart" and the seemingly less than human humanity of London, "the whole *swarm* of its inhabitants." This is a question Wordsworth pauses to take up somewhat abstractly in Book VIII—"Love of Nature Leading to Love of Mankind"—before proceeding to the more disturbing memories of France and the French Revolution in Books IX and X.

When Wordsworth says "slaves unrespited of low pursuits," he is contrasting the historical reality of human passion with his idealization of his own life: "Pure passions, virtue, knowledge, and delight/ The holy life of music and of verse."[29] He means "slaves" in a sense that could be called Platonic: "slaves of appetite." Man without "religious dignity of mind," he had said in Book IV, is "a pageant plaything with vile claws." But this strong reaction to passion makes clearer the conflict he felt between the *ascesis* of the poet and his own sexuality. In Book IV Wordsworth also recalled how "revelry" (its "manliness and freedom") had seduced him from his "habitual quest" as an "unworldly-minded youth, given up/ To Nature and to Books." The poet now writing Book VII, however, does not want it to seem that passion was a problem for this young poet of the Dawn Dedication who was then taking the high and "natural" view of London; rather, it was

[29] *Ibid.*, I, 54-55.

natural that his own sexuality did *not* trouble him. But it is in Book VII that humanity seems sexual to Wordsworth in disturbing ways.

Let us recall here that we find the story of "The Maid of Buttermere" in Book VII, as well as his observation in the theater lobby of the Beautiful Boy and his harlot mother. While observing the unconscious appeal of the mother-child-death associations of these two stories to Wordsworth, we may fail to notice how sexuality has attracted his attention. Still, the Maid of Buttermere was seduced and betrayed by a city man; and Wordsworth identifies himself with both the Maid and her babe significantly, himself shocked by such men. In the other story, the mother of the Beautiful Boy has an unnatural—that is, too openly sexual—appearance ("on her cheek the tints were false/ A painted bloom"); and the child is surrounded by a ring of "dissolute men and shameless women."[30] The mother, inattentive, unheedful of danger to the child, is a woman giving herself to vanity and to men; and again Wordsworth identifies the child with himself. It is possible that Wordsworth is distorting natural adult sexuality in recollection, making it seem "unnatural," because unconsciously "natural" means "filial" to him. The aversion expressed here is something to be remarked but questioned, because the poet who speaks of purified passions in relation to Nature and love makes all desire seem incestuous. But just as in Book IV when he disapproves in retrospect of indulgence in "revelry," it is impossible to know what exactly the young man may have felt different from what the poet imagines he is recollecting.

Turning, then, from Wordsworth's official version of his youth in *The Prelude* to his early poem "Descriptive Sketches," we are surprised by the discrepancy. "Descriptive Sketches," which was inspired by his college vacation tour through the Alps in 1791, was first published in 1793. Eventually, Wordsworth was to tone down the ardor of youth

30 *Ibid.*, VII, 386-387.

in the poem, revising it soberly, but in the original one hears that

> Soft bosoms breathe around contagious sighs
> And amorous music on the water dies;
>
> (114-115)

What may have been personal experience has certainly been set down here as a recollection of Pope in tranquillity, an echo made more perceptible by the heroic couplets. Further on, again echoing Pope in a passage eventually deleted,[31] these lines appear, perhaps the most erotic lines written by Wordsworth:

> Farewell! those forms that, in thy noon-tide shade,
> Rest, near their little plots of wheaten glade;
> Those steadfast eyes, that beating breasts inspire
> To throw the 'sultry ray' of young Desire;
> Those lips, whose tides of fragrance come and go,
> Accordant to the cheek's unquiet glow;
> Those shadowy breasts in love's soft light array'd,
> And rising, by the moon of passion sway'd.
> —Thy fragrant gales and lute-resounding streams,
> Breathe o'er the failing soul voluptuous dreams;
> While Slavery, forcing the sunk mind to dwell
> On joys that might disgrace the captive's cell,
> Her shameless timbrel shakes along thy marge,
> And winds between thine isles the vocal barge.
> Yet, arts are thine that rock th' unsleeping heart,
> And smiles to Solitude and Want impart.
>
> (148-163)

31 See Alexander Pope, "The Rape of the Lock," II, 49-50:

> While melting music steals upon the sky,
> And soften'd sounds along the waters die.

Also, in *The Dunciad* (B), IV, 304-306:

> To isles of fragrance, lily silvered vales,
> Diffusing languor in the panting gales:
> To lands of singing, or of dancing slaves,
> Love-whispering woods, and lute-resounding waves.
>
> (*Poems of Alexander Pope*, ed. J. Sutherland, vol. V, p. 374.)

Since these lines seem to express the young man's impulses, we may surmise that in talking retrospectively of London Wordsworth voiced a moral aversion to sexuality more strongly than he felt it at the time. In "Descriptive Sketches," he pictures himself as a sorrowing young man with a secret grief, itself perhaps a youthful poetic and melancholic pose, but revealingly expressed;

> But doubly pitying Nature loves to show'r
> Soft on his wounded heart her healing pow'r,
> Who plods o'er hills and vales his road forlorn,
> Wooing her varying charms from eve to morn.
>
> (13-16)

"Wooing" Nature (we may recall an "appetite; a feeling and a love" from "Tintern Abbey") has a sensual satisfaction and a preoccupying anticipation of greater delight from her; and yet it also implies reluctance or reserve about actual people. The observer, observed by maidens, is the youth projecting his own unconscious thoughts about himself into them; what shows here is his curiosity about his own reticence, his awareness of Nature's younger rivals:

> The maidens eye him with inquiring glance,
> Much wondering what sad stroke of crazing Care
> Or desperate Love could lead a wanderer there,
> Me, lur'd by hope her sorrows to remove,
> A heart, that could not much itself approve,
> O'er Gallia's wastes of corn dejected led,
> Her road elms rustling thin above my head,
> Or through her truant pathway's native charms,
> By secret villages and lonely farms,
> To where the Alps, ascending white in air,
> Toy with the Sun, and glitter from afar.
>
> (42-52)

If the sensuality of "voluptuous dreams" or of waking fancies was really felt, then his characteristic reserve with people *was* a burden to him. Beneath the need to celebrate the bond and the intimacy with Nature was the desire for sexual manhood, which was to be expressed indirectly in "Resolution and Independence." "By our own spirits are we deified," he says then, acknowledging his own imagination at work in Nature's intentions and discerning Providence in his encounter with the old man whose providential wisdom is manly resolution and independence.

How much, as a young man in London, did Wordsworth feel the burden of Nature in his psyche? Years later, after his crisis over the the French Revolution and his restoration by Nature, he tries to imagine a simple consistency of character for the young poet and the young man in London. Perhaps conscious artifice and unconscious deception make the bond between Nature and the poet "now" appear more harmonious than it was then in his young manhood. Still, for someone as unprepared as Wordsworth for the life of London, the city must have been shocking; but it is likely that he distorts his recollection of it by imagining that he could only have been shocked. He says, simply, that he lived:

> Frugal as there was need, and though self-will'd,
> Yet temperate and reserv'd, and wholly free
> From dangerous passions.
>
> (VII, 70-73)

It is in Book VII also that he recollects his first observation of a fallen woman, "woman to open shame/ Abandon'd and the pride of public vice,"[32] and he says explicitly that he experienced the feeling of division between "humanity" and "the human form" in consequence. This fits the sentiment of the book, the division between the poet, who has felt "grandeur" in the beatings of his heart in consequence of purified passions, and "the swarm" of London's inhabitants, the "slaves unrespited of low pursuits." What he loved about humanity or Man, Book VIII will attempt next to explain, but the *need* to explain makes it seem like a problem discovered in his attempt to extend his story be-

[32] *The Prelude,* VII, 418-419.

yond the innocent Dawn Dedication. Passion—in some of its manifestations sexual—seems to be the dividing line between an idealization of Man, of which the Poet remains the type to Wordsworth, and men. Seemingly, for consistency if for no other reason, Wordsworth had to make Nature's poet react to displays of passion with aversion.

CHAPTER VII

MEN AND HISTORY

1. Ideals of Mind, Man, and Self

Despite Wordsworth's hope of giving a satisfying account of the growth of a poet's mind, our thoughts about the epistemological limits of art are provoked early by him. Still, the imaginative daring of his attempt to invent himself appeals to one's curiosity in exactly the way "romantic" evokes, even from its detractors, a suspicious fascination. Perhaps the egoism that animates an aspiration to godly self-knowledge is, to use Wordsworth's phrase, "heroic argument"; but after listening to these matters by suspending our disbelief, we do not accord them belief. Despite our acknowledgment that the artist may imagine himself as his own hero and may appreciate the complexity of himself, we resist the hubristic rhetoric of Romanticism. Whether we believe in the mystery of God or not, in art we feel more comfortable with the thought that Oedipus suffers, Sophocles imagines, and Apollo alone understands than with the thought that the man who suffered and the artist who creates may *become* the god who understands. Much of the modern reaction to Romanticism, divided as it may seem, agrees in its rejection of the rhetorical pose of the artist. Wordsworth, however, tried to hold to his ideal of the godly Poet, though with increasing uncertainty about himself. Having hoped to confirm himself in the pose of the Poet struck with such assurance in the introduction to the projected *Recluse* in 1798, he confirmed instead the doubts that had prevented him from continuing in that spirit at that time.

The problem for the critic is to determine how, and perhaps why, Wordsworth failed his own expectations. It is in Book XIII of *The Prelude* that Wordsworth presents, with stronger feeling and greater clarity than anywhere else in the poem, the image of wholeness and completion in the ideal Poet—an image drawn from his own experience and reflections, which nevertheless eludes him personally. The Mount Snowdon vision, originally intended more confidently for the conclusion of the projected five-book *Prelude*, follows the largely unsuccessful account of his ordeal in Books IX to XII. The failure of the artist who created to understand the man who suffered results in this uncertainty about the identity of the godly poet who understands. Though Wordsworth had proposed in Book I to "fix the wavering balance" of his mind, he hesitates to idealize himself in Book XIII as he idealizes the Poet:

> Such minds are truly from the Deity,
> For they are Powers; and hence the highest bliss
> That can be known is theirs, the consciousness
> Of whom they are habitually infused
> Through every image, and through every thought,
> And all impressions . . .
>
> (XIII, 106-111)

Wordsworth did not feel that he understood after all.

The ascent into the moonlight on Mount Snowdon with the resulting vision, is his last treatment of Imagination in *The Prelude*. No one reading it could fail to notice its similarity to the Imagination-Revelation passages in his account of crossing the Alps in Book VI. The language here echoes the earlier passages ("vapors," "usurp'd," "gloomy," "the roar of waters, torrents, streams," "Roaring with one voice," "the dark abyss"). The physical setting of a mountain being climbed is the same, and the natural scene is presented even more explicitly as an analogue of "the one great mind." The travellers are climbing, each "in commerce with his private thoughts," when suddenly the moon illuminates the landscape. What he saw appeared to Wordsworth:

> The perfect image of a mighty Mind,
> Of one that feeds upon infinity,
> That is exalted by an under-presence,
> The sense of God, or whatso'er is dim
> Or vast in its own being. . . .
>
> (XIII, 69-73)

In the 1850 version, this reads:

> That feeds upon infinity, that broods
> Over the dark abyss, intent to hear[1]
> Its voices issuing forth to silent light
> In one continuous stream.
>
> (XIV, 71-74; 1850 version)

And the revision adds the recurrent word "abyss" to this emblem of the mind.

In examining the treatment of this analogy in Book VI, however, we found that Wordsworth presents a series of recollections—of himself climbing and being lost in the Alps; of the Traveller in the mountain of the mind halted near the edge of the mind's abyss, from which Imagination arises; and of the effect of experiencing the intensity of Imagination in the mind. Then, in recollecting his descent through the Alps, he depicts the mountain metaphorically as a mind and the natural sounds of the scene as inspired voices issuing from the earth. He could hear the approach of Revelation (the "ghostly language of the ancient earth") the symbols of the Apocalypse. But one must *put* the whole poetic experience together;[2] one interprets in sequence the

[1] Wordsworth is picturing the Holy Spirit and echoing *Paradise Lost*, I, 20-23:

> . . . and with mighty wings outspread
> Dove-like satst brooding on the vast Abyss
> And mad'st it pregnant: what in me is dark
> Illumine . . .

[2] See above, Chap. IV, pp. 136ff.

effects and implications of the separate metaphors with which Wordsworth transmutes recollected experience into vision. The account is powerful but brain-teasing: one may experience the exhilaration of it, but one must decide in an analytical way what it means and how it is significant.

The account of the ascent of Mount Snowdon is more immediately satisfying; it puts the reader more clearly in the recollected situation and re-enacts the process of realization. In dramatic and vivid utterance, Wordsworth leads us through description to his metaphorical transmutation of the scene into vision:

> When at my feet the ground appear'd to brighten,
> And with a step or two seem'd brighter still;
> Nor had I time to ask the cause of this,
> For instantly a Light upon the turf
> Fell like a flash: I look'd about, and lo!
> The Moon stood naked in the Heavens, at height
> Immense above my head, and on the shore
> I found myself of a huge sea of mist,
> Which, meek and silent, rested at my feet:
> A hundred hills their dusky backs upheaved
> All over this still Ocean, and beyond,
> Far, far beyond, the vapours shot themselves,
> In headlands, tongues, and promontory shapes,
> Into the Sea, the real Sea, that seem'd
> To dwindle, and give up its majesty,
> Usurp'd upon as far as sight could reach.
> Meanwhile, the Moon look'd down upon this shew
> In single glory, and we stood, the mist
> Touching our very feet; and from the shore
> At distance not the third part of a mile
> Was a blue chasm; a fracture in the vapour,
> A deep and gloomy breathing-place through which
> Mounted the roar of waters, torrents, streams,
> Innumerable, roaring with one voice.
> The universal spectacle throughout

Was shaped for admiration and delight,
Grand in itself alone, but in that breach
Through which the homeless voice of waters rose,
That dark deep thoroughfare had Nature lodg'd
The Soul, the Imagination of the whole.
(XIII, 36-65)

It is straight description until the mention of the "roar of waters" roaring "with one voice" and the "voice of waters" brings to mind: "And I heard a voice from heaven, as the voice of many waters . . . ," signifying Revelation.[3]

What is the Revelation, however? Except for Wordsworth's conviction, induced by his own imagination, that he is seeing outside himself the "perfect image of a mighty mind" engaged in commerce with its private thoughts" (as he himself had been preoccupied in thought while climbing the mountain), there is no revelation. There is only the belief, described a few lines later, in the power of a mighty mind to reveal its depths to its own attentive consciousness through the power Wordsworth calls Imagination and attributes to "higher minds." Out of "their native selves" such higher minds—those of poets—can use "all the objects of the universe" to make similar "transformations." That is, they can use imagery in this very way to express and to realize the depths of the mind, or, as he says a few lines later, "to hold communion with the invisible world." Actually, we have heard this said before, earlier, and specifically about himself during his college years:

now I felt
The strength and consolation which were mine.
As if awaken'd, summon'd, rous'd, constrain'd,
I look'd for universal things; perused
The common countenance of earth and heaven;

[3] In the King James Version, this reads: ". . . and his voice as the sound of many waters." The Revelation of John, I: 15.

> And, turning the mind in upon itself,
> Pored, watch'd, expected, listen'd; spread my
> thoughts
> And spread them with a wider creeping; felt
> Incumbences more awful, visitings
> Of the Upholder of the tranquil Soul,
> Which underneath all passion lives secure
> A steadfast life. But peace! it is enough
> To notice that I was ascending now
> To such community with highest truth.
> (III, 107-120)

There is a plain enough history of such feelings; as early as Book III he recalls the ascent to highest truth and the grandeur of the lonely prophet who meditates upon the mountain. In Book XIII, the meditation is recollected; it "rose" within him; and "rose" is significantly repeated in this way three lines after the "voice of waters rose" like Revelation in the scene. He is talking with powerful conviction about "mind," his own mind idealized in projected form, and his own feelings about something to be revealed, imagined, and realized.

Certainly such striking imagery induces belief momentarily in the reader that Wordsworth is presenting a Revelation rather than simply describing how one might occur. "Even the grossest minds," he says, "must see and hear/ And cannot chuse but feel"; and under the spell of the passage, its poetic transformation of the scene into the psychic terrain of a visionary mind, we find ourselves feeling that the poet is describing the habit of his own mind,

> one that feeds upon infinity,
> That is exalted by an under-presence,
> The sense of God, or whatso'er is dim
> Or vast in its own being.

In the 1850 version, clarifying this without changing the spirit of the earlier version, he puts it in this way:

it appeared to me the type
Of a majestic intellect, its acts
And its possessions, what it has and craves,
What in itself it is, and would become.
There I beheld the emblem of a mind
That feeds upon infinity, that broods
Over the dark abyss, intent to hear
Its voices issuing forth to silent light
In one continuous stream; a mind sustained
By recognitions of transcendent power,
In sense conducting to ideal form,
In soul of more than mortal privilege.
(XIV, 66-77: 1850 version)

While in the 1805 version he finds exaltation in "an under-presence/ The sense of God, or whatso'er is dim/ Or vast in its own being," in the later version, he makes it seem that the mind so described ("in soul of more than mortal privilege") is aspiring to a perfect clarity with which it "would become" godly. But was *his* mind really like this, "intent to hear/ Its voices issuing forth"?

The passage just quoted from Book III shows how long he has been aware of "whatso'er is dim or vast in his own being," and there are many examples, some of which we have examined in related contexts, of an "underpresence" and the "sense of God" within him. The recesses of the heart, the points within the soul where all stand single, the caverns of the mind that sun can never penetrate, and "the mind's abyss"[4] are all metaphorical representations of dim and vast areas in his own being, locations for "the invisible world," in which the poetic self must seek what may be revealed or imagined. But beyond these metaphors, and beyond flashes, usurpations, and glimpses, the mysterious objects of the invisible world remained a mystery.

In some crucial way that he could not account for, he

[4] See *The Prelude*, I, 233; III, 186-187; III, 246-247; VI, 594: 1850 version.

did not fulfill what he wished to call his destiny in his heroic argument; and he had to acknowledge the discrepancy between himself and his ideal of the Poet made biographically and imaginatively from his own experience. It was not mere modesty. Later, in making another ideal claim about himself, he begins: "I myself am one of the happiest of men. . . ."[5] But the discrepancy indicated at the end of *The Prelude* shows that he knew what the Poet may be, but not wholly what he himself was. He asks:

> Oh! who is he that has his whole life long
> Preserved, enlarged this freedom in himself?
> For this alone is genuine Liberty.
> Witness, ye Solitudes! where I received
> My earliest visitations, careless then
> Of what was given me, and where now I roam,
> A meditative, oft a suffering Man,
> And yet, I trust, with undiminish'd powers,
> Witness, whatever falls my better mind,
> Revolving with the accidents of life,
> May have sustain'd, that, howsoe'er misled,
> I never, in the quest of right and wrong,
> Did tamper with myself from private aims;
> Nor was in any of my hopes the dupe
> Of selfish passions . . .
>
> (XIII, 120-134)

The ideal Poet ("by sensible impressions not enthrall'd," the consciousness of who he is "habitually infused/ Through every image, and through every thought,/ And all impressions") is said to be strong in the intensity of emotion, cheerful "in every act of life," true in moral judgment, and unfailing in delight in the external world. But Wordsworth sees himself differently. A "meditative, oft a suffering man," he is a man of powers, but one who in the accidents of life has taken falls and been misled. He had even been enthralled by sensible impressions, and had lived

[5] Robinson, *Selections*, #49.

through a period of cheerlessness, of deadness of emotion, and of despair in moral judgment. In the 1850 version, he distinguishes himself more explicitly from his ideal:

> A humbler destiny have we retraced,
> And told of lapse and hesitating choice,
> And backward wanderings along thorny ways . . .
> (XIV, 136-138: 1850 version)

His failure to attain a godly clarity of mind may remind us of his recollection in Book VII of the Blind Beggar in London. The "fixed face and sightless eyes" had seemed another "type or emblem" of the mind ("of the utmost that we know/ Both of ourselves and of the universe").[6] Wordsworth had felt "admonish'd from another world."

Having noted the discrepancy between Wordsworth and the ideal of himself as the Poet in Book XIII, let us note, too, the discrepancy between people as they are in History and society and Wordsworth's ideal of Man; for in a way not immediately apparent the parallel discrepancies are not accidental. The early books of *The Prelude* present the boy in solitude or the boy among his comrades in the vale; we next learn of the young man at Cambridge tentatively encountering the world beyond the vale. At the beginning of Book VIII, recalling the annual fair held at the foot of Helvellyn, Wordsworth pauses to give his most idealized picture of people in the pastoral world of the vale. By presenting his love of human nature in this way, retrospectively, Wordsworth intended to intimate a whole history of deep if unrealized feelings about other people in his narrative, an aspect of his growth neglected in the narrative until then. The retrospect was to provide a necessary transition thematically to his account of how his sympathies were "naturally" engaged by the French Revolution. The fair, juxtaposed plainly with the account of Bartholomew Fair

[6] *The Prelude*, VII, 615-622. Again, Wordsworth's use of "waters"—"My mind did at this spectacle turn round/ As with the might of waters . . ."—recalls "the sound of many waters" (Revelation, I: 15).

which concludes Book VII, vividly presents the theme of Book VIII mentioned in the subtitle: "Love of Nature Leading to Love of Mankind." These pastoral people, Wordsworth now wishes to show, were real to him; in Nature, he knew their *human* nature and worth as simply as he knew their human form. But at one point in Book VII we observed how, in contrast, a painful observation of fallen woman made him say:

> a barrier seem'd at once
> Thrown in, that from humanity divorced
> The human Form, splitting the race of Man
> In twain, yet leaving the same outward shape.
> (VII, 423-426)

That is, Wordsworth recorded the shock of discovering that there were conditions in which people could look like people, but not seem like people to him. And puzzled by the difference between human nature as he had experienced it in the vale and as he had observed it "melted and reduced to one identity"[7] in London, Wordsworth wished to believe that Nature made human nature beautiful and that History debased human nature, just as the city debased Nature. So long as it seemed to him that human nature in revolutionary France had much in common with human nature in the vale, Wordsworth's natural conviction was strong; however, his *subsequent* discoveries about human nature led to his despair about Nature and natural sympathies.

True, in Book VIII, Wordsworth attempts only to suggest how the basis of a profound love of mankind was laid by Nature all but imperceptibly for the child, who was largely given over to his "animal activities, and all/ Their trivial pleasures." And he says explicitly that intermediary to his love of mankind was the long period of intimacy with Na-

[7] *The Prelude*, VII, 702-703. See, too, the sonnet "Composed Upon Westminster Bridge," where Wordsworth's surprise at finding the city beautiful at dawn makes him acknowledge its power to evoke a natural response from him. David Ferry, in *The Limits of Mortality*, pp. 12-15, has an interesting interpretation of the poem.

ture, when she was to him: "A passion . . ./ A rapture often, and immediate joy/ Ever at hand." But the love of mankind, to which he says he was led by Nature, has an abstractness about it that seems almost as exclusive of actual people as his reserve with people seen so plainly in his accounts of Cambridge and London. We must look carefully at the mankind that Wordsworth felt he was prepared by Nature to love.

He recalls "the Paradise/ Where I was rear'd," comparing it favorably with fabled gardens of the Orient:

> in Nature's primitive gifts
> Favor'd no less, and more to every sense
> Delicious, seeing that the sun and sky,
> The elements and seasons in their change
> Do find their dearest Fellow-Labourer there,
> The heart of Man, a district on all sides
> The fragrance breathing of humanity,
> Man free, man working for himself, with choice
> Of time, and place, and object; by his wants,
> His comforts, native occupations, cares,
> Conducted on to individual ends
> Or social, and still followed by a train
> Unwoo'd, unthought-of even, simplicity,
> And beauty, and inevitable grace.
>
> (VIII, 145-158)

In the imagery of this recollected Paradise, the image of Man free and working for himself is perfectly consonant with Nature. Although the sentiment is heavy here and the verse sickly sweet, the picture is idyllic. Man seems here unfallen from Paradise, living in eighteenth century rural England a pastoral life so suggestively literary that Wordsworth had to insist upon the simple reality of his shepherds by making explicit distinctions:

> Not such as in Arcadian Fastnesses
> Sequester'd, handed down among themselves,
> So ancient Poets sing, the golden Age . . .
>
> (VIII, 183-185)

"nor such . . . as Shakespeare in the wood of Arden placed . . . Nor such as Spenser fabled. . . ." But if we think of this Paradise as the poet's recollected vale of childhood, we may see how much the idyll depends upon the perceiver, whether as child at the time or as poet cherishing his recollection.

Later in the book, when Wordsworth writes once again of the stunning meanness of life in London, he remembers having drawn support from this recollected image of man for his vision of "what we may become":

> Neither guilt nor vice,
> Debasement of the body or the mind,
> Nor all the misery forced upon my sight,
> Which was not lightly passed, but often scann'd
> Most feelingly, could overthrow my trust
> In what we may become, induce belief
> That I was ignorant, had been falsely taught,
> A Solitary, who with vain conceits
> Had been inspired, and walk'd about in dreams,
> When from that awful prospect overcast
> And in eclipse, my meditations turn'd,
> Lo! everything that was indeed divine
> Retain'd its purity inviolate
> And unencroach'd upon, nay, seem'd brighter far
> For this deep shade in counterview, that gloom
> Of opposition, such as shew'd itself
> To the eyes of Adam, yet in Paradise,
> Though fallen from bliss . . .
>
> (VIII, 802-819)

And while the recollection of "Paradise" may remind us primarily of the poet's way of valuing what the child once seemed to have, the allusion to *Paradise Lost* perhaps reminds us of Adam's task in the fallen world of History, to find a "paradise within thee, happier far."[8] The poet has proposed a similar task to himself, in part consciously and in large part unconsciously.

[8] *Paradise Lost*, XII, 587.

Wordsworth is writing of how he, like Milton, had become a partisan of a worldly revolution whose success might have transformed History and prepared man's redemption from the fallen world. Certainly, for the time that Wordsworth believed in the eventual success of the revolution, he must have felt strongly that the amelioration of man's historical lot would give greater scope to the Poet as Redeemer of the spirit. The Poet would stir in Man his lost memories of Paradise, Man newly freed from bondage[9] and able to listen. Not everyone was to be transported from History to the Lake Country, of course; but in a condition of greater freedom and with the opportunity to discover the natural humanity of the self, Man might seem to himself born again, and thereby might experience feelings and powers now lost to him. In a condition of natural affection, he would experience the world again with new-born wonder and delight, as did the Blest Babe.

Wordsworth's first impressions of revolutionary France are all presented in imagery of rural festivity and human warmheartedness comparable to that of the Helvellyn Fair. But, like Milton, Wordsworth learned tragically that the ideals of the Revolution were not to be presently realized in History, and he doubted man's redemption; yet after his own crisis and recovery, he attempted to maintain that there was redemptive work for the Poet yet to do. The poet who recollected the "paradise within" sought first to affirm and then to employ the powers that such recollection keeps alive:

> Prophets of Nature, we to them will speak
> A lasting inspiration, sanctified
> By reason and by truth; what we have loved,
> Others will love; and we may teach them how;
> Instruct them how the mind of man becomes

[9] The situation of man freed from bondage would be the same as that imagined by Wordsworth in Biblical terms for himself at the very beginning of *The Prelude* (I, 1-25).

A thousand times more beautiful than the earth
On which he dwells . . .

(XIII, 442-448)

Egoistic as it must seem to us, his desire to realize the ideal of the Poet in himself seemed to him an earnest of human nature, an indication of "what we may become."

It is plain that when Wordsworth recalls his early idealization of Man, he recalls at the same time his discovery of personal grandeur; for what Man may feel ideally, the Poet feels habitually. Hence:

Then rose
Man, inwardly contemplated, and present
In my own being, to a loftier height;
As of all visible natures crown; and first
In capability of feeling what
Was to be felt; in being rapt away
By the divine effect of power and love,
As, more than anything we know instinct
With Godhead, and by reason and by will
Acknowledging dependency sublime.

(VIII, 631-640)

It might seem, then, that Wordsworth loved man in order to idealize himself, so it is not surprising to find in Book VIII that his most loved image of Man, that of the Shepherd, meets this peculiar requirement. Considering the psychology of this, one expects that the subject of love of mankind will involve implicitly attitudes towards the father, but one need only observe that in Book VIII the subject of fathers becomes prominent for the first time in *The Prelude*. In what might again be called a preconscious or latently associational way, Wordsworth expresses a good deal of unconscious feeling about fathers and sons while dealing simultaneously with the ideal of Man and the ideal of himself.

We have noted that, to the growing boy, the Nature in

which things happen had a vastness greater than "Nature," the personified Presence. So, too, there was more to the boy, "companionless" in his solitude, than that aspect of himself the poet has so far presented with emphasis. When Wordsworth writes of rugged mountain nature:

> Yet hail to You,
> Your rocks and precipices, Ye that seize
> The heart with firmer grasp! your snows and streams
> Ungovernable, and your terrifying winds,
> That howl'd so dismally when I have been
> Companionless, among your solitudes.
> There 'tis the Shepherd's task the winter long
> To wait upon the storms . . .
>
> (VIII, 353-360)

he is acknowledging another aspect of his life in Nature. The wind did not always excite his imagination in a "visionary" way; sometimes, apparently, its terrifying and dismal howl produced another feeling of solitude in Nature within him. Although the child was often excited in imagination and accompanied by a Presence in Nature, he also knew himself to be in many ways simply alone in the external world and alone in himself. How successfully the poet presents and interprets his awareness of this greater vastness of the world and of the self is what we seek to determine in his account of growth. But we should notice first that the solitude spoken of here *is* significantly different from the solitude in which a relatedness with a Presence in Nature is maintained ("the religious love in which I walk'd with Nature"). Neither the holy calm of the morning vale, nor the visionary sense of the windy darkness in the midnight storm is being evoked by "companionless, among your solitudes," but rather a difficult prospective sense of life, of the world and of himself in it.

Here, the Shepherd becomes Wordsworth's image of Man companionless in Nature in a life "of hope and hazard" as the boy's experience leads him to an awareness of the hopes and hazards of living. Between ages nine and thirteen Wordsworth lived apart from his own father, at school, while his father's employment kept him in London. It was a period when the boy's being much on his own must have forced upon him feelings about being entirely on one's own, feelings which even the other meaning of solitude could not wholly offset. The necessity of further growth to manhood must inevitably have distressed him with his uncertainties about the nature of manhood. The account of his father's death (the second "spot of time"[10]) suggests that the boy already had some unrealized "anxiety of hope," an expectation that greater closeness to his own father would relieve him of the unconscious burdens of his growth. But the narrative presents no specific account of stress in the years between thirteen and seventeen when, after his father's death, a crisis about being alone and about being himself must surely have occurred.[11] At seventeen, carried beyond the vale by circumstance, he appears "as in a dream" at Cambridge, to be prepared for the future life of a man in accordance with the wishes of his guardians; but at Cambridge he lives, instead, an imaginative life apart, already proof against the "injurious sway of circumstances."[12]

His habitual distance from other people, I think, is significantly related to the fact of the father's absence; for it is through closer identification with the father that boys acquire an extended sense of the values and goals of their

[10] *Ibid.*, XI, 345ff.

[11] See Erik Erikson, *Childhood and Society*, part III, chap. 7. There is normally a crisis in growth in adolescence (the ego repudiating certain past identifications and integrating the remaining ones into an identity). I assume that Wordsworth must have experienced considerable distress between the ages of thirteen and seventeen as to who he was and what he was to be. We see his resolution of the crisis in his firm recollection that at age seventeen the matter seemed a foregone conclusion, a decision made by Nature for him. So as not to experience a frightening confusion of identity, Wordsworth held to earlier identifications and remodellings of the ego, and he accepted as inevitable (and even in some ways desirable) his unlikeness to other young men.

[12] *The Prelude*, III, 102-103: 1850 version.

society. Children imitate the acceptable ways of expressing desires and of complying with those of others; but the disapproval, everywhere expressed by Wordsworth, of the social life from which he felt distant is of its passionate meanness; and he gives many specific examples of what was acceptable to others but not to him. Significantly, however, he gives no examples in Book VII of what worthy people may have been doing in, say, London, had he come there with any expectation of employing or enjoying himself among them, because he was unprepared to notice what he was unable to imagine. So we have raised the question of London's reality, or rather London's dream-like unreality to Wordsworth, and must continue to make the connection between Wordsworth's dreams and the aversions he felt while awake.[13]

Except on one occasion, however, Wordsworth does not tell us his dreams.[14] If the disturbing passion of human life unconsciously reminds him of "troubled dreams," he nevertheless specifically denies that he was ever, like most people, subject to selfish passions:

> Witness, whatever falls my better mind,
> Revolving with the accidents of life,
> May have sustain'd, that, howsoe'er misled,
> I never, in the quest of right and wrong,
> Did tamper with myself from private aims;
> Nor was in any of my hopes the dupe
> Of selfish passions; nor did wilfully
> Yield ever to mean cares and low pursuits . . .
> (XIII, 128-135)

While observing the effect on him of the discrepancy between his ideal of Man and the sordid reality of people,

[13] Coleridge's poem, "Pains of Sleep," shows the degree to which the character of the dreamer and the contents of his dreams were still regarded as distinct by the older generation of Romantics. Compare this with Keats's "Hyperion: A Dream," which is the fragment of a revision of *The Fall of Hyperion.*

[14] See below, pp. 351ff.

we should observe at the same time the discrepancy between his ideal of himself as Poet and the reality of himself he finally accepts in the poem. For if there is a close coincidence between his ideal of Man and his ideal of the Poet, it is indeed likely that his reactions to the nightmarish reality of human passion can tell us a lot about what was less than ideal about Wordsworth, just as his dreams could. Despite his vision of a majestic intellect able to reveal "whatso'er is dim/ Or vast in its own being" to its own attentive consciousness brooding over the dark abyss, his failure to imagine his own passions indicates something about passion which remained impenetrably dim and vast in his own being, formidable as a source of feeling, as a rising pressure within, portentous of impending revelations, but inaccessible to his consciousness by the strength with which it was resisted.

We may suppose, however, that there were many troubled dreams about life and his own passionate demands on it—dreams disowned by the waking self with the same aversion Wordsworth expressed for "the little busy passions" of others "thrust upon" his view in daily life.[15] We have noted that when he recalls being brought near "to guilt and wretchedness" ("as in a dream"), he associates an "indefinite terror and dismay" with thoughts of human life *and* with "storms and angry elements" in Nature. The thoughts of human life are "gloomier far"—

> a dim
> Analogy to uproar and misrule,
> Disquiet, danger, and obscurity.
> (VIII, 662-664)

But in the Shepherd, his first ideal of Man, he perceived a purity—or imagined an almost inhuman purity—corresponding to his own.

The Shepherd, who is perceived against a background of Nature that includes "storms and angry elements," seems to

15 *The Prelude*, VIII, 641-648.

stand reassuringly as a symbolic image of the superego, here a benign emblem of the *unconscious* mastery of what is frightening and unknown to the boy about life and himself. But the poet, who did not finally see the objects of the invisible world and who never subsequently imagined or revealed to himself the "stormy" passions within, did not see the rest of his own nature, either, against which "character" is outlined and over which self-knowledge might give real mastery.

First, however, we should look carefully at the idealization of the Shepherd, which is presented in this way:

> A rambling Schoolboy, thus
> Have I beheld him, without knowing why
> Have felt his presence in his own domain,
> As of a Lord and Master; or a Power
> Or Genius, under Nature, under God,
> Presiding; and severest solitude
> Seem'd more commanding oft when he was there.
> Seeking the raven's nest, and suddenly
> Surpriz'd with vapours, or on rainy days
> When I have angled up the lonely brooks
> Mine eyes have glanced upon him, few steps off,
> In size a giant, stalking through the fog,
> His Sheep like Greenland Bears; at other times
> When round some shady promontory turning,
> His Form hath flash'd upon me, glorified
> By the deep radiance of the setting sun:
> Or him have I descried in distant sky,
> A solitary object and sublime,
> Above all height! like an aerial Cross,
> As it is stationed on some spiry Rock
> Of the Chartreuse, for worship. Thus was Man
> Ennobled outwardly before mine eyes,
> And thus my heart at first was introduc'd
> To an unconscious love and reverence
> Of human Nature; hence the human form

To me was like an index of delight,
Of grace and honour, power and worthiness.
(VIII, 390-416)

The poet writing this is particularly concerned with the present and with the self-sufficiency of the poet. The Poet, in Book XIII, is to be a similar figure of "grace and honour, power and worthiness." No longer a schoolboy, he will himself stand between earth and heaven on the summit of Mount Snowdon, and also will seem

a Lord and Master; or a Power
Or Genius, under Nature, under God
Presiding . . .

While this is said here simply of the Shepherd as an image—in a way that makes the "unconscious love and reverence/ Of human Nature" seem a matter of mere imagery—it will be said again in Book XIII of the ideal Poet. The mind's visionary lordliness over its inner psychic terrain corresponds to its mastery of the physical world that it "transforms" with Imagination. Here, however, Wordsworth recalls how the boy seems to have been equally impressed with the size and beauty, the elevation and the companionless autonomy of the image of man in vast Nature. The Shepherd is recollected as himself almost an elemental power and form among elemental powers and forms, as Wordsworth will later speak of the ideal Poet. A future similarity of Poet and Shepherd, of the ideal of self and the ideal of Man, was prepared by an initial perception of difference, just as in the comparisons made between child and father in the play fantasies of children.

This worshipful image of Man, so little suggestive of actual personality, is further distinguished by Wordsworth from the Shepherd's own personality as Wordsworth recollects the child's lack of interest:

But, for the purposes of kind, a Man
With the most common; Husband, Father; learn'd,

Could teach, admonish, suffer'd with the rest
From vice and folly, wretchedness and fear;
Of this I little saw, car'd less for it,
But something must have felt.

(VIII, 423-428)

Although Wordsworth is thankful

That Men did at the first present themselves
Before my untaught eyes thus purified,
Remov'd, and at a distance that was fit,

(VIII, 438-440)

it is plain that he is only interested in the image. The specific content of human worth, of "what we may become," has nothing to do with tending sheep or with the personalities or interests of common shepherds, but rather with closeness to Nature, freedom and self-employment. Again, by noting the peculiar poetic consistency of Wordsworth's characterizations, we may see how easily Wordsworth assimilates his ideal of Man to himself. As early as Book III and Cambridge, he has employed the image of the Shepherd to characterize himself in terms of freedom, naturalness, elevation, vision, detachment and aspiration; and in a way that also prefigures the Mount Snowdon emblem of a visionary mind and a majectic intellect:

Hitherto I had stood
In my own mind remote from human life,
At least from what we commonly so name,
Even as a shepherd on a promontory,
Who, lacking occupation, looks far forth
Into the endless sea, and rather makes
Than finds what he beholds. And sure it is
That this first transit from the smooth delights,
And wild outlandish walks of simple youth,
To something that resembled an approach
Towards mortal business; to a privileg'd world
Within a world, a midway residence

With all its intervenient imagery,
Did better suit my visionary mind,
Far better, than to have been bolted forth,
Thrust out abruptly into Fortune's way
Among the conflicts of substantial life;
By a more just gradation did lead on
To higher things, more naturally matur'd,
For permanent possession, better fruits
Whether of truth or virtue, to ensue.

(III, 543-563)

2. Some Versions of Father and Son

While the observations made and to be made about Wordsworth's fatherless freedom will in part explain the poet's need to invent himself, it is nevertheless plainly enough revealed in this part of *The Prelude* that Wordsworth felt unconsciously drawn to the subject of fathers and sons. For instance, despite the child's apparent indifference to the Shepherd as "Husband, Father," Wordsworth reveals that the companionless boy had feelings about men and fathers that were more complicated than the argument of Book VIII indicates. He did not simply acquire an ideal image of Man in Nature, through which to imagine himself as presiding Genius. At one point, Wordsworth tells a tale he had heard from his "household Dame" about a shepherd and his son, a curious but simple story of a boy going with his father to seek a lost sheep, separating from his father and getting into a terrifying circumstance from which his father providentially rescues him. Having espied the lamb on a small island in a swollen flood stream, the boy leaps to the island, and in doing so startles the lamb, which tries to leap to the further shore but is "borne headlong by the roaring flood" instead. The boy, having in effect taken the lamb's place, cannot summon up the courage to leap back again; his heart faints with fear while the current of the stream grows stronger every minute. The shepherd finds the boy and, stretching out his staff towards him, "bade him leap, which word scarce said/ The boy was safe within his father's arms." Wordsworth says nothing else about the story, but instead talks generally about shepherds.

It is interesting, though, that the boy knew where to find the lamb because he knew, as the woman telling the story explained:

> that tho' the storm
> Drive one of those poor Creatures miles and miles,
> If he can crawl he will return again
> To his own hills, the spots where, when a Lamb,
> He learn'd to pasture at his Mother's side.
> (VIII, 253-257)

The lamb had an instinctive sense of place, of which the boy seems to have had an intuitive knowledge. In his description of himself in Book VIII, Wordsworth seems very like both the lamb and the boy:

> Dear native Regions, wheresoe'er shall close
> My mortal course, there will I think on you;
> Dying, will cast on you a backward look;
> Even as this setting sun (albeit the Vale
> Is no where touched by one memorial gleam)
> Doth with the fond remains of his last power
> Still linger, and a farewell lustre sheds
> On the dear mountain-tops where first he rose.
> (VIII, 468-475: 1850 version)

But Wordsworth is not finding this sentiment on his lips for the first time; it is being adapted from one of Wordsworth's earliest poems, written when he was a sixteen-year-old boy:

> Dear native regions, I foretell,
> From what I feel at this farewell,
> That wheresoe'er my steps may tend,
> And whensoe'er my course shall end,
> If in that hour a single tie

Survive of local sympathy
My soul will cast the backward view,
The longing look alone on you.[16]

These verses were written at a time in his youth when his own father was dead and he was seeking a father in the love and approval of a much-loved schoolmaster, whom he remembers in this way in Book x:

He loved the Poets, and if now alive,
Would have loved me, as one not destitute
Of promise, nor belying the kind hope
Which he had form'd, when I at his command,
Began to spin, at first, my toilsome Songs.
(x, 511-515)

Everything associated in this way with the simple story suggests that the poet preconsciously identifies himself with the boy, a possibility further evidenced by another memory recorded by Wordsworth in the Dove Cottage Papers recalling an experience of his in the Alps:

"On my return I found the difficulty of recrossing the stream much increased and being detained among the large stones in its channel I perceived the water swell every moment which with the dizziness of sight produced by the dashing of the foam placed me in a position of considerable danger. Returning down the valley, from a bridge under the arch of which about two hours before we observed such a quantity of water rolling over our late resting-place as would have swept us away before it."[17]

The appropriateness of Wordsworth's telling the story of the boy in *The Prelude* is, I think, that in this way he is imaginatively or preconsciously remembering danger and isolation in association with his seeming to want to be on his own. When the endangered shepherd boy finds safety

[16] See *The Prelude*, p. 583.
[17] Wordsworth, *Dove Cottage Papers*, quoted by Moorman, *Wordsworth*, p. 146.

in his father's arms, we may think of the poet Wordsworth interpolating a tale that he considers very touching because it shows the natural lovableness of the Shepherd, his image of Man; and we may think, too, of the boy to whom the story was originally told, unconsciously comparing the Shepherd with his own absent father. It was upon his father's employment that his own sustenance depended, but it was by his absent father that he was denied what he felt he needed more—the providential and sustaining love of the Shepherd who seeks his endangered son. One must think, then, of the youth's perplexity—of gratitude and unexpressed love, of anger and resentment, of guilt for such conflict and perhaps of an indefinite "terror and dismay" at intimations of these confused and stifled passions. We shall seek the evidence for this in Books IX and X.

While contemplating London once again in Book VIII, Wordsworth concludes the book with a picture of human worth effectively set off from the inhuman tenor of the city:

> 'Twas a Man,
> Whom I saw sitting in an open Square
> Close to an iron paling that fenced in
> The spacious Grass-plot; on the corner stone
> Of the low wall in which the pales were fix'd
> Sate this one Man, and with a sickly babe
> Upon his knee, whom he had thither brought
> For sunshine, and to breathe the fresher air.
> Of those who pass'd, and me who look'd at him,
> He took no note; but in his brawny Arms
> (The Artificer was to the elbow bare,
> And from his work this moment had been stolen)
> He held the Child, and, bending over it,
> As if he were afraid both of the sun
> And of the air which he had come to seek,
> He eyed it with unutterable love.
>
> (VIII, 844-859)

The father who steals these moments from his work to be with his child gets from Wordsworth a kind of praise accorded to no other man in his many characterizations of London life. No other man is set off by such epic regard for his humanity, his "courage, and integrity, and truth/ And tenderness. . . ." But while such expressions may reveal Wordsworth's unconscious love and unconscious resentment for his own father, we should nevertheless emphasize that the seemingly unprovidential absence of his father forced the boy to conceive of himself uniquely. The boy himself takes the place left empty in his life by his father, and imagines rather than learns what a man is. This is how Wordsworth came to idealize mankind by idealizing himself. As Jean-Paul Sartre puts it, recalling his own fatherless freedom: "A father would have weighted me with a certain stable obstinacy. Making his moods my principles, his ignorance my knowledge, his disappointments my pride, his quirks my law, he would have inhabited me."[18] Although we would say that Wordsworth's was an unfortunate psychic circumstance, which unconsciously he resented, he remembers, as a defense against his fears, that his prolonged youthful intimacy with Nature made him feel *strong*. These are his "God-like hours" as a natural being "in the strength of Nature." So it could seem to him that Man was "distant, but a grace/ Occasional, an accidental thought," and also that when Man rose, he rose

> inwardly contemplated, and present
> In my own being, to a loftier height;
> As of all visible natures crown.
>
> (VIII, 632-634)

When one considers that the ego seems to know nothing of what is repressed, it could well seem that safe from "vulgar man," the innocent heart bears up and lives, preparing, like the infant Hermes, to sing the beautiful song of itself.

But grown up and aware of the significant difference be-

[18] J.-P. Sartre, *The Words*, tr. Bernard Frechtman, p. 55.

tween himself as he imagined himself a "chosen son" and most people he met in the world beyond the vale, Wordsworth tried with imagination to decrease the distance between himself and people. As early as Book VIII, speaking of London as the imperial home of passion, he recalls having craved more power to augment his own, as the larger world he observed widened the purview of his imagination. Despite what we might call the evidence of his distance from people and from the life of London, he believed that he found in himself, in response to the vastness of the city, an answering "capaciousness and amplitude of mind." Strange as it is to hear him say so, he says: "such a place must needs/ Have pleased me in those times"[19]; and he seems to recall embracing a common humanity experienced there:

> Such is the strength and glory of our Youth.
> The Human nature unto which I felt
> That I belong'd . . .
>
> (VIII, 760-763)

He is trying to account for the natural engagement of his imagination by the scene and circumstance of this period of his life, but we must observe how he felt the engagement to have occurred, and should not be suprised to find that it is through a large, if uncertain, analogy with Nature that he accounts for it:

> And less
> Than other minds I had been used to owe
> The pleasure which I found in place or thing
> To extrinsic transitory accidents,
> To records or traditions; but a sense
> Of what had been here done, and suffer'd here
> Through ages, and was doing, suffering, still
> Weigh'd with me, could support the test of
> thought,
> Was like the enduring majesty and power

[19] *The Prelude*, VIII, 753-754.

Of independent nature; and not seldom
Even individual remembrances,
By working on the Shapes before my eyes,
Became like vital functions of the soul;
And out of what had been, what was, the place
Was throng'd with impregnations, like those wilds
In which my early feelings had been nurs'd,
And naked valleys, full of caverns, rocks,
And audible seclusions, dashing lakes,
Echoes and Waterfalls, and pointed crags
That into music touch the passing wind.
(VIII, 777-796)

To perceive an individual thing was to perceive a whole complex of things in association with it, much as his mind had perceived things in Nature.

There is just the suggestion of Apocalyptic language here, too, both in the way he describes the city "revealing" itself and its human past and in the portentous imagery associated to it from Nature and his own past. This is his imaginative way of recalling his own curiosity about the larger mystery of human nature to which he felt he "belong'd" and which he was now to experience. He may have imagined that the city would reveal to him some truth about humanity here, where, closed in upon itself, human nature had made its own habitat and where the history of human suffering was everywhere apparent. Or is it that in writing this, Wordsworth was preconsciously feeling that there was after all something more to be imagined or revealed here about himself? That he momentarily associates the "unnatural" imagery of the vast city with "those wilds/ In which my early feelings had been nurs'd" may suggest to us that his imagination seeks to relate something about human suffering in History to something about his own traumatically "privileged" history in Nature not indicated by the pleasurable and visionary experiences he dwells on. The vastness of Nature, its awful powers and forms, its fearful storms and angry elements, we have said, are analogous to passions suffered and suppressed within himself, to desire and anger and conscience, to the trouble of dreams, and whatsoe'er is dim or vast in his own being; and the sufferings of the city, entered into imaginatively, correspond to an unacknowledged pathos of his own, as we observed earlier about the "still, sad music of humanity" in "Tintern Abbey."

He believes, however, that he was embracing a common humanity imaginatively and that, at the same time, he was sufficiently distinguished from people by his possession of imagination, which can see likeness with a sense of difference:

> Thus here imagination also found
> An element that pleas'd her, tried her strength,
> Among new objects simplified, arranged,
> Impregnated my knowledge, made it live,
> And the result was elevating thoughts
> Of human Nature.
>
> (VIII, 797-802)

The description that follows places him, like Adam, in the fallen world of History that he is now to experience. His belief in "what we may become" is an expression of personal aspiration inclusive of people but at the same time distinguished from their actuality as people:

> Neither guilt nor vice,
> Debasement of the body or the mind,
> Nor all the misery forced upon my sight,
> Which was not lightly passed, but often scann'd
> Most feelingly, could overthrow my trust
> In what we may become, induce belief
> That I was ignorant, had been falsely taught,
> A Solitary, who with vain conceits
> Had been inspired, and walk'd about in dreams.

When from that awful prospect overcast
And in eclipse, my meditations turn'd,
Lo! everything that was indeed divine
Retain'd its purity inviolate
And unencroach'd upon, nay, seem'd brighter far
For this deep shade in counterview, that gloom
Of opposition, such as shew'd itself
To the eyes of Adam, yet in Paradise,
Though fallen from bliss . . .

(VIII, 802-819)

It was in France, however, that his deeper experience of people began.

In Revolutionary France, for a while, people seemed to him more easily characterized by his own ideal of Man while he responded imaginatively to their aspirations. One must always wonder how much and in what ways Wordsworth "approached" realities through imagination, but having, as he says, "approached the shield of human Nature from the golden side,"[20] for a while he found in the people's aspirations his own reflection. He was never to see his image in their subsequent violence.

In explaining his unenthusiastic initial response to the French Revolution, Wordsworth adduces his lack of surprise. Nature had prepared him to understand it immediately; it was almost as if it had been a simple expectation of his:

the events
Seem'd nothing out of nature's certain course,
A gift that rather was come late than soon.

(IX, 251-253)

Characteristically preoccupied, he responded to Paris with reserve; it was revolutionary Paris, but the poet was slow in feeling the large resemblance of aspirations he was to feel presently:

20 *The Prelude*, X, 663-664.

I look'd for something that I could not find,
Affecting more emotion than I felt.

(IX, 70-71)

We may wonder, too, how exactly the transition from resident alien to Patriot was effected (and Wordsworth makes it seem at least as much attributable to tedium as to interest), but he recalls some figures specifically. Significantly, they are not people his own age, but older men.

Wordsworth first describes a man (left unnamed) whom he knew in a group of Royalist officers in Blois. Of the group, he says, in a way plainly recalling Milton's description of the desperate devils' synod in Book II of *Paradise Lost*:

they had yet
One spirit ruling in them all, alike
(Save only one, hereafter to be nam'd)[21]
Were bent upon undoing what was done:
This was their rest, and only hope, therewith
No fear had they of bad becoming worse,
For worst to them was come, nor would have stirr'd,
Or deem'd it worth a moment's while to stir,
In anything, save only as the act
Look'd thitherward.

(IX, 133-142)

This Royalist officer is then described:

One, reckoning by years,
Was in the prime of manhood, and erewhile
He had sate Lord in many tender hearts,

[21] The synod in Hell is in *Paradise Lost*, II, 51ff. Here, the phrase "save only one" alludes to Beaupuis. Beaupuis, whom Wordsworth singles out for epic remembrance, is introduced in this cryptic and parenthetical way, among the Royalist officers Wordsworth had known at Blois. It is somewhat confusing to find "one" repeated a few lines later referring to someone else. The "one" of line 142 is the very opposite of the patriot Beaupuis, but the confusion, the blurring and splitting, makes one think of ambivalence, and Wordsworth was certainly ambivalent in his relations with other men.

Though heedless of such honours now, and chang'd:
His temper was quite master'd by the times,
And they had blighted him, had eat away
The beauty of his person, doing wrong
Alike to body and to mind: his port,
Which once had been erect and open, now
Was stooping and contracted, and a face,
By nature lovely in itself, express'd
As much as any that was ever seen,
A ravage out of season, made by thoughts
Unhealthy and vexatious. At the hour,
The most important of each day, in which
The public News was read, the fever came,
A punctual visitant, to shake this Man,
Disarm'd his voice, and fann'd his yellow cheek
Into a thousand colours; while he read,
Or mused, his sword was haunted by his touch
Continually, like an uneasy place
In his own body.

(IX, 142-163)

The destroyed beauty of his person, the mind tormented by vexatious thoughts, the uneasy motion of his body and the vengeful fingering of his sword are all suggestive of Milton's Satan, yet withal of a virile and impressive man consumed within by passion. Wordsworth finds him and his type, their belief and their commitments, a mockery of History. They are afflicted by "strife and passion," whereas the people are said to have caught "the flame from Heaven."[22] This flame, one supposes, is holy passion or human passion, like Wordsworth's own, purified to holiness.

Describing his imaginative sympathy with this inspired and aspiring people, he says:

To aspirations then of our own minds
Did we appeal; and finally beheld

[22] *The Prelude*, IX, 375.

A living confirmation of the whole
Before us in a People risen up
Fresh as the morning Star: elate we look'd
Upon their virtues, saw in rudest men
Self-sacrifice the firmest, generous love
And continence of mind, and sense of right
Uppermost in the midst of fiercest strife.
(IX, 387-395)

And speaking as one whose own privileged youth had left him inexperienced in the other meanings of "privilege" in historical societies ("It was my fortune scarcely to have seen/ Through the whole tenor of my Schoolday time/ The face of one, who, whether Boy or Man,/ Was vested with attention or respect/ Through claims of wealth or blood . . ."[23]), he recalls realizing the deception of History and of written histories:

Now do I feel how I have been deceived,
Reading of Nations and their works, in faith,
Faith given to vanity and emptiness . . .
(IX, 172-174)

But his father had daily looked upon such faces of privilege and had served in a world so historically determined; and in fact Wordsworth's financial circumstance had been affected seriously by aristocratic abuse. The small patrimony of the Wordsworth children was for years entangled in proceedings initiated to recover the money of his father's estate from his eccentric employer, Lord Lonsdale.[24]

In France he seemed to discover a hierarchy of victimization in History that he had not been made to consider before—from the king down, a structure of privileges and abuses. The young poet may have felt free as "a natural

[23] *The Prelude*, IX, 221-225.

[24] Wordsworth's father had been forced by Lord Lonsdale to loan his savings to him. These savings were not repaid to the Wordsworth children when their father died, leaving them orphans dependent upon the family of their deceased mother.

being in the strength of Nature," but he would have to locate every man he knew or had known, somewhere between the autocratic king and the "abject multitude." He was first to consider abuses in the structure of French society, and only afterwards was he to be made to turn his thoughts upon England. But it is no wonder that he treasured the image of the Shepherd—"Man free and working for himself"—and must have unconsciously compared that ideal of Man, the image of his ideal of himself, with men *and* with his own father whose life was spent absent in servitude.

When Wordsworth recalls the period of his republicanism in France, he is recalling imagining himself a French patriot with a patriot's grievance against the king. Abstractly, he rejected monarchy, and in describing the King—the symbol of Authority and metaphorically the father of his people—he describes him in a way that makes all his subjects children: "where will of One/ Is law for all,"[25] as the paternal will was law to children and the family. Does the king not gather, then, to his symbolic person all the ambivalent feelings men feel and have felt about fathers and authority? If, somewhat abstractly, Wordsworth would see the King overthrown in the name of a finer ideal of Man, we cannot ignore the degree of self-assertion and the idealization of himself we have so far seen expressed by Wordsworth in that finer ideal. But we know, too, of other feelings. The "indefinite terrour and dismay" he felt in contemplating human life, its passions and its dim analogy to "storms and angry elements," to "uproar and misrule." His own passionate self had been subdued before, as in the Boat-Stealing episode, which results in troubled dreams. We shall have occasion to examine further his reactions to the September Massacres, the execution of the King, the Reign of Terror, and the ascendancy of Robespierre, as historical events with deep psychic consequences for him.

We should observe first, however, how the important fig-

25 *The Prelude*, IX, 503-504.

ure, Beaupuis, is also an image of the father. The mind, precipitated by circumstance into an experience of reality it could not anticipate, nevertheless comes prepared to find again the reassurances with which it has lived securely. There had been for Wordsworth the reassuring, permissive and inciting Presence of Nature in his past, and so in France Nature seemed still to be leading him on. And there had been the Shepherd whose tutelary presence was impressive but unthreatening to the boy, like that of the father in the pre-Oedipal period of growth—"remov'd and at a distance that was fit."[26] Other fragments of the one father, divided by a divided psyche, are now to be encountered in the world beyond the vale. They have "lived" elsewhere, as in a kind of unconscious mythology: the angry father lives in dreams, the debased (or castrated) father worked in London, the kingly father lives in History. But the closer contact with the father desired by the boy and revealed by the poet in the interpolated tale of the Shepherd and his Son is most significantly revealed in Wordsworth's account of his friendship with Beaupuis.

Strong in knowledge and in human sentiment, Beaupuis is nevertheless meek in manner and even Christ-like:

> A meeker Man
> Than this liv'd never, or a more benign
> Meek, though enthusiastic to the height
> Of highest expectation. Injuries
> Made *him* more gracious, and his nature then
> Did breathe its sweetness out most sensibly
> As aromatic flowers on alpine turf
> When foot hath crush'd them.
>
> (IX, 297-304)

Injuries made him "more gracious." Of high birth, he is nevertheless bound as "by some invisible tie" to the "mean and the obscure/ And all the homely in their homely

[26] *Ibid.*, VIII, 488-489.

works."[27] As a man who lays down his life for his people freely chosen by him in love, he makes us think of Christ and the Good Shepherd. He also makes us think simply of Wordsworth's idealized Shepherd. Wordsworth perceives Beaupuis suffused by

> a kind of radiant joy
> That cover'd him about when he was bent
> On works of love or freedom,
>
> (IX, 321-323)

which may remind us of the "radiance" in which the Shepherd was perceived by Wordsworth and of the "aerial Cross" of the Chartreuse with which Wordsworth associated the form of the Shepherd:

> His Form hath flash'd upon me, glorified
> By the deep radiance of the setting sun:
> Or him have I descried in distant sky,
> A solitary object and sublime,
> Above all height! like an aerial Cross,
> As it is stationed on some spiry Rock
> Of the Chartreuse, for worship. Thus was Man
> Ennobled outwardly before mine eyes,
> And thus my heart at first was introduc'd
> To an unconscious love and reverence
> Of human Nature.
>
> (VIII, 404-414)

It was by Beaupuis that Wordsworth was tutored in the subjects of freedom and human dignity. Beaupuis seems to be the first man (other than perhaps Wordsworth's old schoolmaster, under whom Wordsworth has begun to write youthful verses) to whom Wordsworth submitted himself to learn. "Oft in solitude/ With him did I discourse," Wordsworth says; and the Shepherd, who had seemed a tutelary spirit of the landscape to the companionless boy in his solitude, seems to have taken on a personality and taken a per-

[27] *Ibid.*, IX, 311-325.

sonal interest in the young man. One suspects that until Wordsworth had talked at length with Beaupuis, freedom had meant "a boy's will," and human dignity, good opinions of oneself.

How vulnerable to human nature Wordsworth was because of this very habit of finding reassurances for his own idealization of himself, Wordsworth was never to understand. His fervor, as he recalls it, has a simple beauty and a naïveté that reminds us, as Erik Erikson has written, that fidelity develops in adolescence and expresses a youth's demand that the world be worthy of his commitment to it.[28] But youth's demand expresses as often its incomprehension of complex historical realities and of present opportunities:

> If Nature then be standing on the brink
> Of some great trial, and we hear the voice
> Of One devoted, one whom circumstance
> Hath call'd upon to embody his deep sense
> In action, give it outwardly a shape,
> And that of benediction to the world;
> Then doubt is not, and truth is more than truth,
> A hope it is and a desire, a creed
> Of zeal by an authority divine
> Sanction'd of danger, difficulty or death.
>
> (IX, 404-413)

So Wordsworth says of the Revolution, in verse that awkwardly recaptures something of the ardor:

> that 'twas a cause
> Good, and which no one could stand up against
> Who was not lost, abandon'd, selfish, proud,
> Mean, miserable, wilfully deprav'd,
> Hater perverse of equity and truth.
>
> (IX, 288-292)

[28] See Erik Erikson, "Human Strength and the Cycle of Generations," in *Insight and Responsibility*.

In the fulfillment of its promise he could accept himself as a man among men; in the meantime, as a patriot among patriots, he began to find the external world more real. For a while, he felt the pleasure of worldly aspiration and expectation, seeking satisfaction, as he says:

> in the very world which is the world
> Of all of us, the place in which, in the end,
> We find our happiness, or not at all.
> (x, 726-728)

To him, the revolution promised to change a reality that most profoundly affronted his identity.

BEFORE proceeding to the period of crisis in his life, Wordsworth pauses to relate the tale of "Vaudracour and Julia" in his narrative, a tale told him by Beaupuis. Ourselves recollecting the interpolated tales of "The Maid of Buttermere" and the Shepherd and his son should find it easier to imagine why Wordsworth included this tale for psychological reasons than why Beaupuis related it to him. The tale is, as almost every commentator observes, preposterous in the extreme. It has been argued by some that Wordsworth included the tale as an oblique account, through a limited verisimilitude, of his own love affair with Annette Vallon at that time,[29] an episode in his life which either the prevailing decorum of biography or at least an understandable reticence prevented him from disclosing. Wordsworth's autobiography has not the candor of Rousseau's. But whether the tale is an allusion to undiscussable matters or simply, as he says, an exemplary tale told him and repeated, we shall consider his version meaningful to him personally, serving conscious, and probably unconscious, purposes. It is certainly the story of a father and a son.

[29] See, for instance, E. Legouis, *William Wordsworth and Annette Vallon* and *Wordsworth in a New Light.* Also, E. de Selincourt's comments in *The Prelude,* pp. 591-592.

As early as Book VIII, Wordsworth says that in his young manhood his mind turned "instinctively to human passions" and that his "Fancy" seized upon the most accidental facts around him to invent tales of passionate distress while he wandered alone in nature. There is no record, other than "Descriptive Sketches," of how he may have figured personally in his own passionate fancies, but while the corrected image he presents in *The Prelude* would suggest that he did not, his life in France shows what we have observed above, that he tried to approach social realities by first imagining his involvement with other people. In any event, scholarship has long since established that Wordsworth himself was about to experience passionate love; the somewhat prudishly recollected college student and moralistic observer of London was to act the romantic youth in the enchanted land of France soon after his arrival there.

He begins by recalling that while strolling with Beaupuis, engaged in intimate ethical discourse, his mind wandered fancifully to the same subject. Perhaps Beaupuis told his tale in response to one of the youth's errant fancies, employing romance to lead him back to the subject of historical abuses. When Wordsworth speaks, in an artificial and "literary" way in Book IX, of Francis I and his mistress bound in "chains of mutual passion," History is momentarily forgotten by the young man who has enjoyed reading romances and even reading History "romantically." Regarding kings, "their vices and their better deeds," in this way, he says that imagination could at times mitigate "the bigotry of a youthful patriot's mind" and imbue certain historical spots with "chivalrous delights." We may think of the world of romance, of Mallory, Ariosto, Sidney, and Spenser, where kings and knights are subjected to temptations and sometimes are derelict to higher duties. For the young man undergoing a similar temptation and succumbing to it, imagination may be charitable to those whose wills entrammeled them in passion.

But what was the appeal of "Vaudracour and Julia" to

Wordsworth? His version of the story appealed to him as it has to no one else. The editor, Ernest de Selincourt, says of it that "as a whole it is among the weakest of his attempts in narrative verse"; that Wordsworth "completely fails in presenting a character so unlike his own"; and that the story is ludicrous, reaching "a climax of absurdity difficult to parallel in our literature."[30] The tale *is* hopelessly inept. It is indecisive about what feelings it would arouse; whatever the facts may have been, they are unsuccessfully transmuted into an illusion of reality to which we may accord poetic belief. But the story contains elements of Wordsworth's psychology unobserved by Wordsworthians, and deserves closer scrutiny.

The story is of a noble youth who falls in love with his childhood playmate and neighbor, but is denied permission by his father to marry beneath his class. Opposing his father's wishes and remaining true to his now-pregnant beloved, Vaudracour commits manslaughter in self-defense; and in the "tragic" outcome, he is eventually separated from Julia, she from her babe, and Vaudracour from his sanity. The father in the story, a figure of noble birth and prerogative, is invested with ruling powers one associates with society rather than simply with family; and Wordsworth must intend the reader to feel that the father's unsympathetic treatment of his son and of Julia also reflects the callousness of History, of French society that forbade marriages between classes. Human and natural worth is not appreciated. Wordsworth's talk of the youthfulness of the son Vaudracour, of his ardor and his willingness to "entrust himself/ To Nature for a happy end of all," *is* intended to convey Vaudracour's natural worth, which is not unlike Wordsworth's, as Wordsworth remembers himself in his youth and especially in revolutionary France. And Julia, the beloved, who is like a "vision" and who makes the earth live "in one great presence of the spring," opening "all paradise" to him, seems to concentrate in one person

[30] See *The Prelude*, pp. 591-593, footnotes to IX, 553-554.

for him the human reality of love. The language of description may recall for us, from other contexts, what deep sources of affection he is drawing upon to convey the worth of the beloved and of their love.

Nevertheless, her lack of social position makes Julia inconsiderable to the father. This is not an allegory, but Julia does sound very like The People, which is only to say that personal histories are usually social history implicitly:

> a bright Maid, from Parents sprung
> Not mean in their condition; but with rights
> Unhonour'd of Nobility, and hence
> The Father of the young Man, who had place
> Among that order, spurn'd the very thought
> Of such alliance.
>
> (IX, 564-569)

While Vaudracour often finds natural sympathy for his love among kindly townspeople, it is plain that the father has too much "influence" in the state for his son to find any real social acceptance except through him; but

> The Father threw out threats that by a mandate
> Bearing the private signet of the State
> He should be baffled of his mad intent,
> And that should cure him . . .
>
> (IX, 665-668)

Yet it is surprising to find how powerless the son really is. Though he begs, he cannot persuade his father to grant him any kind of recognition and support, even after offering to renounce his rights of primogeniture; and then, having "conceived a terror" of his father's dire threats, he goes about armed to defend himself. When set upon by his father's hirelings ("the instruments of ruffian power"), he is driven to act "in the impulse of his rage," killing one and wounding another; but although he opposes his father's autocratic wishes impulsively, he cannot realize within himself the intention of opposing him on principle. When Julia expresses "vehement indignation" at his father, Vaudracour shows his inner meekness before an authority that feels "natural" to him. He is unable to distinguish with any conviction the alternative meaning of "natural" on which he has acted in loving her or in defending himself:

but the Youth
Check'd her, nor would hear of this; for thought
Unfilial, or unkind, had never once
Found harbour in his breast. The Lovers thus
United once again together lived
For a few days, which were to Vaudracour
Days of dejection, sorrow and remorse
For that ill deed of violence which his hand
Had hastily committed: for the Youth
Was of a loyal spirit, a conscience nice
And over tender for the trial which
His fate had call'd him to.[31]

(IX, 713-724)

Before the law, to whom the son then "peacefully resign'd his person," he is a criminal; but again, through friends and influence at court, the father has power to secure the liberty of his son on his promise to comply with his father's wishes; it is as if the law existed simply to enforce such natural compliances as those of sons with fathers.

Whether Vaudracour realized it or not, however, he *was* acting on some principle of nature, though plainly it was a strong principle weakly held: it could not survive his own dismay at seeing it applied. After the "ill deed of violence," Vaudracour says of himself: "a murderer, Julia, cannot love/ An innocent woman," as if he were annunciating a natural truth. What is significant here is how Wordsworth regards Vaudracour, not what Vaudracour does or does not

31 See Goethe's essay on Hamlet, in which he characterizes him as "a soul unfit" for a great burden because of a too great sensitivity, in *Wilhelm Meister's Apprenticeship*, IV, chap. xiii, tr. Thomas Carlyle, London, 1795.

do. For what the story actually does is set in opposition two powerful feelings about what is "natural": the natural worth of human beings, their love and the passion necessary to assert and defend that worth and the "natural" feeling that seems to attach to the settled order of things in society from deep in the psyche. Were Wordsworth able to imagine the conflict and resolve it in Vaudracour's favor, he could have told the same story with a very different effect—so as to incite a reader to feel passionately the tragic conflict in the youth who must oppose the settled order of things in opposing his father's autocratic wishes for the sake of something naturally finer. Instead, Wordsworth exasperates his reader with Vaudracour's pathetic fecklessness because the unrealized conflict about what is natural was his own and the subject of passion in himself one that he eschewed.

Beyond Julia and the possible allusion to Annette Vallon, in the story, there were the principles of the French Revolution with which Wordsworth had associated natural human worth and the natural and pure love of mankind. Here it is necessary to observe how *The Prelude* shows that Wordsworth naively anticipated that those principles, philosophically argued and affirmed by every human heart, would prove irresistible in transforming society: the unnatural opposition would be weak, whereas the revolutionists would feel the pure passion of "the flame from heaven" as he imagined it. He was appalled to discover the repressive violence of the continental *and English* regimes, on the one hand, and the violent and factious advocacy of the revolutionists, on the other. We shall presently observe how deeply the experience of Nature had been for Wordsworth the experience of *English* nature, secured by the settled order of things, by English institutions and allegiances which all unawares he had always felt as "natural."[32] To

[32] F. R. Leavis, *Revaluation*, p. 171. Dr. Leavis also applies the words "nature" and "natural" to Wordsworth in ways that make plain how profoundly English was the Nature of Wordsworth's youth. But Dr. Leavis limits the meanings of "Nature" for Wordsworth in this way:

understand Wordsworth's crisis, we may learn from Vaudracour's plight as Wordsworth imagines it, and see there what Wordsworth feels about Nature and society.

Erik Erikson has said that a child experiences a crisis of passion and restraint in the anal period of growth, which results in a seemingly natural resolution observable in the child's behavior—a free compliance, a purposive willing of order.[33] The early resolution of this crisis is the basis of his subsequent acceptance of himself in a context of laws and codes later in life; and this crisis is one that occurs earlier than that of Oedipal conflict. Although conscience forms and develops in relation to the father in society as a result of Oedipal resolution, its rudiments are pre-Oedipal. Vaudracour, who in effect does not *want* to be like his father, reveals this by rejecting the social code by which he is himself identified and expected to live; and, in conflict with that code and its laws, he is thrown back upon an earlier conflict within himself, between passion and restraint, personal will and the settled order of things. It is at least *possible* that in adult life the early conflict, re-experienced symbolically in great historical issues can be again resolved, but with a difference. By using violence in the name of principles, by willing a subsequent compliance with a finer order, and by persisting in establishing it, men may alter their historical circumstances and even their own personalities and the potential of personality in their children.[34] But Vaudracour is a pathetically marginal figure, unable to imagine anything; and Wordsworth is unable

---

"a congenial social environment, with its wholesome simple pieties and the traditional sanity of its moral culture, which to him were Nature." In contrast, I mean to emphasize that psychologically the experience of family is primary and that "Nature" for Wordsworth is filial before it is national. In Wordsworth's use of the word "Nature," the evocative imagery may indeed be English, but the "Presence" regularly evoked is filial.

[33] See Erik Erikson, *Childhood and Society*, part III, chap. 7.

[34] This, for instance, is the reasoning of Brutus in *Julius Caesar*, as well as of Freud in *Civilization and Its Discontents* and of Erikson in *Young Man Luther*.

to imagine that he should. Yet it is Wordsworth who imagined himself a revolutionist and who, at this point in *The Prelude,* is about to deal with his own crisis over principles and passions, social orders and revolutions.

Wordsworthians cannot see any significant resemblance between Vaudracour and Wordsworth, but I think that plainly some elements of the tale touch Wordsworth's unconscious imagination of himself and appeal to him in that way. Most significantly, the mother of the baby takes on the aspect of the mother of her lover as well. He is seen

> Propping a pale and melancholy face
> Upon the Mother's bosom, resting thus
> His head upon one breast, while from the other
> The Babe was drawing in its quiet food.
> (IX, 811-814)

It seems to me that this scene recalls an idealized unrelinquished love, a lost relationship with continuing unconscious force in the poet. If we think of Wordsworth feeling a deep sympathy for the circumstance of poor Vaudracour in a way that readers do not, we must wonder where such feelings come from that cause him to picture the pathos in exactly this way. When childish Vaudracour says, "Julia how much thine eyes have cost me," we may be hearing Wordsworth's unconscious feelings of reproach, those of the sorrowing child who, like Vaudracour, had been too much dependent on looks of love that promised "all paradise" and the "one great presence of the spring." When Wordsworth describes the painful, seemingly pointless, and unnatural separation of the mother and her babe-like lover sulking on her breast, he may be unconsciously recalling the repressed trauma of separation closely resembling this:

> Nor could they frame a manner soft enough
> To impart the tidings to the Youth; but great
> Was their astonishment when they beheld him
> Receive the news in calm despondency,

Composed and silent, without outward sign
Of even the least emotion.

(IX, 847-852)

What Wordsworth here "imagines" for Vaudracour, I think, "reveals" a moment of his own past, unconsciously "true" or "compelling" to Wordsworth. The gratuitous death of the babe (who "by some mistake/ Or indiscretion of the Father, died")[35] may remind us that we have already seen the unconscious desire for death associated with babes in Wordsworth; also, the unconscious grievance against his own unnurturing father in tales associated with the years after his mother's death in which he lived apart from his father as a school child. The hopeless hermetic solitude and the imbecile mind of Vaudracour ("in those solitary shades/ His days he wasted, an imbecile mind") may recall to us the potential of extreme psychic withdrawal observed in Wordsworth as early as "Tintern Abbey," with its implication of psychosis. And, finally, the specific denial of any intention in the story ("Theirs be the blame who caused the woe, not mine") is the simplest denial of possible unconscious intentions in telling it.

Perhaps there is an oblique allusion made to his own love affair in this story which concludes Book IX. We tend to accept the likelihood upon reading at the beginning of Book X of his own unavoidable departure from the Loire Valley, where he left behind the pregnant Annette. It is not until after his second description of revolutionary Paris that he tells Coleridge how reluctantly he left for England, "Compelled by nothing less than absolute want/ Of funds for my support."[36] Otherwise, he says, despite his alien status and his unfittedness for any significant role, he would have remained in France, an active patriot. But unprepared to imagine war between his native England and his spiritually espoused France, he could not foresee the length of his separation from Annette at that time. Delay and cir-

35 *The Prelude*, IX, 906-907.
36 *Ibid.*, X, 191-192.

cumstances were to make it permanent and leave him even more significantly alone for the ensuing events of History.

3. "Depressed, bewildered thus . . ."

There is disagreement among scholars as to the precise date of Wordsworth's crisis, its apparent and real causes, the forms it took and its duration.[37] The different interpretations reflect the tenuous relationship in the text between the presentation of fact and the interpretation of self based on it. Book X of the 1805 version (divided into Books X and XI to make up the fourteen-book 1850 version) falters very noticeably as narrative. States of mind are recorded, past ones mediated by present reflections, but set down in unspecific relation to each other and to the events also recorded. Despite the uncertain chronology, Wordsworth's account does allow us to distinguish intensities of crisis in a period that shows the "hopes and hazards" of living once associated by the boy with the manhood of the Shepherd. The account extends from the period in which Wordsworth approached the fallen world of History through imagination to the point at which he "yielded up moral questions in despair."[38] We should note, then, that the first stage of crisis begins with his shock at England's joining the "confederated host" of Europe against France; and we should observe, too, that the shock is anticipated by a feeling of dread he had about the events in France.

Wordsworth's account of parting from the Loire valley with the knowledge that "the king had fallen," his pleasure in learning that France had taken the name of a Republic, and his enthusiastic touring of revolutionary Paris seem like a partisan patriot's natural responses; but we have observed Wordsworth's temperamental distance from people and we may suspect that Wordsworth is not entirely "natural" in the role he assumed imaginatively. He seems to himself just like any other person responding to an his-

[37] *Ibid.*, pp. 603-606. This is well summarized by the editor.
[38] *Ibid.*, X, 901.

torical event of great consequence, but we must wonder what would account for that transformation of character. We should attempt to see how the appearance of the world may have changed so that its apparent difference may account for his.

When Wordsworth says:

> Bliss was it in that dawn to be alive,
> But to be young was very heaven . . .
> (x, 693-694)

a long description follows of the kind of transformed historical world his temperament was prepared to enter with natural conviction:

> Not favour'd spots alone, but the whole earth
> The beauty wore of promise, that which sets,
> To take an image which was felt, no doubt,
> Among the bowers of paradise itself,
> The budding rose above the rose full blown.
> What temper at the prospect did not wake
> To happiness unthought of? The inert
> Were rouz'd, and lively natures rapt away:
> They who had fed their childhood upon dreams,
> The Play-fellows of Fancy, who had made
> All powers of swiftness, subtlety, and strength
> Their ministers, used to stir in lordly wise[39]
> Among the grandest objects of the sense,
> And deal with whatsoever they found there
> As if they had within some lurking right
> To wield it; they too, who, of gentle mood,
> Had watch'd all gentle motions, and to these
> Had fitted their own thoughts, schemers more mild,
> And in the region of their peaceful selves,
> Did now find helpers to their hearts' desire,

[39] This seems again to be recalling the mind of Prospero and the world of the island in *The Tempest* as the place and analogue of Imagination.

And stuff at hand, plastic as they could wish
Were call'd upon to exercise their skill,
Not in Utopia, subterraneous Fields,
Or some secreted Island, Heaven knows where,
But in the very world which is the world
Of all of us, the place in which, in the end,
We find our happiness, or not at all.
(x, 702-728)

The "schemers more mild," like this poet who has lived "in the region of [his] peaceful [self]," now were to find "helpers to their hearts' desire"; and we can imagine how attractive the thought was to him. Beyond this pleasant notion, one may hear very distinctly in this passage an echo of the lines written as an introduction to the projected *Recluse* and recall the poet's hope of finding Beauty "a living Presence" in the world after facing the incapacitating fears of life "in the Mind of Man." If in 1798, the plan was for a personal meditation in retirement, in 1792 the historical world had seemed rather to be offering itself for action. One would have some difficulty, however, while thinking of the whole French Revolution and its principal characters, in designating the moment when it might have seemed to men acquainted with History that their most ideal aspirations were being realized with such felicity; but this only serves to emphasize the kind of demand Wordsworth was making on the world. When he speaks of History looking in promise like the "bowers of Paradise," we are aware that "Paradise" has not a merely literary weight for him as description, but rather a complex psychic reference of its own.

He continues:

Why should I not confess that earth was then
To me what an inheritance new-fallen
Seems, when the first time visited, to one
Who thither comes to find in it his home?
He walks about and looks upon the place

With cordial transport, moulds it, and remoulds,
And is half pleased with things that are amiss,
'Twill be such joy to see them disappear.

An active partisan, I thus convoked
From every object pleasant circumstance
To suit my ends; I moved among mankind
With genial feelings still predominant . . .
(x, 729-740)

The "active partisan" described in his account of his return to revolutionary Paris is here further characterized by a peculiar analogy, that of a young man entering into his inheritance. This may rightly characterize a recollected *feeling* of his, that of discovering later than most that the visible world is "his" if he is able to regard it as such; but at the same time it is a crude analogy for revolutionary times and is at odds with other significant recollections of his own past states of feeling. Eventually, Wordsworth came to feel that he misled himself and was in part misled by the appearances of events, but if the text reveals how, it does so without Wordsworth accurately accounting for it.

"Inheritance" suggests a settled and orderly transference of property and implies a passing of generations that seem at once natural and social. The abrupt confrontations of orders in the French Revolution, explicit in its principles, could never have seemed so, except to one who characteristically denies the intensity and meaning of passion, its basic self-interest, and its potential of violence. So it is that his revolutionary ardor made little of the "Massacres" and much of the "venerable name/ Of a Republic" recently assumed:

lamentable crimes
'Tis true had gone before this hour, the work
Of massacre, in which the senseless sword
Was pray'd to as a judge; but these were past,

Earth free from them for ever, as was thought,
Ephemeral monsters, to be seen but once;
Things that could only shew themselves and die.

(x, 31-37)

But in no accidental way, his psyche did not make little of the recent events. The figure of the king attracts his attention, not as a hated historical symbol, but as a domestic figure, pathetically husband and father, and in a way that makes clear that not "inheritance" but violent dispossession is the case:

The Prison where the unhappy Monarch lay,
Associate with his Children and his Wife
In bondage; and the Palace lately storm'd
With roar of cannon, and a numerous Host.
I crossed (a black and empty area then)
The Square of the Carousel, few weeks back
Heap'd up with dead and dying, upon these
And other sights looking as doth a man
Upon a volume whose contents he knows
Are memorable, but from him lock'd up,
Being written in a tongue he cannot read,
So that he questions the mute leaves with pain
And half upbraids their silence.

(x, 42-54)

The metaphor of "reading" may simply characterize Wordsworth's inability to infer the preceding events precisely from the marks left by them; but there is just the suggestion, too, that the language he cannot read is metaphorically of human passion and violence, which is why Wordsworth, more than another man, cannot understand what is before his eyes. But he then recollects feeling dread that disturbed and prevented sleep, and, echoing *MacBeth,* he recalls that he "seem'd to hear a voice that cried,/ To the whole City, 'Sleep no more.' "[40] If murder leads to murder and the kill-

[40] *The Prelude,* x, 76-77. See, too, *MacBeth,* II, ii, 33ff.

ing of a king has profound psychic consequences as well as political and historical ones, did Wordsworth himself feel that in some way he had "murther'd sleep"?[41] What the patriots have done, has the youthful partisan not willed?

There are, however, two other peculiarities in this passage, of perhaps less apparent reference. He says:

> the fear gone by
> Press'd on me almost like a fear to come;
> I thought of those September Massacres,
> Divided from me by a little month,
> And felt and touch'd them, a substantial dread;
> The rest was conjured up from tragic fictions,
> And mournful Calendars of true history,
> Remembrances and dim admonishments.
> (x, 62-69)

"Dim admonishments" may now remind us of several other contexts in which "dim" and "admonishments" are used, sometimes as that very phrase: the "apt admonishment" from the Old Leech-Gatherer; the "dim and undetermined sense of unknown modes of being" in the Boat-Stealing episode; the admonishment "from another world" in the Blind Beggar incident; and especially the "dim/ Analogy to uproar and misrule/ Disquiet, danger and obscurity," examined above. All suggest "unknowns" that qualify Wordsworth's special regard for himself as distinct from common humanity, all come in contexts that connect Wordsworth's own passions with dream-like circumstances in reality. Here, again, in Paris, reality is becoming a bad dream that brings bad dreams, and in a way that identifies MacBeth with the youth of pure passions. But very peculiarly, Wordsworth seems to be echoing something else from Shakespeare as well. He says:

> '*The horse is taught his manage,* and the wind
> Of heaven wheels round and treads in his own steps,

[41] MacBeth, II, ii, 40.

Year follows year, the tide returns again,
Day follows day, all things have second birth;
The earthquake is not satisfied at once.'

(x, 70-74)

The versification seems to resemble some of the involuted metaphorical passages of *MacBeth*, and Wordsworth seems to be mulling over a thought that is like a free elaboration of a thought or phrase recollected from Shakespeare. While his uneasy feelings of dread plainly tell him that what has happened will probably happen again, the phrase "The horse is taught his manage" barely seems to cooperate with the other examples in conveying that impression.

Without attempting to interpret its possible import, de Selincourt rightly identifies the phrase as I, i, 1-13 of *As You Like It*.[42] Again, it is an example of a preconscious association of a context (about inheritances) with the psychic circumstance that Wordsworth is only partially describing:

> *Orlando*: As I remember, Adam, it was upon this fashion: bequeathed me by will but poor a thousand crowns, and, as thou sayest, charged my brother, on his blessing, to breed me well; and there begins my sadness. My brother Jaques he keeps at school, and report speaks goldenly of his profit. For my part, he keeps me rustically at home, or, to speak more properly, stays me here at home unkept; for call you that keeping for a gentleman of my birth, that differs not from the stalling of an ox? His horses are bred better; for, besides that they are fair with their feeding, *they are taught their manage*, and to that end riders dearly hired; but I, his brother, gain nothing under him but growth; for the which his animals on his dunghills are as much bound to him as I. Besides this nothing that he so plentifully gives me, the something that nature gave

[42] *The Prelude*, p. 595. Neither the reference to *MacBeth*, nor the echo of *As You Like It*, is commented on by the editor.

> me his countenance seems to take from me. He lets me feed with his hinds, bars me the place of a brother, and, as much as in him lies, mines my gentility with my education. This is it, Adam, that grieves me; and the spirit of my father, which I think is within me, begins to mutiny against this servitude. I will no longer endure it, though yet I know no wise remedy how to avoid it.
>
> (I, i, 1-25)

Some of our previous observations should suggest why key elements of *As You Like It* should bring the play to mind. The discussion here is between a gentle youth on his own in the world and Old Adam, who remembers a golden way of life which, with the death of the youth's father, has passed. The resolution of the play depends upon Arden and the beneficent influence of pastoral Nature that may be felt there; Arden recalls the Golden Age in Nature and sets that idealization in opposition to the historical world where human nature is corrupted in the life of the court. The play recalls a good father, but shows the effect of an unfortunate inheritance in the abuse of Orlando by his brother Oliver. So, too, in the present there are a good duke and good father and a bad duke and bad father, brothers divided by the envy of one of them. As in *The Tempest,* an inherited kingdom has been usurped by one brother from a gentler and naturally finer brother. The subject of fathers and brothers, authorities and revolutionists, is one that Wordsworth never clarifies, but the passages on Paris and the recent massacres mentioned here immediately precede what was for Wordsworth the terrible subject of Robespierre, a fact of considerable importance.

It is someone like Robespierre rather than Beaupuis who comes to inherit the revolution, yet in Wordsworth's account, it is Beaupuis who stands out as a man so gentle that Wordsworth could and did idealize revolutionists. Perhaps the Girondists in their brief hour enhanced that effect of his eager imagination; yet they proved to be as vulnerable to circumstances as his own idealizations were to be. When his ideal image of Man, the Shepherd, seemed to "become" Beaupuis, Wordsworth perhaps persuaded himself that revolutionary ardor is man's desire to obliterate all authoritarian distinctions—between classes of society, between generations, between master and servant, man and boy, king and subject, father and son; whereas others, more opportunistic, sought wealth, power and rank. It seems to be what "liberty, equality, and *fraternity*" really meant to Wordsworth, though he confused most men with himself by imagining that it meant exactly to them what it felt like to him. Unconsciously he hoped to find that the personalities of men were changing just as they seemed to wish to change their society; *they* wanted to be less like what History had made them, more like what Nature had made him. In the Shepherd he had imagined himself ideally; approaching manhood did not mean adjusting to a father's ways, but simply fulfilling Nature's and his own. And then Beaupuis seemed to be telling him he was right, that the revolution ideally expressed man's desire to reclaim human nature from History and become Nature's children again. How much it must have seemed the triumph of Nature, then—just as it must have seemed to him that Beaupuis was the "good" father who wanted only to be a "brother." The success of the revolution would be a regression fulfilled: an inheritance as large as may be imagined, everyone a lord and master, no contrary wills, all passions pure and fulfilled. As for leaders, brother revolutionists would advance men like Beaupuis who could be trusted in the place of the symbolic father-king, who has been proved to be no father at all. Poets, too, would find honorable employment, as older brothers experienced in the benign ways of Nature. It is not a little bit fantastic. And it is upon these expectations that the dreadful scene in Paris casts a gloom.

Wordsworth had wished to see the revolution as an event

in the "certain course" of Nature[43] and wished especially to find the principles proclaimed by the revolution true: liberty, equality, and *fraternity*. Freud, on the same subject, explains that the uncertain cohesiveness of brothers is that of sons banded in opposition to the father, collectively aggrieved by his oppression, but individually envious of his power. Each would wish to supplant him in his role after they have deposed him, though only by banding together and seeming to contemn the role itself could they effect his deposition.[44] Passions find reasons but remain passions; and the French, with passionate factious strife and legalistic reasoning, replaced a king with autocrats like Robespierre and Napoleon. Wordsworth's hopes for the revolution rose and fell, his feelings divided between love of the principles and loathing for Robespierre. But whether one considers the forceful disinheritance of the king or the nature of the revolutionary inheritors, it seems a denial of reality that Wordsworth could hope that the transition to a Republic would resemble an inheritance, though he felt in a way it did.

The passage from Shakespeare tells of a share in an inheritance denied one by the abusiveness of an unnatural brother, a feeling that Wordsworth is to record as his own in relation to Robespierre. Orlando then speaks of "mutiny against this servitude" and of knowing as yet "no wise remedy to avoid it"; such was soon to be Wordsworth's case. Wordsworth quickly sensed danger to his own psyche in the revolution as it came under the will of Robespierre; he felt, as he says, powerless to affect its course, though he does *not* say, until after he had found good reason to abandon the revolution to its historical fate, that he wavered quite early in his feelings about it. But as early as his return to Paris, when he was so pleased by the name of "republic" he was

43 *The Prelude*, IX, 251-252: "the events/ Seem'd nothing out of Nature's certain course."

44 See Freud, *Totem and Taboo*.

reacting with deep dread to the implications of his own imaginative commitment to the revolution, and already feeling unconsciously that he wanted "to avoid" the consequences. Passion, even to effect principle, frightened him; Robespierre, who seemed without principles, terrified him.

Robespierre is a foil to Beaupuis and Wordsworth. In a sense Louvet, who had answered Robespierre's public challenge to any man "who had an ill surmise of him/ To bring his charge in openness,"[45] is also a foil to Wordsworth himself. It is not that Wordsworth should have said publicly at the time what in retrospect he remembers having felt in sympathy with Louvet: "I, Robespierre, accuse thee!"[46] Of course, how could he? But rather that he was unable to assess realities when psychic imperatives required that he deny them to preserve his own stability. Unlike Louvet, he anticipated Robespierre's fall "with a revelation's liveliness" because he felt

> that tyrannic Power is weak,
> Hath neither gratitude, nor faith, nor love,
> Nor the support of good or evil men
> To trust in, that the Godhead which is ours
> Can never utterly be charm'd or still'd,
> That nothing hath a natural right to last
> But equity and reason, that all else
> Meets foes irreconcilable, and at best
> Doth live but by variety of disease.
>
> (x, 168-176)

Despite his insight into the worsening circumstance of the revolution, he maintained that the ideals of the revolution would assert themselves with irresistible strength:

> That Man was only weak through his mistrust
> And want of hope, where evidence divine
> Proclaim'd to him that hope should be most sure,
> That, with desires heroic and firm sense,

[45] *The Prelude,* x, 94-95. [46] *Ibid.,* x, 100.

A Spirit thoroughly faithful to itself,
Unquenchable, unsleeping, undismay'd,
Was as an instinct among Men, a stream
That gather'd up each petty straggling rill
And vein of water, glad to be roll'd on
In safe obedience, that a mind whose rest
Was where it ought to be, in self-restraint,
In circumspection and simplicity,
Fell rarely in entire discomfiture
Below its aim, or met with from without
A treachery that defeated it or foil'd.

(x, 144-158)

He is committed now to seeing revolutionary man in his own image. The alternative estimate would require a reassessment of himself, but especially a reassessment of Nature, her efficacy and her intentions, one that briefly and desperately he undertook at a later moment of crisis.

Still, he knew that Paris was like London in its way:

That great Emporium, Chronicle at once
And Burial-place of passions and their home
Imperial and chief living residence.

(VIII, 749-751)

The destiny of the revolution would be controlled from a Paris always passionate in its vicissitudes: "Liberty, and Life, and Death would soon/ To the remotest corners of the land/ Lie in the arbitrement of those who ruled/ The capital City. . . ."[47] He saw Louvet "left alone without support/ Of his irresolute friends"[48]; and just as in London where earlier he had felt a craving for greater Power, Wordsworth felt his want of it in Paris:

yea I could almost
Have pray'd that throughout earth upon all souls
By patient exercise of reason made

[47] *Ibid.*, x, 108-111. [48] *Ibid.*, x, 102-103.

Worthy of liberty, upon every soul
Matured to live in plainness and in truth
The gift of tongues might fall, and men arrive
From the four quarters of the winds to do
For France what without help she could not do,
A work of honour . . .

(x, 117-125)

"The gift of tongues" reminds us of the Epistles of St. Paul and the ecstatic possession experienced by the faithful, perhaps like the flame Wordsworth had imagined the people catching "from Heaven."[49] But Wordsworth could only imagine wishfully a "natural" inspiration he could not himself have transmitted. To be inspiring to a people so situated, he would have had to be a power comparable to Nature (which is how he later describes the ideal Poet in Book XIII). But of himself at the time he observes accurately his mere mortality, his historical insignificance, and his tentative ardor:

Yet did I grieve, nor only griev'd, but thought
Of opposition and of remedies,
An insignificant Stranger, and obscure,
Mean as I was, and little graced with power
Of eloquence even in my native speech,
And all unfit for tumult or intrigue,
Yet would I willingly have taken up
A service at this time for cause so great,
However dangerous . . .

(x, 129-137)

He continues, some lines later:

In this frame of mind,
Reluctantly to England I return'd,
Compell'd by nothing less than absolute want
Of funds for my support, else, well assured

[49] St. Paul, I Corinthians, 14: 1-22, especially 20-22. And *The Prelude*, IX, 375.

That I both was and must be of small worth,
No better than an alien in the Land,
I doubtless should have made a common cause
With some who perish'd, haply perish'd, too,
A poor mistaken and bewilder'd offering,
Should to the breast of Nature have gone back
With all my resolutions, all my hopes,
A Poet only to myself, to Men
Useless, and even, beloved Friend! a soul
To thee unknown . . .

(x, 189-202)

The poet withdraws from France with a feeling of dread. The crisis came in England.

To speak psychologically of "denial" almost inevitably suggests insincerity, unless one insists upon the dominant unconscious factors of all character. Wordsworth expressed sincerely what he was compelled to feel about his character in relation to circumstance. Beyond this, we may question the capacity for *fidelity* to specific commitments in a young man whose most profound commitment is to a deep and prior reality, one that takes precedence over any sense of the external world that runs counter to it; and we have said, too, that it was the appearance of the world that seemed to have changed as Wordsworth seemed to accept its greater reality in revolutionary France. The French Revolution seemed to serve his needs. The coincidence of needs and circumstances should be remarked, for the needs would persist unabated whether the circumstances changed or remained constantly favorable. The circumstances changed. At the time, Wordsworth had to deal with the changes under the pressure of need, though he was later to attempt to account for his crisis in terms of circumstance—what events had brought. In the ensuing crisis, the most acceptable forms that his needs had taken in his growth were to be called in question; and this portion of *The Prelude* shows the strain of his attempt to account for that critical period in which he was questioning the very forms that he has been laboring in the poem to formulate and affirm. A natural sympathy with the French Revolution is a very late form of the psychic need expressed in his deep attachment to Nature, but the crisis it seemed to cause was profound.

After his return to England came the shock of England's joining the "confederated host" of nations against France. He says:

> Not in my single self alone I found,
> But in the minds of all ingenuous Youth,
> Change and subversion from this hour. No shock
> Given to my moral nature had I known
> Down to that very moment; neither lapse
> Nor turn of sentiment that might be nam'd
> A revolution, save at this one time,
> All else was progress on the self-same path
> On which with diversity of pace
> I had been travelling; this a stride at once
> Into another region.
>
> (x, 232-242)

Here, within a matter of a few lines, the two metaphors of growth—the journey-metaphor and the soul-tillage-metaphor—will come suddenly together. His growth had seemed to him a consistent if various journey and seemed at the same time rooted in Nature; his being had been rooted in English Nature, a fact with unanticipated significance which was to reveal itself in a perplexing experience of sustained inner violence:

> for I felt
> The ravage of this most unnatural strife
> In my own heart; there lay it like a weight
> At enmity with all the tenderest springs
> Of my enjoyments. I, who with the breeze
> Had play'd, a green leaf on the blessed tree
> Of my beloved country; nor had wish'd

For happier fortune than to wither there,
Now from my pleasant station was cut off,
And toss'd about in whirlwinds.

(x, 250-259)

Exulting in the overthrow of English troops, he experienced a "conflict of sensations without name"; and while sitting in a congregation of worshipers "bending all/ To their great Father," he, "like an uninvited guest . . . fed on the day of vengeance yet to come."[50] He could not join the prayer for English success. This fidelity of poetic characterization—for that was Wordsworth's true fidelity—seems at once Greek and tragic; for in it we see Wordsworth remembering wishing for the English what he felt was happening to himself.

Aeschylus gave the Athenians the figure of Orestes to contemplate. Covered with his mother's blood, which is his own blood, Orestes is the victim of opposed loyalties, both promising insanity. In conflicts involving the symbols fixed deep in one's psyche, there are no wounds inflicted that are not in the same act or wish inflicted on oneself. In modern England, as in the primitive tribe or in the more sophisticated family of Greek civic tragedy, the nation's sons are felt to be family; and one cannot violate family. So while Wordsworth felt violated by the actions of others, he felt it in accordance with his own destructive passion. His sole defense against feeling violent was in insisting upon his unselfish devotion to the principles of the revolution as a pledge in love to a humanity greater than England, could the English but accept, in the name of Nature, this whole human family:

Oh! Much have they to account for, who could tear
By violence at one decisive rent
From the best Youth in England, their dear pride,
Their joy, in England; this, too, at a time

[50] *The Prelude*, x, 266ff.

In which worst losses easily might wear
The best of names, when patriotic love
Did of itself in modesty give way
Like the Precursor when the Deity
Is come, whose harbinger he is, a time
In which apostacy from ancient faith
Seem'd but conversion to a higher creed. . . .
(x, 276-286)

Circumstances had exposed him now to filial hatreds, his own and others; and just as with the imageless character of the dreams troubled by passion, it seems appropriate that Wordsworth report here "a conflict of sensations without name."

Despite his willingness to admit in retrospect how unrealistic were his aspirations and how misguided his consequent thoughts and feelings, he was never to question his character, nor its peculiar vulnerability to circumstances. But like the "sunset canon" that he remembers from these days when the British fleet, as yet unengaged in the war, lay at anchor off the quiet shore, he was to himself a regular disquietude:

While the Orb went down
In the tranquillity of Nature, came
That voice, ill requiem! seldom heard by me
Without a spirit overcast, a deep
Imagination, thought of woes to come,
And sorrow for mankind, and pain of heart.
(x, 302-307)

His "deep imagination, thoughts of woe to come" should recall his having thought of human life with "an indefinite terror and dismay," a "dim analogy of uproar and misrule/ Disquiet, danger, and obscurity"[51]; but here, his dread of what will happen ("sorrow for mankind, and pain of heart") barely conceals his own violent wishes, his venge-

[51] *Ibid.*, VIII, 657-664.

ful "conflict of sensations without name." His descriptions of the events in France as the war progressed and of the state of his psyche are nightmarish, fulfilling the dark forboding of the sunset canon.

The disturbed tranquillity of Nature presaging displays of passion reminds us, too, of a more explicitly characterized and much earlier sense of his own passionate self as once it had caused the trouble of his dreams in boyhood:

> In thought and wish
> That time, my shoulder all with springes hung,
> I was a fell destroyer. On the heights
> Scudding away from snare to snare, I plied
> My anxious visitation, hurrying on,
> Still hurrying, hurrying onward; moon and stars
> Were shining o'er my head; I was alone,
> And seem'd to be a trouble to the peace
> That was among them. . . .
>
> (I, 316-324)

And it is more than curious that his account of France—"thus beset by foes on every side/ The goaded land waxed mad"[52]—presents a picture of unrelieved frenzy, and settles, with only slight hesitation at its incongruity, on the analogy of a child passionately enjoying himself:

> the blind rage
> Of insolent tempers, the light vanity
> Of intermeddlers, steady purposes
> Of the suspicious, slips of the indiscreet,
> And all the accidents of life were press'd
> Into one service, busy with one work;
> The Senate was heart-stricken, not a voice
> Uplighted, none to oppose or mitigate;
> Domestic carnage now filled all the year
> With Feast-days; the old Man from the chimney-nook,
> The Maiden from the bosom of her Love,

[52] *Ibid.*, x, 312-313.

> The Mother from the Cradle of her Babe,
> The Warrior from the Field, all perish'd, all,
> Friends, enemies, of all parties, ages, ranks,
> Head after head, and never heads enough
> For those that bade them fall: they found their joy,
> They made it, ever thirsty as a Child,
> If light desires of innocent little Ones
> May with such heinous appetites be match'd,
> Having a toy, a wind-mill, though the air
> Do of itself blow fresh, and make the vane
> Spin in his eye sight, he is not content
> But with the plaything at arm's length he sets
> His front against the blast, and runs amain,
> To make it whirl the faster. . . .
>
> (x, 322-346)

But the child, seemingly mindless in its play, is made by the force of the association to seem possessed by destructive rather than innocent passion. The poet, awe-struck by the historical spectacle, seems to invert his habitual recollection of innocence. In *The Prelude,* the angry child who suffered remains largely hidden in the account of growth, but turns up enigmatically in this kind of preconscious association with the troubled matters of the recent past.

It was the terrible, if brief, reign of Robespierre, the "cruel son," that strained Wordsworth's convictions. Out of all proportion to what Wordsworth was prepared to suffer for the sake of his convictions, including the experience of Wordsworth himself being the "cruel son" in relation to his own native England, Robespierre's domestic management of revolutionary France seemed maddeningly to be passion unbridled in the name of Reason. The strain for Wordsworth was that of attempting to affirm and defend the reasoned principles of the revolution and the love that had inspired them, while discovering in displays of violence the intensity of passion from which these principles might at the moment seem inseparable. How could a believer and a patriot dissociate himself from the conduct of his cause? How could a reasonable man and Nature's gentlest being accept these manifestations of destructive passion, fearfully beyond his own? If Beaupuis, like the Shepherd, seems to be compatible with Wordsworth's natural idealization of himself, Robespierre may have been the extreme of what Wordsworth repressed and denied in himself. Wordsworth felt no need to compare his own sequestered position with Robespierre's public dominance, his own "vengeance" with Robespierre's "heinous appetites," but the force of the comparison was felt by him. One may suppose that no fine distinctions were being made between Robespierre and gentler-natured revolutionists in the England in which Wordsworth was living at the time. Wordsworth writes of this period of crisis:

> Most melancholy at that time, O Friend!
> Were my day-thoughts, my dreams were miserable;
> Through months, through years, long after the last
> beat
> Of those atrocities (I speak bare truth,
> As if to thee alone in private talk)
> I scarcely had one night of quiet sleep
> Such ghastly visions had I of despair
> And tyranny, and implements of death,
> And long orations which in dreams I pleaded
> Before unjust Tribunals, with a voice
> Labouring, a brain confounded, and a sense
> Of treachery and desertion in the place
> The holiest that I knew of, my own soul.
>
> (x, 369-381)

Having connected troubled dreams with passion, and both with conscience in relation to the father, we may speculate about the psychic implications of these recurrent dreams of "unjust tribunals."

In the simplest sense, the dreams draw manifestly upon the events in France. One can see Wordsworth defending the Girondists, charged with treason by Robespierre, before tribunals executing Robespierre's will. It is as if Wordsworth were pleading against Robespierre, in the name of the principles of the revolution, before Robespierre—the accuser and the judge seemingly one and the same. We have said, citing Erikson, that the subsequent "natural" belief in law and order is the result of an early resolution of crisis between impulse and restraint in the crises of growth and that the feeling of control achieved is naturally earlier and deeper than the social uses to which it is put. After the conflict with the father in the Oedipal period, identification with the father "socializes" the capacity for self-control as conscience. To Wordsworth, however, Robespierre was the figure of unrestraint, not only perverting the attempt at principled reform but violating its basis in Nature. The revolution, as Wordsworth understood it, sought to justify itself by its proposed naturalness in a humane new order. As we understand it, that justification appeals to fugitive feelings deeper than conscience as conscience is normatively developed socially in association with the father and the settled order of things. But Robespierre was the bad and passionate son who fills the vacant seat of the dispossessed father and looses an autocratic will terribly upon his brother revolutionists. The hierarchy of victimization remains, attended by a new rhetoric, and the hated abuses are intensified rather than rectified. It is impossible, I think, that Wordsworth did not feel in some way that his own ardent adherence to the principles of the revolution had implicated him in the ascendancy and conduct of Robespierre; for however reasoned the principles were, the revolution required a corresponding passion. When one thinks of any abrogation of legality made passionately in the name of a higher, or really a "deeper," natural feeling, the disruption of order in society must be seen as the paradox it is for sensitive minds.

Wordsworth, whose father was a lawyer in the older order of society, had more cause than most to re-experience the tribunals in Paris in dreams about profound social disruption, violent passions, and betrayal. Yet how often he has said, with some false modesty, that he lacked the power of eloquence to persuade or inspire people, as when he says: "Mean as I was, and little graced with power/ Of eloquence even in my native speech,/ And all unfit for tumult and intrigue. . . ."[53] We should observe precisely, however, that he does not hesitate to make the claim of supreme eloquence for the Poet and for himself ideally in poetry. He claims incapacity only in the imagined situation of action, himself called upon to speak inspiringly, persuasively, forensically. It is a small point, but indicative, that the letter he wrote as a challenging statement of his beliefs—"Letter to the Bishop of Llandaff"—written in 1793 was withheld by him from publication.[54] Reading it, one learns that it was not a want of eloquence, but rather a discreet refusal or a psychic inability that restrained him, which is suggestively similar to his inability or unwillingness to compete for anything at college. Perhaps the lines in *The Prelude,* "I doubtless should have made a common cause/ With some who perish'd, haply perish'd, too . . . ," are making false claims in retrospect. He did not act in the overthrow of authority; he seems, in his crisis, unwilling to claim that his forensic skills have any worth; and in his dreams he feels powerless to defend his principles in court against the accuser-as-judge who is perverting them. But in his dreams he is made *to do* what in reality he was so reluctant to do—experience the distressful feelings that attend assertion or passionate advocacy. Perhaps he did have a natural conviction of law and order to which to appeal, one prior to and deeper than the "court of conscience" ordinarily associated with the father; perhaps at the same time he could have shown reform to be innocent of the mad passions of the usurping son Robespierre, who had put

53 *Ibid.,* x, 132-134.

54 Wordsworth, *Prose Works,* vol. I, pp. 1-23, "Letter to the Bishop of Llandaff."

nothing better than "unjust tribunals" in the place of the traditional "court of conscience"; but perhaps, too, in his dreams he was being brought closer to the realization that his convictions were uncertainly founded and were unattended by irresistible powers. Indeed, in these dreams, he felt that his "natural" convictions were betraying him to circumstantial realities he could not influence, control, or evade.

Wordsworth concludes the passage by speaking of a feeling of betrayal, though he does not elaborate upon it:

> and a sense
> Of treachery and desertion in the place
> The holiest that I knew of, my own soul.

In MS D2 he wrote "blank desertion" for "desertion"; and here, I think, is an indication of the unconsciously felt "betrayal" by Nature. The "holiest place," his own soul, is the source of the deep natural conviction to which he would appeal; he felt the treachery *there*. Three lines later he makes a characteristic use of "holy":

> When I began at first, in early youth
> To yield myself to Nature, when that strong
> And holy passion overcame me first . . .
>
> (x, 382-384)

Wordsworth's passions, like his convictions, seemed holy to him in seeming natural; they had been brought early under a due restraint, and purified. Nature "led" him to his passionate advocacy of the principles of the revolution. "Blank desertion" may then recall for us an earlier experience of being "led" by her into an experience of passion from which he believed he gained the instruction intended by her, the restraint and purity of which he speaks. We have looked at the Boat-Stealing episode and may say that, despite his interpretation of Nature's beneficent intentions, he experienced a "betrayal" by her permissive incitement resulting in his terror and troubled dreams. He encounters the paternal figure of the mountain peak and acquires, he says, "a dim and undetermin'd sense/ Of unknown modes of being" and a profound feeling of "blank desertion." The rationalization of what he has projected into external reality and experienced there draws attention away from the psychic sequence: incitement, desire, desertion, and terror. But we may find in this episode, in small, the same unconscious intention revealed later, in large and with less easily rationalized effects, in the ordeal of the revolution: to repeat the basic trauma of betrayal.

But Robespierre's fall and death in 1794 were sufficient to renew in him the expectation of a natural fulfillment of his hopes, the arrival of "golden times" in History.[55] Power, it seemed, would now revert to Nature, leaving an "interregnum's open space for her to stir about in, uncontroll'd."[56] It may seem odd to the reader that Wordsworth could be so credulous. Although the mere fact that he was young seems to satisfy Wordsworth in retrospect as explanation enough, youth alone may not account for the mistakes made in youth. Other youthful partisans had seen realities they could not discount. The hopes of some, Wordsworth says, did not "outlast the shock" of Robespierre's conduct; Wordsworth's hopes did, and so he and people like himself bore "the deepest feeling of the grief" during that period. "Trust in Man" remained; his belief that "tyrannic power is weak" sustained him through his miserable days and nights; and at the fall of Robespierre he could say: "Thus far our trust is verified." "Trust" here denies the feeling of treachery; it opposes insight with a stronger psychic need to persist in believing what he wished were true. He had so far extended that belief that he had found a way of accepting the "visible world"—"which is the world/ Of all of us, the place in which, in the end/ We find our happiness, or not at all"[57]—and now, having so thoroughly subjected History to Nature in his own mind, he could not tol-

[55] *The Prelude*, x, 543.
[56] *Ibid.*, x, 610-613.
[57] *Ibid.*, x, 726-728.

erate contradiction. The period of renewed hope was brief; the despair which soon followed brought to its crisis the ordeal he had unconsciously sought.

Before accounting for the experience of despair, Wordsworth gives a general recapitulation of the events leading up to the moment when France herself betrayed the Revolution and him. The recapitulation is accurate enough in outline, though certainly it seems simpler and more restrained in manner than the account that precedes it in Books IX and X. It approaches the historical moment of crisis in this way:

> An active partisan, I thus convoked
> From every object pleasant circumstance
> To suit my ends; I moved among mankind
> With genial feelings still predominant;
> When erring, erring on the better part,
> And in the kinder spirit; placable,
> Indulgent oft-times to the worst desires
> As on one side not uninform'd that men
> See as it hath been taught them, and that time
> Gives rights to error; on the other hand
> That throwing off oppression must be work
> As well of licence as of liberty;
> And above all, for this was more than all,
> Not caring if the wind did now and then
> Blow keen upon an eminence that gave
> Prospect so large into futurity,
> In brief, a child of nature, as at first,
> Diffusing only those affections wider
> That from the cradle had grown up with me,
> And losing, in no other way than light
> Is lost in light, the weak in the more strong.
>
> In the main outline, such, it might be said,
> Was my condition, till with open war
> Britain opposed the Liberties of France;

This threw me first out of the pale of love;
Sour'd and corrupted upwards to the source
My sentiments, was not, as hitherto,
A swallowing up of lesser things in great;
But change of them into their opposites,
And thus a way was opened for mistakes
And false conclusions of the intellect,
As gross in their degree and in their kind
Far, far more dangerous. What had been a pride
Was now a shame; my likings and my loves
Ran in new channels, leaving old ones dry,
And hence a blow which, in maturer age,
Would but have touch'd the judgment struck more deep
Into sensations near the heart: meantime,
As from the first, wild theories were afloat,
Unto the subtleties of which, at least,
I had but lent a careless ear, assured
Of this, that time would soon set all things right,
Prove that the multitude had been oppressed,
And would be so no more.

But when events
Brought less encouragement, and unto these
The immediate proof of principles no more
Could be entrusted, while the events themselves,
Worn out in greatness, and in novelty,
Less occupied the mind, and sentiments
Could through my understanding's natural growth
No longer justify themselves through faith
Of inward consciousness, and hope that laid
Its hand upon its object, evidence
Safer, of universal application, such
As could not be impeach'd, was sought elsewhere.
(x, 737-791)

It had become more difficult for him to dismiss the charges against France by indicting her antagonists in her place;

and when the French became "oppressors in their turn,"[58] violating innocent nations to serve their own interests, Wordsworth read the doom of France. The safer evidence he sought for the "proof of principles" led him to Godwinism.

He never *says* that he felt betrayed by Nature, and the very inertia of his ensuing despair, when Godwinism too had failed to satisfy his needs, seems to have prevented the expression of strong feeling. His profound despondency after "yielding up moral questions in despair"[59] was a dull and sustained resistance to seeing the resemblance of his present situation to the traumatic moment of the past; yet, in the 1850 version, he seems to make the connection poetically, without realizing it, when he says:

> Depressed, bewildered thus, I did not walk
> With scoffers, seeking light and gay revenge
> From indiscriminate laughter, nor sate down
> In reconcilement with an utter waste
> Of intellect . . .
>
> (XI, 321-325: 1850 version)

Here, he echoes *exactly* the words of the Blest Babe passage that describe the idealized relationship which had been disrupted traumatically: "No outcast he, bewilder'd and depress'd. . . ." As opposed to the Blest Babe, the child at the traumatic moment of his life had felt outcast, bewildered, and depressed. And now, as in the past, the strongest feelings of betrayal were left unexpressed. Like Vaudracour receiving the news of his impending separation from Julia "in calm despondency/ Composed and silent, without outward sign/ Of even the least emotion . . . ," he does not say what he feels. It was his sister Dorothy who was to break in upon his despondency, like Nature or Mother, but more devoted, more present, and more dependable than either; she reassured him, renewing his trust in a way that no man

[58] *Ibid.*, X, 792. See footnote, pp. 603-606.
[59] *Ibid.*, X, 901.

could expect, and few have found. It is no wonder that his restoration seemed to him a kind of miracle.

Although the very moment of the crisis *is* recollected briefly, the feelings suggested by the account are left as unexplored by Wordsworth in poetry as they were probably resisted at the time. And although he does not say that he felt intolerable feelings of betrayal by Nature, his descriptions show how he had tried to rationalize the deepening distrust that resulted in despair. He had sought to substitute reason for emotion, understanding for feeling. While seeking to "abstract the hopes of man/ Out of his feelings, to be fix'd thenceforth/ For ever in a purer element,"[60] he was again turning away from the reality other people accepted. In the past he had turned his mind in upon itself to resist "the injurious sway of place or circumstance"[61]; but whereas in the past he had sought "solace" and reassurance in an inner and prior reality from which he drew his "natural" convictions, he was now dissociating himself equally from the tyranny of circumstance and the false assurance of a "providential" Nature. In his thinking, he employed "such means/ As did not lie in Nature." In his determination to understand human nature, social freedom, and History, he was briefly attempting to stand utterly alone.

Of course the account he gives of this in retrospect recalls the attempt as vain and misguided, which is only natural from one who feels himself now to have been saved by Nature from such an error. The tone of heavy irony is barely restrained in his patronizing exclamations: "What delight! How glorious!" Having experienced despair and having found again his trust in Nature, he does not enter again into the spirit of free inquiry of that period either very willingly or very imaginatively. And yet, even this retrospective glimpse of his Godwinism, apologetic as he is to Nature for having for a while ceased to trust her,

60 *Ibid.*, x, 808-810.
61 *Ibid.*, iii, 102-103: 1850 version.

suggests that whatever exactly Godwinism was to Godwin and his followers, it was psychically something else to Wordsworth. To adapt his own words here, it was the attempt to realize with the independent intellect the truth of his *own* circumstance:

What delight!
How glorious! in self-knowledge and self-rule,
To look through all the frailties of the world,
And, with a resolute mastery shaking off
The accidents of nature, time, and place,
That make up the weak being of the past,
Build social freedom on its only basis,
The freedom of the individual mind,
Which, to the blind restraint of general laws
Superior, magisterially adopts
One guide, the light of circumstances, flash'd
Upon an independent intellect. . . .
(x, 819-830)

The passage, lines of which appear in Wordsworth's tragedy, *The Borderers,* does seem to describe his attempt consciously to understand the ordeal he has unconsciously sought. However ironically he now recalls his past presumption, the single word "flash'd" may remind us of the Imagination passage ("but with a flash that has reveal'd/ The invisible world . . .") and of the high poetic aspiration of Wordsworth's mind to achieve a godly clarity of mind in such moments of sudden illumination. Perhaps the true understanding of social freedom does require what is here regarded ironically by Wordsworth in his own experience: "the freedom of the individual mind" from the "accidents of nature, time, and place"—that is, from everything that engages feeling blindly to circumstances, past or present, communally or neurotically.

The account Wordsworth is giving testifies to a dramatic failure of conscious questioning on his part, or rather to the success of unconscious resistance in defending the ego from an opposed unconscious intention. We may be at a loss to account for Wordsworth's failure to imagine or disclose the repressed matters that seem so dynamically present in the ordeal he is recalling, but I think we may infer the reason from the analogy of tragedy. Although the circumstance of Oedipus's life was fated, and his character would have to be consistent with the fulfillment of the oracle, not all of his character as we know its tragic greatness—its excellence and its vulnerability—is clearly implied by the oracle. What the oracle states could have been fulfilled in a far cruder way. It is the play itself that persuades us that only this character with its initiative, individuality, intelligence, pride, and violent passion could have had this fate, its excellence and its vulnerability equally implicated in the horrible greatness that results. Without his concern for his people as children, his determination to employ his masterful intelligence in solving the neglected royal mystery of Thebes, his violence and suspicion directed at Creon and Teiresias, his threats to the Shepherd and the Paedogogue, his assurance of the personal worth that won him his queen and his title, his acceptance of his pathos and guilt, and his tender concern for his own children—Oedipus's story could simply be a terrible hard luck story rather than a display of human greatness. And yet, when the Shepherd has said, "No man living is more wretched than Oedipus"[62]; and the chorus has lamented that he has been afflicted with "heavier punishment than a mortal man can bear"; and Oedipus has asked, "Is there a sorrow greater? What has God done to me?" he concludes: "Of all men, I alone can bear this guilt," his greatness confirmed by his very ability to rise to the occasion once more, to accept and bear what mortals believe themselves and each other incapable of bearing. There is in such self-abasement the dignity we associate with tragedy; he accepts as his character's burden all of what is dim and vast in Fate as it reveals what is dim and vast in human nature, his own.

[62] Sophocles, *Oedipus Rex,* Scene IV. In *The Oedipus Cycle,* tr. D. Fitts and R. Fitzgerald, these quotations are from pp. 62, 68, and 72.

We may apply this to Wordsworth's account of his ordeal, first by observing of his tragedy, *The Borderers,* that he imagined in it not a tragic hero, but a villain and a victim. It is from the villain Oswald, however, that the lines about the "light of circumstances" and "an independent intellect" come, when he has deceived the youthful hero Marmaduke, as Wordsworth had felt deceived. In 1795-96, when Wordsworth was living at Racedown with Dorothy and, under her influence, was recovering from his despair, he was intent upon dissociating himself further from what had caused his despair. He did so by imagining a terrible figure, Oswald, who *wished to repeat* his own tragic experience by forcing it upon someone else, an innocent and idealistic youth. In the light of my interpretation of Wordsworth's unconscious intentions, it must seem that Wordsworth divides himself here, dissociating his "evil" unconscious with its mad and malign interest in the truth, from his good and youthful character which ought not to be polluted by it. In the play, the pollution happens, however, though with no possibility of self-knowledge. The Iago-like Oswald does not seem intimately connected to the psychology of his Marmaduke; and Marmaduke—ironically both cursed and exiled by himself from companionship with men—wanders off at the end of the play like Oedipus, whom he does not resemble at all in character and whom he resembles in circumstance only because Wordsworth is crudely borrowing tragic effects from Sophocles.

Before his account of the fall of Robespierre, Wordsworth gives what may be the wisest estimate of History and of revolution given in his time:

> Then was the truth received into my heart,
> That under heaviest sorrow earth can bring,
> Griefs bitterest of ourselves or of our kind,
> If from the affliction somewhere do not grow
> Honour which could not else have been, a faith,
> An elevation, and a sanctity,

If new strength be not given, or old restored
The blame is ours not Nature's. When a taunt
Was taken up by Scoffers in their pride,
Saying 'behold the harvest which we reap
From popular Government and Equality,'
I saw that it was neither these, nor aught
Of wild belief engrafted on their names
By false philosophy, that caus'd the woe,
But that it was a reservoir of guilt
And ignorance, fill'd up from age to age,
That could no longer hold its loathsome charge,
But burst and spread in deluge through the Land.
(x, 423-440)

The thought that people are not equal to their ideals and that the burdens of History may be too great for "Nature" to rectify does not lead him to deeper discoveries about himself or force him to make any personal disclosures. In fact, in saying this he seems to avoid saying anything about the feelings that the coming ordeal was to bring upon him—that he had felt personally betrayed by his ideals and had wanted to blame Nature. Certainly there is Robespierre to blame in retrospect and the inertia of History to blame generally; also there are the English statesmen whose conduct he characterized in this striking way:

Our Shepherds (this say merely) at that time
Thirsted to make the guardian Crook of Law
A tool of Murder; they who ruled the State,
Though with such awful proof before their eyes
That he who would sow death, reaps death, or
worse,
And can reap nothing better, child-like long'd
To imitate, not wise enough to avoid,
Giants in their impiety alone,
But, in their weapons and their warfare base
As vermin working out of reach, they leagu'd

Their strength perfidiously, to undermine
Justice, and make an end of Liberty.
(x, 646-657)

It does seem like an unconscious irony that he should use "Shepherds," a rather trite figure of speech for statesmen, and in so doing choose the very image of his ideal of Man, animating it metaphorically as a figure threatening violence. The Shepherd with his crook, associated in memory with Wordsworth's "unconscious love and reverence of human nature," his childhood and innocence, is transformed by murderous rage; and here, too, the use of "child-like" imitation inverts the memory of innocent play, just as we observed earlier in:

ever thirsty as a Child,
If light desires of innocent little Ones
May with such heinous appetites be match'd . . .
(x, 338-340)

We have again the unexpected analogy of innocent and destructive passions. How peculiarly his imagination of the angry figure of the Shepherd evokes the association of anger in the child. Beyond this, being led by recollection in his narrative to unpleasant memories, Wordsworth feels distress at something like *unholy* passion rising in his imagination:

But this is passion over-near ourselves,
Reality too close and too intense,
And mingled up with something, in my mind,
Of scorn and condemnation personal,
That would profane the sanctity of Verse.
(x, 641-645)

To talk of betrayals and violence is to feel an unfamiliar answering passion within.

Wordsworth recounts how, in the name of an abstraction, the ideal of Man, he employed his intellect in a Godwinian pursuit of truth. He does not himself make explicit the connection between the ideal of Man and the ideal of himself as they had formed in him, so he never says that in examining Man for the discrepany between the ideal and the reality—questioning "impulse, motive, right and wrong"—he was interrogating himself. From an "inquiry" to the strange image of dissecting a "living body," from questioning to an "Interrogation," from Interrogation to Arraignment and Prosecution in Court, the Godwinian pursuit of truth becomes more frantic. The gathering desperation and the resulting despair are hardly those of intellectual unsuccess. What he pictures here, however, is the kind of scrutiny that was *not* being turned directly on the ideal and the reality of himself:

> I took the knife in hand
> And stopping not at parts less sensitive,
> Endeavoured with my best of skill to probe
> The living body of society
> Even to the heart; I push'd without remorse
> My speculations forward; yea, set foot
> On Nature's holiest places. Time may come
> When some dramatic Story may afford
> Shapes livelier to convey to thee, my Friend,
> What then I learn'd, or think I learn'd, of truth,
> And the errors into which I was betray'd
> By present objects, and by reasoning false
> From the beginning, inasmuch as drawn
> Out of a heart which had been turn'd aside
> From Nature by external accidents,
> And which was thus confounded more and more,
> Misguiding and misguided. Thus I fared,
> Dragging all passions, notions, shapes of faith,
> Like culprits to the bar, suspiciously
> Calling the mind to establish in plain day
> Her titles and her honours, now believing,
> Now disbelieving, endlessly perplex'd

With impulse, motive, right and wrong, the ground
Of moral obligation, what the rule
And what the sanction, till, demanding *proof*,
And seeking it in everything, I lost
All feeling of conviction, and, in fine,
Sick, wearied out with contrarieties,
Yielded up moral questions in despair . . .
(x, 873-901)

Here *he* is accuser and judge, not realizing the sense in which he is the accused himself. "Dragging all passions, notions, shapes of faith/ Like culprits to the bar," he resorts to the image of a tribunal, himself at once violent and strangely like Robespierre. He presides over the pretensions of Man, demanding to know what the true connection is between principles and passions. It is in the answer to exactly that question about the history of his own character, the fiction of the self, that the truth resides; for his story unconsciously reveals how the ego, like Man in History, will persist in maintaining itself in real or imagined "privileges," employing what repressive forces are necessary to keep down threats to its rule. The spectacle he witnessed of the historical multitudes and their spokesmen revolutionists making a mockery of the principles of the revolution is an analogue of the passionate self that he could not accept as his own. Yet the passionate self, like people in History, is a reality with an historical heritage of its own: denied and subjected, ignorant and abused, distrusting, unreasoning and strong, it can, in moments of insurrection, drive the ego itself in an assault upon its own ideals, demanding an end to unjustly burdensome pretensions of superior worth. The questions of History and of a personal history *might* have come to a common crisis in the poet's mind in his attempt to understand the dimness and the vastness of his own being through the vulnerability of his character to circumstance. Instead, Wordsworth never sounds less convincing than when he gives this picture of himself:

Above all how much
Still nearer to ourselves we overlook
In human nature and that marvellous world
As studied first in my own heart, and then
In life among the passions of mankind
And qualities commix'd and modified
By the infinite varieties and shades
Of individual character. Herein
It was for me (this justice bids me say)
No useless preparation to have been
The pupil of a public School, and forced
In hardy independence, to stand up
Among conflicting passions, and the shock
Of various tempers, to endure and note
What was not understood though known to be;
Among the mysteries of love and hate,
Honour and shame, looking to right and left,
Uncheck'd by innocence too delicate
And moral notions too intolerant,
Sympathies too contracted. Hence, when call'd
To take a station among Men, the step
Was easier, the transition more secure,
More profitable also; for the mind
Learns from such timely exercise to keep
In wholesome separation the two natures,
The one that feels, the other that observes.

(XIII, 306-331)

CHAPTER VIII

CONCLUSION: ARAB, WANDERER, DRUID, CHRISTIAN

The conclusion of the poem, with the discrepancy we have observed between the Poet described ideally and Wordsworth declared as simply himself, indicates what Wordsworth must have felt to be the failure of his intentions. But if we say that his poetic obsession failed to reveal its meaning to him and that his unconscious intention to reveal the truth to himself was never successfully expressed, we are nevertheless saying that a stronger and opposite unconscious intention succeeded instead. The negative aspect of the repetition compulsion had effectively resisted and denied the trauma; it had rationalized the traces of repressed matters that had remained in memory, revealing them only in disguised form. Wordsworth was depressed by the result, but the depression did not last. He busied himself with new plans, even though he was never to feel qualified to write *The Recluse,* for which *The Prelude* was to have prepared him. *The Prelude* afforded him relief from a poetic obsession, though he continued with a milder compulsion to revise the text of the poem as long as he lived. If *The Prelude* never gave him the freedom that true conscious understanding might have brought, it did give him an acceptable version of himself as "a meditative, oft a suffering man," but a man generally convinced of his happiness. He had become a poet with a new sense of purpose. It is with an examination of this revision of his role that I wish to conclude this study.

As early as Book v of the poem, Wordsworth presents the Arab Dream. In a context which associates the questionable survival of poetry itself with the wish of mortals to survive no matter what ("abject, depress'd, forlorn, disconsolate"),[1] the Arab Dream, as we shall see, is a symbolic picture of an obsession. Wordsworth's account of his own "survival" since childhood, though thoroughly rationalized by him as his "privileged" growth, was an obsession with the plight of the child "outcast . . . bewildered and depressed."[2] We may recall here from our analysis of the first "spot of time" how the picture of a constricted landscape showed us the child traumatically isolated with no model and no "guide"; and recall, too, that it was from the analogy he subsequently discovered between the winds of Nature and the voices heard in poetry that Wordsworth was to gain the only "guide" to survival he could accept: following the poets was to be his "visionary" way in life. We have also observed that the memory of that first experience of his lonely plight is characterized by its "dreariness" and that he further associates with that "spot of time" the profound feeling of relief found in love by recollecting his visit to the same lonely moor years later in the presence of his loved ones, his sister and Mary, who was to be his wife. We have already made some significant connections between his marriage and the revision of his role as poet, and here we shall consider further the obsession from which he found relief.

The dream itself—in the 1805 version told to him by a philosophical friend and related as the friend's experience; in the 1850 version presented as his own—was no doubt not his own dream. Scholarship has shown the extreme likelihood that Coleridge told him of a dream of Descartes' that resembled his own musings and became "his" dream through poetic license.[3] In the dream, the Arab's mission is

1 *The Prelude*, v, 27. 2 *Ibid.*, II, 261.
3 *Ibid.*, p. 539. Footnote to v, 55-139.

to preserve the shell of Poetry and the stone of Geometry from the universal destruction at hand, an Apocalypse foretold by the blast from the shell. The stone and the shell are described in this way:

> The one that held acquaintance with the stars,
> And wedded man to man by purest bond
> Of nature, undisturbed by space or time;
> Th' other that was a God, yea many Gods,
> Had voices more than all the winds, and was
> A joy, a consolation, and a hope.
>
> (v, 104-109)

We need only hear mention of the God or Gods perceived in poetic utterance and the "voices more than all the *winds*" to recall a rich train of associations within the poem that suggest the psychic meaning of the shell to Wordsworth; if it symbolizes poetry, it symbolizes in "his" dream what poetry meant to him. Actually, some simple tracing of the subject of geometry in the poem would show its comparable relevance. For instance, when in Book x Wordsworth says he "yielded up moral questions in despair," he adds immediately:

> And for my future studies, as the sole
> Employment of the enquiring faculty,
> Turn'd towards mathematics, and their clear
> And solid evidence . . .
>
> (x, 902-905)

In Book I, he speaks of his hope to fix in poetry "those phantoms of conceit," "the many feelings that oppress'd my heart"[4]; and in Book VI he makes clear that geometry substitutes pure designs for oppressive imagery in "a mind beset/ With images and haunted by itself." ("Haunted" is also the word used by Wordsworth to describe the child at play finding "presences" everywhere in Nature.)

[4] *The Prelude*, I, 129-133.

Geometry affords neutral subject matter to the obsessively burdened mind, and brings relief from sorrow:

> And as I have read of one by shipwreck thrown
> With fellow Sufferers whom the waves had spar'd
> Upon a region uninhabited
> An island of the Deep, who having brought
> To land a single Volume and no more,
> A treatise of Geometry, was used,
> Although of food and clothing destitute,
> And beyond common wretchedness depress'd,
> To part from company and take this book,
> Then first a self-taught pupil in those truths,
> To spots remote and corners of the Isle
> By the sea side, and draw his diagrams
> With a long stick upon the sand, and thus
> Did oft beguile his sorrow, and almost
> Forget his feeling; even so, if things
> Producing like effect, from outward cause
> So different, may rightly be compar'd,
> So was it with me then, and so will be
> With Poets ever. Mighty is the charm
> Of those abstractions to a mind beset
> With images, and haunted by itself;
> And specially delightful unto me
> Was that clear Synthesis built up aloft
> So gracefully even then when it appear'd
> No more than as a plaything, or a toy
> Embodied to the sense, not what it is
> In verity, an independent world
> Created out of pure Intelligence.
>
> (VI, 160-187)

Wordsworth's image of the mathematical mind was the statue of Newton at Cambridge standing alone in the night as Wordsworth has also described himself ("for I would walk alone/ In storm and tempest, or in starlight nights/

Beneath the quiet heavens . . ."). Of Newton's statue, he says:

> And from my pillow, looking forth by light
> Of moon or favouring stars, I could behold
> The antechapel where the statue stood
> Of Newton with his prism and silent face,
> The marble index of a mind for ever
> Voyaging through strange seas of Thought, alone.
> (III, 58-63: 1850 version)

But more than the similarity of two figures in the night is suggested here. Although Newton's thought dealt with the entire universe, his *thinking* (*voyaging* "through strange seas of Thought, alone") was a prolonged solitude, his mind turned in upon its solitary thoughts. Wordsworth's description of him should suggest to us both Wordsworth's journey-metaphor and the inner world he himself explored in solitude:

> turning the mind in upon itself,
> [I] pored, watch'd, expected, listen'd; spread my thoughts
> And spread them with a wider creeping; felt
> Incumbences more awful, visitings
> Of the Upholder of the tranquil Soul.
> (III, 112-116)

The difference between Newton and Wordsworth is that one was preoccupied by pure images that stand for things, the other by "phantoms of conceit" that stand for feelings about things. For Wordsworth, Geometry and Poetry had a common psychic function; and the Arab is the symbolic guardian of both of these pure activities, with their obsessive meanings in the poem.

The dream, even though adapted by Wordsworth, has a perfect congruence with his own experience, even to the extent that the poem shows him to be both obsessed and finally able to separate himself from his obsession. The

Arab and the Dreaming Man come together in their common terror over survival, and finally part on the very issue of Wordsworth's life that the poem records. With our observations about the first "spot of time" in mind, we should place the Arab and the Dreaming Man in relation to Wordsworth by these lines:

> Much rejoic'd
> The Dreaming Man that he should have a Guide
> To lead him through the Desart . . .
>
> (v, 81-83)

Taken together, they suggest that Wordsworth felt his visionary way was both an anxious errand and his only way out of a barren circumstance. And so, keeping in mind the descriptions of himself in his experiences of solitude or the description of the imaginary Hermit withdrawn into a cave in "Tintern Abbey," we should see a recognizable aspect of Wordsworth's psychology revealed in his description of the Arab as he has "fancied him a living man":

> A gentle Dweller in the Desart, craz'd
> By love and feeling and internal thought,
> Protracted among endless solitudes;
> Have shap'd him, in the oppression of his brain,
> Wandering upon his quest, and thus equipp'd.
> And I have scarcely pitied him; have felt
> A reverence for a Being thus employ'd;
> And thought that in the blind and awful lair
> Of such a madness, reason did lie couch'd.
>
> (v, 144-152)

Speaking through symbols, Wordsworth can say without realizing it that in part he still feels the urgency that attaches fugitively to the visionary way, having himself been "craz'd/ By love and feeling and internal thought/ Protracted among endless solitudes"; and he can call it "madness" at this point because it is from that obsessive pursuit of true consciousness (in which Reason does lie couched) that he had turned away to find relief from his own "visionary dreariness" in the actual presence of loved ones, in the companionship of marriage and domesticity. He expresses his affinity with the Arab in this way:

> Enow there are on earth to take in charge
> Their Wives, their Children, and their virgin
> Loves,
> Or whatsoever else the heart holds dear;
> Enow to think of these; yea, will I say,
> In sober contemplation of the approach
> Of such great overthrow, made manifest
> By certain evidence, that I, methinks,
> Could share that Maniac's anxiousness, could go
> Upon like errand.
>
> (v, 153-161)

But it is the Arab Wordsworth imagines and dissociates from himself, not Wordsworth, who continues to live the fixated and lonely life of an obsessive mind.

In the dream, the approaching Apocalypse—"the waters of the deep gathering upon us"—joins the Arab and the Dreaming Man in a common peril:

> A wish was now ingender'd in my fear
> To cleave unto this Man, and I begg'd leave
> To share his errand with him. On he pass'd
> Not heeding me; I follow'd, and took note
> That he look'd often backward with wild look,
> Grasping his twofold treasure to his side.
> —Upon a Dromedary, Lance in rest,
> He rode, I keeping pace with him.
>
> (v, 115-122)

The peril recollected and imagined in the dream resembles Wordsworth's recollections and imaginings at the beginning of Book v: conscious thoughts about the survival of poetry itself and about human survival; and obsessive unconscious thoughts about a traumatic experience of death which have persisted since childhood in the survivor. The Arab, as a projection of one aspect of Wordsworth himself, looks backwards over his own shoulder and actually makes the Dreaming Man look backwards, too, while rushing onwards; and again the dream adapted by Wordsworth is perfectly congruent with his own experience—his poetry as a retrospective process seems to go onwards by looking backwards. Apocalyptic destruction would restore "true" Life by destroying temporal life and the world of the self; it would restore the soul to its prior reality—a concern we have seen to be peculiarly Wordsworth's as he deals in a psychic way with the realities of world, self, and soul. But the Dreaming Man is passed and distanced by the Arab; he wakes in terror, and Wordsworth resumes the narrative with his own waking thoughts.

The impending Apocalypse—that is, Revelation—as the poem elsewhere suggests, would be a revelation of a death behind him in the past and of a desired *life beyond it.* If we think of the life-beyond-death in a psychological way as his unconscious recollection of existence "prior" to the traumatic loss of his mother in death, we should not suppose that existence to be simply that of the eight-year-old boy as he was; for we have observed in the first "spot of time" the degree of separation from the mother accepted by the young horseman already proudly identified with men. His past existence is, rather, what it has subsequently become under the pressure of regressive need in a continuing allegiance to the pleasure-principle; it is an unconsciously idealized existence like that imagined as the secure relationship of Blest Babe and Mother in Book II; or like the union yearned for in "Tintern Abbey" as the visionary coalescence of the "living soul" and the deep "life of things." The feeling of "something ever more about to *be*" in the Imagination passage of Book VI expresses his desire for a wholeness of being as soul; and his realization there about "Our being's heart and home" at once anticipates an eternity of bliss beyond time and death and recollects a reality of joy associated with the mother, deeper than that accessible to ordinary consciousness and felt to be prior to it.

The whole context of Book v, I think, supports this interpretation of a death in the past as the impending revelation. The remainder of the book, Wordsworth's ensuing thoughts about poetry, includes the death-and-union fantasy of "There was a boy"; the only explicit mention of the death of Wordsworth's mother ("early died my honor'd mother . . ."), with the use of the journey-metaphor we have explored ("she left us destitute, and as we might/ Trooping together . . ."); and his account of his seemingly first encounter with Death itself in the form of the drowned man when, wandering in the new vale after his mother's death, the child was "seeking I knew not what."[5] In this last incident cited from Book v, the somewhat dream-like experience of confronting the evidence of drowning and death is the child's; it seems to me the biographical version of the matters presented in the Arab dream: the picture of the drowning world and the impending revelation of death. Here, again, with books as the nominal subject of Book v, Wordsworth further suggests that the face of Death could be looked upon and its reality accepted as in art ("for my inner eye/ Had seen such sights before . . ."). Wordsworth, of course, remained wholly unconscious of the latently associational aspect of Book v in general and of the boy's experience in particular, but the experience must have had a profound and mysterious effect on his feelings about art, about what can be seen with "the inner eye."

There was, after all, a profound mystery involved; but even Wordsworth's intuitive understanding of how the mind may be repossessed by earlier emotions recollected in tranquillity and his uncommon sensitivity to the disturbances of spirit within himself did not make it much more likely that by contemplating traces of traumata held in memory he would actually bring on revelations. Yet the possibility, at once small and real, may be seen vividly in

[5] *Ibid.*, v, 389-422; v, 256-260; and v, 450-481.

the symbolism of the Arab Dream. If in this way one can understand Wordsworth's unconscious identification with the Arab, one can more readily sympathize with his need to distinguish himself from the Arab finally, for the Arab now seemed to Wordsworth "Craz'd/ By love and feeling and internal thought/ Protracted among endless solitudes." The Dreaming Man, left behind by the Arab, awakes; and Wordsworth accepts the distinctness of his life and his dream.

THE WANDERER, like the Hermit, the Recluse, the Lonely Traveller, and the Arab, is another poetic version of the life Wordsworth might have led. Of these several figurative types, only the Arab is not identified by a capitalized noun that immediately describes both a way of life and a fixed state of soul. As Wordsworth worked on the lengthy *Excursion,* he invented other figurative types, adding the Solitary and the Parson to the Wanderer. In the poem's several voices we hear caricatures of different aspects of Wordsworth's personality talking to each other solemnly, morally, piously. Indeed, the poem becomes the wax gallery of aspects of his personality, with the lifeless figure of the Wanderer as its principal attraction.

Whether or not there was an original for the Wanderer as described, other than a projection of Wordsworth himself, we shall never know. There seems to have been a favorite old man, an itinerant figure and perhaps a storyteller from Wordsworth's boyhood,[6] but the poetic connections we can make between the Wanderer and Wordsworth himself are surer and more revealing. Earlier we discussed the Hermit in "Tintern Abbey" and the Wordsworth who

6 "The character I have represented in his person is chiefly an idea of what I fancied my own character might have been in his circumstances." Wordsworth then describes "a Scotchman" named Patrick, a pedlar, of whose gentle and religious character he learned from Sara, his sister-in-law. Another model for the Wanderer was a "packman" Wordsworth had known in his boyhood, from whom Wordsworth heard tales of life beyond the vale. See Wordsworth, *Prose Works,* p. 196.

sought a "hermitage" at the beginning of *The Prelude*.[7] The Recluse, who was to resemble both Wordsworth and the Hermit in paradoxical ways, never really emerged as a personna for the poet. And the Lonely Traveller, whom we have since observed as Wordsworth's figure of his poetic self "in the Mind of Man," reaches an impasse in *The Prelude*; he might have found what Wordsworth was unconsciously seeking in the abyss of the mind, but he did not. The Lonely Traveller was not to survive *The Prelude,* just as the intense inwardness of Wordsworth's poetic obsession did not. The peculiar "outwardness" of the Wanderer, then, is in point here; for he might have sufficed for Wordsworth as a later characterization of himself as man and poet in place of Hermit, Recluse, or Lonely Traveller. Wordsworth might well have chosen to wander alone through life collecting exemplary tales of human suffering and endurance, but unlike the celibate Wanderer he imagined, Wordsworth married and settled down.

Parts of the idealized descriptions of the Wanderer to be found in Book I of *The Excursion* were in fact written first for *The Prelude* as self-description and put afterwards into the later poem as descriptions of someone else. While there are peculiarities in the description of the Wanderer that make him little distinct from Wordsworth himself for the reader of *The Prelude,* it should be remembered that *The Excursion* was published in Wordsworth's lifetime and *The Prelude* was not. In the Wanderer, contemporary readers were given a perhaps fictionalized Wordsworth, but with no disturbing contrast. A Scot by birth, the Wanderer tended cattle in the highlands as a boy, briefly tried teaching in a rural school as a young man, but then became a pedlar. He retired from peddling when he had acquired means from it to support himself without it. Having never married and having no settled domicile, he continued to wander, an itinerant knower-of-people in their more settled and distressing lives, an observer of life, uninvolved but wise.

7 See above, pp. 46ff. and 90ff.

Most of the descriptions of his youth, of his feelings and interests, seem to fit those of Wordsworth's youth; the reader of *The Prelude* will perhaps find the many echoes too striking to believe the Wanderer's distinctness from Wordsworth at all, despite a few discrepant facts.

Beyond this, Wordsworth tells us that there are poets "sown by Nature" who do not write; and that this man is one such. Some there are, he says, who in youth lack "culture and the inspiring aid of books" and who have "a temper too severe/ Or a nice backwardness afraid of shame." But the Wanderer in his youth, it turns out, read exactly what Wordsworth had read—romances, for instance, histories, the Bible, and Milton; he has, if anything, a less severe temper than Wordsworth often claims for himself in *The Prelude*, and as affable story-teller he seems not at all reticent, nor "afraid of shame" in uttering some of the platitudes which the Wordsworth of 1814 has invented for him in *The Excursion*. Wordsworth seems intent upon contemplating and projecting himself prospectively in a different circumstance of life, but different from himself only to the extent of some apparently not very crucial facts of biography.

There is one passage describing the Wanderer, however, which is crucial:

> From his native hills
> He wandered far; much did he see of men,
> Their manners, their enjoyments, and pursuits,
> Their passions and their feelings; chiefly those
> Essential and eternal in the heart,
> That, 'mid the simpler forms of rural life,
> Exist more simple in their elements,
> And speak a plainer language. In the woods,
> A lone Enthusiast, and among the fields,
> Itinerant in this labour, he had passed
> The better portion of his time; and there
> Spontaneously had his affections thriven

Amid the bounties of the year, the peace
And liberty of nature; there he kept
In solitude and solitary thought
His mind in a just equipoise of love.
Serene it was, unclouded by the cares
Of ordinary life; unvexed, unwarped
By partial bondage. In his steady course,
No piteous revolutions had he felt,
No wild varieties of joy and grief,
Unoccupied by sorrow of its own,
His heart lay open; and, by nature tuned
And constant disposition of his thoughts
To sympathy with man, he was alive
To all that was enjoyed where'er he went,
And all that was endured; for in himself
Happy, and quiet in his cheerfulness,
He had no painful pressure from without
That made him turn aside from wretchedness
With coward fears. He could *afford* to suffer
With those whom he saw suffer. Hence it came
That in our best experience he was rich,
And in wisdom of our daily life.
For hence, minutely, in his various rounds,
He had observed the progress and decay
Of many minds, of minds and bodies too;
The history of many families;
How they had prospered; how they were
o'erthrown
By passion or mischance, or such misrule
Among the unthinking masters of the earth
As makes the nations groan.

(*The Excursion,* I, 340-381)

When one has studied the uncanny resemblance of Wordsworth and the Wanderer and at the same time the very basic difference between them, one may pause over the kind of detail that is easily overlooked at first. Why was the Wanderer, who seems to have had an ecstatic love of Nature in a youth described in very "Wordsworthian" language, *not* subject to "wild varieties of joy and grief" as Wordsworth was? For one thing, *unlike* Wordsworth—and it may be the most significant small detail Wordsworth imagined in his biographical sketch of this persona—the Wanderer did not lose his mother and father at an early age, especially not his mother, and so was not situated in life and in Nature in quite the same way Wordsworth was. The "equipoise of love," which Wordsworth imagines as the condition of the Wanderer's mind "in solitude and solitary thought," suggests to me the idealized description of calmness and serenity Wordsworth imagines as the equipoise of the Blest Babe and the Mother; and it seems to me as falsely ascribed to the grown man as the Wanderer himself seems unreal. Wordsworth has imagined someone equally free from adult selfhood ("the cares of ordinary life") and from the "visionary" search in which we have observed Wordsworth. If the Wanderer is not convincing as a character, it is because Wordsworth cannot really imagine what it would be like to be at once superficially very like himself and profoundly unlike himself; for the Wanderer is a version of Wordsworth stripped of his most vital quality, his obsession, while remaining different from everyone else too. Hence, he becomes the spokesman for the Christian Wordsworth seeking an appropriate Christian selflessness at exactly the time from which scholars date Wordsworth's decline: Wordsworth begins to seem no longer "Wordsworth." But the mysteries of joy and grief may suggest to us what Nature was to the younger Wordsworth and was not to the more Christian Wanderer. Many may love Nature in their way, but only some are "privileged" to feel uniquely loved by her and inspired by her ghostly language to write visionary poetry. The vital Wordsworth was different from the lifeless Wanderer for whom he imagined an uncommon sensitivity to Nature because Wordsworth's experience of Nature, his "privilege," was not simply his uncommon sensitivity.

VIII. CONCLUSION

I have attempted to account for Nature in Wordsworth's life in a radical way, relating Wordsworth's adult experiences to the repressed traumatic matters of his "privileged" childhood. When I have spoken of Wordsworth's unconscious dependency on the mother in Nature, his unconscious fear of her undependability, or of his unconscious intention to repeat an early trauma of betrayal, I have been aware that my interpretation has emphasized the pathology of a "case"; but in doing so, I have hoped to avoid obscuring the really dynamic factors of his special circumstance. The "special" case is distinguished from the general case of Man primarily by the access it affords to closer observation, but the attempt to understand "pathology" is the attempt to illuminate the human case, and not to reduce the special one. It should hardly still need saying that both the popular understanding and the common stigma of "abnormality" are irrelevant to a consideration in depth of human psychology; and that even the distinction of illness from health is at best a quantitative one. Wordsworth was, for what I would call the most creative period of his life, abnormal but able to maintain himself through his own robust efforts; he sought, in a radical and highly personal way, an uncommon understanding of himself in the world as "a soul of more than mortal privilege." It would be useless to discount as merely Romantic and rhetorical his analogy of the Poet and God, for it was profoundly opposed to what most people believed to be the normal relationship of Man and God as Wordsworth well knew. To speak of pathology here, however, is to attempt to account for what seems his unique vitality, his compulsion to find his God in his own genius. To Blake, preoccupied with larger issues than his own personality, normality was that pathetic reduction of the eternal life of vision to the myopic life of the temporal and material commonplace; his explanation of the divinity of Man in Jesus was that Imagination had allowed Jesus to know—in the Blakean sense of know through *images,* and hence, *imagine*—himself as God; for God to Blake was primarily Poetic Genius. Unlike Wordsworth, he made no later adjustments to the commonplace.

Wordsworth became more "normal" after his marriage and during the Christian period of his life; that is, he came to share more of the communal features and the communal understanding of life in his culture; but he did so by abandoning his preoccupation with those peculiar perceptions of his own divided being which, for the most creative period of his life, had obsessed him. Wordsworth's eyes, Matthew Arnold thought, averted their ken from half of human fate when he became more piously preoccupied with himself, but only in the visionary passages do we approach what it was of life that Wordsworth had attempted to see and to see whole. The "wholeness" of life, as I have argued, was the "wholenesss" of being he sought in those startling moments of perception when Imagination and Memory make consciousness aware of something to be realized from the unconscious depths of the mind. Wordsworth had lived many years with an uncommonly urgent awareness of the feeling ("the soul—an impulse to herself"[8]) that not to know all of one's psychic reality is to know external reality in partial and unsatisfying ways. Wordsworth's "eyes" looked most intently at the external world during the period of his creative life in which he tried to recollect his experience of it, whether of Nature, the City, or History, in order to "imagine" all of himself clearly, in order to reveal a reality he felt to be immanent beneath the habitual perception and the habitual perceiver.

Christian writers have often written of human life as a lingering mortal illness; "illness" conveys the "sickness unto death," life as the fevered awareness of its own deathward progression. Psychoanalysis addresses itself to the feeling of sickness in life in another way, and finds, perhaps

[8] "On Man, on Nature, and on Human Life . . . ," *Poetical Works*, p. 590.

quantitatively more evident in the neurotic individual, that human life as it is universally dominated by repression is a mortal neurosis. While Christianity seeks to satisfy man's persistent wish for a life that he feels his soul has once "known" and may know again, psychoanalysis seeks to account for those feelings in another way, examining simultaneously the recollected knowing, the fevered awareness and the persistence of unconscious wishing. Wordsworth, as a Romantic who sought a personal revelation of himself, anticipated this. To speak of a *poetic* obsession, then, is to imply the compelling need of one man to experience and to articulate in wholly personal imagery the mystery of his being. The possible realization by the adult poet of the traumatic nature of his own childhood would fulfill his own unconscious intentions; he would use his imaginative power to expose his own past weakness and fear, which were humanly and rightly the fear and weakness of a child undergoing a terrible experience. In doing so, he would realize his ideal of himself as the Poet who has access to the "invisible world" and whose wholeness of being is his understanding of his own mystery. What is abnormal is the individual transformation of the human neurosis of life into art, for such a personal obsession is not to be contrasted with freedom from obsession, but rather with the communal forms of obsession in which people have shared "the burthen of the mystery" impersonally. The abnormality of a poetic obsession is also to be contrasted with the abnormal individual states of neurosis and psychosis which produce fantasy but not art. The aging Wordsworth, cultivating a Christian selflessness and impersonality, effected normality through resignation, with great difficulty, and wrote bad poetry.

It is the relationship of the Wanderer to Wordsworth and to the Poet described ideally in the Mount Snowdon vision that concerns us now. F. R. Leavis, with whom I have basically disagreed, finds the Wanderer to be "very much in the nature of an idealized self-portrait" for Wordsworth: "this clearly is what he would have liked to be."[9] Certainly he is different from Wordsworth in one of the key ways that the ideal Poet would be different, for both are said to enjoy a freedom from the kinds of error and suffering that Wordsworth understood as his own and recorded in *The Prelude*. But there is a crucial difference: the ideal Poet would be Wordsworth's own age, a still young man with a soul of more than mortal privilege and a majestic intellect looking prospectively at life, confirmed in its extraordinary powers. The ideal Poet so endowed would attempt to dispel the fears "in the Mind of Man" and speak of "joy in widest commonality spread."[10] He was certainly the young man's ideal of himself, his anticipated wholeness of being implying a corresponding belief in the realizable fullness of human life, "of what we may become." Failing his ideal, for Wordsworth, was failing what he had wished to be "now." The Wanderer, however, is an old man; and except for seeming in Wordsworth's imagination more generously sympathetic to human suffering than Wordsworth perhaps feared he himself could be, he is hardly what Wordsworth would have *liked* to be. The Wanderer seems to pursue human misery, though it is fairer to say that he merely finds it everywhere as Wordsworth imagines his experiences for him. Wordsworth's imagination of life has changed, and the Wanderer is its diminished vehicle.

And the Wanderer is an anomaly. Despite Wordsworth's attempt to imagine plausibly the life of the non-participating observer, and to induce belief in the sympathetic wisdom of his detachment, the Wanderer has no life because he really has had no life. His true being—the inner mystery we associate with Wordsworth—remains invisible, or is non-existent. Trying to imagine a being exempt from "the cares of ordinary life," Wordsworth creates an imper-

[9] See Leavis, *Revaluation*, pp. 177-179. Also see above Chap. IV, pp. 151-152.

[10] *Poetical Works*, p. 590.

sonal presence, not a distinct person—himself as a mere figment of himself. It is as if in the Wanderer Wordsworth imagined all too well what he would find in life were he, like the Wanderer, to live exempt from its ordinary attachments while compelled by habit to observe it: Joy is brief, happiness uncertain, change brings losses and sorrows. Destruction by social evils and historical circumstance is everywhere apparent, but the Wanderer brings word that even Nature's processes, as in his story of Margaret, are relentless and indifferent to human life, encroaching upon the neglected garden and cottage, dragging Margaret back to the earth, covering the traces. The reality of grief remains, to be broken like the Host among the communicants of the story. Wordsworth, as he became more Christian, believed this; but in his actual life he wished to protect himself from what he contemplated through the Wanderer in poetry. In poetry he sought instruction in "frequent sights of what is to be borne"; in his life, he said conversationally, "I am myself one of the happiest of men. . . ."[11]

The Wanderer's life takes root nowhere, in place or in marriage; his way is the journey, his style sympathetic observation, his gesture departure. It seems to me that Wordsworth chose in his life between the two key metaphors he employs habitually in his tale of growth, rootedness and tillage on the one hand, journey on the other. Settling was accepting exactly the revision of his role in life suggested by the relief felt from "visionary dreariness" at the end of the first "spot of time," and further suggested by the distinction between marriage and the anxious errand of the Arab in the dream. Wordsworth's returning to the Lakes and settling near the original vale suggests that a new beginning in the old setting may lay the ghosts—or the haunting Presences—which have persisted obsessively in mind as insubstantial "phantoms of conceit." But having distinguished the Wanderer's way through life from Words-

[11] Robinson, *Selections*, #49.

worth's, we should see how tenuously distinct they were spiritually in Wordsworth's Christian period. The poet in *The Excursion,* who seems to be instructed by the greater wisdom of the Wanderer, modestly conceals whose wisdom it is the Wanderer speaks. How could Wordsworth "understand" things the way a man who has lived so lonely a life understands them?

In his poetry, Wordsworth seems to go from a prolonged youth into an early old age, a characterization of him which even the physical description of him at age thirty-five fits.[12] But unlike the Wanderer, he did *live* the middle years of his life as man, husband, and father, although it would not do to claim too much for his life and marriage. Observed closely, his later life suggests the ways in which problems, partially eased, partially resolved, take new forms rather than pass away. It was not for him to choose, as Yeats says, "perfection of the life or of the work," for he seemed quite unable to grow into the fullness of either. He lived domestically surrounded by women who loved and indulged him, all devotedly ministering to his needs—wife, sister, sister-in-law, daughter, spinster secretary. Their solicitude satisfied many more needs than one associates with those of man, husband, and father, for he was above all to them their Poet. He had replaced the one maternal Presence in Nature with several useful human ones in his household. If in the past the one had inspired his poetry, in the present the several set it down at his dictation and made from his many scribbled revisions all of the fair-copy manuscripts that survive. He became in many ways more preoccupied with himself, but less fruitfully so than in the period of *The Prelude* when his still questioning spirit was poetically obsessed. It was as if, assured of his common humanity by the close proximity of people in the most intimate human relations with him, he could withdraw much of the time into the temperamental loneliness of his spirit; his preoccupations deepened and narrowed with the years into a

[12] *Ibid., passim.*

pious concern with his own soul. Christian wayfarers in the brief transit of this life live the paradox of mortality, knowing their specific relations with the things and people of this world, providing nevertheless for a personal salvation elsewhere.

"Points have we all within our souls/ Where all stand single"[13] came to have a pious rather than a heuristic meaning for him. There was no longer something to be suddenly discovered, but in Dr. Johnson's phrase, "much to be regularly endured."[14] But still, in comparison to his Wanderer, whose life he imagined as a theatergoer's in the theater of the world, Wordsworth participated in life, in both its opportunities and its obligations; and his family life afforded him relief, when he needed it, from his poetic and religious contemplation of human suffering and mortality. Wordsworth's constant use of the theater as a metaphor in *The Prelude* for his own youthful experience of the world beyond the vale revealed his basic disbelief in life's reality and his more than just imaginative distance from it. The difference, then, between the Wanderer and Wordsworth seems to be a qualitative one that preserves the basic quantities that have been rearranged; for we must observe that the Christian Wordsworth, as man, husband, and father, still maintained a noticeable distance from life and a disbelief in the reality of this world. He seems, however, to have been more able to accept the ultimate Christian loneliness than the immediate human one, here, as in the Arab dream.

WORDSWORTH finished *The Prelude* in a perplexed state of mind. Following upon the jumbled chronology of Books IX and X and Wordsworth's uncertain mastery of the matters he treats in them, Books XI and XII seem fragmentary, random in their recollections, and heavy with pronouncements. Since *The Prelude* does not present an exploration

[13] *The Prelude,* III, 186-187.

[14] Samuel Johnson, *Rasselas,* end of Chapter Eleven.

and an achieved understanding of Wordsworth's "mysterious" self, because Wordsworth approached but did not penetrate that mystery, we have emphasized the analogous mysteries of people and of Wordsworth in a different way. There is for him the mystery of other people as they are perceived to be oppressively concentrated in the nightmarish city, passionately dissatisfied or deluded in History; and there is the mystery of Wordsworth himself to himself. The divided ego cannot see clearly, or really at all, the analogous nature of this hydra of humanity and its own passionate self, of which it remains unconscious. But as the likelihood of further discovery diminished for Wordsworth, a theme emerges in the later books of *The Prelude* which may account in part for his perplexity of mind and the conclusion's fragmentary nature. Nature and her maternal providence had been his principal themes through the poem; but gradually God's paternal providence, with its possibly greater if more severe solicitude, qualified the pronouncements Wordsworth had intended to make. "There's not a man that lives," Wordsworth had said in book III,

> who hath not had his godlike hours,
> And knows not what majestic sway we have,
> As natural beings in the strength of nature.
> (III, 192-194)

The end of the poem, in the spirit of the Blind Beggar incident in Book VII, is heavier with his feeling of being "admonish'd from another world."

To understand the shift of emphasis from Nature to God, which is perfectly explicit in the poem, we must examine the effective cause of his perplexity. Here, then, we should interpose the fact of the death by shipwreck and drowning of Wordsworth's sea-captain brother John in 1805. A gentler being, Wordsworth felt, there had never been than this silent lover of Nature, his youngest brother. Wordsworth's grief brought on a profound state of mourning, and much of his time was spent inquiring into the precise circumstances of the shipwreck, especially since there was some public question of both John's valor and competence. Relieved to find his brother's innocence as great as he had thought it, Wordsworth may well have set his own exacerbated spirit to brooding on the real question of guilt that had been raised. And who *was* guilty?

"Peele Castle," written in 1805, while Wordsworth was finishing *The Prelude,* is a severe and beautiful poem. It may remind us of "Resolution and Independence," written some years earlier. For in the earlier poem Wordsworth says, "My whole life I have lived in pleasant thought/ As if life's business were a summer mood" and "far from the world I walk and from all care"; while in the later poem, remembering a summer by the sea, he says, "I could have fancied that the mighty deep/ Was even the gentlest of all gentle things," and recalls himself, "Beside a sea that could not cease to smile;/ On tranquil land, beneath a sky of bliss." Both poems characterize a condition of life, a habitual way of perceiving it and of occupying oneself securely in it; and both present moments of realization when events or perplexing thoughts impinge upon that contentment, dispelling it, and making it and the conceptions of the self based on it seem to have been delusive.

In a way that should not really seem odd to us, it is striking that for Wordsworth at thirty-five years old, this loss, this seemingly first occasion for profound mourning, should seem to falsify his belief in his privileged existence—"the fond illusion of my heart"—and make the poet forsake his "dream," his contentment in the solitude of Nature. We are reminded of a vague sense of grief and of loss expressed and denied in the past—for instance, as it was expressed without a clear object in "Tintern Abbey" and denied there: "not for this/ Faint I, nor mourn, nor murmur. . . ." And we are led again to imagine his grief and rage at the death of his mother and his subsequent denial of pain, anger, and loss. I have used Wordsworth's description of Vaudracour in Book IX to suggest how the child Wordsworth suppressed his feelings in the past and how they were unconsciously recollected by the poet:

> everyone was overwhelm'd with grief
> Nor could they frame a manner soft enough
> To impart the tidings to the Youth; but great
> Was their astonishment when they beheld him
> Receive the news in calm despondency,
> Composed and silent, without outward sign
> Of even the least emotion.
>
> (IX, 846-852)

But in the present, with the death of John, the adult gives expression to feelings that at once resemble those of the past and are significantly different from them. With the death of John, Wordsworth felt in another way the "betrayal" by Nature of the gentle heart that loved her. Wordsworth had not yet expressed his feelings about the fact that death awaits us all in nature; but significantly death here is *not* the natural mortal limit of human life. Death might conclude life gently "in smoothe old age," as Homer says of Nestor and Odysseus and as death was to take Wordsworth himself at eighty, but this early and violent death in Nature, seemingly effected by Nature herself, takes away a loved one before his time. The similarity of this death to the early death of a young mother is striking, and it may remind us, too, of the indifference of Nature to Margaret, another young mother, in Book I of *The Excursion.* But the child who sought to deny the loss of the mother, and who had conceived of a maternal and providential Nature in doing so, could not accept his irrational and distressing feelings of betrayal by the mother herself. The adult, however, while not returning to those repressed feelings, could not now avoid the very human feelings about Nature and natural life he had not allowed himself to experience before, and thus is "humanized" in his distress. Nature as a substitute for mother was, after all, different from the mother; and here Wordsworth begins to accept that significant difference, though he would never really understand why he had felt "betrayed." Providence will seem less natural and maternal; the soul will be more on its own in a forced autonomy from Nature.

But "Peele Castle" also offers a very striking example of psychic defenses at work, one that goes far to explain the Wordsworth who was to set his house in Christian order; for the castle here draws upon the recurrent image of the dwelling place of the spirit. We may recall the trust in Nature he hoped he was expressing in "Tintern Abbey" when he said to Dorothy: "When thy mind shall be a mansion for all lovely forms,/ Thy memory be as a dwelling place/ For all sweet sounds and harmonies . . ."; or when, recalling the loss of his parents, he said: "The props of my affections were remov'd,/ And yet the building stood, as if sustain'd/ By its own spirit." Here, recalling the summer and the seaside, he recalls the castle; and as he opens a nostalgic dialogue with the scene itself, half-forgetting his present feelings, half yearning to be deceived again in the way he describes that past, he says "Wher'ere I looked, thy image still was there." Recalling serenity and the deceptive look of tranquillity and permanence, he thinks of castle and sea joined, the form of the castle, something like the Blest Babe, sleeping on the glassy calm of the sea; the sea, like the child's view of the mother, seemed "even the gentlest of all gentle things." Had he painted the scene then, he says, realizing now the falseness of the picture, he would have added "The light that never was, on sea or land/ The consecration and the poet's dream." Now, in contrast, those who inhabit such a dream—"*Housed* in a dream, at distance from the kind"—are to be pitied, he says; and he claims instead, with "a quiet mind," the absoluteness of loss: "The feeling of my loss will ne'er be old."

While the plain insistence on loss and the pained admission of betrayal stand out, the approval he gives to Beaumont's picture of the castle should be further questioned. The storm rages; the ship—the "hulk that labors in the deadly swell"—is very like John's ship, which foundered in a storm just off shore; and storm and sea are a picture of violent Nature. But is the violence, seemingly so animated with human rage, only Nature's? Wordsworth speaks of a calm mind, and then, the tone of the poem changing, like Lear he out-storms Nature in his description. Of course, Beaumont painted the picture (one can imagine any amateur and Romantic picture of a storm here), but as Wordsworth describes it, it is the passionate expressiveness that pleases him; it is a passionate and angry work. All the habitually unacknowledged passions—the tension, anger, fear, and violence that he has sometimes seen in "storms and angry elements" but repressed in himself—are at the artist's command here; yet Wordsworth, dissociating himself from the expressiveness he both praises and recreates in words, chooses the castle instead to identify with, "cased in the unfeeling armor of old time." There are two ways of looking at this: one is that humans must endure the rage of Nature, even becoming unfeeling to endure; the other is that this violence is unconsciously projected rage, so that Wordsworth feels he can say he does not feel. His calm mind is maintained by the unfeeling armor of his own firm defenses; there is almost unbearable anger, associated with betrayal, pain, death and loss, but it is not his now—*and it never has been.* The poem expresses present loss, but holds down stronger feelings from the past; for his need now is to learn to express love and reverence for God and not personal revelations from the unconscious.

It was, however, perplexing to Wordsworth to be writing the end of *The Prelude* with the logical fulfillment of its earlier claims about Nature at a time when his feelings were changing. As he turned more towards God with poems like "Ode to Duty" (1805), his feelings about God, psychically referring themselves to the father, led him towards that greater autonomy of the Christian soul, as in psychology it is the autonomy that comes in growth with due regard for the father. So it is that the two "spots of time" written as early as 1800, were put now into Book XI, in 1805, having been left out of the earlier books which dealt with ages six and thirteen. Our analysis of the first "spot of time" ("At a time/ When scarcely . . . my hand could hold a bridle"[15]) showed it to include, along with its recollection of strength, a present acknowledgment of "dreariness" at the remembered prospect for life of the child; and we have since emphasized that Wordsworth found relief from his visionary obsession in a new love found in the world, which in part eased the unconscious dependency on the mother and Nature. The second "spot of time" ("One Christmas time/ The day before the holidays began . . ."[16]) carries the desired relief further. In it, Wordsworth not only reveals the "anxiety of hope" felt in the past in relation to the father sending for the thirteen-year-old boy (at Christmas, but symbolically at puberty), but he also expresses his present conviction about God as Providence, found in these later books of the poem. He remembers and includes now his having felt "chastisement" on the occasion of his father's death:

> With trite reflections of morality,
> Yet in the deepest passion, I bow'd low
> To God, who thus corrected my desires;
> (XI, 373-375)

Here—rather than, say, in Book III or Book VI—the feeling of having been admonished from another world seems more relevant to Wordsworth, even if it does not really fit any more certainly with the thematic logic of the poem than does the Blind Beggar incident in Book VII. In Book XII he adds to his description of the poet those wordless poets whose contemplation (in "the language of the heavens") brings them close to God through their humility:

> Others, too,
> There are among the walks of homely life

15 *The Prelude*, XI, 279ff.

16 *Ibid.*, XI, 345ff.

Still higher, men for contemplation framed,
Shy, and unpractis'd in the strife of phrase,
Meek men, whose very souls perhaps would sink
Beneath them, summon'd to such intercourse;
Theirs is the language of the heavens, the power,
The thought, the image, and the silent joy;
Words are but under-agents in their souls;
When they are grasping with their greatest
  strength
They do not breathe among them . . .
(XII, 264-274)

With what sounds like a new ease of *expressing* reverence to the paternal God who is above Nature and in "another world," he goes on:

this I speak
In gratitude to God, who feeds our hearts
For his own service, knoweth, loveth us
When we are unregarded by the world.
(XII, 274-277)

It is from such a Being in another world that comes chastisement, admonishment, and providential love.

As for his relationship with this world—with Nature as it has seemed a pure Presence or as it has been domestically an English one; with men as they have been symbolic images like the Shepherd, political images like gentle Beaupuis, or passionate images of alter egos like Robespierre; with society as it has been considered abstractly and generally in History or specifically in France and England—he presents a vision of Druidism that allows him to bring together Nature, Society, Religion, Men, and History in relation to the Poet. And while this vision does not astound us with its wisdom (it is, in fact, one of those passages in Wordsworth which one is most in danger of neglecting altogether), it is a remarkable example of ego synthesis: in place of the whole truth he had sought, he now places a partial truth by which he can live. Thus, the divided ego, even as it abandons the unconscious intention of curing itself by a radical introspection, synthesizes its experience, gathering its various kinds of strength as it arrives at an acceptable understanding of what they are. The Poet will not be a soul of more than mortal privilege, but he will be a poet and find his place among men, distinguished from them by his greater awareness of his mystery and theirs, but identified with them in a community of spirit. The long Druid passage indicates the kind of qualified success Wordsworth attempts, and I think achieves, at this late moment of the poem while writing in perplexity at the end of a long labor. This was to be the "normality" he achieved and maintained with difficulty.

From his despair he had found relief in his relationship with Dorothy and, through her, with Nature. He describes this period with more directness and candor in Book XI, in 1805, than in the parts of "Tintern Abbey" it calls to mind from 1798.[17] He had told Coleridge that "there is/ One great society alone on earth/ The noble living and the noble dead"[18]; but unsure of how to value things of diminished and only relative worth, he had been living emotionally apart from that great society, too. His uncertainty in this matter reveals his greater uncertainty of his own relative worth; for how shall the person ennobled by his ideals survive them? He tells us, in Book XI:

> that I could no more
> Trust the elevation which had made me one
> With the great Family that here and there
> Is scatter'd through the abyss of ages past,
> Sage, Patriot, Lover, Hero; for it seem'd
> That their best virtues were not free from taint
> Of something false and weak, which could not
> stand
> The open eye of Reason.
>
> (XI, 60-67)

[17] *The Prelude*, XI, 1-41 and 138-195.

[18] *Ibid.*, X, 969-970.

He continues:

> Then I said,
> Go to the Poets, they will speak to thee
> More perfectly of purer creatures, yet
> If Reason be nobility in man,
> Can aught be more ignoble than the man
> Whom they describe, would fasten if they may
> Upon our love by sympathies of truth.
> (XI, 67-73)

It is striking that he can say this and not apply it to himself as, in effect, one of the "purer creatures" of imagination, of which he as poet has been speaking. Instead, in describing the activity of his distrustful mind, he seems to be remembering Prospero again, the poet-wizard with a vision of life, the figure who is so potent in his art but who lives at an enforced distance from humankind; but the comparison is strange and forced.

Wordsworth was using reason to disillusion himself as poet, as if Prospero were disabusing himself about the uses of imagination:

> as by simple waving of a wand
> The wizard instantaneously dissolves
> Palace or grove, even so did I unsoul
> As readily by syllogistic words
> Some charm of Logic, ever within reach,
> Those mysteries of passion which have made,
> And shall continue evermore to make,
> (In spite of all that Reason hath perform'd
> And shall perform to exalt and to refine)
> One brotherhood of all the human race
> Through all the habitations of past years
> And those to come, and hence an emptiness
> Fell on the Historian's Page, and even on that
> Of Poets, pregnant with more absolute truth.
> The works of both wither'd in my esteem,

> Their sentence was, I thought, pronounc'd; their
> rights
> Seem'd mortal, and their empire pass'd away.
>
> (XI, 79-95)

But then, before describing his own restoration, he asks this question, expressing reverence for the "God of love" in the "life of Nature:"

> What then remained in such eclipse? what light
> To guide or chear? The laws of things which lie
> Beyond the reach of human will or power;
> The life of nature, by the God of love
> Inspired, celestial presence ever pure;
> These left, the Soul of Youth must needs be rich,
> Whatever else be lost, and these were mine,
> Not a deaf echo, merely, of the thought
> Bewilder'd recollections, solitary,
> But living sounds.
>
> (XI, 96-105)

But what of the poet-wizard?

His vision of the Druids in Book XII returns to the subject of fearful passions. He presents a vision of communality, *including* in the ritual the poet-wizard, whose story in *The Prelude* would otherwise be one of early joys, unworldly wisdom, mixed allegiances, dreamlike confrontations, angry estrangements, and despondent isolation. Unlike Prospero, he has not understood human nature by coming to understand the role of his own *character* in his sufferings, but through this vision he expresses his desire to live among men and make use of his powers to articulate his and their common suffering. He then exhorts Coleridge, his brother poet, as he will again exhort him in the closing lines of the poem, to remember that poets, like Biblical prophets and like the Druid priests, must preside over the mystery of communal life, which they neither govern nor renounce, but with persistence instruct.

He writes:

that the genius of the Poet hence
May boldly take his way among mankind
Wherever Nature leads, that he hath stood
By Nature's side among the men of old,
And so shall stand for ever. Dearest Friend,
Forgive me if I say that I, who long
Had harbour'd reverentially a thought
That Poets, even as Prophets, each with each
Connected in a mighty scheme of truth,
Have each for his peculiar dower, a sense
By which he is enabled to perceive
Something unseen before; forgive me, Friend,
If I, the meanest of this Band, had hope
That unto me had also been vouchsafed
An influx, that in some sort I possess'd
A privilege, and that a work of mine,
Proceeding from the depth of untaught things,
Enduring and creative, might become
A power like one of Nature's. To such mood,
Once above all, a Traveller at that time
Upon the Plain of Sarum was I raised;
There on the pastoral Downs without a track
To guide me, or along the bare white roads
Lengthening in solitude their dreary line,
While through those vestiges of ancient times
I ranged, and by the solitude o'ercome,
I had a reverie and saw the past,
Saw multitudes of men, and here and there,
A single Briton in his wolf-skin vest
With shield and stone-axe, stride across the Wold;
The voice of spears was heard, the rattling spear
Shaken by arms of mighty bone, in strength
Long moulder'd of barbaric majesty.
I called upon the darkness; and it took,
A midnight darkness seem'd to come and take
All objects from my sight; and lo! again
The desart visible by dismal flames!

It is the sacrificial Altar, fed
With living men, how deep the groans, the voice
Of those in the gigantic wicker thrills
Throughout the region far and near, pervades
The monumental hillocks; and the pomp
Is for both worlds, the living and the dead.
At other moments, for through that wide waste
Three summer days I roam'd, when 'twas my chance
To have before me on the downy Plain
Lines, circles, mounts, a mystery of shapes
Such as in many quarters yet survive,
With intricate profusion figuring o'er
The untill'd ground, the work, as some divine,
Of infant science, imitative forms
By which the Druids covertly express'd
Their knowledge of the heavens, and imaged forth
The constellations, I was gently charm'd,
Albeit with an antiquarian's dream,
And saw the bearded Teachers, with white wands
Uplifted, pointing to the starry sky
Alternately, and Plain below, while breath
Of music seem'd to guide them, and the Waste
Was chear'd with stillness and a pleasant sound.
(XII, 294-353)

Again, there is the Traveller; and there are key words we recognize, rich from associated contexts—no guide, solitude, the dreary line, darkness, the two worlds, objects taken from the sight. The rite that follows begins with strong and primitive men, themselves the distant fathers of England, engaged in a worship that makes continuing life from destruction and makes Nature resound with human passion fitting itself into the continuing patterns of the season and the starry skies. Wordsworth presents the vision vividly, though he makes it seem less important to himself by claiming for it only the charm of an "antiquarian's dream"; still it is as if Wordsworth were admitting in imagination to the tragic ritual. He was admitting, that is, to the extent that he was able, the importance of the identification with men, though it was never to be an identification deeply and fully made. Here he imagines the Poet-priest participating in the rite, just as his own concern with the communality of human life and of human grief in "Peele Castle" had led him to say, "A deep distress hath humanized my soul."

In "Peele Castle," he says:

> Farewell, farewell, the heart that lives alone
> Housed in a dream, at distance from the kind!
> Such happiness, wherever it be known,
> Is to be pitied; for 'tis surely blind.
> But welcome fortitude, and patient cheer,
> And frequent sights of what is to be borne!
> Such sights, or worse, as are before me here.—
> Not without hope we suffer and we mourn.

Having called on darkness in the Druid vision, he sees something like the "invisible world" again revealed, the light of sense having gone out, taking "all objects from my sight." When he says "and the pomp/ Is for both worlds, the living and the dead," the Poet is like one of "the bearded teachers" who, with their wands uplifted, resemble Prospero, this time "souling" rather than "unsouling" the groves. The rite being imagined affirms what the poet accepts:

> Those mysteries of passion which have made,
> And shall continue evermore to make,
> (In spite of all that Reason hath perform'd
> And shall perform to exalt and to refine)
> One brotherhood of all the human race
> Through all the habitations of past years
> And those to come.
>
> (XI, 84-90)

Hence, he can accept as a sustaining belief the "one great society alone on earth/ The noble living and the noble dead." Having relocated himself with an imagined role in "the great family" and still maintaining a difference, he can share common acceptances in this life with other people who have with him a common humanity in "those mysteries of passion." His acceptance of human suffering and mortality seems now to admit that what is dead is dead, which takes at least one burden off the heart and mind that had tried to deny death. Beyond this vision of the Druid rite of continuous life, there was to be his Christian vision of providential and continuous life beyond death.

Nature, then, was to have a more neutral psychic function. However suggestive of maternal solicitude, Nature neither withholds him in a dream apart from life, nor betrays him in any personal way. Death, believed by him to be providentially ameliorated by God, is no longer denied by the inhuman analogy of the Poet and God. That analogy, which mortality could not sustain and which true conscious understanding would not have needed, was transformed rather than wholly relinquished. The "emblem of a mind" presented in Book XIII is Wordsworth's fullest expression of an aspiration from which he finally dissociated himself, that of a soul, as it might have been his soul, to be of "more than mortal privilege." But Wordsworth, dissociated from his ideal of himself and relieved of the burden of a fixated obsession with death, could accept in its place the Christian expectation of an eventual resurrection from death. The soul would be brought to perfection in God's will and God's understanding. In the Snowdon vision, the emblem of a mighty mind, the night setting, the intimation of a godly clarity of mind and of a perfect understanding despite the darkness may recall St. Paul's promise to the faithful in salvation:

> Charity
> Beareth all things, believeth all things, hopeth all
> things, endureth all things.

Charity never faileth: but whether *there be* prophecies,
They shall fail; where *there be* tongues, they shall cease;
Whether *there be* knowledge, it shall vanish away.
For we know in part, and we prophesy in part.
But when that which is perfect is come, then that
Which is in part shall be done away.
When I was a child, I spake as a child;
I understood as a child, I thought as a child: but when I became a man, I put away childish things.
For now we see through a glass, darkly; but then face to face: now I know in part; but then shall I know even as also I am known.[19]

The humility, which is Christian, may be contrasted with the simple matter-of-factness of Aristotle's description of the contemplative life and the pursuit of self-knowledge:

"However, such a life would be more than human. A man who would live it would do so not insofar as he is human, but because there is a divine element in him. . . . So if it is true that intelligence is divine in comparison with man, then a life guided by intelligence is divine in comparison with human life. We must not follow those who advise us to have human thoughts, since we are only men, and mortal thoughts, as mortals should; on the contrary, we should try to become immortal as far as that is possible and do our utmost to live in accordance with what is highest in us. . . . One might regard it as each man's true self, since it is the controlling and better part. It would therefore be strange if a man chose not to live his own life but someone else's."[20]

The Prelude is the record of an attempt to live in accord with a high estimate of human worth. At the same time, it

[19] I Corinthians 13: 7-12.
[20] Aristotle, *Ethics*, tr. Ostwald, p. 290.

is a poetic attempt at curing the self of a specific trauma, and sheds light on what some have considered the general human trauma of self-consciousness. Inevitably, *The Prelude* is a poetic display of profound egoism, one increasingly qualified by the poet and finally renounced, but one that endures because the process is set above the person, as every sympathetic reader will attest. The personality of Wordsworth is intimately necessary, but subordinately so, to the account he wished to give of Imagination. What may be imagined in the sublime egoism of poetry confers a dignity on the mind attempting to imagine of itself something worthy of the power by which it is possessed. Despite Wordsworth's later Christian resignation, this is a feeling one has about Wordsworth in relation to his art evoked by the peculiarity of his appropriate name.

APPENDIX

The history of Wordsworthian scholarship and criticism hardly needs rehearsing in an appendix to a book like this. While the bibliography will suggest the range of related readings, I hope that the argument presented will have been taken for what it is, an attempt at a different kind of interpretation. As for the vicissitudes of Wordsworth's popularity and the history of preoccupations through which he has been interpreted, they are matters of common knowledge easily enough obtained with some research.[1] Instead, I would like briefly to distinguish between the interpretation presented here and some few other modern and cognate theories of his personality.

While aptly describing aspects of Wordsworth's mind and poetic practice in *Revaluation*, F. R. Leavis reacts strongly both to the amateur religionists who mystify themselves and others in talking of Wordsworth's mysticism and to the literary psychologists who would explain him differently. With the abruptness of one who believes that everything relevant to the practice of literary criticism can and should be generated from within the study of literature, he dismisses "psychoanalytics" out of hand, enjoins critics from considering further the many passages in Wordsworth's poetry that are plainly expressive of Wordsworth's personal psychology, and reproves some who did.[2] One such critic whom Leavis treats curtly is Herbert Read, whose book, *Wordsworth*, in 1930, was a significant modern attempt to deal with Wordsworth's personality, to get at what Read called the man behind the myth, the legend, the mask.

For many readers today, Wordsworth has been rescued by modern curiosity from the fate of being an acknowledged but unread major author of the early modern period; he

1 See Bibliography below. For accounts of his popularity, see especially the books by James V. Logan and by Elsie Smith.

2 F. R. Leavis, *Revaluation*, p. 168.

is a challenge to their ingenuity. For them, after all of Wordsworth's explanation of himself as the poet in *The Prelude* and despite all the scholarly and critical elaborations of Wordsworth, Wordsworth remains to be explained; there are questions that are epistemological in nature and they are inseparable from the man and his manner. Wordsworth's art is not easily explained by the facts of his life, nor does his art, even at its most confessional, satisfy one's curiosity about the life being thus transmuted into artifact. Anyone who has read some of the scholarly works on Wordsworth's life and art—of which, say, *The Early Life of William Wordsworth* by Émile Legouis has proven a durable example—has known the frustration of curiosity I speak of and the scholar's set of mind that Mr. Read called in question. The speculations about Wordsworth that rarely vary from Wordsworth's own surmises in *The Prelude,* the observations of Wordsworth that are essentially paraphrases of Wordsworth's representation of himself in *The Prelude,* the substantiations of interpretations that are no more than quotations from *The Prelude*—all such deference to Wordsworth has left Wordsworth himself very much in control of the "Wordsworth" one hears of, and as much so after Matthew Arnold as before, after George McLean Harper[3] as before.

In contrast, Mr. Read's approach to Wordsworth was refreshing. He raised psychological questions about Wordsworth's representation of himself and spoke to them directly: "It is often said that all fiction is disguised autobiography; it is as true to say that all autobiography is disguised fiction." And without impugning Wordsworth's sincerity, he says: "Sincerity is not truth; it is only conviction—a state of belief directed towards some arbitrary end."[4] But

[3] See George McLean Harper, *William Wordsworth, His Life Works, and Influence.* It was Professor Harper who first made available the facts of Wordsworth's love affair in France; see *Wordsworth's French Daughter.*

[4] Herbert Read, *Wordsworth,* London, 1930, p. 50.

while the book has many virtues and while Mr. Read must have made some of his readers in the 1930's aware of the inadequacies of the many pat assumptions of Wordsworth scholarship, the book does not wear well; despite its novel attempt at a modern view, its psychological view of Wordsworth is simplistic, its pronouncements about the psychology of creativity dubious.

Mr. Read's psychological view of Wordsworth hinges on his understanding of guilt. He seeks to explain how it was that Wordsworth at twenty-seven "first realized that intimate communion with natural beauty which was to be the mainspring of his poetry and the source of his original philosophy,"[5] and he finds that: "It came as an aftermath, as an issue from the emotional storm that descended on him in France. As that storm subsided, the outraged feelings sought compensation in memories; and then, at first slowly, then riotously, the treasure of his unconscious mind, so richly stored in childhood, was opened and given forth in the poetry of one wonderful decade."[6]

The storm alluded to is, of course, Wordsworth's love affair with Annette Vallon and his involvement in the revolutionary affairs of France. To Read, the love affair is the key to Wordsworth's psychology:

> "It transformed his being; I think that this passion and all its melancholy aftermath was the deepest experience of Wordsworth's life—the emotional complex from which all his subsequent career flows in its intricacy and uncertainty. It was this experience which Wordsworth saw fit to hide—to bury in the most complete secrecy and mask with a long sustained hypocrisy."[7]

But at the time that Read was writing, the fact of the love affair had still the somewhat exaggerated importance of a new and quite disturbing discovery about Wordsworth; and while many of Read's observations about Wordsworth's

[5] *Ibid.*, p. 61. [6] *Ibid.*, p. 60. [7] *Ibid.*, p. 96.

subsequent behavior in relation to the affair seem accurate enough, his understanding of Wordsworth's unconscious guilt, its relation to his art and to the ultimate failure of his poetic impulse, assumes too much and explains too little.

The love affair and the subsequent guilt were, in psychoanalytic terms, "overdetermined." Indeed, Read's picture of the young Wordsworth who went to France from Cambridge is itself an idealized conception of a young man whose adversities were all before him and whose subsequent responses and reactions to life are difficult to comprehend in one "so blessed with early liberty." Read describes him:

> "Wordsworth reached his twenty-first year without ever having had to submit to any repressive discipline. It would be difficult to find, among our famous men, one so blessed with early liberty. This youth, eager in mind and body, reached the fullness of his manhood in passion and in pride unchecked. At the end of his time at Cambridge we can be sure that he had already freed his mind from the repressive conventions of his religion. He faced the world, his poise maintained only by his instinctive reserve. It is no wonder that this last barrier fell before the emotional storms that then descended upon him."[8]

Unfortunately, that view of Wordsworth as blessed with early liberty is as uncritically accepted by Read from Wordsworth as are the most conventional scholarly views of Wordsworth. Read quotes Wordsworth's *Autobiographical Memoranda*: " 'Of my earliest days at school I have little to say, but that they were very happy ones, chiefly because I was left at liberty, then and in the vacations, to read whatever books I liked. . . .' "[9] And a general description of freedom follows, with Read observing how the school children "lodged with the cottagers of Hawkeshead, free from the jealous restrictions that too often make a home a prison."

[8] *Ibid.*, p. 69.

[9] *Ibid.*, p. 51.

Although he mentions the death of Wordsworth's mother when Wordsworth was eight, he makes no significant connection between her death and Wordsworth's earliest days at school which followed immediately thereupon. What seems to have been lost to Read is any awareness of the traumatic nature of such an event—the repressions, fixations, denials, and distortions that attend such traumatic events in a child's life and the hysteria and unconscious obsessions that affect the life of the grown man, and more than likely his poetic practice. Had Read's view been psychoanalytic in fact, rather than eclectic in his use of some psychoanalytic concepts, the resulting picture of Wordsworth would have been significantly different.

To TURN from Read to F. W. Bateson is to turn to a more deliberately psychological view. Bateson's book, *Wordsworth: A Reinterpretation*, was, to my thinking, a welcome book when it appeared in 1954. In it he attempts boldly to match the traditional critics in their observations of Wordsworth's stylistic evolution and particular achievement, while at the same time advancing a basically modern psychological hypothesis about the poetry in relation to the poet. He calls in question the literary humanist's reliance on intuition as to what poets and people are like.

What makes Mr. Bateson's account of Wordsworth so interesting is the cultural, literary, and biographical evocation of a major poet with whom Mr. Bateson's mind engages interrogatively, speculatively, and at times theoretically. It is plain that modern depth psychology has enlightened Mr. Bateson's critical approach; he is keenly aware of trauma, unconscious motives, neurotic isolation, incipient disintegrations, incestuous attachments, and regressive modes. He sees Wordsworth's subjectivity as at once a sickness and an attempt at cure; he sees the poetry as the expression of an impelling need "to integrate the more subjective or inward-looking and the more objective or outward-looking aspects of his personality." ("The poetry, it turns out, was not so much autobiography as a technique of self-preservation and self-recreation."[10]) With such observations, I basically agree, and at the time that I first read them some years ago was grateful for the simple directness with which he made such observations and ignored the traditional pieties surrounding Wordsworth. In questioning the nature of the poet, it was plain that here was a critic able to argue a plausible Wordsworth along other lines, one who could make use of newer hypotheses about a poet's growth and about our human psychology than those found in the intuitive psychologizing of the literary humanists.

To distinguish my approach from Mr. Bateson's, I should say first that his is a reading of the life tracing the evolution and exhaustion of a literary style through the phases of the poet's experience and making use of poetry and biographical data; mine is primarily a reading of *The Prelude* and of the character revealed in it, the poet remembering, explaining, imagining, and inventing himself. While there are many common features of psychological assumption and critical method, the problems posed are different and the executions inevitably so. Indeed, some of the theoretical assumptions are different, too; for Mr. Bateson, in trying to fix some peculiarity of a group of poems or of a period, relies more heavily on the immediate biographical context for local explanations than I think justifiable; and in consequence he makes use of a psychological vocabulary descriptively rather than theoretically. While I find many of the insights valuable (e.g. his description of the incipient incestuousness in Wordsworth's and Dorothy's intimacy, as well as his description of Wordsworth's resolution of that crisis[11]), I find others labored and implausible (e.g. his theory about Wordsworth's adolescent love affair with "Mary of Esthwaite Water"[12]).

Finally, I must go further and say that he too underestimates the traumatic effect of the death of Wordsworth's

[10] F. W. Bateson, *Wordsworth; A Reinterpretation*, p. 186.

[11] *Ibid.*, pp. 143ff. and 183ff. [12] *Ibid.*, pp. 65-70.

mother when Wordsworth was eight. I am surprised to find that he can restrict his understanding of Wordsworth's "neurosis"[13] to the extreme uncongeniality of the loveless home at Penrith afforded him by his mother's relatives after her death in the periods when he was not at school. Perhaps it is only on the assumption of the traumatic effect of that significant death that *The Prelude* opens up to the kind of interpretation I make of the unconscious wishes and processes revealed in it, but that assumption allows for an exploration of the "subjective inwardness" of Wordsworth's mind as I think Mr. Bateson's assumptions do not, and leads to an extended interpretation of what Mr. Bateson also rightly calls Wordsworth's "technique of self-preservation and self-recreation." For it is in relation to the desperate circumstance in which those obscure processes of mind first began to fashion a personal myth, a fiction of the self, that the "egotistical sublime" of the poetry is best understood.

ANOTHER book I must mention here is David Ferry's *The Limits of Mortality*. While it deserves consideration on its own merits as a sustained and precise inquiry into Wordsworth's imagination, it is relevant here in another way, although it is not explicitly psychological in its approach to Wordsworth. Professor Ferry's method of close reading questions the manifest text for its latent implications and finds a Wordsworth at odds with himself and at odds with the more official versions of "Wordsworth." In that way, while concerning himself primarily with Wordsworth's metaphysical realities and the relationship between what he calls the "mystical" and the "sacramental" imaginations, he shows convincingly at several points that a constellation of wishes in the poet, amounting to a spiritual attitude, remained permanently at odds with many of the surface appearances of Wordsworth's poetry. It is not my intent to discuss in what sense Professor Ferry's interpretations and my own are like and unlike; at their most like, they are as

13 *Ibid.*, p. 77.

unlike as similar observations made for widely different purposes of explanation. But Professor Ferry's precise descriptions of the metaphysical realities he discerns in Wordsworth reveal aspects of the poet's psyche and prove congenial to a reader whose orientation is psychological.

NEXT, there is the work of Geoffrey Hartman, principally *Wordsworth's Poetry, 1787-1814*. First, it is only fair to say that no brief consideration of Professor Hartman's book can even suggest the wealth of its observations or the scope and brilliance of the book. Moreover, to consider the book for the sake of distinguishing his approach from mine hardly provides the occasion for showing what I think it is worth, so I shall say at the outset that it is the best book on Wordsworth I have read. The ease with which he brings his cultural and literary historical erudition to bear on the central figure of English Romantic poetry and his patient attention to every aspect of style are admirable; and his command of related religious matters must leave scholars who have found the subject of mysticism and vision unavoidable in discussing Wordsworth feeling that Professor Hartman has written the book they would like to see written or have tried to write.

Of his book in relation to mine, I will suggest that the arguments do not diverge essentially in their observations of crucial phenomena, as alternative arguments often do and as arguments about Wordsworth have. Instead, the difference lies in the terms of description applied, or rather in the assumptions about meaning that dictate the choice of certain significant terms. Anyone patient enough to attend to approximately parallel interpretations can understand the terms crucial to one argument in the terms of the other, but it is plain that the convictions with which the respective terms were chosen differ significantly.

It is a question in my own mind whether or not a discussion of Freudian and Jungian psychology would be useful here, though some mention of those designations seems unavoidable. While Professor Hartman makes Jungian assumptions about growth, traumatic events, and change, he has not written a Jungian interpretation of Wordsworth; he has written a work of literary criticism and scholarship, verging, as he says, on a phenomenology of mind. He has tried to relate the poetry and the personality of Wordsworth developmentally and has considered carefully the role of the poet and the function of poetry; it is while speaking developmentally of Wordsworth's experience that he touches on significant Jungian terms for describing and explaining growth. So, too, I hope that my study of Wordsworth, while more evidently Freudian than Professor Hartman's is Jungian, will not seem "merely" psychoanalytic; it is meant to be literary in ways that Freudian analyses may not often be, and makes use of Freudian concepts in ways that practicing psychoanalysts might not with their patients or in their writings on artists.

Since reading Professor Hartman's book, I have tried to fix precisely that matter of conviction that basically distinguishes the one interpretation from the other. I think the preference for Freudian or Jungian psychology reflects a deeper concern about the nature of reality. When, for instance, I read Professor Hartman's descriptions of Wordsworth's "Apocalyptic imagination" in relation to Nature, they seem accurate to me as descriptions of the workings of Wordsworth's mind, and in that sense, acceptable. I am aware of attempts on my own part to find a suitable language of description, one responsive to the vitality and suggestiveness of Wordsworth's own language, and like Professor Hartman, find myself employing language very like Wordsworth's own. But even allowing for the similarities of description in rendering Wordsworth's sense of natural bond and specific place, of acute self-consciousness, of constriction, fixity, and obsessive fixation, of unconscious attachment to Nature and of unconscious desire for liberation by the imagination, and fear of it—there is still a difference; and the difference lies in the working concept of "mind" by which the scholar seeks to explain aspects of mental process and their ground in "being."

Professor Hartman says in the preface:

"One term, not technical, requires special comment. By 'apocalyptic,' as in 'apocalyptic imagination,' I intend the Apocalypse of St. John (the Book of Revelation), and, more generally, the kind of imagination that is concerned with the supernatural and especially the Last Things. The term may also describe a mind which actively desires the inauguration of a totally new epoch, whether preceding or following the end of days. And since what stands between us and the end of the (old) world is the world, I sometimes use 'apocalyptic' to characterize any strong desire to cast out nature and to achieve an unmediated contact with the principle of things."[14]

I am alerted here to an operant concept of mind unmistakably different from my own and ultimately unreconcilable with it for the purposes of explanation. However tentatively the ensuing attempt at cumulative explanation may proceed, the implications from the outset are plain. In dealing with the matter of human separation from the unconscious life in nature and, especially in this poet's case, with the imaginative experiences in seeking and resisting the consciousness of that separation, it is the scholar's working concept of mind that reveals itself. True, Professor Hartman speaks here of "the kind of imagination that is concerned with the supernatural and especially the Last Things," and subsequently maintains his own critical detachment from Wordsworth's concerns; but it is soon plain that it is no part of his intention to explain "soul" or "Apocalypse" in psychological terms while explaining the psychology of Wordsworth's conflicted concern with them. In using Wordsworth's own terms much of the time, Professor Hartman remains closer than I do to the actual form Wordsworth gave to the expression of his deepest spiritual

[14] Geoffrey Hartman, *Wordsworth's Poetry*, p. x.

and psychological concerns, but that is because for him too they are realities that abide.

Professor Hartman is in the company of those literary scholars and some scholars of comparative religion who have found modern psychological thinking, principally Jung's, congenial to their interest in the relationship between the inspired imagination and the continuing reality of the supernatural. But to Freudians, as to Freud, "supernatural" has plainly the connotation of illusory, and "Apocalyptic" is at most a metaphor for possible psychic "revelations" from the personal unconscious. So it is, in my account, my intention to interpret psychologically what Wordsworth means by Nature, soul, and Apocalypse in various contexts, and to try to show how his recurrent patterns of metaphor link associated contexts and reveal aspects of the poet's personal psychology.

Jungians have held that Freud's insights were seriously limited by his over-insistence on his hypotheses—hypotheses, it seemed to Jung, that came prematurely to function doctrinally as an expression of Freud's personality; the claim against Freudians, then, is that their analyses are "reductive" in seeking to explain character and behavior psychogenetically in terms of infantile sexuality and traumata, principally through the Oedipus complex, and on the basis of a limited clinical empiricism. In contrast, Freudians have held that Jung cut himself off from the basic concepts of psychoanalysis and that Jungian psychology is vague and "expansive"; if its descriptions of types of personality seem empirical, its further discussion of individuation and the relation of conscious ego to unconscious self merely rests on vague postulates about human consciousness, the experience of the race, and the mysteriousness of the unknown. Since I find myself at least as interested in Jung's postulates and their application to myth and literature as I am in Freud's notions of an archaic heritage or his later thoughts about the pre-Oedipal period and his metapsychological speculations about entropy, I am anxious to leave aside the history of the failures of imagination on the parts of principals and disciples alike in their dealings with each other's merits. But we should see here the practical consequences of the Jungian and Freudian assumptions of Professor Hartman's study and mine.

When, for instance, Professor Hartman speaks of the early poems, like "The Vale of Esthwaite," he says of Wordsworth:

"He is desperately unsure not only of whether his imagination can pass from nature to man but also of whether it can stay with nature itself. His doubts do not come as yet from any broad conceptual scheme concerning the origin of the poetic impulse. But having lost father and mother, and deprived of sister and everything that used to be home, he is in danger of being detached from the 'social chain.' His dilemma is increased by the fact that nature itself is not—or no longer—sufficient for a mind awakened, by these separations, to its independence. Though he insists that nothing 'from the social chain can tear/ This bosom link'd forever there,' his imagination is unable to stay with the only society (Esthwaite Valley) he knows. The gentlest of valleys, his home for the last eight years, begins to haunt him—or rather, it is his mind which haunts supernaturally through nature, as the gothic and 'terrific' scenes of the poem reveal."[15]

In this passage he mentions the loss of mother, father, and home, and he connects these losses to Wordsworth's intense but untenable dependency on nature; but he takes these traumatic separations to be ancillary to a generic crisis, the basic human experience of separation, that of the awakened human consciousness from nature, and, ultimately, of the soul from the material world. What meaning such traumatic losses have is to be found in that generic crisis and in that ultimate necessity, and not, as I would think, conversely. It is not that Professor Hartman is not

[15] *Ibid.*, p. 77.

sensitive to the early traumatic losses in Wordsworth's life—in fact, he sees in Wordsworth's early experiences a dangerous predisposition to lose "the reality principle" itself—but he shows no theoretical concern with their psychological significance, for that, after all, would require a Freudian hypothesis and an acknowledgement of psychic determinism. Instead of pursuing the suggestion that Wordsworth's mind is "haunted" by unconscious projections into nature experienced as mysterious perceptions and seeking to determine the content of those projections, Professor Hartman sees the mind's growing awareness of its separateness from nature as a supernatural experience, as well as, psychologically, part of Wordsworth's personal history.

While it is the intent of both arguments to trace Wordsworth's increasing self-consciousness, his crises and his encounters with the unconscious self, his attraction to and his fear of his own imagination, his failure to accept his own attempts at revelation and freedom, Professor Hartman's argument is sustained by the "expansive" suggestiveness of its Jungian assumptions, and mine relates later crises of experience "reductively" to earlier ones along Freudian lines.

FINALLY, it was while this manuscript was being prepared for the press that a book published in 1968 by Professor Wallace W. Douglas was called to my attention: *Wordsworth: The Construction of a Personality.* Just as with Professor Hartman's book, which I did not read until my own was written, it proved a pleasant surprise, a confirmation of certain basic intuitions about the appropriateness of applying psychoanalytic concepts to Wordsworth. Professor Douglas gives the most succinct and plausible account in psychological terms of the dynamics of Wordsworth's growth that I have read. There are many points of similarity in our respective interpretations, especially in point of passages cited for what they reveal about the psychological mechanisms through which Wordsworth dealt with the unbroken unconscious dependency on the mother who died. I am particularly struck with the treatment of Wordsworth's pre-Oedipal relationship with his mother and with the discussion of the importance of Ann Tyson (Wordsworth's "frugal Dame") in the Hawkeshead days.

While Professor Douglas, in a sense, makes less of the trauma of loss itself than I do, he gives a very interesting and complex account, influenced by the work of Melanie Klein, of Wordsworth's ego remodelled to incorporate the mother lost in death; as he says, "not the external mother, whether good or bad, but rather the inner mother, the possessively absorbed object of love and need."[16] Briefly to suggest Professor Douglas's fine insight, I shall conclude by quoting at length a partial statement of his thesis, which follows the observation that "all the content of Wordsworth's life and poetry suggests that for many years the dominant factor in his behavior was the mechanism with which he sought to correct and control his relationship to the mother of his infantile experience." He then says of Wordsworth:

"I think that in Wordsworth the normal process of internalization became, or was transformed into, a mechanism to achieve absolute possession and total affective gratification. In this way the loss of the mother was prevented or compensated for, but I think that the mechanism could have had only partial and temporary successes in controlling or masking the ambivalences and conflicts that were produced by the very existence of such demands, let alone their satisfaction. The decisive fact is that Wordsworth's self had been constituted as a depository of attitudes, values and feelings taken from the mother. Wordsworth's self was enough like what he felt his mother was and wanted so

[16] This and the following quotations are from page 133. See especially pp. 133-136.

that she was in feeling (if not in fact) contained within him."

It is from this that Professor Douglas goes on to explain Wordsworth's "great fantasy of Nature" in terms of the ambivalences felt for the mother incorporated within. While my own interpretation differs somewhat, I think the two compatible, and have learned a considerable amount from his.

BIBLIOGRAPHY

I. Wordsworth and Related Readings

Abercrombie, Lascelles. *The Art of Wordsworth.* New York, 1952.

Abrams, Meyer. *The Mirror and The Lamp.* New York, 1953.

———, ed. *English Romantic Poets.* New York, 1960.

Arnold, Matthew. "Wordsworth," in *Essays in Criticism, 2nd Series.* London, 1900.

Barzun, Jacques. *Classic, Romantic, and Modern.* 2nd ed., Boston, 1961.

Bate, Walter Jackson. *From Classic to Romantic.* Cambridge, 1946.

Bateson, F. W. *Wordsworth: A Reinterpretation.* London, 1954.

Beatty, Arthur. *William Wordsworth.* 3rd edn., Madison, 1960.

Bloom, Harold. *The Visionary Company.* New York, 1961.

Bowra, E. M. *The Romantic Imagination.* Cambridge, 1949.

Bradley, A. C. *Oxford Lectures.* London, 1909.

Brooks, Cleanth. *The Well-Wrought Urn.* New York, 1947.

Brower, Reuben A. *The Poetry of Robert Frost.* New York, 1964.

Bush, Douglas. *Mythology and The Romantic Tradition in English Poetry.* Cambridge, 1937.

Coleridge, Samuel Taylor. *Biographia Literaria,* ed. J. Shawcross. Oxford, 1907.

———. *Collected Letters of Samuel Taylor Coleridge,* ed. Earl Leslie Griggs. 4 vols., New York, 1956-1959.

———. *Passages from His Prose and Table Talk,* ed. W. H. Dirks. London, 1894.

Danby, John F. *The Simple Wordsworth.* New York, 1960.

Darbishire, Helen. *Wordsworth.* London, 1953.

Davie, Donald. *Articulate Energy*. London, 1955.
de Selincourt, Ernest. *The Early Wordsworth*. Oxford, 1936.
———. *Wordsworth and Other Studies*. Oxford, 1947.
Douglas, Wallace W. *Wordsworth: The Construction of a Personality*. Kent, Ohio, 1968.
Empson, William. *English Pastoral Poetry*. New York, 1938.
———. *Seven Types of Ambiguity*. 2nd edn., New York, 1947.
Ferry, David. *The Limits of Mortality*. Middletown, 1959.
Fink, Zera S. *The Early Wordsworthian Milieu*. Oxford, 1958.
Garrod, H. W. *Wordsworth: Lectures and Essays*. Oxford, 1923.
Grierson, Herbert J. C. *Milton and Wordsworth: Poets and Prophets*. New York, 1937.
Harper, George McLean. *Wordsworth: His Life, Works, and Influence*. New York, 1916.
———. *Wordsworth's French Daughter*. Princeton, 1921.
Hartman, Geoffrey. *The Unmediated Vision*. New Haven, 1954.
———. *Wordsworth's Poetry 1787-1814*. New Haven, 1964.
Havens, R. D. *The Mind of a Poet*. Baltimore, 1941.
Hazlitt, William. *The Complete Works of William Hazlitt*, ed. P. P. Howe, based on edn. of A. R. Waller and A. Glover. 21 vols., London, 1930-1934. (Vols. 5, 11 and 17 are cited.)
Herford, C. H. *The Age of Wordsworth*. London, 1901.
James, D. G. *Scepticism and Poetry*. London, 1937.
Jones, John. *The Egotistical Sublime*. London, 1954.
Keats, John. *Letters*, ed. Maurice Buxton Forman. 4th edn., London, 1952.
Knight, G. Wilson. *The Starlit Dome: Studies in the Poetry of Vision*. Oxford, 1941.
Knight, William. *The Life of William Wordsworth*. Edinburgh, 1889.
Kroeber, Karl. *Romantic Narrative Art*. Madison, 1960.

Langbaum, Robert. *The Poetry of Experience.* London, 1957.

Leavis, F. R. *Revaluation: Tradition and Development in English Poetry.* London, 1936; New York, 1947.

Legouis, Émile. *The Early Life of William Wordsworth,* tr. J. W. Mathews. London, 1897.

———. *William Wordsworth and Annette Vallon.* London, 1922.

———. *Wordsworth in a New Light.* Cambridge, 1923.

Lindenberger, H. *On Wordsworth's Prelude.* Princeton, 1963.

Logan, James V. *Wordsworthian Criticism.* Columbus, 1947.

Margoliouth, H. M. *Wordsworth and Coleridge, 1795-1834.* New York, 1953.

Meyer, G. W. *Wordsworth's Formative Years.* Ann Arbor, 1943.

Miles, Josephine. *Eras and Modes in English Poetry.* Berkeley, 1957.

Moorman, Mary. *William Wordsworth: A Biography.* Oxford, 1957.

Pater, Walter. *Appreciations.* London, 1889.

Perkins, David D. *The Quest for Permanence.* Cambridge, 1959.

Pottle, F. A. "Wordsworth and Freud, or The Theology of the Unconscious," *Bulletin of the General Theological Seminary,* 34, 1948.

Potts, A. F. *Wordsworth's Prelude.* Ithaca, 1953.

Praz, Mario. *The Romantic Agony,* tr. Angus Davidson. London, 1933.

Read, Herbert. *Wordsworth.* London, 1930.

———. *The True Voice of Feeling.* New York, 1953.

Richards, I. A. *Coleridge on Imagination.* London, 1934; Bloomington, 1960.

Robinson, H. C. *Blake, Coleridge, Wordsworth, Lamb: Selections from the Literary Remains of H. C. Robinson,* ed. Edith J. Morley. Manchester, 1922.

Smith, Elsie. *An Estimate of Wordsworth by His Contemporaries, 1793-1822*. Oxford, 1932.

Sperry, Willard. *Wordsworth's Anti-Climax*. New York, 1935.

Stephen, Leslie. *Hours in a Library*. Vol. 3, new edn., New York, 1907.

Trilling, Lionel. *The Liberal Imagination*. New York, 1950.

Whitehead, Alfred North. *Science and the Modern World*. New York, 1929.

Willey, Basil. *The Seventeenth-Century Background*. London, 1934.

———. *The Eighteenth-Century Background*. London, 1949.

Wimsatt, W. S. *The Verbal Icon*. Lexington, 1954.

Wordsworth, Dorothy. *Journals of Dorothy Wordsworth*, ed. E. de Selincourt. London, 1941.

Wordsworth, William. *The Early Letters of William Wordsworth and Dorothy Wordsworth*, ed. E. de Selincourt. Oxford, 1935.

———. *The Prelude; or Growth of a Poet's Mind*, ed. E. de Selincourt. 2nd edn., rev. Helen Darbishire. Oxford, 1959.

———. *The Poetical Works of William Wordsworth*, ed. Thomas Hutchinson, rev. E. de Selincourt. London, 1960.

———. *The Prose Works of William Wordsworth*, ed. A. Grosart. 3 vols., London, 1876.

2. Selected Psychological Works

Bergler, Edmund. *Counterfeit Sex*. New York, 1951.

Brown, Norman O. *Life Against Death*. New York, 1959.

Erikson, Erik H. *Childhood and Society*. New York, 1963.

———. *Identity, Youth and Crisis*. New York, 1968.

———. *Insight and Responsibility*. New York, 1964.

———. "The Problems of Ego Identity," *Journal of the American Psychoanalytical Association, 4*, 1956.

———. *Young Man Luther.* New York, 1958.

Fenichel, Otto. *The Psychoanalytic Theory of Neurosis.* New York, 1945.

Freud, Anna. *The Ego and the Mechanisms of Defense,* tr. C. M. Baines. New York, 1946.

Freud, Sigmund. The Standard Edition of the Complete Psychological Works of Sigmund Freud, translated from the German under the General Editorship of James Strachey in collaboration with Anna Freud. 24 vols. London, 1953-. Abbreviated as CW. The following works are cited in this book:

"Civilization and Its Discontents," CW XXI, pp. 57-145.

"The Dissolution of the Oedipus Complex," XIX, 171-179.

"The Ego and the Id," XIX, 1-66.

"The Future of an Illusion," XXI, 1-56.

"The Infantile Genital Organization," XIX, 139-145.

"Infantile Sexuality," VII, 173-206.

"Instincts and Their Vicissitudes," XIV, 109-140.

"The Interpretation of Dreams," IV (entire vol.) and V, 339-627.

"Moses and Monotheism," XXIII, 1-137.

"Mourning and Melancholia," XIV, 237-258.

"New Introductory Lectures on Psycho-Analysis," XXII, 1-182.

"A Note on the Unconscious in Psycho-Analysis," XII, 255-266.

"On Narcissism," XIV, 67-102.

"Psycho-Analysis," XVIII, 235-254.

"Repression," XIV, 141-158.

"A Special Type of Choice of Object Made by Men," XI, 163-175.

"Totem and Taboo," XIII, 1-162.

"The Unconscious," XIV, 159-215.

Greenacre, Phyllis. *The Quest for the Father.* New York, 1963.

———. *Trauma, Growth, and Personality.* New York, 1952.

Hartmann, Heinz. *Ego Psychology and the Problem of Adaptation*. New York, 1958.

———. *Essays on Ego Psychology*. New York, 1964.

———, with E. Kris and R. M. Lowenstein, "Some Psychoanalytic Comments on Culture and Personality," in *Psychoanalysis and Culture*, ed. G. B. Wilbur and W. Muensterberger. New York, 1951.

Hendricks, Ives. *Facts and Theories of Psychoanalysis*. New York, 1934.

Klein, Melanie, and Joan Riviere. *Love, Hate, and Reparation*. London, 1962.

Kris, Ernst. *Psychoanalytic Explorations in Art*. New York, 1952.

Kubie, Lawrence. *Neurotic Distortion of the Creative Process*. New York, 1961.

Lewin, Bertram D. *The Image and the Past*. New York, 1969.

———. *Dreams and the Uses of Regression*. New York, 1958.

Rappaport, David. *The Organization and Pathology of Thought*. New York, 1951.

——— and M. Gill. "The Points of View and Assumptions of Metapsychology," *International Journal of Psycho-Analysis* (London), *40* (1959), 1-110.

Schactel, Ernest. "On Memory and Childhood Amnesia," in *Psychological Offprint Series*. New York, 1951.

Trilling, Lionel. "Art and Neurosis" and "Freud and Literature" in *The Liberal Imagination*. New York, 1950.

———. *Freud and the Crisis of Our Culture*. Boston, 1955.

3. Other Works Cited

Aristotle. *The Ethics*, tr. Martin Ostwald. Indianapolis, 1962.

Blake, William. *The Poetry and Prose of William Blake*, ed. Geoffrey Keynes. London, 1939.

Boswell, James. *Life of Johnson,* ed. G. B. Hill, rev. L. F. Powell. 6 vols., Oxford, 1934-1950.

Collins, William. *The Poems of William Collins,* ed. Christopher Stone. London, 1907.

Keats, John. *The Poetical Works of John Keats,* ed. H. W. Garrod. London, 1961.

Milton, John. *Paradise Lost,* ed. Merritt Hughes. New York, 1935.

Pope, Alexander. *Poems of Alexander Pope; The Dunciad,* ed. James Sutherland. New Haven, 1953.

Sartre, Jean-Paul. *The Words,* tr. Bernard Frechtman. New York, 1966.

Sophocles. *The Oedipus Cycle,* tr. Dudley Fitts and R. Fitzgerald. New York, 1939.

INDEX